THE LOEB CLASSICAL LIBRARY

FOUNDED BY JAMES LOEB

TACITUS

II

LCL 111

TACITUS

THE HISTORIES

BOOKS I–III

WITH AN ENGLISH TRANSLATION BY

CLIFFORD H. MOORE

HARVARD UNIVERSITY PRESS
CAMBRIDGE, MASSACHUSETTS
LONDON, ENGLAND

First published 1925
Reprinted 1936, 1952, 1956, 1962, 1968, 1980, 1992, 1996

ISBN 0-674-99123-0

Printed in Great Britain by St Edmundsbury Press Ltd, Bury St Edmunds, Suffolk, on acid-free paper. Bound by Hunter & Foulis Ltd, Edinburgh, Scotland.

CONTENTS

INTRODUCTION

Life and Works of Tacitus

Our scanty knowledge of the life of Cornelius Tacitus is derived chiefly from his own works and from the letters of his intimate friend, the younger Pliny. The only certain dates are the following: in 78 A.D. he married the daughter of Gnaeus Julius Agricola, whose life he later wrote;[1] in 88 he was praetor and a member of the college of the XVviri, but he may have been appointed to this sacred office before this year.[2] The consulship he obtained in 97 (or 98),[3] and between 113–116 (or 111–112) he governed the province of Asia as proconsul.[4] His earlier political career can be determined with somewhat less

[1] *Agric.* 9: consul (77 A.D.) egregiae tum spei filiam iuveni mihi despondit et post consulatum collocavit; et statim Britanniae praepositus est.

[2] *Ann.* xi. 11: is quoque (Domitianus) edidit ludos saeculares, iisque intentius adfui sacerdotio quindecimvirali praeditus ac tunc praetor.

[3] Pliny, *Epist.* II. i. 6: laudatus est (Verginius Rufus) a consule Cornelio Tacito; nam hic supremus felicitati eius cumulus accessit, laudator eloquentissimus. The question as to the year obviously depends on the date of the death of Verginius. For the literature on the dispute see Schanz: *Geschichte der röm. Litteratur*, § 427.

[4] See an inscription from Mylasa, published in the *Bulletin de Correspondance Hellénique*, 1890, p. 621 f.

accuracy from his own words: dignitatem nostram a Vespasiano inchoatam, a Tito auctam, a Domitiano longius provectam non abnuerim.[1] According to this we may conjecture that he had been tribunus militum laticlavius, and had held some of the offices of the vigintivirate under Vespasian (69–79); the quaestorship then would have come to him between 79 and 81.

From the above facts we can believe that Tacitus was born not far from 55–56 A.D. This date fits the course of his political career; besides, we know that he was only a few years older than his devoted friend, the younger Pliny, who was born in 61 or 62.[2] The place of his birth is unknown, and in fact his praenomen is uncertain; the codex Mediceus I gives it as Publius, but Apollinaris Sidonius, writing in the fifth century, names him Gaius.[3] His father may have been a procurator of Belgic Gaul.[4] Certainly the historian was descended from well-to-do, if not wealthy, parents, for he enjoyed the best education of his day, had the full political career of the nobility, and early married well. Moreover, his attitude of mind is always that of a proud and aristocratic Roman, without sympathy or interest in the

[1] *Hist.* i. 1.

[2] Plin., *Epist.* VII. XX. 3; erit rarum et insigne duos homines aetate dignitate propemodum aequales, non nullius in litteris nominis—cogor enim de te quoque parcius dicere quia de me simul dico—alterum alterius studia fovisse. equidem adulescentulus cum iam tu fama gloriaque floreres, te sequi, tibi 'longo sed proximus intervallo' et esse et haberi concupiscebam. (Written probably in 107.)

[3] *Epist.* IV. 14. 1; 22. 2. Cf. Mommsen, *Hermes*, III., p. 108, 1; Studemund, *ibid.* viii. 232 f.

[4] Pliny, *N.H.* vii. 76.

affairs of the lower classes; his occasional admiration for an independent and free spirit in foreigners is prompted by his desire to secure a clear contrast for Roman vices.

The influence of Tacitus's rhetorical studies is clearly seen in all his writings, and he won reputation as an orator.[1] It was natural, then, that his earliest extant work, the *Dialogus de Oratoribus*, should be an inquiry into the reasons for the decay of oratory under the empire. Modelled on Cicero's rhetorical works, it shows in form and style the effects of its author's study. The scene of the dialogue is placed in the year 74–75 A.D., but the date of composition is unknown; apparently it was not published until after Domitian's death (96). His other works belong to the field of history. Two small volumes preceded his larger studies. The *Agricola* is an encomiastic biography of his father-in-law, Gnaeus Julius Agricola. A considerable portion of this little book is given to a description of Britain and to an account of the Roman conquest, so that a triple interest—in geography and ethnography, history, and biography—is secured on the reader's part. The book was composed, or at least published, in 98 A.D.[2] The *Germania*, published at about the same time, gives an ethnographic account of Germany, in which the Romans then had an especial interest because of Trajan's projected expedition thither. There is idealization of the Germanic peoples at the expense of the Romans, but also much

[1] Cf. Pliny, *Epist.* II. i. 6, quoted above, and *ibid.* II. xi. 17: respondit Cornelius Tacitus eloquentissime et, quod eximium orationi eius inest, σεμνῶς.

[2] *Agricola*, 3. 44.

sober and valuable matter with regard to the Germanic tribes; the booklet is the earliest significant account that we possess of these peoples, for the chapters dealing with Germany in the sixth book of Caesar's *Gallic War* are too slight to give us more than a glimpse of the Germanic peoples and their ways.

However, as early as Tacitus was writing his *Agricola,* he was planning a larger historical work which should deal with his own era.[1] But with the passage of time his plan was somewhat changed: he first composed the *Histories,* a translation of which is here presented. This work began with January 1, 69 A.D., and was carried through to the death of Domitian (96). Then he turned to an earlier time, and wrote a history of the period from the death of Augustus to the end of 68. He seems to have entitled this work *Ab excessu divi Augusti,* but he refers to it also as *Annales,* and this is the name by which it is generally known. Our slight evidence shows that Tacitus was working on his *Histories* between the years 104 and 109; the latest chronological reference in the *Annals* is to 117. Apparently death prevented him from carrying out his cherished purpose of writing the history of the happy reigns of Nerva and Trajan.

The fourteen books of the *Histories* covered the period from January 1, 69, to the death of Domitian in 96, as stated above; of these only Books I.–IV. are preserved complete, while Book V. breaks off with chapter 26, at about August, 70 A.D.

[1] *Agric.* 3: Non tamen pigebit vel incondita ac rudi voce memoriam prioris servitutis ac testimonium praesentium bonorum composuisse.

The first book contains an account of the brief reign of Galba, of the adoption of Piso as his successor, and of the revolution that placed Otho in the imperial power and cost Galba and Piso their lives (1–49). Then follow (50–90) the story of the uprising of the legions in Germany, where Vitellius was proclaimed emperor, the advance of these troops toward Italy, and Otho's preparations to oppose them.

With the beginning of the second book (1–10) Tacitus directs our attention to the East, where Vespasian and his son Titus begin to play an important rôle. He then turns back to Italy and to the struggle between the opposing forces of Otho and Vitellius, which ends with Otho's defeat at the battle of Bedriacum and his suicide (11–50). The rest of the book (51–101) contains an account of the reign of Vitellius, which is quickly threatened by the proclamation in Egypt and Syria of Vespasian as emperor. The general Mucianus, as chief of Vespasian's forces, advances toward the West. The legions of Moesia, Pannonia, and Dalmatia join Vespasian's cause. The news from the East finally causes Vitellius to despatch some forces to the north of Italy.

The third book gives an account of the struggle between the adherents of Vespasian and those of Vitellius. This finally comes to a close with the defeat of the latter, who meets a miserable end at the hands of a mob of soldiers and civilians.

With the fourth book we find Vespasian supreme. On January 1, 70, the emperor and his son Titus entered on office as consuls, although both were still in the East. The greater part of the book, however (12–37; 54–79; 85–86), is taken up with

an account of the threatening uprising of the Batavians under Civilis; this story is continued in the fifth book (14–26), although the opening chapters (1–13) claim a greater interest from the modern reader with their history of the expedition led by Titus against Jerusalem.

In time of composition the *Histories* lie between the three minor works with which Tacitus began his literary career and the *Annals*, the maturest product of his mind and pen. As is to be expected, the *Histories* are written in a style that has not yet fully attained the extreme compression of his latest work; but nevertheless examples of the flowing period here are few, and the sentences are frequently overweighted with their content. Connectives are comparatively rare; the reader must often find for himself the connection of thought. In diction Tacitus avoids, when possible, the commonplace and vulgar, without, however, seeking for what is strange and unnatural. He employs poetic turns and phrases, being greatly influenced by his predecessors, especially by Sallust and by Vergil. Yet the poetic eloquence that often marks his style is all his own, as are the sharp epigrammatic sentences that form so striking a characteristic of his pages.

In form the *Histories* are annalistic, often interrupting the narrative to preserve the order of events. To the modern reader this procedure is disturbing, but we must remember that it was one of the canonical forms of history in antiquity.

Tacitus was a man of deep feeling and strong individuality. Eager as he was to write "sine ira et studio,"[1] he was yet unable to do so; we may well

[1] *Ann.* I. 1. 6.

conjecture that if we had to-day his account of the reign of Domitian, we should find that the man mastered the historian there as in his extant accounts of the reigns of Tiberius and of Nero. Conscious that the Empire did not offer him the great themes of the Republic, he sought after the springs of action that are hidden in men's hearts. Human motives interest him so much that he sometimes does not give due weight to the influence of events themselves. He is the most individualistic, the most psychological of ancient historians, and in writing his history of the early empire he has endeavoured to write the history of the human soul.[1] Like most historians of antiquity, he is also a moralist, who regards it as his duty to hold vice up to scorn and to praise virtue.[2] With his age he is inclined to believe in astrology, prodigies and fate; but on these points he often finds himself puzzled.

We may and must at times doubt Tacitus's interpretation of his facts; but his genius is such that he gives a mordant vividness to his pictures and descriptions. He writes with grim feeling because he is impassioned by his own experiences and knows what a tyrant is. His terse and epigrammatic style, unparalleled before or since, and the manner in which his personality pervades his work have made his fame secure.

[1] Cf. *Hist.* ii. 74–76.

[2] *Ann.* III. 65. 1: praecipuum munus annalium reor ne virtutes sileantur utque pravis dictis factisque ex posteritate et infamia metus sit.

BIBLIOGRAPHY

Manuscripts

The text of the *Histories* depends on a single manuscript, the Mediceus II (M), known also as the Laurentianus 68, 2, in which are found as well *Annals* XI–XVI and Apuleius, *De Magia, Metamorphoses,* and *Florida.* This manuscript was written in the eleventh century in Langobard script at Monte Cassino. It is published in facsimile with an introduction by Enrico Rostagno: *Codices graeci et latini photographice depicti,* VII. 2, Leiden, 1902. All other manuscripts are copies of the Mediceus and comparatively useless, except to supply the text in two passages that are now missing in the parent manuscript: I. 69–75 and I. 86–II. 2.

Printed Editions

The editio princeps brought out by Vindelinus de Spira in Venice in 1470 contained *Annals XI–XVI, Histories, Germania,* and *Dialogus.* The first edition of all the works was by Beroaldus, published at Rome in 1515.

Modern editions are numerous. The text edition

of Halm, 4th ed., Leipsic, 1884, has long been the standard; but it has now been somewhat replaced for the *Histories* by that of Van der Vliet, Groningen, 1900, and by C. D. Fisher's in the Oxford Classical Texts, 1910.

Among annotated editions of the *Histories* the following may be named: E. Wolff, Berlin, 1886, 1888; C. Heraeus, Leipsic[5], 1904; A. D. Godley, London, 1887, 1890; and W. A. Spooner, London, 1891.

For studying the language of Tacitus, Gerber and Greef, *Lexicon Taciteum,* 2 vols., Leipsic, 1903, is indispensable.

Translations

The earliest English translation of the *Histories* (I.–IV.) was made by Sir Henry Savile, London, 1591. The translation of the complete works by Arthur Murphy, London (1793), 1811, long remained the standard English translation.

More modern and better translations are by Church and Brodribb, London (1864), 1905; W. Hamilton Fyfe, Oxford, 1912; and G. G. Ramsay, London, 1915. That by H. W. Quill, London, 1892, 1896, may also be mentioned, but it is inferior to those just named. In French there is an excellent rendering by Burnouf, Paris, 1914. Although the following translation was made in the first draft largely in Italy with none of these renderings at hand, it probably owes more to them all than the translator is aware; for whatever he has taken, consciously or unconsciously, he is sincerely grateful.

It is unnecessary to say anything on the diffi-

culties of translating Tacitus to those who have attempted to render even a small portion of his work ; and the experiment is earnestly recommended to all who would entertain a kindly charity toward one who has dared to face the tempting but impossible task.

ADDENDUM (1980)

Editions with Commentary:

H. Heubner: I (1963); II (1968); III (1972); IV (1976), Heidelberg

K. Wellesley: III (1972)

Commentary:

G. E. F. Chilver: A Historical Commentary on Tacitus' *Histories I and II*, Oxford 1980

Studies:

Sir Ronald Syme: *Tacitus*, 2 volumes, Oxford 1958

Sir Ronald Syme: *Ten Studies in Tacitus*, Oxford 1970

Surveys of Scholarship:

Classical World (*Weekly*): volumes 48 (1954) 121; 58 (1964) 69; 63 (1970) 253; 71 (1977) 1

F. D. R. Goodyear: Tacitus: *Greece and Rome Surveys 4*, Oxford 1970

HISTORICAL NOTE

To understand the events narrated in the opening chapters of the *Histories* it is necessary to have in mind the events that led up to the death of Nero and the acceptance of the imperial office by Galba.

As a result of the discontent with Nero, Servius Sulpicius Galba had been proclaimed *imperator* by his troops in Hither Spain early in April, 68. Galba was now in his seventy-third year. He was of high birth and had been consul thirty-five years before; under Caligula he had distinguished himself when governor of Gaul by repelling the German invasion in 39 A.D., and at Caligula's death he had declined to listen to his friends who urged him to claim the imperial power. Later the Emperor Claudius sent him to govern the province of Africa, then distressed by the poor discipline prevailing among the soldiers and threatened by barbarian raids. After restoring discipline and securing peace, for which accomplishments he was highly honoured, Galba retired from public life, but in 60 he was recalled by Nero, who sent him to govern Hispania Tarraconensis.

Early in the year 68 Galba had been approached by Vindex, governor of Gallia Lugdunensis, who proposed that they should revolt and that Galba should

be emperor. The old man was too cautious to embark then upon so dangerous an enterprise, but after the revolt under Vindex had broken out he began to fear for his own safety; claiming that his life was sought by Nero, he called his troops together and addressed them on the state of the empire. Although they proclaimed him emperor (*imperator*), Galba styled himself only the representative of the Senate and the people (*legatus senatus populique Romani*). He was supported by Otho, governor of Lusitania, and Caecina, quaestor of Baetica. After the rebellion under Vindex had been crushed and Vindex himself had committed suicide, Galba's situation seemed desperate, but Nero's hesitation and levity saved him. Finally, Nympidius Sabinus, prefect of the praetorian guards, embraced Galba's cause for his own purposes; Nero was condemned to death by the Senate, and met his end in the suburban villa of his freedman Phaon on the night of June 9. Seven days later the news reached Galba at Clunia in Spain, whereupon he assumed the imperial name. His progress to Rome was slow; pretenders in Spain and Gaul had to be put down, and claimants from Germany and Africa disposed of; in October he entered Rome, after overcoming the real, or supposed, opposition of some marines at the Mulvian Bridge.

THE HISTORIES OF TACITUS

BOOK I

CORNELII TACITI

HISTORIARUM

LIBER I

I. Initium mihi operis Servius Galba iterum Titus Vinius consules erunt. Nam post conditam urbem octingentos et viginti prioris aevi annos multi auctores rettulerunt, dum res populi Romani memorabantur pari eloquentia ac libertate: postquam bellatum apud Actium atque omnem potentiam ad unum conferri pacis interfuit, magna illa ingenia cessere; simul veritas pluribus modis infracta, primum inscitia rei publicae ut alienae, mox libidine adsentandi aut rursus odio adversus dominantis. Ita neutris cura posteritatis inter infensos vel obnoxios. Sed ambitionem scriptoris facile averseris,[1] obtrectatio et livor pronis auribus accipiuntur; quippe adulationi foedum crimen servitutis, malignitati falsa species libertatis inest. Mihi Galba Otho Vitellius nec beneficio nec iniuria cogniti. Dignitatem nostram

[1] averseris *Pichena*: adverseris *M*.

---

[1] Jan. 1, 69 A.D.

[2] To be meticulously exact, the period was 822 years, according to the Varronian date of the founding of Rome, 753 B.C., which was generally accepted in Tacitus's day.

[3] Tacitus thus dates the beginning of the Empire at 31 B.C.; yet the position of Augustus was not made wholly constitutional until January, 27 B.C.

THE HISTORIES OF
TACITUS

BOOK I

I. I BEGIN my work with the second consulship of Servius Galba, when Titus Vinius was his colleague.[1] Many historians have treated of the earlier period of eight hundred and twenty years from the founding of Rome, and while dealing with the Republic they have written with equal eloquence and freedom.[2] But after the battle of Actium, when the interests of peace required that all power should be concentrated in the hands of one man,[3] writers of like ability disappeared; and at the same time historical truth was impaired in many ways: first, because men were ignorant of politics as being not any concern of theirs; later, because of their passionate desire to flatter; or again, because of their hatred of their masters. So between the hostility of the one class and the servility of the other, posterity was disregarded. But while men quickly turn from a historian who curries favour, they listen with ready ears to calumny and spite; for flattery is subject to the shameful charge of servility, but malignity makes a false show of independence. In my own case I had no acquaintance with Galba, Otho, or Vitellius, through either kindness or injury at their hands. I

a Vespasiano inchoatam, a Tito auctam, a Domitiano longius provectam non abnuerim: sed incorruptam fidem professis neque amore quisquam et sine odio dicendus est. Quod si vita suppeditet, principatum divi Nervae et imperium Traiani, uberiorem securioremque materiam, senectuti seposui, rara temporum felicitate ubi sentire quae velis et quae sentias dicere licet.

II. Opus adgredior opimum casibus,[1] atrox proeliis, discors seditionibus, ipsa etiam pace saevum. Quattuor principes ferro interempti: trina bella civilia, plura externa ac plerumque permixta: prosperae in Oriente, adversae in Occidente res: turbatum[2] Illyricum, Galliae nutantes, perdomita Britannia et statim omissa[3]: coortae in nos Sarmatarum ac Sueborum gentes, nobilitatus cladibus mutuis Dacus, mota prope etiam Parthorum arma falsi Neronis ludibrio. Iam vero Italia novis cladibus vel post longam saeculorum seriem repetitis adflicta. Haustae

[1] opimum *codd. dett.*: opibus *M*.
[2] prospere Inorientem adversae in occidentes. returbatum *M*.
[3] omissa *Lipsius*: missa *M*.

---

[1] Tacitus must have been quaestor under Vespasian or Titus, for he was praetor in 88, and consul in 97 A.D.

[2] So far as we know, Tacitus never carried out his plan. After finishing his *Histories*, which covered the years 69–96 A.D., he turned back and wrote the *Annals*, embracing the years 14–68 A.D.

[3] Galba, Otho, Vitellius, and Domitian.

[4] Two of the three civil wars were those of Otho against Vitellius and of Vitellius against Vespasian; the third was probably that of Domitian against the revolting governor of

cannot deny that my political career owed its beginning to Vespasian; that Titus advanced it; and that Domitian carried it further;[1] but those who profess inviolable fidelity to truth must write of no man with affection or with hatred. Yet if my life but last, I have reserved for my old age the history of the deified Nerva's reign and of Trajan's rule, a richer and less perilous subject, because of the rare good fortune of an age in which we may feel what we wish and may say what we feel.[2]

II. The history on which I am entering is that of a period rich in disasters, terrible with battles, torn by civil struggles, horrible even in peace. Four emperors fell by the sword;[3] there were three civil wars, more foreign wars, and often both at the same time. There was success in the East, misfortune in the West. Illyricum was disturbed, the Gallic provinces wavering, Britain subdued and immediately let go.[4] The Sarmatae and Suebi rose against us; the Dacians won fame by defeats inflicted and suffered; even the Parthians were almost roused to arms through the trickery of a pretended Nero.[5] Moreover, Italy was distressed by disasters unknown before or returning after the lapse of ages. Cities

Upper Germany, L. Antonius Saturninus, in 89 A.D. Suet. *Dom.* 6 f.; Dio Cassius, lxvii. 11.

The foreign wars were against the Rhoxolani (i. 79) and the Jews (v. 1). The successes in the East were won in the latter war, while the disasters in the West were caused by the revolt of Civilis and his Batavians, as is narrated below, especially iv. 12–37, 54–79; v. 14–26.

The subjugation of Britain was accomplished by Agricola, the father-in-law of Tacitus, in 77–84 A.D.; in the later years of Domitian's reign some parts of the province apparently were lost.

[5] See Suet. *Dom.* 6; *Ner.* 57.

aut obrutae urbes, fecundissima Campaniae ora; et urbs incendiis vastata, consumptis antiquissimis delubris, ipso Capitolio civium manibus incenso. Pollutae caerimoniae, magna adulteria: plenum exiliis mare, infecti caedibus scopuli. Atrocius in urbe saevitum: nobilitas, opes, omissi gestique honores pro crimine et ob virtutes certissimum exitium. Nec minus praemia delatorum invisa quam scelera, cum alii sacerdotia et consulatus ut spolia adepti, procurationes alii et interiorem potentiam, agerent verterent cuncta odio et terrore. Corrupti in dominos servi, in patronos liberti; et quibus deerat inimicus per amicos oppressi.

III. Non tamen adeo virtutum sterile saeculum ut non et bona exempla prodiderit. Comitatae profugos liberos matres, secutae maritos in exilia coniuges: propinqui audentes, constantes generi, contumax etiam adversus tormenta servorum fides; supremae clarorum virorum necessitates fortiter toleratae[1] et laudatis antiquorum mortibus pares exitus. Praeter multiplicis rerum humanarum casus caelo terraque prodigia et fulminum monitus et futurorum praesagia, laeta tristia, ambigua manifesta; nec enim umquam atrocioribus populi Romani cladibus magisve iustis indiciis adprobatum est non esse curae deis securitatem nostram, esse ultionem.

[1] necessitates fortiter toleratae *codd. dett.*: necessitates ipsa necessitas fortiter tolerata *M*.

---

[1] The reference is to the eruption of Vesuvius in 79 A.D. Pliny, *Epist.* vi. 16 and 20.

[2] By the fire of 69 (iii. 71), and by the conflagration under Titus, 80 A.D. Dio Cassius, lxvi. 24.

on the rich fertile shores of Campania were swallowed up or overwhelmed;[1] Rome was devastated by conflagrations, in which her most ancient shrines were consumed and the very Capitol fired by citizens' hands.[2] Sacred rites were defiled; there were adulteries in high places. The sea was filled with exiles, its cliffs made foul with the bodies of the dead. In Rome there was more awful cruelty. High birth, wealth, the refusal or acceptance of office—all gave ground for accusations, and virtues caused the surest ruin. The rewards of the informers were no less hateful than their crimes; for some, gaining priesthoods and consulships as spoils, others, obtaining positions as imperial agents and secret influence at court, made havoc and turmoil everywhere, inspiring hatred and terror. Slaves were corrupted against their masters, freedmen against their patrons; and those who had no enemy were crushed by their friends.

III. Yet this age was not so barren of virtue that it did not display noble examples. Mothers accompanied their children in flight; wives followed their husbands into exile; relatives displayed courage, sons-in-law firmness, slaves a fidelity which defied even torture. Eminent men met the last necessity with fortitude, rivalling in their end the glorious deaths of antiquity. Besides the manifold misfortunes that befell mankind, there were prodigies in the sky and on the earth, warnings given by thunderbolts, and prophecies of the future, both joyful and gloomy, uncertain and clear. For never was it more fully proved by awful disasters of the Roman people or by indubitable signs that the gods care not for our safety, but for our punishment.

IV. Ceterum antequam destinata componam, repetendum videtur qualis status urbis, quae mens exercituum, quis habitus provinciarum, quid in toto terrarum orbe validum, quid aegrum fuerit, ut non modo casus eventusque rerum, qui plerumque fortuiti sunt, sed ratio etiam causaeque noscantur. Finis Neronis ut laetus primo gaudentium impetu fuerat, ita varios motus animorum non modo in urbe apud patres aut populum aut urbanum militem, sed omnis legiones ducesque conciverat, evulgato imperii arcano posse principem alibi quam Romae fieri. Sed patres laeti, usurpata statim libertate licentius ut erga principem novum et absentem; primores equitum proximi gaudio patrum; pars populi integra et magnis domibus adnexa, clientes libertique damnatorum et exulum in spem erecti: plebs sordida et circo ac theatris sueta, simul deterrimi servorum, aut qui adesis bonis per dedecus Neronis alebantur, maesti et rumorum avidi.

V. Miles urbanus longo Caesarum sacramento imbutus et ad destituendum Neronem arte magis et impulsu quam suo ingenio traductus, postquam neque dari donativum sub nomine Galbae promissum

---

[1] Galba was the first to be proclaimed emperor outside Rome.

IV. Before, however, I begin the work that I have planned, I think that we should turn back and consider the condition of the city, the temper of the armies, the attitude of the provinces, the elements of strength and weakness in the entire world, that we may understand not only the incidents and the issues of events, which for the most part are due to chance, but also their reasons and causes. Although Nero's death had at first been welcomed with outbursts of joy, it roused varying emotions, not only in the city among the senators and people and the city soldiery, but also among all the legions and generals; for the secret of empire was now disclosed, that an emperor could be made elsewhere than at Rome.[1] The senators rejoiced and immediately made full use of their liberty, as was natural, for they had to do with a new emperor who was still absent. The leading members of the equestrian class were nearly as elated as the senators. The respectable part of the common people and those attached to the great houses, the clients and freedmen of those who had been condemned and driven into exile, were all roused to hope. The lowest classes, addicted to the circus and theatre, and with them the basest slaves, as well as those men who had wasted their property and, to their shame, were wont to depend on Nero's bounty, were cast down and grasped at every rumour.

V. The city soldiery had long been accustomed to swear allegiance to the Caesars, and had been brought to desert Nero by clever pressure rather than by their own inclination. Now when they saw that the donative, which had been promised in

neque magnis meritis ac praemiis eundem in pace quem in bello locum praeventamque gratiam intellegit apud principem a legionibus factum, pronus ad novas res scelere insuper Nymphidii Sabini praefecti imperium sibi molientis agitatur. Et Nymphidius quidem in ipso conatu oppressus, set[1] quamvis capite defectionis ablato manebat plerisque militum conscientia, nec deerant sermones senium atque avaritiam Galbae increpantium. Laudata olim et militari fama celebrata severitas eius angebat aspernantis veterem disciplinam atque ita quattuordecim annis a Nerone adsuefactos ut haud minus vitia principum amarent quam olim virtutes verebantur. Accessit Galbae vox pro re publica honesta, ipsi anceps, legi a se militem, non emi; nec enim ad hanc formam cetera erant.

VI. Invalidum senem Titus Vinius et Cornelius Laco, alter deterrimus mortalium, alter ignavissimus, odio flagitiorum oneratum contemptu inertiae destruebant. Tardum Galbae iter et cruentum, inter-

[1] set *Rhenanus*: et *M.*

---

[1] Nymphidius had promised the praetorians 7,500 drachmas ($1,500) each, and 1,250 drachmas ($250) to each legionary, the former sum being the largest gift ever promised the soldiers. Plut. *Galba* 2.

[2] Nymphidius had soon come to feel that his services were not duly appreciated by Galba and that Titus Vinius and Cornelius Laco had supplanted him in Galba's regard. He next gave out that he was the son of Caligula (Tac. *Ann.* xv. 72; Plut. *Galba*, 9) and wished to persuade the praetorians to proclaim him emperor in Galba's place; but they refused, and when he tried to force himself into the praetorian camp, they killed him. Plut. *Galba*, 14; Suet. *Galba*, 11.

[3] On Titus Vinius, see i. 48, below; Laco, who had been

Galba's name, was not given them,[1] that there were not the same opportunities for great services and rewards in peace as in war, and that the legions had already secured the favour of the emperor whom they had made, inclined as they were to support a revolution, they were further roused by the criminal action of Nymphidius Sabinus, the prefect, who was trying to secure the empire for himself.[2] It is true that Nymphidius was crushed in his very attempt, but, though the head of the mutiny was thus removed, the majority of the soldiers were still conscious of their guilt, and there were plenty of men to comment unfavourably on Galba's age and greed. His strictness, which had once been esteemed and had won the soldiers' praise, now vexed them, for they rebelled against the old discipline; through fourteen years they had been trained by Nero to love the faults of the emperors not less than once they respected their virtues. Besides, there was the saying of Galba's to the effect that he was wont to select, not buy, his soldiers—an honourable utterance in the interests of the state, but dangerous to himself; for everything else was at variance with such a standard.

VI. Galba was weak and old. Titus Vinius and Cornelius Laco, the former the worst of men, the latter the laziest, proved his ruin, for he had to bear the burden of the hatred felt for the crimes of Titus and of men's scorn for the lethargy of Cornelius.[3] Galba's approach to Rome had been slow and

appointed prefect of the praetorian guard in place of Nymphidius, played a prominent part in Galba's brief reign, and was killed by Otho at the same time as his imperial master. See i. 46; Plut. *Galba*, 27.

fectis Cingonio Varrone consule designato et Petronio Turpiliano consulari: ille ut Nymphidii socius, hic ut dux Neronis, inauditi atque indefensi tamquam innocentes perierant. Introitus in urbem trucidatis tot milibus inermium militum infaustus omine atque ipsis etiam qui occiderant formidolosus. Inducta legione Hispana, remanente ea quam e classe Nero conscripserat, plena urbs exercitu insolito; multi ad hoc numeri e Germania ac Britannia et Illyrico, quos idem Nero electos praemissosque ad claustra Caspiarum et bellum, quod in Albanos parabat, opprimendis Vindicis coeptis revocaverat: ingens novis rebus materia, ut non in unum aliquem prono favore ita audenti parata.

VII. Forte congruerat ut Clodii Marci et Fontei Capitonis caedes nuntiarentur. Macrum in Africa haud dubie turbantem Trebonius Garutianus procurator iussu Galbae, Capitonem in Germania, cum similia coeptaret, Cornelius Aquinus et Fabius Valens legati legionum interfecerant antequam iuberentur. Fuere qui crederent Capitonem ut avaritia et libidine

---

[1] Cingonius Varro had actually composed the speech with which Nymphidius addressed the praetorians. Plut. *Galba*, 14. Petronius Turpilianus, consul in 61 A.D., had been governor of Britain 61–63 (Tac. *Ann.* xiv. 39; *Agri.* 16); he was selected by Nero as general against Vindex and Galba, but had come to an agreement with the latter. Zonares, xi. 13, p. 570D.

[2] The Claustra Caspiarum seem to be the pass which was also called Portae Caucasiae (Plin. *N.H.* VI. xiii. 40); it is that which leads to-day to Tiflis.

[3] Clodius Macer was governor of Africa. Cf. below, i. 73; Suet. *Galba*, 11; Plut. *Galba*, 6. 13. Fonteius Capito,

bloody: the consul-elect, Cingonius Varro, and Petronius Turpilianus, an ex-consul, had been put to death, Cingonius because he had been an accomplice of Nymphidius, Petronius as one of Nero's generals:[1] they were killed unheard and undefended, so that men believed them innocent. Galba's entrance into Rome was ill-omened, because so many thousands of unarmed soldiers had been massacred, and this inspired fear in the very men who had been their murderers. A Spanish legion had been brought to Rome; the one that Nero had enrolled from the fleet was still there, so that the city was filled with an unusual force. In addition there were many detachments from Germany, Britain, and Illyricum, which Nero had likewise selected and sent to the Caspian Gates[2] to take part in the campaign which he was preparing against the Albani; but he had recalled them to crush the attempt of Vindex. Here was abundant fuel for a revolution; while the soldiers' favour did not incline to any individual, they were ready for the use of anyone who had courage.

VII. It happened too that the executions of Clodius Macer and Fonteius Capito were reported at this same time.[3] Macer, who had unquestionably been making trouble in Africa, had been executed by Trebonius Garutianus, the imperial agent, at Galba's orders. Capito, who was making similar attempts, had been executed in Germany by Cornelius Aquinus and Fabius Valens, the commanders of the legions, before they received orders to take such action. There were some who believed that, although Capito's character was defiled and

consul in 67 A.D., was governor of Lower Germany. i. 58; iii. 62.

foedum ac maculosum ita cogitatione rerum novarum abstinuisse, sed a legatis bellum suadentibus, postquam impellere nequiverint, crimen ac dolum ultro compositum, et Galbam mobilitate ingenii, an ne altius scrutaretur, quoquo modo acta, quia mutari non poterant, comprobasse. Ceterum utraque caedes sinistre accepta, et inviso semel principi seu bene seu male facta parem invidiam[1] adferebant. Venalia cuncta, praepotentes liberti, servorum manus subitis avidae et tamquam apud senem festinantes, eademque novae aulae mala, aeque gravia, non aeque excusata. Ipsa aetas Galbae inrisui ac fastidio erat adsuetis iuventae Neronis et imperatores forma ac decore corporis, ut est mos vulgi, comparantibus.

VIII. Et hic quidem Romae, tamquam in tanta multitudine, habitus animorum fuit. E provinciis Hispaniae praeerat Cluvius Rufus, vir facundus et pacis artibus, bellis inexpertus. Galliae super memoriam Vindicis obligatae recenti dono Romanae civitatis et in posterum tributi levamento. Proximae tamen Germanicis exercitibus Galliarum civitates non eodem honore habitae, quaedam etiam finibus

[1] parem invidiam *Bezzenberger* : praeminuit iam *M.*

---

[1] Cluvius Rufus, now governor of Hispania Tarraconensis, wrote an account of the reigns of Nero, Galba, Otho, and Vitellius. He is one of the few authorities whom Tacitus mentions by name.

[2] In 48 A.D. Claudius had granted full citizenship to the Gallic nobility of Gallia Comata (*Ann.* xi. 23 f.). This privilege Galba extended to all citizens in the Gallic tribes and communities that had favoured Vindex and himself; and at the same time he reduced the tribute 25 per cent. i. 51; Plut. *Galba*, 18.

stained by greed and lust, he had still refrained from any thought of a revolution, but that the commanders who urged him to begin war had purposely invented the charge of treason against him when they found that they were unable to persuade him; and that Galba, either by his natural lack of decision, or to avoid a closer examination of the case, had approved what was done, regardless of the manner of it, simply because it could not be undone. But both executions were unfavourably received, and now that the emperor was once hated, his good and evil deeds alike brought him unpopularity. Everything was for sale; his freedmen were extremely powerful, his slaves clutched greedily after sudden gains with the impatience natural under so old a master. There were the same evils in the new court as in the old: they were equally burdensome, but they did not have an equal excuse. Galba's very years aroused ridicule and scorn among those who were accustomed to Nero's youth, and who, after the fashion of the vulgar, compared emperors by the beauty of their persons.

VIII. Such were the varied sentiments at Rome, natural in a city with so vast a population. Of the provinces, Spain was governed by Cluvius Rufus, a man of ready eloquence, expert in the arts of peace but untrained in war.[1] The Gallic provinces were held to their allegiance, not only by their memory of the failure of Vindex, but also by the recent gift of Roman citizenship, and by the reduction of their taxes for the future;[2] yet the Gallic tribes nearest the armies of Germany had not been treated with the same honour as the rest; some had actually had their lands taken from them, so that they felt equal

ademptis pari dolore commoda aliena ac suas iniurias metiebantur. Germanici exercitus, quod periculosissimum in tantis viribus, solliciti et irati, superbia recentis victoriae et metu tamquam alias partis fovissent. Tarde a Nerone desciverant, nec statim pro Galba Verginius. An imperare noluisset dubium: delatum ei a milite imperium conveniebat. Fonteium Capitonem occisum etiam qui queri non poterant, tamen indignabantur. Dux deerat abducto Verginio per simulationem amicitiae; quem non remitti atque etiam reum esse tamquam suum crimen accipiebant.

IX. Superior exercitus legatum Hordeonium Flaccum spernebat, senecta ac debilitate pedum invalidum, sine constantia, sine auctoritate: ne quieto quidem milite regimen; adeo furentes infirmitate retinentis ultro accendebantur. Inferioris Germaniae legiones diutius sine consulari fuere, donec missu Galbae A. Vitellius aderat, censoris Vitellii ac ter consulis filius: id satis videbatur. In Britannico

---

[1] The Lingones and Treveri, who had supported Verginius, are meant. i. 53f.

[2] The district along the Rhine was divided for administrative and military purposes into Upper Germany and Lower Germany. Upper Germany extended on both sides of the Rhine from Vindonissa (Windisch, near Lake Constance) to Mogontiacum (Mayence); Lower Germany from Mogontiacum to the North Sea, but included little territory on the east bank of the Rhine. Usually there were four legions in each district; but at this time there were only three in Upper Germany.

[3] Aulus Vitellius had enjoyed the favour of Caligula, Claudius, and Nero in turn. In 48 A.D. he had been consul ordinarius with L. Vipstanus Poblicola; he had been proconsul of Africa, apparently in 60–61, and in the following year he served in the same province as *legatus* of his brother,

irritation whether they reckoned up their neighbours' gains or counted their own wrongs.[1] The armies in Germany were vexed and angry, a condition most dangerous when large forces are involved.[2] They were moved by pride in their recent victory and also by fear, because they had favoured the losing side. They had been slow to abandon Nero; and Verginius, their commander, had not pronounced for Galba immediately; men were inclined to think that he would not have been unwilling to be emperor himself; and it was believed that the soldiers offered him the imperial power. Even those who could not complain of the execution of Fonteius Capito were none the less indignant. But they had no leader, for Verginius had been taken away under the cloak of friendship. The fact that he was not sent back, but was actually brought to trial, the soldiers regarded as an accusation against themselves.

IX. The army in Upper Germany despised their commander, Hordeonius Flaccus. Incapacitated by age and lameness, he had neither courage nor authority. Even when the soldiers were quiet he had no control; once exasperated, the feebleness of his restraint only inflamed them further. The soldiers of Lower Germany were a considerable time without a general of consular rank, until Galba sent out Aulus Vitellius, the son of that Vitellius who had been censor and three times consul: his father's honours seemed to give him enough prestige.[3] In

who then was governor. He was a member of most of the important priesthoods, and also held the office of commissioner of public works at Rome. Tacitus characterizes him below, ii. 86.

exercitu nihil irarum. Non sane aliae legiones per omnis civilium bellorum motus innocentius egerunt, seu quia procul et Oceano divisae, seu crebris expeditionibus doctae hostem potius odisse. Quies et Illyrico, quamquam excitae a Nerone legiones, dum in Italia cunctantur, Verginium legationibus adissent: sed longis spatiis discreti exercitus, quod saluberrimum est ad continendam militarem fidem, nec vitiis nec viribus miscebantur.

X. Oriens adhuc immotus. Syriam et quattuor legiones obtinebat Licinius Mucianus, vir secundis adversisque iuxta famosus. Insignis amicitias iuvenis ambitiose coluerat; mox attritis opibus, lubrico statu, suspecta etiam Claudii iracundia, in secretum Asiae sepositus[1] tam prope ab exule fuit quam postea a principe. Luxuria industria, comitate adrogantia, malis bonisque artibus mixtus: nimiae voluptates, cum vacaret; quotiens expedierat, magnae virtutes: palam laudares, secreta male audiebant: sed apud subiectos, apud proximos, apud collegas variis inlecebris potens, et cui expeditius fuerit tradere imperium quam obtinere. Bellum Iudaicum Flavius Vespa-

[1] sepositus *Acidalius*: repositus *M.*

---

[1] The legions here referred to had been withdrawn on account of Vindex's revolt.

[2] Licinius Mucianus had been consul under Nero, and in 67 was appointed governor of Syria. After Vespasian claimed the imperial power Mucianus became his strongest supporter; the details are given below, Books II–IV.

the army stationed in Britain there were no hostile feelings; and indeed no other legions through all the confusion caused by the civil wars made less trouble, either because they were farther away and separated by the ocean, or else they had learned in many campaigns to hate the enemy by preference. There was quiet in Illyricum also, though the legions which Nero had called from that province, while they delayed in Italy, had made overtures to Verginius through their representatives;[1] but the various armies, separated by long distances—which is the most effective means of maintaining the fidelity of troops—did not succeed in combining either their vices or their strength.

X. The East was as yet undisturbed. Syria and its four legions were held by Licinius Mucianus, a man notorious in prosperity and adversity alike.[2] When a young man he had cultivated friendships with the nobility for his own ends; later, when his wealth was exhausted, his position insecure, and he also suspected that Claudius was angry with him, he withdrew to retirement in Asia and was as near to exile then as afterwards he was to the throne. He displayed a mixture of luxury and industry, of affability and insolence, of good and wicked arts. His pleasures were extravagant if he was at leisure; whenever he took the field, he showed great virtues. You would have praised his public life; but his private life bore ill repute. Yet by diverse attractions he gained power with his subordinates, with those close to him, and with his associates in office; and he was a man who found it easier to bestow the imperial power than to hold it himself. The war against the Jews was being directed with three legions

sianus (ducem eum Nero delegerat) tribus legionibus administrabat. Nec Vespasiano adversus Galbam votum aut animus: quippe Titum filium ad venerationem cultumque eius miserat, ut suo loco memorabimus. Occulta fati et ostentis ac responsis destinatum Vespasiano liberisque eius imperium post fortunam credidimus.

XI. Aegyptum copiasque, quibus coerceretur, iam inde a divo Augusto equites Romani obtinent loco regum: ita visum expedire, provinciam aditu difficilem, annonae fecundam, superstitione ac lascivia discordem et mobilem, insciam legum, ignaram magistratuum, domi retinere. Regebat tum Tiberius Alexander, eiusdem nationis. Africa ac legiones in ea interfecto Clodio Macro contenta qualicumque principe post experimentum domini minoris. Duae Mauritaniae, Raetia, Noricum, Thraecia et quae aliae procuratoribus cohibentur, ut cuique exercitui vicinae, ita in favorem aut odium contactu valentiorum agebantur. Inermes provinciae atque ipsa in primis Italia, cuicumque servitio exposita, in pretium belli cessurae erant. Hic fuit rerum Romanarum status,

---

[1] Titus Flavius Vespasianus was born at Reate in 9 A.D. Up to the present he had spent his life as a soldier and administrator in Thrace, Crete, Germany and Britain; he had been aedile in 38, praetor in 40, and consul in 51 A.D.; and in 66 he was appointed general by Nero to conduct the war against the Jews.

[2] On the position and importance of Egypt, see *Ann.* ii. 59: "For Augustus had made it one of the secret principles of his power to keep Egypt to himself and not to allow senators or eminent knights to enter it without his permission. His purpose was to save Italy from the danger of being starved; indeed Italy was at the mercy of any man who once got control of Egypt, for the province is the key

by Flavius Vespasianus,[1] whom Nero had selected as general. Neither Vespasian's desires nor sentiments were opposed to Galba, for he sent his son, Titus, to pay his respects and to show his allegiance to him, as we shall tell at the proper time. The secrets of Fate, and the signs and oracles which predestined Vespasian and his sons for power, we believed only after his success was secured.

XI. Egypt, with the troops to keep it in order, has been managed from the time of the deified Augustus by Roman knights in place of their former kings.[2] It had seemed wise to keep thus under the direct control of the imperial house a province which is difficult of access, productive of great harvests, but given to civil strife and sudden disturbances because of the fanaticism and superstition of its inhabitants, ignorant as they are of laws and unacquainted with civil magistrates. At this time the governor was Tiberius Alexander, himself an Egyptian. Africa and its legions, now that Clodius Macer had been killed, were satisfied with any emperor after their experience of a petty tyrant. The two provinces of Mauritania, Raetia, Noricum, Thrace and the other districts which were in charge of imperial agents, were moved to favour or hostility by contact with forces more powerful than themselves, according to the army near which each was. The provinces without an army, and especially Italy itself, were exposed to slavery under any master and destined to become the rewards of war.

This was the condition of the Roman state when

to both sea and land; and a small force there could resist large armies."

cum Servius Galba iterum Titus Vinius consules inchoavere annum sibi ultimum, rei publicae prope supremum.

XII. Paucis post kalendas Ianuarias diebus Pompei Propinqui procuratoris e Belgica litterae adferuntur, superioris Germaniae legiones rupta sacramenti reverentia imperatorem alium flagitare et senatui ac populo Romano arbitrium eligendi permittere quo seditio mollius acciperetur. Maturavit ea res consilium Galbae iam pridem de adoptione secum et cum proximis agitantis. Non sane crebrior tota civitate sermo per illos mensis fuerat, primum licentia ac libidine talia loquendi, dein fessa iam aetate Galbae. Paucis iudicium aut rei publicae amor: multi stulta spe, prout quis amicus vel cliens, hunc vel illum ambitiosis [1] rumoribus destinabant, etiam in Titi Vinii odium, qui in dies quanto potentior eodem actu invisior erat. Quippe hiantis in magna fortuna amicorum cupiditates ipsa Galbae facilitas intendebat, cum apud infirmum et credulum minore metu et maiore praemio peccaretur.

XIII. Potentia principatus divisa in Titum Vinium consulem Cornelium Laconem praetorii praefectum; nec minor gratia Icelo Galbae liberto, quem anulis

[1] ambitiosis *Agricola*: ambitionis *M.*

Servius Galba, chosen consul for the second time, and his colleague Titus Vinius entered upon the year that was to be for Galba his last and for the state almost the end.

XII. A few days after the first of January a despatch was brought from Pompeius Propinquus, imperial agent in Belgic Gaul, saying that the legions of Upper Germany had thrown off all regard for their oath of allegiance and were demanding another emperor, but that they left the choice to the senate and the Roman people, that their disloyalty might be less seriously regarded. This news hastened Galba's determination. He had already been considering with himself and his intimates the question of adopting a successor; indeed during the last few months nothing had been more frequently discussed throughout the state, first of all because of the licence and the passion which men now had for such talk, and secondly because Galba was already old and feeble. Few were guided by sound judgment or real patriotism; the majority, prompted by foolish hope, named in their selfish gossip this man or that whose clients or friends they were; they were also moved by hatred for Titus Vinius, whose unpopularity increased daily in proportion to his power. Moreover, Galba's very amiability increased the cupidity of his friends, grown greedy in their high good fortune; since they were dealing with an infirm and confiding man, they had less to fear and more to hope from their wrong-doings.

XIII. The actual power of the principate was divided between Titus Vinius the consul and Cornelius Laco the praetorian prefect, nor was the influence of Icelus, Galba's freedman, less than

donatum equestri nomine Marcianum vocitabant. Hi discordes et rebus minoribus sibi quisque tendentes, circa consilium eligendi successoris in duas factiones scindebantur. Vinius pro M. Othone, Laco atque Icelus consensu non tam unum aliquem fovebant quam alium. Neque erat Galbae ignota Othonis ac Titi Vinii amicitia; et rumoribus nihil silentio transmittentium, quia Vinio vidua filia, caelebs Otho, gener ac socer destinabantur. Credo et rei publicae curam subisse, frustra a Nerone translatae si apud Othonem relinqueretur. Namque Otho pueritiam incuriose, adulescentiam petulanter egerat, gratus Neroni aemulatione luxus. Eoque Poppaeam Sabinam, principale scortum, ut apud conscium libidinum deposuerat, donec Octaviam uxorem amoliretur. Mox suspectum in eadem Poppaea in provinciam Lusitaniam specie legationis seposuit. Otho comiter administrata provincia primus in partis transgressus nec segnis et, donec bellum fuit, inter praesentis splendidissimus, spem adoptionis statim conceptam acrius in dies rapiebat, faventibus

---

[1] Icelus had hurried from Rome to Galba in Spain with the news of Nero's death, and had been rewarded with the gold ring and the privilege of wearing the narrow purple stripe (*angustus clavus*) on his tunic, that were prerogatives of the equestrian order. He then became one of Galba's chief advisers; he was later executed by Otho. Plut. *Galba*, 7; Suet. *Galba*, 14. 22.

theirs. He had been presented with the ring of a knight, and people called him Marcianus, an equestrian name.[1] These three quarrelled with one another, and in small matters each one worked for himself; but in the question of choosing a successor they were divided into two parties. Vinius favoured Marcus Otho; Laco and Icelus agreed not so much in favouring any particular person as in supporting someone other than Otho. Galba was not ignorant of the friendship between Otho and Titus Vinius; and the common gossip of people, who let nothing pass in silence, was already naming Otho the son-in-law and Vinius the father-in-law, because the former was a bachelor and Vinius had an unmarried daughter. I can believe that Galba cherished also some thought for the state, which had been wrested from Nero in vain if it were to be left in the hands of an Otho. For Otho had spent his boyhood in heedlessness, his early manhood under no restraint. He had found favour in Nero's eyes by imitating his extravagance; therefore Nero had left with him, privy as he was to his debaucheries, Poppaea Sabina, the imperial mistress, until he could get rid of his wife Octavia. Later the emperor suspected him in relation to this same Poppaea and removed him to the province of Lusitania, ostensibly as governor. He administered the province acceptably, but he was the first to join Galba's party and he was not an inactive partisan. So long as war lasted he was the most brilliant of all Galba's immediate supporters, and now, as soon as he had once conceived the hope of being adopted by Galba, he desired it more keenly every day that passed. The majority of the soldiers favoured him, and Nero's

plerisque militum, prona in eum aula Neronis ut similem.

XIV. Sed Galba post nuntios Germanicae seditionis, quamquam nihil adhuc de Vitellio certum, anxius quonam exercituum vis erumperet, ne urbano quidem militi confisus, quod remedium unicum rebatur, comitia imperii transigit; adhibitoque super Vinium ac Laconem Mario Celso consule designato ac Ducenio Gemino praefecto urbis, pauca praefatus de sua senectute, Pisonem Licinianum accersiri iubet, seu propria electione sive, ut quidam crediderunt, Lacone instante, cui apud Rubellium Plautum exercita cum Pisone amicitia; sed callide ut ignotum fovebat, et prospera de Pisone fama consilio eius fidem addiderat. Piso M. Crasso et Scribonia genitus, nobilis utrimque, vultu habituque moris antiqui et aestimatione[1] recta severus, deterius interpretantibus tristior habebatur: ea pars morum eius quo suspectior sollicitis adoptanti placebat.

XV. Igitur Galba, adprehensa Pisonis manu, in hunc modum locutus fertur: "Si te privatus lege

[1] aestimatione *Beroaldus*: extimatione *M.*

---

[1] M. Salvius Otho, born 32 A.D., had governed Lusitania well for ten years (59–68 A.D.) under Nero, but had promptly joined Galba's cause and had accompanied him to Rome. For a somewhat different account of his relation to Poppaea, see *Ann.* xiii. 45.

[2] The expression "imperial comitia" is ironical, in imitation of "consular comitia," etc., which described the ordinary elections. The date of the adoption was January 10.

court was inclined to him because he was like Nero.[1]

XIV. But after Galba received word of the disloyal movement in Germany, though he had as yet no certain news with regard to Vitellius, he was distressed as to the possible outcome of the army's violence, and had no confidence even in the soldiers within the city. So he held a kind of imperial comitia, which he regarded as his only remedy.[2] Besides Vinius and Laco, he called Marius Celsus, the consul-elect, and Ducenius Geminus, the city prefect. He first spoke briefly of his own advanced years, then directed that Licinianus Piso should be called in, either because he was his own choice, or, as some believed, owing to the insistence of Laco, who had formed an intimate friendship with Piso at the house of Rubellius Plautus. But Laco cleverly supported Piso as if he were a stranger, and Piso's good reputation added weight to Laco's advice. Piso was the son of Marcus Crassus and Scribonia, thus being noble on both sides;[3] his look and manner were those of a man of the ancient school, and he had justly been called stern; those who took a harsher view regarded him as morose, but this element in his character, which caused the anxious to suspect him, recommended him to Galba for adoption.

XV. Then Galba, according to report, took Piso's hand and spoke to this effect: "If as a private citizen I were adopting you according to curiate

[3] Piso, born 38 A.D., was long an exile under Nero (i. 48), and therefore had held no civil offices in the State. His father, mother, and one brother had been put to death by Claudius, a second brother killed by Nero.

curiata apud pontifices, ut moris est, adoptarem, et mihi egregium erat Cn.[1] Pompei et M. Crassi subolem in penatis meos adsciscere, et tibi insigne Sulpiciae ac Lutatiae decora nobilitati tuae adiecisse: nunc me deorum hominumque consensu ad imperium vocatum praeclara indoles tua et amor patriae impulit ut principatum, de quo maiores nostri armis certabant, bello adeptus quiescenti offeram, exemplo divi Augusti qui sororis filium Marcellum, dein generum Agrippam, mox nepotes suos, postremo Tiberium Neronem privignum in proximo sibi fastigio conlocavit. Sed Augustus in domo successorem quaesivit, ego in re publica, non quia propinquos aut socios belli non habeam, sed neque ipse imperium ambitione accepi, et iudicii mei documentum sit non meae tantum necessitudines, quas tibi postposui, sed et tuae. Est tibi frater pari nobilitate, natu maior, dignus hac fortuna nisi tu potior esses. Ea aetas tua quae cupiditates adulescentiae iam effugerit, ea vita in qua nihil praeteritum excusandum habeas. Fortunam adhuc tantum adversam tulisti: secundae res acrioribus stimulis animos explorant, quia miseriae tolerantur, felicitate corrumpimur. Fidem, libertatem, amicitiam, praecipua humani animi bona, tu quidem eadem constantia retinebis, sed alii per obsequium imminuent: inrumpet adulatio, blanditiae et[2] pessimum

[1] Cn. *Freinsheim*: nunc *M*.
[2] et *add. Freudenburg*.

---

[1] To give validity to the adoption of a mature person the approval of the curiae and of the pontifices was necessary. The curiate assembly had lost its political power in 286 B.C., but it was still represented by thirty lictors, assembled by the pontifices. Galba, as pontifex maximus, dispensed with the usual forms.

law before the pontifices, as is customary,[1] it were both an honour to me to bring into my house a descendant of Gnaeus Pompey and Marcus Crassus, and a distinction for you to add the glories of the Sulpician and Lutatian houses to your own high rank. But as it is, called to the imperial office, as I have been, by the consent of gods and men, I have been moved by your high character and patriotism to offer you in peace the principate for which our forefathers fought, and which I obtained in war. Herein I follow the example of the deified Augustus, who placed in high station next his own, first his sister's son Marcellus, then his son-in-law Agrippa, afterwards his grandsons, and finally Tiberius Nero, his step-son. But Augustus looked for a successor within his own house, I in the whole state. I do this not because I have not relatives or associates in arms; but I did not myself gain this power by self-seeking, and I would have the character of my decision shown by the fact that I have passed over for you not only my own relatives, but yours also. You have a brother as noble as yourself and older, worthy indeed of this fortune, if you were not the better man. You have reached an age which has already escaped from the passions of youth; your life is such that you have to offer no excuses for the past. Thus far you have known only adversity; prosperity tests the spirit with sharper goads, because we simply endure misfortune, but are corrupted by success. Honour, liberty, friendship, the chief blessings of the human mind, you will guard with the same constancy as before; but others will seek to weaken them by their servility. Flattery, adulation, and that worst poison

veri adfectus venenum, sua cuique utilitas. Etiam si[1] ego ac tu simplicissime inter nos hodie loquimur, ceteri libentius cum fortuna nostra quam nobiscum; nam suadere principi quod oporteat multi laboris, adsentatio erga quemcumque principem sine adfectu peragitur.

XVI. "Si immensum imperii corpus stare ac librari sine rectore posset, dignus eram a quo res publica inciperet: nunc eo necessitatis iam pridem ventum est ut nec mea senectus conferre plus populo Romano possit[2] quam bonum successorem, nec tua plus iuventa quam bonum principem. Sub Tiberio et Gaio et Claudio unius familiae quasi hereditas fuimus: loco libertatis erit quod eligi coepimus; et finita Iuliorum Claudiorumque domo optimum quemque adoptio inveniet. Nam generari et nasci a principibus fortuitum, nec ultra aestimatur: adoptandi iudicium integrum et, si velis eligere, consensu monstratur. Sit ante oculos Nero quem longa Caesarum serie tumentem non Vindex cum inermi provincia aut ego cum una legione, sed sua immanitas, sua luxuria cervicibus publicis depulerunt; neque erat adhuc damnati principis exemplum. Nos bello et ab aestimantibus adsciti cum invidia quamvis egregii erimus.

[1] etiam si *Halm*: etiam *M*.
[2] possit *Rhenanus*: posset *M*.

of an honest heart, self-interest, will force themselves in. Even though you and I speak to each other with perfect frankness to-day, all other men will prefer to deal with our great fortune rather than ourselves. For to persuade a prince of his duty is a great task, but to agree with him, whatever sort of prince he is, is a thing accomplished without real feeling.

XVI. "If the mighty structure of the empire could stand in even poise without a ruler, it were proper that a republic should begin with me. But as it is, we have long reached such a pass that my old age cannot give more to the Roman people than a good successor, or your youth more than a good emperor. Under Tiberius, Gaius, and Claudius we Romans were the heritage, so to speak, of one family; the fact that we emperors are now beginning to be chosen will be for all a kind of liberty; and since the houses of the Julii and the Claudii are ended, adoption will select only the best; for to be begotten and born of princes is mere chance, and is not reckoned higher, but the judgment displayed in adoption is unhampered; and, if one wishes to make a choice, common consent points out the individual. Keep Nero before your eyes. Swelling as he was with pride over the long line of Caesars, it was not Vindex with an unarmed province, nor I with a single legion, but his own monstrous character, his own extravagance, that flung him from the necks of the people; yet never before had there been a precedent for condemning an emperor. We, who have been called to power by war and men's judgment of our worth, shall be subject to envy, no matter how honourable we may prove. Yet do not be

Ne tamen territus fueris si duae legiones in hoc concussi orbis motu nondum quiescunt: ne ipse quidem ad securas res accessi, et audita adoptione desinam videri senex, quod nunc mihi unum obicitur. Nero a pessimo quoque semper desiderabitur: mihi ac tibi providendum est ne etiam a bonis desideretur. Monere diutius neque temporis huius, et impletum est omne consilium si te bene elegi. Utilissimus idem ac brevissimus bonarum malarumque rerum dilectus est, cogitare quid aut volueris sub alio principe aut nolueris; neque enim hic, ut gentibus quae regnantur, certa dominorum domus et ceteri servi, sed imperaturus es hominibus qui nec totam servitutem pati possunt nec totam libertatem."

Et Galba quidem haec ac talia, tamquam principem faceret, ceteri tamquam cum facto loquebantur.

XVII. Pisonem ferunt statim intuentibus et mox coniectis in eum omnium oculis nullum turbati aut exultantis animi motum prodidisse. Sermo erga patrem imperatoremque reverens, de se moderatus; nihil in vultu habituque mutatum, quasi imperare posset magis quam vellet. Consultatum inde, pro rostris an in senatu an in castris adoptio noncuparetur. Iri in castra placuit: honorificum id militibus fore,

frightened if there are still two legions not yet reduced to quiet in a world that has been shaken to its foundations. I myself did not come to the throne in security, and when men hear that I have adopted you, I shall cease to seem an old man—the one charge that is now laid against me. Nero will always be missed by the worst citizens; you and I must take care that he be not missed also by the good. To give you further advice were untimely, and, besides, all the advice I would give is fulfilled if you prove a wise choice. The distinction between good and evil is at once most useful and quickest made. Think only what you might wish or would oppose if another were emperor. For with us there is not, as among peoples where there are kings, a fixed house of rulers while all the rest are slaves, but you are going to rule over men who can endure neither complete slavery nor complete liberty."

Galba spoke further to the same effect, as if he were making an emperor, but everyone else conversed with Piso as if he had been already made one.

XVII. People report that Piso gave no sign of anxiety or exaltation, either before those who were looking on at the time or afterward when the eyes of all were upon him. He answered with the reverence due to a father and an emperor; he spoke modestly about himself. There was no change in his look or dress; he seemed like one who had the ability rather than the desire to be emperor. The question was then discussed whether his adoption should be proclaimed from the rostra or in the senate or in the praetorian camp. It was decided to go to the camp, for this act, they thought, would be a mark of honour toward the soldiers, whose support,

quorum favorem ut largitione et ambitu male adquiri, ita per bonas artis haud spernendum. Circumsteterat interim Palatium publica expectatio, magni secreti impatiens; et male coercitam famam supprimentes augebant.

XVIII. Quartum idus Ianuarias, foedum imbribus diem, tonitrua et fulgura et caelestes minae ultra solitum turbaverunt. Observatum id antiquitus comitiis dirimendis non terruit Galbam quo minus in castra pergeret, contemptorem talium ut fortuitorum; seu quae fato manent, quamvis significata, non vitantur. Apud frequentem militum contionem imperatoria brevitate adoptari a se Pisonem exemplo divi Augusti et more[1] militari, quo vir virum legeret, pronuntiat. Ac ne dissimulata seditio in maius crederetur, ultro adseverat quartam et duoetvicensimam[2] legiones, paucis seditionis auctoribus, non ultra verba ac voces errasse et brevi in officio fore. Nec ullum orationi aut lenocinium addit aut pretium. Tribuni tamen centurionesque et proximi militum grata auditu respondent: per ceteros maestitia ac silentium, tamquam usurpatam etiam in pace donativi necessitatem bello perdidissent. Constat potuisse conciliari animos quantulacumque parci senis liberali-

[1] Exemplo . . . more *Ferretus*: more . . . exemplo *M.*
[2] duoetvicensimam *Pichena*: duodevicensimam *M.*

---

[1] According to the primitive method of raising levies.

when gained through good arts, was not to be despised, however base it was to seek it by bribery and canvassing. In the meantime an expectant crowd had gathered around the palace, impatient to learn the great secret, while the unsuccessful efforts of those who wished to check the rumour only increased it.

XVIII. The tenth of January, a day of heavy rain, was made dreadful by thunder, lightning, and unusual threats from heaven. In earlier times notice of these things would have broken up an election, but they did not deter Galba from going to the praetorian camp, for he despised these things as mere chance; or else the truth is that we cannot avoid the fixed decrees of fate, by whatever signs revealed. Before a crowded gathering of the soldiers, with the brevity that became an emperor, he announced that he was adopting Piso after the precedent set by the deified Augustus, and following the military custom by which one man chose another.[1] And to prevent an exaggerated idea of the revolt by attempting to conceal it, he went on to say that the Fourth and Twenty-second legions had been led astray by a few seditious leaders, but their errors had not passed beyond words and cries, and presently they would be under discipline. He added no flattery of the soldiers, nor made mention of a gift. Yet the tribunes, centurions, and soldiers nearest him answered in a satisfactory manner; but among all the rest of the soldiers there was a gloomy silence, for they felt that they had lost through war the right to a gift which had been theirs even in times of peace. There is no question that their loyalty could have been won by the slightest generosity on the part of this stingy old man. He

tate: nocuit antiquus rigor et nimia severitas, cui iam pares non sumus.

XIX. Inde apud senatum non comptior Galbae, non longior quam apud militem sermo: Pisonis comis oratio. Et patrum favor aderat: multi voluntate, effusius qui noluerant, medii ac plurimi obvio obsequio, privatas spes agitantes sine publica cura. Nec aliud sequenti quadriduo, quod medium inter adoptionem et caedem fuit, dictum a Pisone in publico factumve. Crebrioribus in dies Germanicae defectionis nuntiis et facili civitate ad accipienda credendaque omnia nova cum tristia sunt, censuerant patres mittendos ad Germanicum exercitum legatos. Agitatum secreto num et Piso proficisceretur, maiore praetextu, illi auctoritatem senatus, hic dignationem Caesaris laturus. Placebat et Laconem praetorii praefectum simul mitti: is consilio intercessit. Legati quoque (nam senatus electionem Galbae permiserat) foeda inconstantia nominati, excusati, substituti, ambitu remanendi aut eundi, ut quemque metus vel spes impulerat.

XX. Proxima pecuniae cura; et cuncta scrutantibus iustissimum visum est inde repeti ubi inopiae causa erat. Bis et viciens miliens[1] sestertium donationibus Nero effuderat: appellari singulos iussit,

[1] milies *Lipsius*: mille *M.*

---

[1] A sum roughly equivalent to $100,000,000 of our money, but the vastly greater value of money in antiquity must be taken into account to arrive at a just comparison.

was ruined by his old-fashioned strictness and excessive severity—qualities which we can no longer bear.

XIX. Galba's speech to the senate was as bald and brief as his address to the soldiers. Piso spoke with grace; and the senators showed their approval. Many did this from good-will, those who had opposed the adoption with more effusion, the indifferent—and they were the most numerous—with ready servility, for they had their private hopes in mind and cared nothing for the state. During the four days that followed between his adoption and murder Piso said and did nothing further in public. More frequent reports of the revolt in Germany arrived every day, and since the citizens were ready to accept and believe anything strange and bad, the senate voted to send a delegation to the army in Germany. There was a secret discussion as to whether Piso also should go, that so the mission might be more imposing: the other members would take with them the authority of the senate, Piso the dignity of a Caesar. They voted to send Laco also, the prefect of the praetorian cohort; but he vetoed their plan. The senate had left the choice of members to Galba. With disgraceful lack of firmness he named men, excused them, made substitutions, as they pleaded with him to stay or go, according to their fears or hopes.

XX. The next anxiety was with regard to finances. After full consideration it seemed fairest to look for money from the sources where the cause of the poverty lay. Twenty-two hundred million sesterces had been squandered by Nero in gifts.[1] It was

decima parte liberalitatis apud quemque eorum relicta. At illis vix decimae super portiones erant, isdem erga aliena sumptibus quibus sua prodegerant, cum rapacissimo cuique ac perditissimo non agri aut faenus sed sola instrumenta vitiorum manerent. Exactioni triginta equites Romani praepositi, novum officii genus et ambitu ac numero onerosum : ubique hasta et sector, et inquieta urbs actionibus. Ac tamen grande gaudium quod tam pauperes forent quibus donasset Nero quam quibus abstulisset. Exauctorati per eos dies tribuni, e praetorio Antonius Taurus et Antonius Naso, ex urbanis cohortibus Aemilius Pacensis, e vigilibus Iulius Fronto. Nec remedium in ceteros fuit, sed metus initium, tamquam per artem et formidinem singuli pellerentur, omnibus suspectis.

XXI. Interea Othonem, cui compositis rebus nulla spes, omne in turbido consilium, multa simul exstimulabant, luxuria etiam principi onerosa, inopia vix privato toleranda, in Galbam ira, in Pisonem invidia ; fingebat et metum quo magis concupisceret : praegravem se Neroni fuisse, nec Lusitaniam rursus et alterius exilii honorem expectandum. Suspectum

voted that individuals should be summoned, and that a tenth part of the gifts which Nero had made them should be left with each. But Nero's favourites had hardly one-tenth left, for they had wasted the money of others on the same extravagances as they had their own; the most greedy and depraved had neither lands nor principal, but only what would minister to their vices. Thirty Roman knights were appointed to collect the money. This was a new office, and a burden because of the number and intrigue of its members. Everywhere there were auctions and speculators, and the city was disturbed by lawsuits. And yet there was great joy that those who had received gifts from Nero were going to be as poor as those from whom he had taken the money. During these same days four tribunes were dismissed, Antonius Taurus and Antonius Naso from the praetorian cohorts, from the city cohorts Aemilius Pacensis, and Julius Fronto from the police. This action was no assistance against the rest, but it did arouse their fears: individuals, they thought, were being driven from office craftily and cautiously one by one, because all were suspected.

XXI. In the meantime Otho, who had nothing to hope from a peaceful arrangement, and whose purpose depended wholly on disorder, was spurred on by many considerations. His extravagance was such as would have burdened an emperor, his poverty a private citizen could hardly have borne. He was angry toward Galba and jealous of Piso. He invented fears also to give his greed greater scope. He said that he had been formidable to Nero, and that he could not look again for Lusitania and the honour of a second exile; that tyrants always suspected and

semper invisumque dominantibus qui proximus destinaretur. Nocuisse id sibi apud senem principem, magis nociturum apud iuvenem ingenio trucem et longo exilio efferatum: occidi Othonem posse. Proinde agendum audendumque, dum Galbae auctoritas fluxa, Pisonis nondum coaluisset. Opportunos magnis conatibus transitus rerum, nec cunctatione opus, ubi perniciosior sit quies quam temeritas. Mortem omnibus ex natura aequalem oblivione apud posteros vel gloria distingui; ac si nocentem innocentemque idem exitus maneat, acrioris viri esse merito perire.

XXII. Non erat Othonis mollis et corpori similis animus. Et intimi libertorum servorumque, corruptius quam in privata domo habiti, aulam Neronis et luxus, adulteria, matrimonia ceterasque regnorum libidines avido talium, si auderet, ut sua ostentantes, quiescenti ut aliena exprobrabant, urgentibus etiam mathematicis, dum novos motus et clarum Othoni annum observatione siderum adfirmant, genus hominum potentibus infidum, sperantibus fallax, quod in civitate nostra et vetabitur semper et retinebitur. Multos secreta Poppaeae mathematicos, pessimum principalis matrimonii instrumentum, habuerant: e quibus Ptolemaeus Othoni in Hispania comes, cum superfuturum eum Neroni promisisset, postquam ex

hated the man who was marked out as their successor; this had already injured him with the aged emperor, and was going to injure him still more with the young one, who was cruel by nature and embittered by long exile. An Otho could be murdered; therefore he must be bold and act while Galba's authority was still weak and Piso's not yet established; this time of transition was opportune for great attempts, and a man must not delay when inactivity is more ruinous than rash action. Death nature ordains for all alike; but it differs as it brings either oblivion or glory in after ages; and if the same end awaits the guilty and the innocent, it is the duty of a man of superior vigour to deserve his death.

XXII. Otho's mind was not effeminate like his body. His intimate freedmen and slaves, who had more licence than prevails in private houses, constantly held before his eager eyes Nero's luxurious court, his adulteries, his many marriages, and other royal vices, exhibiting them as his own if he only dared to take them, but taunting him with them as the privilege of others if he did not act. The astrologers also—a tribe of men untrustworthy for the powerful, deceitful towards the ambitious, a tribe which in our state will always be both forbidden and retained—they also urged him on, declaring from their observation of the stars that there were new movements on foot, and that the year would be a glorious one for Otho. Many of these astrologers, the worst possible tools for an imperial consort, had shared Poppaea's secret plans, and one of them, Ptolemy, who had been with Otho in Spain, had promised him that he should survive Nero. Having

eventu fides, coniectura iam et rumore senium Galbae et iuventam Othonis computantium persuaserat fore ut in imperium adscisceretur. Sed Otho tamquam peritia et monitu fatorum praedicta accipiebat, cupidine ingenii humani libentius obscura credendi. Nec deerat Ptolemaeus, iam et sceleris instinctor, ad quod facillime ab eius modi voto transitur.

XXIII. Sed sceleris cogitatio incertum an repens: studia militum iam pridem spe successionis aut paratu facinoris adfectaverat, in itinere, in agmine, in stationibus vetustissimum quemque militum nomine vocans ac memoria Neroniani comitatus contubernalis appellando; alios agnoscere, quosdam requirere et pecunia aut gratia iuvare, inserendo saepius querelas et ambiguos de Galba sermones quaeque alia turbamenta vulgi. Labores itinerum, inopia commeatuum, duritia imperii atrocius accipiebantur, cum Campaniae lacus et Achaiae urbes classibus adire soliti Pyrenaeum et Alpes et immensa viarum spatia aegre sub armis eniterentur.

XXIV. Flagrantibus iam militum animis velut faces addiderat Maevius Pudens, e proximis Tigellini. Is

---

[1] On Tigellinus, see i. 72 below.

won credit by the event, he had then, employing his own conjectures and the gossip of those who compared Galba's old age and Otho's youth, persuaded Otho that he would be called to the imperial office. But Otho accepted his prophecies as if they were genuine warnings of fate disclosed by Ptolemy's skill, for human nature is especially eager to believe the mysterious. And Ptolemy did not fail to do his part; he was already urging Otho even to crime, to which from such aspirations the transition is most easily made.

XXIII. Yet it is uncertain whether the idea of committing crime came suddenly to Otho; he had long been trying to win popularity with the soldiers because he hoped for the succession or was preparing some bold step. On the march, at review, or in camp he addressed all the oldest soldiers by name, and, reminding them that they had attended Nero together, he called them messmates. Others he recognized, some he asked after and helped with money or influence; oftentimes he let drop words of complaint and remarks of a double meaning concerning Galba, and did other things that tended to disturb the common soldiery. For they were grumbling seriously over the toilsome marches, the lack of supplies, and the hard discipline. The men who had been in the habit of going by ship to the lakes of Campania and the cities of Achaia found it hard to climb the Pyrenees and the Alps under arms and to cover endless marches along the high roads.

XXIV. When the minds of the soldiers were already inflamed, Maevius Pudens, one of Tigellinus's nearest friends,[1] added fuel to the fire. Winning

mobilissimum quemque ingenio aut pecuniae indigum et in novas cupiditates praecipitem adliciendo eo paulatim progressus est ut per speciem convivii, quotiens Galba apud Othonem epularetur, cohorti excubias agenti viritim centenos nummos divideret; quam velut publicam largitionem Otho secretioribus apud singulos praemiis intendebat, adeo animosus corruptor ut Cocceio Proculo speculatori, de parte finium cum vicino ambigenti, universum vicini agrum sua pecunia emptum dono dederit, per socordiam praefecti, quem nota pariter et occulta fallebant.

XXV. Sed tum e libertis Onomastum futuro sceleri praefecit, a quo Barbium Proculum tesserarium speculatorum et Veturium optionem eorundem perductos, postquam vario sermone callidos audacisque cognovit, pretio et promissis onerat, data pecunia ad pertemptandos plurium animos. Suscepere duo manipulares imperium populi Romani transferendum et transtulerunt. In conscientiam facinoris pauci adsciti: suspensos ceterorum animos diversis artibus stimulant, primores militum per beneficia Nymphidii ut suspectos, vulgus et ceteros ira et desperatione dilati totiens donativi. Erant quos memoria Neronis

---

[1] The speculatores were picked men, chosen from the praetorians, who formed the bodyguard of the emperor.

over all who were of a restless temper or who needed money and were hot-headed for a revolution, he gradually came to the point, whenever Galba dined at Otho's house, of using the dinner as an excuse for distributing one hundred sesterces to each member of the cohort that stood on guard. This was a kind of gift from the state, but Otho added to its significance by secret gifts to individuals; and he grew so bold in his acts of corruption that when Cocceius Proculus, one of the bodyguard,[1] had a quarrel with his neighbour with regard to boundaries, Otho bought up the neighbour's whole farm with his own money and gave it to Proculus. This was possible through the dullness of the prefect Laco, who equally failed to see what was notorious and what was secret.

XXV. Then Otho put one of his freedmen, Onomastus, in charge of the crime he planned. When Onomastus had won over Barbius Proculus, the officer of the password for the bodyguard, and Veturius, a subaltern of the same, and had learned through various conversations that they were clever and bold, he loaded them with rewards and promises, and gave them money to tamper with the loyalty of a larger number. Two common soldiers thus undertook to transfer the imperial power, and they transferred it. Few were admitted to share the plot. By various devices they worked on the anxieties of the rest—on the soldiers of higher rank by treating them as if they were suspected because of the favours Nymphidius had shown them, on the mass of the common soldiers by stimulating their anger and disappointment that the donative had been so often deferred. There were some who were

ac desiderium prioris licentiae accenderet: in commune[1] omnes metu mutandae militiae terrebantur.

XXVI. Infecit ea tabes legionum quoque et auxiliorum motas iam mentis, postquam vulgatum erat labare Germanici exercitus fidem. Adeoque parata apud malos seditio, etiam apud integros dissimulatio fuit, ut postero iduum die redeuntem a cena Othonem rapturi fuerint, ni incerta noctis et tota urbe sparsa militum castra nec facilem inter temulentos consensum timuissent, non rei publicae cura, quam foedare principis sui sanguine sobrii parabant, sed ne per tenebras, ut quisque Pannonici vel Germanici exercitus militibus oblatus esset, ignorantibus plerisque, pro Othone destinaretur. Multa erumpentis seditionis indicia per conscios oppressa: quaedam apud Galbae auris praefectus Laco elusit, ignarus militarium animorum consiliique quamvis egregii, quod non ipse adferret, inimicus et adversus peritos pervicax.

XXVII. Octavo decimo kalendas Februarias sacrificanti pro aede Apollinis Galbae haruspex Umbricius tristia exta[2] et instantis insidias ac domesticum hostem praedicit, audiente Othone (nam proximus

[1] commune *Rhenanus*: communi *M*. [2] tristitia *M*.

kindled by their memory of Nero and a longing for their former licence: but all had one common fear of some change in their conditions of service.

XXVI. This infection touched the loyalty of the legions also and of the auxiliaries, who were already unsettled, now that it was a matter of common knowledge that the army in Germany was disaffected. And so ready were the ill-disposed for revolt and even the loyal to wink at wrong-doing, that on the fourteenth of January they planned to carry off Otho as he was returning from dinner, and would have done so if they had not been deterred by the uncertainty of night, by the dispersion of the soldiers in detachments scattered through the whole city, and by the difficulties of common action when men are in their cups. They were not influenced by any anxiety for the state, for in their sober senses they were preparing to pollute it with the blood of their emperor; but they feared that in the darkness any man who fell in the way of the soldiers from Pannonia or Germany might be proclaimed as Otho, for the majority did not know him. There were many signs of the outbreak of the revolt, but these were repressed by the plotters. Some things reached Galba's ears, but the prefect Laco made light of them; he was unacquainted with the soldiers' spirit, and he was opposed to any plan, however excellent, which he did not himself propose, and obstinate against those who knew better than himself.

XXVII. On the fifteenth of January, when Galba was sacrificing in front of the temple of Apollo, the seer Umbricius declared that the omens were unfavourable, that a plot was imminent, and that an enemy was in his house. Otho heard this, for he

adstiterat[1]) idque ut laetum e contrario et suis cogitationibus prosperum interpretante. Nec multo post libertus Onomastus nuntiat expectari eum ab architecto et redemptoribus, quae significatio coeuntium iam militum et paratae coniurationis convenerat. Otho, causam digressus requirentibus, cum emi sibi praedia vetustate suspecta eoque prius exploranda finxisset, innixus liberto per Tiberianam domum in Velabrum, inde ad miliarium aureum sub aedem Saturni pergit. Ibi tres et viginti speculatores consalutatum imperatorem ac paucitate salutantium trepidum et sellae festinanter impositum strictis mucronibus rapiunt; totidem ferme milites in itinere adgregantur, alii conscientia, plerique miraculo, pars clamore et gladiis, pars silentio, animum ex eventu sumpturi.

XXVIII. Stationem in castris agebat Iulius Martialis tribunus. Is magnitudine subiti sceleris, an corrupta latius castra et, si contra tenderet, exitium metuens, praebuit plerisque suspicionem conscientiae; anteposuere ceteri quoque tribuni centurionesque praesentia dubiis et honestis, isque habitus animorum fuit ut pessimum facinus auderent pauci, plures vellent, omnes paterentur.

XXIX. Ignarus interim Galba et sacris intentus

[1] adsisterat *M.*

---

[1] The *miliarium aureum* was a column, covered with gilt-bronze, erected by Augustus, on which were engraved the names of the chief cities of the empire and their distances from Rome.

stood next to Galba, and interpreted it by contraries as favourable to himself and auguring well for his purposes. Presently his freedman, Onomastus, announced to him that his architect and the contractors were waiting for him, this having been agreed upon as a sign that the soldiers were already gathering and that the conspiracy was ripe. When some asked Otho why he was leaving, he gave as an excuse that he was buying some properties of whose value he was doubtful because of their age, and therefore he wished to examine them first. Taking the arm of his freedman he walked through the palace of Tiberius to the Velabrum, and then to the golden milestone[1] hard by the temple of Saturn. There twenty-three of the bodyguard hailed him as emperor; when he was frightened because there were so few to greet him, they put him quickly into a chair and with drawn swords hurried him away. About the same number of soldiers joined them as they went, some through knowledge, more through wonder, a part with shouts and drawn swords, a part in silence, ready to take their cue from the result.

XXVIII. Julius Martialis the tribune was the officer of the day in the camp. Terrified by the enormity of the sudden crime, ignorant of the extent to which the camp was disloyal, and fearing death if he opposed, he made the majority suspect him of complicity. All the rest of the tribunes also and the centurions preferred present safety to a doubtful but honourable course. And such was the attitude of their minds that the foulest of crimes was dared by a few, desired by more, and acquiesced in by all.

XXIX. Galba in the meantime was in ignorance.

fatigabat alieni iam imperii deos, cum adfertur rumor rapi in castra incertum quem senatorem, mox Othonem esse qui raperetur, simul ex tota urbe, ut quisque obvius fuerat, alii formidine augentes, quidam minora vero, ne tum quidem obliti adulationis. Igitur consultantibus placuit pertemptari animum cohortis, quae in Palatio stationem agebat, nec per ipsum Galbam, cuius integra auctoritas maioribus remediis servabatur. Piso pro gradibus domus vocatos in hunc modum adlocutus est: "Sextus dies agitur commilitones, ex quo ignarus futuri, et sive optandum hoc nomen sive timendum erat, Caesar adscitus sum. Quo domus nostrae aut rei publicae fato[1] in vestra manu positum est, non quia meo nomine tristiorem casum paveam, ut qui adversas res expertus cum maxime discam[2] ne secundas quidem minus discriminis habere: patris et senatus et ipsius imperii vicem doleo, si nobis aut perire hodie necesse est aut, quod aeque apud bonos miserum est, occidere. Solacium proximi motus habebamus incruentam urbem et res sine discordia translatas: provisum adoptione videbatur ut ne post Galbam quidem bello locus esset.

XXX. "Nihil adrogabo mihi nobilitatis aut modestiae; neque enim relatu virtutum in comparatione Othonis opus est. Vitia, quibus solis gloriatur,

[1] fato *Puteolanus*: fatum *M*.
[2] discam *Freinsheim*: dicam *M*.

Intent upon his sacrifices, he was importuning the gods of an empire which was already another's, when a report was brought to him that some senator or other was being hurried to the camp. Afterwards rumour said that it was Otho; and at the same time people came from the whole city—some, who had happened to meet the procession, exaggerating the facts through terror, some making light of them, for they did not even then forget to flatter. On consultation it was decided to try the temper of the cohort that was on guard at the palace, but not through Galba himself, whose authority was kept unimpaired for more serious measures. Piso, standing on the steps of the palace, called the soldiers together and spoke as follows: "It is now five days, my comrades, since, in ignorance of the future, I was adopted as Caesar, not knowing whether this name was one to be desired or feared. The fate of our house and the State depends on you. I say this not because I fear misfortune on my own account, for I have known adversity, and at the present moment I am learning that prosperity brings no less danger. But I grieve for the fate of my father, the senate, and the very empire, if we must either ourselves die to-day or kill others—an act which brings equal sorrow to the good. In the last uprising we were solaced by the fact that the city was unstained by blood and the government transferred without dissension: adoption seemed to provide against any occasion for war even after Galba's death.

XXX. "I make no claim of high birth or character for myself, and I need not catalogue virtues when the comparison is with Otho. His faults, which are

evertere imperium, etiam cum amicum imperatoris ageret. Habitune et incessu an illo muliebri ornatu mereretur imperium? Falluntur quibus luxuria specie[1] liberalitatis imponit: perdere iste sciet, donare nesciet. Stupra nunc et comissationes et feminarum coetus volvit animo: haec principatus praemia putat, quorum libido ac voluptas penes ipsum sit, rubor ac dedecus penes omnis; nemo enim umquam imperium flagitio quaesitum bonis artibus exercuit. Galbam consensus generis humani, me Galba consentientibus vobis Caesarem dixit. Si res publica et senatus et populus vacua nomina sunt, vestra, commilitones, interest ne imperatorem pessimi faciant. Legionum seditio adversus duces suos audita est aliquando: vestra fides famaque inlaesa ad hunc diem mansit. Et Nero quoque vos destituit, non vos Neronem. Minus triginta transfugae et desertores, quos centurionem aut tribunum sibi eligentis nemo ferret, imperium adsignabunt? Admittitis exemplum et quiescendo commune crimen facitis? Transcendet haec licentia in provincias, et ad nos scelerum exitus, bellorum ad vos pertinebunt. Nec est plus quod pro caede principis quam quod innocentibus datur, sed proinde a nobis donativum ob fidem quam ab aliis pro facinore accipietis."

[1] specie *Rhenanus*: speciem *M*.

the only things in which he glories, were undermining the empire even when he pretended to be the friend of the emperor. Was it by his bearing and gait or by his womanish dress that he deserved the throne? They are deceived who are imposed upon by extravagance under the garb of generosity. He will know how to ruin, he will not know how to give. Adulteries and revelries and gatherings of women fill his thoughts: these he considers the prerogatives of imperial power. The lust and pleasure of them will be his, the shame and disgrace of them will fall on every Roman; for imperial power gained by wicked means no man has ever used honourably. The consent of all mankind made Galba Caesar, and Galba made me so with your consent. If the State and the Senate and People are but empty names, it is your concern, comrades, that the emperor should not be made by the worst citizens. A revolt of the legions against their generals has been sometimes heard of; your loyalty and good name have remained unimpaired down to the present day. It was Nero, too, who deserted you, not you Nero. Shall less than thirty renegades and deserters, men whom no one would allow to choose a centurion or tribune, bestow the empire? Will you allow this precedent, and by inaction make their crime yours? Such licence will spread to the provinces, and the consequence of their crimes will fall on us, the resulting wars on you. The reward given the assassins for the murder of the emperor will not be greater than that which will be bestowed on those who refrain from crime; nay, you will receive no less a gift from us for loyalty than you will from others for treason."

XXXI. Dilapsis speculatoribus cetera cohors non aspernata contionantem, ut turbidis rebus evenit, forte[1] magis et nullo[2] adhuc consilio rapit signa[3] quam,[4] quod postea creditum est, insidiis et simulatione. Missus et Celsus Marius ad electos Illyrici exercitus, Vipsania in porticu tendentis; praeceptum Amullio Sereno et Domitio Sabino primipilaribus, ut Germanicos milites e Libertatis atrio accerserent. Legioni classicae diffidebatur,[5] infestae ob caedem commilitonum, quos primo statim introitu trucidaverat Galba. Pergunt etiam in castra praetorianorum tribuni Cetrius Severus, Subrius Dexter, Pompeius Longinus, si incipiens adhuc et necdum adulta seditio melioribus consiliis flecteretur. Tribunorum Subrium et Cetrium adorti milites minis, Longinum manibus coercent exarmantque, quia non ordine militiae, sed e Galbae amicis, fidus principi suo et desciscentibus suspectior erat. Legio classica nihil cunctata praetorianis adiungitur; Illyrici exercitus electi Celsum infestis[6] pilis proturbant. Germanica vexilla diu nutavere, invalidis adhuc corporibus et

1 evenit forte *Pichena*: eventior te *M.*
2 nullo *Freinsheim*: nonnullo *M.*
3 rapit signa *Meiser*: par signas *M.*
4 quam *add. Heinsius.*
5 diffidebatur *Acidalius*: diffidebat *M.*
6 festum incestis *M.*

---

1 This was on the west side of the *Campus Agrippae*, a piazza laid out by Agrippa on the Campus Martius, and finished and dedicated by Augustus in 7 B.C.

2 This building, which held the archives and offices of the censors, had been restored by Asinius Pollio, who in 39 B.C.

XXXI. The members of the bodyguard slunk away, but the rest of the cohort did not refuse to hear his speech, and, as frequently happens in times of excitement, they seized their standards haphazard, without any plan as yet, rather than, as was afterwards believed, to conceal their treachery. Celsus Marius was sent to the picked troops from Illyria, who were encamped in the Vipsanian Colonnade;[1] Amullius Serenus and Domitius Sabinus, centurions of the first rank, were ordered to summon the German troops from the Hall of Liberty.[2] The legion of marines was not trusted, for they were still hostile to Galba, because he had immediately massacred their comrades when he first entered the city.[3] The tribunes, Cetrius Severus, Subrius Dexter, and Pompeius Longinus, went even into the praetorian camp to see if the mutiny were still incipient and not yet come to a head, so that it could be averted by wiser counsels. Subrius and Cetrius the soldiers attacked and threatened, Longinus they forcibly restrained and disarmed; this action was prompted by his fidelity to his emperor, which was due not to his military position, but to his friendship for Galba; therefore the mutineers regarded him with the greater suspicion. The legion of marines without hesitation joined the praetorians. The picked troops from Illyria drove Celsus away at the point of their spears. The German detachments hesitated for a long time; they were still weak physically and were kindly

established in it the first public library at Rome. It was apparently on or near the site on which Trajan later built his forum.

[3] Cf. chap. 6 above.

placatis animis, quod eos a Nerone Alexandriam praemissos atque inde reversos[1] longa navigatione aegros impensiore cura Galba refovebat.

XXXII. Universa iam plebs Palatium implebat, mixtis servitiis et dissono clamore caedem Othonis et coniuratorum exitium[2] poscentium ut si in circo aut[3] theatro ludicrum aliquod postularent: neque illis iudicium aut veritas, quippe eodem die diversa pari certamine postulaturis, sed tradito more quemcumque principem adulandi licentia adclamationum et studiis inanibus.

Interim Galbam duae sententiae distinebant: Titus Vinius manendum intra domum, opponenda servitia, firmandos aditus, non eundum ad iratos censebat: daret malorum paenitentiae, daret bonorum consensui spatium: scelera impetu, bona consilia mora valescere, denique eundi ultro, si ratio sit, eandem mox facultatem, regressus, si paeniteat, in aliena potestate.

XXXIII. Festinandum ceteris videbatur antequam cresceret invalida adhuc coniuratio paucorum: trepidaturum etiam Othonem, qui furtim digressus, ad ignaros inlatus, cunctatione nunc et segnitia

[1] reversos *Döderlein*: rursus *M.*
[2] exitium *Acidalius*: exitum *M.*
[3] aut *ed. Spirensis*: a *M.*

---

[1] Cf. Juvenal x. 54–77.

disposed towards Galba, for Nero had sent them to Alexandria, and then on their return, when sick from their long voyage, Galba had taken great pains to care for them.

XXXII. The whole mass of the people, with slaves among them, filled the palace. There were discordant cries demanding Otho's death and the execution of the conspirators, exactly as if the people were calling for some show in the circus or the theatre; there was neither sense nor honesty in their demands, for on this very same day they would have clamoured for the opposite with equal enthusiasm;[1] but they acted according to the traditional custom of flattering the emperor, whoever he might be, with fulsome acclamations and senseless zeal.

In the meantime Galba was torn between two proposals: Titus Vinius urged the necessity of staying in the palace, arming the slaves for defence, blocking the entrances, and not going to the infuriated troops. Let Galba, he said, give time for the disloyal to repent, for the loyal to come to a common agreement; crimes gained strength by impulsive action, wise counsels through delay; and, after all, he would later have the same opportunity to go on his own motion if it should seem wise, but if he went now and regretted it, his return would depend on others.

XXXIII. All the rest thought that he should act immediately, before the conspiracy, as yet weak and confined to a few, should gain strength. They declared that Otho would lose heart. He had slipped away by stealth, had presented himself to people who did not know him, and now, because

terentium tempus imitari principem discat. Non expectandum ut compositis castris forum invadat et prospectante Galba Capitolium adeat, dum egregius imperator cum fortibus amicis ianua ac limine tenus domum cludit, obsidionem nimirum toleraturus. Et praeclarum in servis auxilium si consensus tantae multitudinis et, quae plurimum valet, prima indignatio elanguescat.[1] Proinde intuta quae indecora; vel si cadere necesse sit, occurrendum discrimini: id Othoni invidiosius et ipsis honestum. Repugnantem huic sententiae Vinium Laco minaciter invasit, stimulante Icelo privati odii pertinacia in publicum exitium.

XXXIV. Nec diutius Galba cunctatus speciosiora suadentibus accessit. Praemissus tamen in castra Piso, ut iuvenis magno nomine, recenti favore et infensus Tito Vinio, seu quia erat seu quia irati ita volebant; et facilius de odio creditur. Vixdum egresso Pisone occisum in castris Othonem vagus primum et incertus rumor: mox, ut in magnis mendaciis, interfuisse se quidam et vidisse adfirma-

[1] indignatio elanguescat *I. Gronovius*: indignatione languescat *M.*

---

[1] Cf. Suet. *Galba*, 19, for a different account.

of the hesitancy and inactivity of those who were wasting their time, he was having an opportunity to learn to play the emperor. There must be no waiting for Otho to settle matters in the camp, invade the forum, and go to the Capitol under the very eyes of Galba, while that most noble emperor with his valiant friends barred his house and did not cross his threshold, being ready, no doubt, to endure a siege! It was a brilliant backing, too, that they would find in slaves, if the united sentiment of the whole people and their first indignation, which is the strongest, should be allowed to cool! The dishonourable, therefore, was the dangerous resolve; even if they must fall, they should go forth to meet the danger; that would bring more disrepute on Otho and honour to themselves. When Vinius opposed this view Laco attacked him with threats, goaded on by Icelus, who persisted in his personal enmity towards Vinius to the ruin of the state.

XXXIV. Galba did not delay any longer, but favoured those who offered the more specious advice.[1] Yet Piso was sent first to the camp, for he was young, had a great name, and enjoyed fresh popularity; he was also an enemy of Titus Vinius; either that was a fact, or else in their anger the opponents of Vinius wished to have it so: and it is so much easier to believe in hatred. Piso had hardly left the palace when a report was brought, vague and uncertain at first, that Otho had been killed in the camp. Presently, as is natural in falsehoods of great importance, some appeared who declared that they had been present and had seen the murder. Between those who rejoiced in the news and those who were indifferent

bant, credula fama inter gaudentis et incuriosos. Multi arbitrabantur compositum auctumque rumorem mixtis iam Othonianis, qui ad evocandum Galbam laeta falso vulgaverint.

XXXV. Tum vero non populus tantum et imperita plebs in plausus et immodica studia sed equitum plerique ac senatorum, posito metu incauti, refractis Palatii foribus ruere intus ac se Galbae ostentare, praereptam sibi ultionem querentes, ignavissimus quisque et, ut res docuit, in periculo non ausurus, nimii verbis, linguae feroces; nemo scire et omnes adfirmare, donec inopia veri et consensu errantium victus sumpto thorace Galba inruenti turbae neque aetate neque corpore resistens[1] sella levaretur. Obvius in Palatio Iulius Atticus speculator, cruentum gladium ostentans, occisum a se Othonem exclamavit; et Galba "Commilito," inquit, "quis iussit?" insigni animo ad coercendam militarem licentiam, minantibus intrepidus, adversus blandientis incorruptus.

XXXVI. Haud dubiae iam in castris omnium mentes tantusque ardor ut non contenti agmine et corporibus in suggestu, in quo paulo ante aurea Galbae statua fuerat, medium inter signa Othonem

[1] resistens *Faernus*: sistens *M.*

to it, the story was believed. Many thought this rumour had been invented and exaggerated by Otho's partisans who were already in the crowd and spread abroad the pleasant falsehood in order to lure Galba from his palace.

XXXV. Then indeed it was not the people only and the ignorant mob that burst into applause and unrestrained enthusiasm, but many of the knights and senators as well. They laid aside all fear and became incautious, broke down the doors of the palace and burst in, presenting themselves to Galba and complaining that they had been robbed of vengeance. They were all rank cowards, and, as the event proved, men who would show no courage in time of danger, but who now were exceedingly bold with words and savage of tongue. No one knew; everyone affirmed. Finally, overcome by the dearth of truth and by the common error, Galba put on his breastplate; then since his years and strength were unequal to resisting the inrushing crowds, he was raised aloft in a chair. Julius Atticus, one of the bodyguard, met him in the palace, and exhibiting his bloody sword cried out that he had killed Otho. "Who gave you orders, comrade?" said Galba; for Galba showed a remarkable spirit in checking licence on the part of the soldiers; before threats he was unterrified, and incorruptible against flattery.

XXXVI. There was no longer any doubt as to the sentiments of all the soldiers in the camp. Their enthusiasm was so great that they were not satisfied with carrying Otho on their shoulders as they advanced, but they placed him on a platform where shortly before the gilded statue of Galba had stood, and surrounded him with the standards and

vexillis circumdarent. Nec tribunis aut centurionibus adeundi locus: gregarius miles caveri insuper praepositos iubebat. Strepere cuncta clamoribus et tumultu et exhortatione mutua, non tamquam in populo ac plebe, variis segni adulatione vocibus, sed ut quemque adfluentium militum aspexerant, prensare manibus, complecti armis, conlocare iuxta, praeire sacramentum, modo imperatorem militibus, modo milites imperatori commendare. Nec deerat Otho protendens manus adorare vulgum, iacere oscula et omnia serviliter pro dominatione. Postquam universa classicorum legio sacramentum eius accepit, fidens viribus, et quos adhuc singulos exstimulaverat, accendendos in commune ratus pro vallo castrorum ita coepit.

XXXVII. "Quis ad vos processerim, commilitones, dicere non possum, quia nec privatum me vocare sustineo princeps a vobis nominatus, nec principem alio imperante. Vestrum quoque nomen in incerto erit donec dubitabitur imperatorem populi Romani in castris an hostem habeatis. Auditisne ut poena mea et supplicium vestrum simul postulentur? Adeo manifestum est neque perire nos neque salvos esse nisi una posse; et cuius lenitatis est Galba, iam fortasse promisit, ut qui nullo exposcente tot milia innocentissimorum militum trucidaverit. Horror animum subit quotiens recordor feralem introitum et

ensigns. Neither tribune nor centurion was allowed to approach him: the common soldiery kept calling out that they must beware of their commanders above all. There was utter confusion, with shouts and tumult and mutual exhortation—not such as one sees in a gathering of the people and populace, when there are various cries and half-hearted flattery, but they seized everyone they saw coming over to them, embraced them with their arms, placed them next to them, repeated the oath of allegiance, now recommending the emperor to the soldiers, now the soldiers to the emperor. Otho did not fail in his part: he stretched out his hands and did obeisance to the common soldiers, threw kisses, and played in every way the slave to secure the master's place. After the entire legion of marines had sworn fidelity to him, enthusiastic in his strength and thinking that he must now encourage in a body those whom he had hitherto incited as individuals, he began to speak from the wall of the camp as follows:

XXXVII. "Comrades, I cannot tell who I am who come before you, because I may not call myself a private citizen after you have named me emperor, nor emperor while another holds the imperial power. Your name, also, will be uncertain so long as there is any doubt whether you have an emperor or an enemy of the Roman people in your camp. Do you hear how men demand my execution and your punishment in the same breath? So clear it is that we can neither die nor be safe except together: and so merciful is Galba that perhaps he has already made promises such as befit the man who massacred all those thousands of innocent soldiers when no man demanded it. Horror comes over me whenever I recall

hanc solam Galbae victoriam, cum in oculis urbis decimari deditos iuberet, quos deprecantis in fidem acceperat. His auspiciis urbem ingressus, quam gloriam ad principatum attulit nisi occisi Obultronii Sabini et Cornelii Marcelli in Hispania, Betui Cilonis in Gallia, Fontei Capitonis in Germania, Clodii Macri in Africa, Cingonii in via, Turpiliani in urbe, Nymphidii in castris? Quae usquam provincia, quae castra[1] sunt nisi cruenta et maculata aut, ut ipse praedicat, emendata et correcta? Nam quae alii scelera, hic remedia vocat, dum falsis nominibus severitatem pro saevitia, parsimoniam pro avaritia, supplicia et contumelias vestras disciplinam appellat. Septem a Neronis fine menses sunt, et iam plus rapuit Icelus quam quod Polycliti et Vatinii et Aegiali perdiderunt.[2] Minore avaritia ac licentia grassatus esset T. Vinius si ipse imperasset: nunc et subiectos nos habuit tamquam suos et vilis ut alienos. Una illa domus sufficit donativo quod vobis numquam datur et cotidie exprobratur.

XXXVIII. "Ac ne qua saltem in successore Galbae spes esset accersit ab exilio quem tristitia et avaritia sui simillimum iudicabat. Vidistis, commilitones, notabili tempestate etiam deos infaustam

[1] in castris *M.*
[2] perdiderunt *Ritter*: perierunt *M.*

---

[1] Favourite freedmen of Nero, whose inclination indulged their greed.

his fateful entrance, and the single victory that he won, when he gave orders that those who surrendered should be decimated in the sight of the whole city; they were the very men whom he had received under his protection in answer to their appeals. Such were the auspices under which he entered the city. Now what glory has he brought to the principate, except the murder of Obultronius Sabinus and Cornelius Marcellus in Spain, of Betuus Cilo in Gaul, of Fonteius Capito in Germany, of Clodius Macer in Africa, of Cingonius on the way to Rome, of Turpilianus in the city, of Nymphidius in the camp? What province is there anywhere, what camp, that is not bloodstained and defiled, or, as Galba would say, purged and disciplined? For what other men call crimes he calls 'remedies,' falsely naming cruelty 'strictness,' avarice 'frugality,' the punishment and insults you suffer 'discipline.' It is seven months since Nero met his end, and already Icelus has stolen more than all that a Polyclitus and a Vatinius and an Aegialus squandered.[1] Titus Vinius would have proceeded with less greed and lawlessness if he had been emperor himself; now he keeps us under his heel as if we were his slaves, and regards us as cheap because we belong to another. Galba's house alone is equal to paying the donative which is never given to you, but daily thrown in your teeth.

XXXVIII. "Furthermore, to prevent your having any hope even in his successor, Galba summoned from exile the man whose gloom and greed he reckoned made him most like himself. Comrades, you saw how even the gods by a wonderful storm expressed their disapproval of this ill-starred adop-

adoptionem aversantis.[1] Idem senatus, idem populi Romani animus est: vestra virtus expectatur, apud quos omne honestis consiliis robur et sine quibus quamvis egregia invalida sunt. Non ad bellum vos nec ad periculum voco: omnium militum arma nobiscum sunt. Nec una cohors togata defendit nunc Galbam sed detinet: cum vos aspexerit, cum signum meum acceperit, hoc solum erit certamen, quis mihi plurimum imputet. Nullus cunctationis locus est in eo consilio quod non potest laudari nisi peractum." Aperire deinde armamentarium iussit. Rapta statim arma, sine more et ordine militiae, ut praetorianus aut legionarius insignibus suis distingueretur: miscentur auxiliaribus galeis scutisque, nullo tribunorum centurionumve adhortante, sibi quisque dux et instigator; et praecipuum pessimorum incitamentum quod boni maerebant.

XXXIX. Iam exterritus Piso fremitu crebrescentis seditionis et vocibus in urbem usque resonantibus, egressum interim Galbam et foro adpropinquantem adsecutus erat; iam Marius Celsus haud laeta rettulerat, cum alii in Palatium redire, alii Capitolium petere, plerique rostra occupanda censerent, plures tantum sententiis aliorum contra dicerent, utque evenit in consiliis infelicibus, optima viderentur quorum tempus effugerat. Agitasse Laco

[1] aversantes *Agricola* : adversantes *M.*

tion. The senate, the Roman people, have the same feelings: they look to brave action on your part, for in you is all strength for honourable plans, and without you purposes, however noble, are of no avail. It is not to war or to danger that I am calling you; all the armed forces are on our side. And that one cohort in civil dress is not now defending Galba, but detaining him; when it has once seen you, has once accepted my watchword, the only rivalry between you will be to see who can put me most in his debt. There is no time for delay in a plan which is not praiseworthy unless put into effect." Then he ordered the armoury to be opened. The soldiers immediately seized arms without regard to military custom or rank, with no desire to distinguish praetorian or legionary by their proper insignia; they wore the helmets and shields of auxiliaries without distinction; there was no tribune or centurion to direct them; each guided and spurred himself on; and the chief incentive of the rascals was the grief of loyal men.

XXXIX. Piso, already terrified by the roar that arose from the growing revolt and by the shouts whose echoes reached even the city, had now caught up with Galba, who had meanwhile left the palace and was approaching the forum. Already Marius Celsus had brought a discouraging report. Thereupon some proposed that Galba return to the palace, others that he try to reach the Capitol, while many urged the necessity of seizing the rostra. But the majority simply opposed the advice of others; and as usually happens in the case of such unfortunate proposals, those plans for which the opportunity was past, now seemed the best. Men say that Laco,

ignaro Galba de occidendo Tito Vinio dicitur, sive ut poena eius animos militum mulceret, seu conscium Othonis credebat, ad postremum[1] vel odio. Haesitationem attulit tempus ac locus, quia initio caedis orto difficilis modus; et turbavere consilium trepidi nuntii ac proximorum diffugia, languentibus omnium studiis qui primo alacres fidem atque animum ostentaverant.[2]

XL. Agebatur huc illuc Galba vario turbae fluctuantis impulsu, completis undique basilicis ac templis, lugubri prospectu. Neque populi aut plebis ulla vox, sed attoniti vultus et conversae ad omnia aures; non tumultus, non quies, quale magni metus et magnae irae silentium est. Othoni tamen armari plebem nuntiabatur; ire praecipitis et occupare pericula iubet. Igitur milites Romani, quasi Vologaesum aut Pacorum avito Arsacidarum solio depulsuri ac non imperatorem suum inermem et senem trucidare pergerent, disiecta plebe, proculcato senatu, truces armis, rapidi equis forum inrumpunt. Nec illos Capitolii aspectus et imminentium templorum religio et priores et futuri principes terruere quo minus facerent scelus cuius ultor est quisquis successit.

[1] postremum *Rhenanus*: posterum *M.*
[2] ostentaverint *M.*

---

[1] Vologaesus became king of the Parthians in the reign of Claudius; Pacorus was king of Media, now apparently subject to the Parthians. Cf. *Annals* xii. and xv.

without Galba's knowledge, considered killing Titus Vinius, either to appease the angry spirits of the soldiers by his punishment or because he believed him privy to Otho's plans, or finally simply because he hated him. Time and place, however, made him hesitate, because when once a massacre has been started, it is hard to check it; moreover his plan was upset by disturbing reports and by the defection of his closest adherents, since the enthusiasm of all who at first had been eager to exhibit their loyalty and spirit was now weakening.

XL. Galba was swept to and fro by the various movements of the surging mob; crowds everywhere filled the public halls and temples, contemplating the grim spectacle. Neither the common people nor the rabble uttered a word, but their faces showed their terror and they turned their ears to catch every sound; there was no uproar, no quiet, but such a silence as accompanies great fear and great anger. Yet Otho received a report that the rabble was being armed; he ordered his adherents to go with all haste and anticipate the danger. So Roman soldiers rushed on as if they were going to drive a Vologaesus or a Pacorus from the ancestral throne of the Arsacidae[1] and were not hurrying to slay their own emperor—an old man all unarmed. They thrust aside the rabble, trampled down senators; terrifying men by their arms, they burst into the forum at full gallop. Neither the sight of the Capitol nor the sanctity of the temples which towered above them, nor the thought of emperors past and to come, could deter them from committing a crime which any successor to the imperial power must punish.

XLI. Viso comminus armatorum agmine vexillarius comitatae Galbam cohortis (Atilium Vergilionem fuisse tradunt) dereptam Galbae imaginem solo adflixit; eo signo manifesta in Othonem omnium militum studia, desertum fuga populi forum, destricta adversus dubitantis tela. Iuxta Curtii lacum trepidatione ferentium Galba proiectus e sella ac provolutus est. Extremam eius vocem, ut cuique odium aut admiratio fuit, varie prodidere.[1] Alii suppliciter interrogasse quid mali meruisset, paucos dies exsolvendo donativo deprecatum: plures obtulisse ultro percussoribus iugulum: agerent ac ferirent, si ita e[2] re publica videretur. Non interfuit occidentium quid diceret. De percussore non satis constat: quidam Terentium evocatum, alii Laecanium; crebrior fama tradidit Camurium quintae decimae legionis militem impresso gladio iugulum eius hausisse. Ceteri crura brachiaque (nam pectus tegebatur) foede laniavere; pleraque vulnera feritate et saevitia trunco iam corpori adiecta.

XLII. Titum inde Vinium invasere, de quo et ipso ambigitur consumpseritne vocem eius instans metus, an proclamaverit non esse ab Othone mandatum ut occideretur. Quod seu finxit formidine seu conscientiam[3] coniurationis confessus est, huc

[1] prodere *M.* [2] e *om. M.*
[3] conscientiam *Acidalius*: conscientia *M.*

---

[1] At this time an enclosed spot in the forum.

XLI. When he saw the armed force close upon him, the standard-bearer of the cohort escorting Galba—it is said that his name was Atilius Vergilio—tore Galba's portrait from the standard and threw it on the ground. This signal made the feeling of all the soldiers for Otho evident; the people fled and deserted the forum; if any hesitated, the troops threatened them with their weapons. It was near the Lacus Curtius[1] that Galba was thrown from his chair and rolled on the ground by his panic-stricken carriers. His last words have been variously reported according to the hatred or admiration of individuals; some say that he asked in an appealing tone what harm he had done and begged for a few days to pay the donative; many report that he voluntarily offered his throat to his assassins, telling them to strike quickly, if such actions were for the state's interest. His murderers cared nothing for what he said. About the actual assassin nothing certain is known: some say that he was one Terentius of the reserve forces, others that his name was Laecanius; a more common story is that a soldier of the Fifteenth legion, Camurius by name, pierced his throat with a thrust of his sword. The rest shamefully mutilated his legs and arms, for his breast was protected, and in their cruel savagery they continued to inflict many wounds on his body even after his head had been cut off.

XLII. Then they attacked Titus Vinius. In his case also there is a question whether his terror of instant death deprived him of speech or whether he cried out that Otho had not given orders for his death. He may have invented this statement in his fear, or he may have thus confessed his com-

potius eius vita famaque inclinat, ut conscius sceleris fuerit cuius causa erat. Ante aedem divi Iulii iacuit primo ictu in poplitem, mox ab Iulio Caro[1] legionario milite in utrumque latus transverberatus.

XLIII. Insignem illa die virum Sempronium Densum aetas nostra vidit. Centurio is praetoriae cohortis, a Galba custodiae Pisonis[2] additus, stricto pugione occurrens armatis et scelus exprobrans ac modo manu modo voce vertendo in se percussores quamquam vulnerato Pisoni effugium dedit. Piso in aedem Vestae pervasit, exceptusque misericordia publici servi et contubernio eius abditus non religione nec caerimoniis sed latebra imminens exitium differebat, cum advenere missu Othonis nominatim in caedem eius ardentis Sulpicius Florus e Britannicis cohortibus, nuper a Galba civitate donatus, et Statius Murcus speculator, a quibus protractus Piso in foribus templi trucidatur.

XLIV. Nullam caedem Otho maiore laetitia excepisse, nullum caput tam insatiabilibus oculis perlustrasse dicitur, seu tum primum levata omni sollicitudine mens vacare gaudio coeperat, seu recordatio maiestatis in Galba, amicitiae in Tito Vinio quamvis immitem animum imagine tristi con-

[1] Caro *Rhenanus*: cario *M*.
[2] a galbae c. a pisonis *M*.

plicity in the plot; but his life and reputation incline us rather to believe that he was privy to the crime of which he was the cause. He fell in front of the temple of the deified Julius at the first blow, which struck him in the back of the knee; afterwards he was run clean through the body by a legionary, Julius Carus.

XLIII. A noble hero on that day our own age beheld in the person of Sempronius Densus. He was a centurion of a praetorian cohort whom Galba had assigned to protect Piso; he drew his dagger, rushed to meet the armed men, upbraided them for their crime, and drawing the attention of the assassins to himself by act and word, gave Piso a chance to escape, although he was wounded. Piso fled into the temple of Vesta, where he was received through the pity of one of the public slaves who hid him in his chamber. It was the obscurity of his hiding-place and not some scruple about the sacred spot or its rites that delayed for a time the end that threatened him; but presently, despatched by Otho who was consumed with a desire for Piso's death above all others, there arrived Sulpicius Florus of the British auxiliaries, recently enfranchised by Galba, and Statius Murcus of the bodyguard; these dragged Piso out and slew him at the door of the temple.

XLIV. No other murder, according to report, gave Otho greater joy; on no other head did he gaze with such insatiable eyes. The reason may have been that now his mind was first free from anxiety and so open to joy, or else that in the case of Galba the memory of his treason, and in the case of Titus Vinius the recollection of his friendship,

fuderat, Pisonis ut inimici et aemuli caede laetari ius fasque credebat. Praefixa contis capita gestabantur inter signa cohortium iuxta aquilam legionis, certatim ostentantibus cruentas manus qui occiderant, qui interfuerant, qui vere qui falso ut pulchrum et memorabile facinus iactabant. Plures quam centum viginti libellos praemium exposcentium ob aliquam notabilem illa die operam Vitellius postea invenit, omnisque conquiri et interfici iussit, non honori[1] Galbae, sed tradito principibus more munimentum ad praesens, in posterum ultionem.

XLV. Alium crederes senatum, alium populum: ruere cuncti in castra, anteire proximos, certare cum praecurrentibus, increpare Galbam, laudare militum iudicium, exosculari Othonis manum; quantoque magis falsa erant quae fiebant,[2] tanto plura facere. Nec aspernabatur singulos Otho, avidum et minacem militum animum voce vultuque temperans. Marium Celsum, consulem designatum et Galbae usque in extremas res amicum fidumque, ad[3] supplicium expostulabant, industriae eius innocentiaeque quasi malis artibus infensi. Caedis et praedarum initium et optimo cuique perniciem quaeri apparebat, sed Othoni nondum auctoritas inerat ad prohibendum scelus: iubere iam poterat. Ita simulatione

[1] honori *Nipperdey*: honore *M.*
[2] flebant *M.*
[3] ad *om. M.*

distressed with gloomy visions even his cruel mind; but over the murder of Piso, his enemy and rival, he thought it lawful and right to rejoice. The victims' heads were displayed on poles among the standards of the cohorts side by side with the eagle of the legion, while those who had committed the murders, those who had been present, and those who, whether truly or falsely, boasted of their share in what they regarded as a splendid and memorable act, vied in exhibiting their bloody hands. More than one hundred and twenty petitions demanding rewards for some notable deed done that day were afterwards found by Vitellius; their authors he ordered to be hunted out and killed without exception, not that he wished to honour Galba, but he acted according to the traditional custom of emperors in thus securing protection for the time being and vengeance for the future.

XLV. The senate and the people seemed wholly changed: all rushed to the camp, striving to pass those next them and to overtake those before; they inveighed against Galba, praised the soldiers' decision, covered Otho's hand with kisses, the extravagance of their acts being in direct proportion to their falsity. Otho did not rebuff individuals, while he sought to check the eager and threatening temper of the soldiers by his words and look. They demanded for punishment Marius Celsus, consul elect, who had been Galba's faithful friend even to the very end; for they hated his energy and upright character as if they were vicious qualities. It was clear that they wished to begin murder, plunder, and the destruction of every honest citizen, but Otho had not yet the influence to forbid crimes: he could, however, already order

irae vinciri iussum et maiores poenas daturum adfirmans praesenti exitio[1] subtraxit.

XLVI. Omnia deinde arbitrio militum acta: praetorii praefectos sibi ipsi legere, Plotium Firmum e manipularibus quondam, tum vigilibus praepositum et incolumi adhuc Galba partis Othonis secutum; adiungitur Licinius Proculus, intima familiaritate Othonis suspectus consilia eius fovisse. Urbi Flavium Sabinum praefecere, iudicium Neronis secuti, sub quo eandem curam obtinuerat, plerisque Vespasianum fratrem in eo respicientibus. Flagitatum ut vacationes praestari centurionibus solitae remitterentur; namque gregarius miles ut tributum annuum pendebat. Quarta pars manipuli sparsa[2] per commeatus aut in ipsis castris vaga, dum mercedem centurioni exsolveret, neque modum oneris quisquam neque genus quaestus pensi habebat: per latrocinia et raptus aut servilibus ministeriis militare otium redimebant. Tum locupletissimus quisque miles labore ac saevitia fatigari donec vacationem emeret. Ubi sumptibus exhaustus socordia insuper elanguerat, inops pro locuplete et iners pro strenuo in manipulum redibat, ac rursus alius atque alius, eadem egestate ac licentia corrupti, ad seditiones et discordias et ad extremum bella civilia ruebant. Sed Otho ne vulgi largitione centurionum animos

[1] auxilio *M*: exilio *M*[1].
[2] manipuli sparsa *Pichena*: manipuli pars *M*.

them. Therefore, pretending to be angry, he ordered the arrest of Celsus, and by declaring that he was to suffer severer punishment, saved him from immediate death.

XLVI. The soldiers' will was henceforth supreme. The praetorians chose their own prefects,—Plotius Firmus, formerly a common soldier, but later chief of the city police, and a partisan of Otho even while Galba lived; as his associate they gave him Licinius Proculus, whose intimacy with Otho made men suspect that he had favoured his plans. As Prefect of the City they selected Flavius Sabinus, thus following Nero's choice, for Sabinus had held the same office under Nero, while many in doing so had an eye on his brother Vespasian. The troops also demanded that the payments usually made to centurions to secure furloughs should be abolished, since they amounted to an annual tax on the common soldiers. A quarter of each company would be away on furlough or loafing about the camp itself, provided the soldiers paid the centurion his price, and no one cared how the burden pressed on the soldiers or how they got their money; in reality it was through highway robbery, petty thieving, and by menial occupations that the soldiers purchased rest from military service. Moreover the richest soldiers would be cruelly assigned to the most fatiguing labour until they bought relief. Then, impoverished and demoralized by idleness, the soldier would return to his company poor instead of well-to-do and lazy instead of energetic; so ruined one after another by the same poverty and lack of discipline, they were ready to rush into mutiny and dissension, and finally into civil war. But Otho wished to avoid alienating the centurions

averteret,[1] fiscum suum vacationes annuas exsoluturum promisit, rem haud dubie utilem et a bonis postea principibus perpetuitate disciplinae firmatam. Laco praefectus, tamquam in insulam seponeretur, ab evocato, quem ad caedem eius Otho praemiserat, confossus; in Marcianum Icelum ut in libertum palam animadversum.

XLVII. Exacto per scelera die novissimum malorum fuit laetitia. Vocat[2] senatum praetor urbanus, certant adulationibus ceteri magistratus, adcurrunt patres: decernitur Othoni tribunicia potestas et nomen Augusti et omnes principum honores, adnitentibus cunctis abolere convicia ac probra, quae promisce iacta haesisse animo eius nemo sensit; omisisset offensas[3] an distulisset brevitate imperii in incerto fuit. Otho cruento adhuc foro per stragem iacentium in Capitolium atque inde in Palatium vectus concedi corpora sepulturae cremarique permisit. Pisonem Verania uxor ac frater Scribonianus, Titum Vinium Crispina filia composuere, quaesitis redemptisque capitibus, quae venalia interfectores servaverant.

XLVIII. Piso unum et tricensimum aetatis annum explebat, fama meliore quam fortuna. Fratres eius Magnum Claudius, Crassum Nero interfecerant: ipse diu exul, quadriduo Caesar, properata adoptione ad

[1] averteret *I. Gronovius*: averteret et *M.*
[2] vacat *M.* [3] omisisse tot fensas *M.*

---

[1] Both the consuls, Galba and Vinius, were now dead.
[2] Gnaeus Pompeius Magnus had married the emperor Claudius's daughter Antonia in 41, but within six years he was put to death. Marcus Licinius Crassus Frugi was charged with treason by the notorious Marcus Aquilius Regulus and executed between 66 and 68. Cf. iv. 42.

by generosity to the rank and file, and so he promised that the imperial treasury should pay for the annual furloughs, a procedure which was undoubtedly useful and which later was established by good emperors as a fixed rule of the service. The prefect Laco, who had been ostensibly banished to an island, was assassinated by a retired soldier whom Otho had despatched to kill him. Marcianus Icelus, being only a freedman, was publicly executed.

XLVII. The day was spent in crimes, and the worst evil was the joy felt over the crimes. The senate was called together by the city praetor;[1] the other magistrates vied in flattery; the senators hurried to their places, and voted Otho the tribunitian power, the title Augustus, and all the honours granted the other emperors; for all did their best to blot out the memory of their former abuse and insults, nor did anyone discover to his sorrow that these random utterances had found lodgment in Otho's mind; whether he had forgotten them or put off his vengeance his reign was too short to show. He was then carried through the heaps of dead bodies, while the forum still reeked with blood, first to the Capitol and then to the Palatine; after that he allowed the bodies to be given up for burial and burning. Piso was laid to rest by his wife Verania and his brother Scribonianus, Titus Vinius by his daughter Crispina, after they had discovered and redeemed their heads, which the assassins had kept for profit.

XLVIII. Piso was near the end of his thirty-first year; his reputation had been better than his fortune. His brother Magnus had been put to death by Claudius, his brother Crassus by Nero.[2] He himself, long an exile, was Caesar for four days; the

hoc tantum maiori fratri praelatus est ut prior occideretur. Titus Vinius quinquaginta septem annos variis moribus egit. Pater illi praetoria familia, maternus avus e proscriptis. Prima militia infamis: legatum Calvisium Sabinum habuerat, cuius uxor mala cupidine visendi situm castrorum, per noctem militari habitu ingressa, cum vigilias et cetera militiae munia eadem lascivia temptasset,[1] in ipsis principiis stuprum ausa, et criminis huius reus Titus Vinius arguebatur. Igitur iussu G. Caesaris oneratus catenis, mox mutatione temporum dimissus, cursu honorum inoffenso legioni post praeturam praepositus probatusque servili deinceps probro respersus est tamquam scyphum aureum in convivio Claudii furatus, et Claudius postera die soli omnium Vinio fictilibus ministrari iussit. Sed Vinius proconsulatu Galliam Narbonensem severe integreque rexit; mox Galbae amicitia in abruptum tractus, audax, callidus, promptus et, prout animum intendisset, pravus aut industrius, eadem vi. Testamentum Titi Vinii magnitudine opum inritum, Pisonis supremam voluntatem paupertas firmavit.

XLIX. Galbae corpus diu neglectum et licentia tenebrarum plurimis ludibriis vexatum dispensator

[1] temptasset *Puteolanus*: temperasset *M*.

---

[1] Under the second triumvirate in 43 B.C. Cf. Dio C. xlvii. 7.

[2] That is, the emperor's cupidity disregarded the provisions of the will.

only advantage he gained over his elder brother by his hasty adoption was that he was killed before him. Titus Vinius lived fifty-seven years; his character varied at different times. His father was of a praetorian family, his maternal grandfather one of the proscribed.[1] He had disgraced himself in his first military service under the legate Calvisius Sabinus, whose wife, prompted by a shameful desire to see the camp, entered it at night disguised as a soldier. After she had interfered with the guard and the other soldiers on duty with unfailing effrontery, she had the hardihood to commit adultery in the general's headquarters. Titus Vinius was charged with complicity in this crime and therefore was ordered by Caligula to be heavily loaded with chains. Later, when times changed, he was released; and then, advancing in office without interruption, he was appointed to the command of a legion after he had been praetor; and though he won success in this position, he later smirched his reputation by an act worthy of a slave; for he was charged with stealing a golden cup at a dinner given by Claudius, so that the next day Claudius ordered Vinius alone to be served with earthenware. But as proconsul of Gallia Narbonensis, Vinius ruled his province with strictness and honesty. Later, through friendship with Galba he was carried to a dangerous height. He was bold, cunning, efficient, wicked or virtuous, according to his inclination at the time; but he always showed the same vigour. His great riches made his will void,[2] but Piso's poverty secured the fulfilment of his last wishes.

XLIX. Galba's body was long neglected and abused with a thousand insults under the licence of

Argius e prioribus servis humili sepultura in privatis eius hortis contexit. Caput per lixas calonesque suffixum laceratumque ante Petrobii tumulum (libertus is Neronis punitus a Galba fuerat) postera demum die repertum et cremato iam corpori admixtum est. Hunc exitum habuit Servius Galba, tribus et septuaginta annis quinque principes prospera fortuna emensus et alieno imperio felicior quam suo. Vetus in familia nobilitas, magnae opes: ipsi medium ingenium, magis[1] extra vitia quam cum virtutibus. Famae nec incuriosus nec venditator; pecuniae alienae non adpetens, suae parcus, publicae avarus; amicorum libertorumque, ubi in bonos incidisset, sine reprehensione patiens, si mali forent, usque ad culpam ignarus. Sed claritas natalium et metus temporum obtentui, ut, quod segnitia erat, sapientia vocaretur. Dum vigebat aetas militari laude apud Germanias floruit. Pro consule Africam moderate, iam senior citeriorem Hispaniam pari iustitia continuit, maior privato visus dum privatus fuit, et omnium consensu capax imperii nisi imperasset.

L. Trepidam urbem ac simul atrocitatem recentis

[1] magnis *M*.

---

[1] According to Plutarch, *Galba* 28, this office was performed by the famous Helvidius Priscus.

darkness. Finally Argius, his steward, one of his former slaves, gave it humble burial in his master's private garden. Galba's head, which had been fixed on a pole and maltreated by camp-followers and servants, was finally found the next day before the tomb of Petrobius—he was one of Nero's freedmen whom Galba had punished—and was placed with the body which had already been burned.[1] This was the end of Servius Galba. He had lived seventy-three years, through the reigns of five emperors, with good fortune, and he was happier under the rule of others than in his own. His family was of the ancient nobility and possessed great wealth. Galba himself was of mediocre genius, being rather free from faults than possessing virtues. He was neither careless of reputation nor one who cared to boast of it. He was not greedy for another's property; he was frugal with his own, stingy with the state's. Kindly and complacent toward friends and freedmen, if he found them honest; if they were dishonest, he was blind even to a fault. But his high birth and the terror which the times inspired masked the truth, so that men called wisdom what was really indolence. While he was vigorous physically, he enjoyed a reputation for his military service in the German provinces. As proconsul he governed Africa with moderation and, when he was already an old man, ruled Hither Spain with the same uprightness. He seemed too great to be a subject so long as he was subject, and all would have agreed that he was equal to the imperial office if he had never held it.

L. Rome was in a state of excitement and horror-stricken not only at the recent outrageous crime,

sceleris, simul veteres Othonis mores paventem novus insuper de Vitellio nuntius exterruit, ante caedem Galbae suppressus ut tantum superioris Germaniae exercitum descivisse crederetur. Tum duos omnium mortalium impudicitia ignavia luxuria deterrimos velut ad perdendum imperium fataliter electos non senatus modo et eques, quis aliqua pars et cura rei publicae, sed vulgus quoque palam maerere. Nec iam recentia saevae pacis exempla sed repetita bellorum civilium memoria captam totiens suis exercitibus urbem, vastitatem Italiae, direptiones provinciarum, Pharsaliam Philippos et Perusiam ac Mutinam, nota publicarum cladium nomina, loquebantur. Prope eversum orbem etiam cum de principatu inter bonos certaretur, sed mansisse G. Iulio, mansisse Caesare Augusto victore imperium; mansuram fuisse sub Pompeio Brutoque rem publicam: nunc pro Othone an pro Vitellio in templa ituros? utrasque impias preces, utraque detestanda vota inter duos, quorum bello solum id scires, deteriorem fore qui vicisset. Erant qui Vespasianum et arma Orientis augurarentur, et ut potior utroque Vespasianus, ita bellum aliud atque alias cladis horrebant. Et ambigua de Vespasiano

---

[1] Cf. chap. 14.

but also at the thought of Otho's former character. Now it was terrified in addition by news with regard to Vitellius, which had been suppressed before Galba's death, so that the citizens believed that only the army of Upper Germany had mutinied.[1] Then the thought that two men, the worst in the world for their shamelessness, indolence, and profligacy, had been apparently chosen by fate to ruin the empire, caused open grief not only to the senators and knights who had some share and interest in the state, but even to the common people. Their talk was no longer of the recent horrors of a bloody peace, but they recalled memories of the civil wars and spoke of the many times the city had been captured by Roman armies, of the devastation of Italy, of the plundering of the provinces, of Pharsalia, Philippi, Perusia, and Mutina, names notorious for public disaster. They said that the world had been well-nigh overturned, even when the principate was the prize of honest men; but yet the empire had remained when Julius Caesar won, and had likewise remained when Augustus won; the republic would have remained if Pompey and Brutus had been successful; but now—should they go to the temples to pray for an Otho or a Vitellius? Prayers for either would be impious and vows for either detestable when, in the struggle between the two, the only thing of which men were certain was that the victor would be the worse. There were some who had forebodings of Vespasian and the armies in the East, and yet although Vespasian was a better man than Otho or Vitellius, they shuddered at another war and another massacre. Indeed Vespasian's reputation was uncertain; he,

fama, solusque omnium ante se principum in melius mutatus[1] est.

LI. Nunc initia causasque motus Vitelliani expediam. Caeso cum omnibus copiis Iulio Vindice ferox praeda gloriaque exercitus, ut cui sine labore ac periculo ditissimi belli victoria evenisset, expeditionem et aciem, praemia quam stipendia malebat. Diu infructuosam et asperam militiam toleraverant ingenio loci caelique et severitate disciplinae, quam in pace inexorabilem discordiae civium resolvunt, paratis utrimque corruptoribus et perfidia impunita. Viri, arma, equi ad usum et ad decus[2] supererant. Sed ante bellum centurias tantum suas turmasque noverant; exercitus finibus provinciarum discernebantur: tum adversus Vindicem contractae[3] legiones, seque et Gallias expertae, quaerere rursus arma novasque discordias; nec socios, ut olim, sed hostis et victos vocabant. Nec deerat pars Galliarum, quae Rhenum[4] accolit, easdem partis secuta ac tum acerrima instigatrix adversum Galbianos; hoc enim nomen fastidito Vindice indiderant. Igitur Sequanis Aeduisque ac deinde, prout opulentia civitatibus

[1] principum Imelius mutus *M*.
[2] dedecus *M*.
[3] contractae *Rhenanus*: confractae *M*.
[4] qua herenum *M*.

---

[1] The Sequani lived in Franche-Comté, Burgundy, and part of Alsace, having as their capital Vensontio (Besançon). The Aeduans were between the Saône and the Loire. Their capital was Augustodunum (Autun).

unlike all his predecessors, was the only emperor who was changed for the better by his office.

LI. I will now relate the origin and causes of the revolt of Vitellius. After Julius Vindex had been slain and all his forces with him, the army, flushed with joy over the booty and glory it had won, as was natural since it had secured a very rich victory without effort or danger, preferred to advance and fight, to secure rewards rather than mere pay. The soldiers had long endured a profitless service which was severe because of the character of the district and of the climate, and also because discipline was strict. But discipline which is stern in time of peace is broken down by civil strife, for there are men on both sides ready to corrupt, and treachery goes unpunished. The army had men, weapons, and horses in abundance for use and for show, but before the war the soldiers had been acquainted with only their own centuries and squadrons, for the armies were then separated by the boundaries of the provinces. But at that time the legions had been mobilized against Vindex, so that they had become acquainted with their own strength and that of the Gallic provinces. Therefore they were again looking for war and new quarrels; they no longer called the Gauls "allies" as before, but "enemies" and "the defeated." In fact that part of the Gallic provinces which borders the Rhine had not failed to attach itself to the same party and at this time was most vigorous in urging the soldiers on against "the Galbans," for they had given them this name in scorn of Vindex. Accordingly, being hostile first of all towards the Sequani and the Aeduans,[1] and then towards other states in pro-

erat, infensi expugnationes urbium, populationes agrorum, raptus penatium hauserunt animo, super avaritiam et adrogantiam, praecipua validiorum vitia, contumacia Gallorum inritati, qui remissam sibi a Galba quartam tributorum partem et publice donatos in ignominiam exercitus iactabant. Accessit callide vulgatum, temere creditum, decimari legiones et promptissimum quemque centurionum dimitti. Undique atroces nuntii, sinistra ex urbe fama; infensa Lugdunensis colonia et pertinaci pro Nerone fide fecunda[1] rumoribus; sed plurima ad fingendum credendumque materies in ipsis castris, odio metu et, ubi viris suas respexerant, securitate.

LII. Sub ipsas superioris anni kalendas Decembris Aulus Vitellius inferiorem Germaniam ingressus hiberna legionum cum cura adierat: redditi plerisque ordines, remissa ignominia, adlevatae notae; plura ambitione, quaedam iudicio, in quibus sordes[2] et avaritiam Fontei Capitonis adimendis adsignandisve militiae ordinibus integre mutaverat. Nec consularis legati mensura sed in maius omnia accipiebantur. Et ut[3] Vitellius apud severos humilis, ita comitatem bonitatemque faventes vocabant, quod sine modo,

[1] facunda *M.*
[2] sordes *Acidalius*: sorde *M.*
[3] ut *add. Rhenanus.*

portion to their wealth, their souls thirsted for the storming of cities, the ravaging of fields, and the looting of houses. Their irritation arose not simply from greed and arrogance—faults especially common to the stronger—but also from the insolent spirit of the Gauls, who as an insult to the army boasted that Galba had remitted a quarter of their tribute and had rewarded them as communities. There was, too, a rumour cleverly spread abroad and rashly believed, that the legions were being decimated and the most active centurions dismissed. From every side came alarming messages and from Rome disturbing reports; the colony of Lyons was hostile and, owing to its persistent loyalty to Nero, was filled with rumours; but the amplest material for imagination and credulity was to be found within the camp itself in the soldiers' hatreds, in their fears, and also, when they considered their own strength, in their self-confidence.

LII. About the first of December in the preceding year Aulus Vitellius had entered Lower Germany and carefully inspected the winter quarters of the legions. Many of the troops had their ranks restored, their disgrace removed, the marks against them cancelled. He did much for his selfish ends, but some things with sound judgment; among these was the honest change he made from the meanness and greed which Fonteius Capito had shown in taking away or bestowing military rank. The acts of Vitellius were not regarded as those simply of a consular legate, but without exception were taken to be more significant; and while the strict thought Vitellius demeaned himself, his partisans called it affability and kindness where he gave away his own

sine iudicio donaret sua, largiretur aliena; simul aviditate imperitandi[1] ipsa vitia pro virtutibus interpretabantur. Multi in utroque exercitu sicut modesti quietique ita mali et strenui. Sed profusa cupidine et insigni temeritate legati legionum Alienus Caecina et Fabius Valens; e quibus Valens infensus Galbae, tamquam detectam a se Verginii cunctationem, oppressa Capitonis consilia ingrate tulisset, instigare Vitellium, ardorem militum ostentans: ipsum celebri ubique fama, nullam in Flacco Hordeonio moram; adfore Britanniam, secutura Germanorum auxilia: male fidas provincias, precarium seni imperium et brevi transiturum: panderet modo sinum et venienti Fortunae occurreret. Merito dubitasse Verginium equestri familia, ignoto patre, imparem si recepisset imperium, tutum si recusasset: Vitellio tris patris consulatus, censuram, collegium Caesaris et imponere iam pridem imperatoris dignationem et auferre privati securitatem. Quatiebatur his segne ingenium ut concupisceret magis quam ut speraret.

LIII. At in superiore Germania Caecina, decorus[2] iuventa, corpore ingens, animi immodicus, scito[3] ser-

[1] imperitandi *Fisher*: imperandi *M.*
[2] decorus *Baiter*: decori *M.*
[3] scito *Lipsius*: cito *M.*

---

[1] Caecina was stationed in Upper Germany, Valens in Lower.
[2] See chaps. 8 and 9 above.
[3] Hordeonius was commander in Upper Germany.
[4] Vitellius's father had been consul in 34; under Claudius he was associated with the emperor in this office in 43 and 47, and also shared the censorship with Claudius in the last year.

property without limit and without judgment and squandered what belonged to others; at the same time their greed for power made them translate his very faults into virtues. There were many in both armies obedient and law-abiding, as well as many unprincipled and energetic. But the commanders of the legions, Alienus Caecina and Fabius Valens, were men of boundless greed and extraordinary recklessness.[1] Valens was hostile to Galba, because Galba had treated with ingratitude his disclosure of Verginius's hesitation[2] and his crushing of Capito's plans. He began to urge Vitellius on and to point out to him the eager spirit of the soldiers, saying that he enjoyed great fame everywhere, that Flaccus Hordeonius[3] would give no occasion for delay, that Britain would join him, the German auxiliaries follow his standard; the loyalty of the provinces he declared weak, the old emperor's rule precarious and sure soon to pass; let him but open his arms and hurry to meet approaching fortune. He maintained that Verginius had hesitated with good reason, for he was of equestrian family, his father was unknown and he would have been unequal to the office if he had got the imperial power, but safe if he refused it; but to Vitellius, his father's three consulships and the censorship in which he had Caesar as colleague[4] had long since given him imperial dignity and had taken away from him the security of a subject. These arguments stirred his sluggish nature to covetousness rather than to hope.

LIII. But in Upper Germany, Caecina, a handsome young man of towering stature and boundless ambition, had won over the support of the soldiers

mone, erecto incessu, studia militum inlexerat. Hunc iuvenem Galba, quaestorem in Baetica impigre in partis suas transgressum, legioni praeposuit: mox compertum publicam pecuniam avertisse ut peculatorem flagitari iussit. Caecina aegre passus miscere cuncta et privata vulnera rei publicae malis operire statuit. Nec deerant in exercitu semina discordiae, quod et bello adversus Vindicem universus adfuerat, nec nisi occiso Nerone translatus in Galbam atque in eo ipso sacramento vexillis inferioris Germaniae praeventus erat. Et Treviri ac Lingones, quasque alias civitates atrocibus edictis aut damno finium Galba perculerat, hibernis legionum propius miscentur: unde seditiosa colloquia et inter paganos corruptior miles; et in Verginium favor cuicumque alii profuturus.

LIV. Miserat civitas Lingonum vetere instituto dona legionibus dextras, hospitii insigne. Legati eorum in squalorem maestitiamque compositi per principia per contubernia modo suas[1] iniurias, modo vicinarum civitatium praemia, et ubi pronis militum auribus accipiebantur, ipsius exercitus pericula et contumelias conquerentes accendebant animos. Nec

[1] modo insuas *M.*

---

[1] The Treviri dwelt in the district about Trèves, which preserves their name, as Langres recalls the Lingones.

by his clever speech and dignified carriage. This youth Galba had put in command of a legion, for when he was quaestor in Baetica, he had not hesitated to join Galba's party. But later, when Galba found that he had embezzled public money, he ordered him to be prosecuted for peculation. Caecina took this hard and decided to embroil everything and conceal his private wounds amid the misfortunes of the state. And there were not lacking seeds of discord in the army, because it had taken part in full force in the war against Vindex and had not gone over to Galba until Nero had been killed, and then had been anticipated in taking the oath of allegiance to Galba by some detachments from Lower Germany. The Treviri, too, and Lingones,[1] as well as other states which Galba had punished with harsh edicts or loss of territory, were closely associated with the legions' winter quarters, with the result that there were seditious conferences and the soldiers were demoralized by mixing with the civilian inhabitants, and the attachment that they apparently showed Verginius was ready to be given to anyone else.

LIV. The community of the Lingones, according to their ancient custom, had sent clasped right hands, an emblem of friendship, as gifts to the legions. Their envoys, assuming the appearance of poverty and sorrow, complained both at headquarters and in the messes of the common soldiers, now of their wrongs, again of the rewards given to neighbouring communities, and, when the soldiers were ready to lend a listening ear, of the dangers and the insults suffered by the army itself, and so inflamed the temper of the troops. In fact, they were not far

procul seditione aberant cum Hordeonius Flaccus abire legatos, utque occultior digressus esset, nocte castris excedere iubet. Inde atrox rumor, adfirmantibus plerisque interfectos, ac ni sibi ipsi[1] consulerent, fore ut acerrimi militum et praesentia conquesti per tenebras et inscitiam ceterorum occiderentur. Obstringuntur inter se tacito foedere legiones, adsciscitur auxiliorum miles, primo suspectus tamquam circumdatis cohortibus alisque impetus in legiones pararetur, mox eadem acrius volvens, faciliore inter malos consensu ad bellum quam in pace ad concordiam.

LV. Inferioris tamen Germaniae legiones sollemni kalendarum Ianuariarum sacramento pro Galba adactae, multa cunctatione et raris primorum ordinum vocibus, ceteri silentio proximi cuiusque audaciam expectantes, insita mortalibus natura, propere sequi quae piget inchoare. Sed ipsis legionibus inerat diversitas animorum: primani quintanique turbidi adeo ut quidam saxa in Galbae imagines iecerint: quinta decima ac sexta decima legiones nihil ultra fremitum et minas ausae initium erumpendi circumspectabant. At in superiore exercitu quarta ac duetvicensima legiones, isdem hibernis tendentes, ipso kalendarum Ianuariarum die dirumpunt ima-

[1] ni sibi ipsi *Halm*: nisi ipsi *M.*

---

[1] Stationed at Bonn and Xanten (Vetera).
[2] At Xanten and Neuss (Novaesium).
[3] At Mayence (Mogontiacum).

from mutiny when Hordeonius Flaccus ordered the envoys to leave and told them to go out of camp by night that their departure might be less noticeable. From this arose a disturbing report, for many maintained that the envoys had been killed; and it was urged that if the soldiers did not take thought for themselves, the most energetic among them and those who complained of present conditions would be put to death under the cover of darkness without the knowledge of their fellows. Thereupon the legions bound themselves by a secret oath; the auxiliary soldiers joined them. These had been at first suspected of planning to attack the legions, because their infantry and cavalry had surrounded the camp; but presently they showed themselves more zealous in the same cause; for the wicked conspire more readily to make war than to preserve harmony in time of peace.

LV. Yet the legions of Lower Germany had taken the usual oath of allegiance to Galba on the first of January, although there was great hesitation and only a few in the front ranks repeated it, while the rest silently waited, each on the courage of his neighbour, it being human nature to follow eagerly a course that one hesitates to begin. But there was a diversity of sentiment in the legions themselves. The First and Fifth [1] were so mutinous that some stoned Galba's images. The Fifteenth and Sixteenth legions,[2] while daring to do nothing worse than murmur and threaten, were seeking some opening for an outbreak. In the Upper army, however, the Fourth and Twenty-second legions, who were wintering in the same camp,[3] on the very first of January tore down the

gines Galbae, quarta legio promptius, duetvicensima cunctanter, mox consensu. Ac ne reverentiam imperii exuere viderentur, senatus populique Romani oblitterata iam nomina sacramento advocabant, nullo legatorum tribunorumve pro Galba nitente, quibusdam, ut in tumultu, notabilius turbantibus. Non tamen quisquam in modum contionis aut suggestu locutus; neque enim erat adhuc cui imputaretur.

LVI. Spectator flagitii Hordeonius Flaccus consularis legatus aderat, non compescere ruentis, non retinere dubios, non cohortari bonos ausus, sed segnis pavidus et socordia innocens. Quattuor centuriones duetvicensimae legionis, Nonius Receptus, Donatius Valens, Romilius Marcellus, Calpurnius Repentinus, cum protegerent Galbae imagines, impetu militum abrepti vinctique. Nec cuiquam ultra fides aut memoria prioris sacramenti, sed quod in seditionibus accidit, unde [1] plures erant omnes fuere.

Nocte quae kalendas Ianuarias secuta est in coloniam Agrippinensem aquilifer quartae legionis epulanti Vitellio nuntiat quartam et duetvicensimam legiones proiectis Galbae imaginibus in senatus ac populi Romani verba iurasse. Id sacramentum inane visum: occupari nutantem fortunam et offerri principem placuit. Missi a Vitellio ad legiones

[1] inde *M*.

[1] Agrippa had allowed the Ubii to move from the right to the left bank of the Rhine in 38 B.C. Their town, *oppidum Ubiorum*, became *colonia Claudia Augusta Agrippinensis* (or *Agrippinensium*) in 50 A.D. See Strabo iv. 3, 4 (194): Dio Cassius xlviii. 49, 3; Tac. *Ann.* xii. 27.

images of Galba, the Fourth legion with greater readiness, the Twenty-second with hesitation at first, but presently in full accord; and they called in their oath on the now forgotten names of the senate and Roman people that they might not seem to give up reverence for the empire. No one of the legates or tribunes made any effort in Galba's behalf; some, as is usual in an uproar, were conspicuous in causing trouble. Yet no one addressed the soldiers in formal speech or from the tribunal, for there was no one as yet to whom claim for such service could be made.

LVI. Hordeonius Flaccus, the consular legate, was a spectator of this disgraceful scene. He did not dare to check those who were in a fury or to restrain the doubtful or even to exhort the loyal, but he was slow to act, timid, and innocent only because of his sloth. Four centurions of the Twenty-second legion, Nonius Receptus, Donatius Valens, Romilius Marcellus, Calpurnius Repentinus, were swept away by the onrush of the soldiers when they tried to protect Galba's images, and were thrown into chains. No man had any loyalty or thought for his former oath, but as happens in mutinies all joined the majority.

On the night which followed January first, an eagle-bearer of the Fourth legion came to Cologne[1] and reported to Vitellius at table that the Fourth and Twenty-second legions had thrown down Galba's statues and taken the oath of allegiance to the senate and the Roman people. Such an oath seemed idle; they decided to seize fortune while in the balance and to offer an emperor to the soldiery. Vitellius sent men to the legions and legates to

legatosque qui descivisse a Galba superiorem exercitum nuntiarent: proinde aut bellandum adversus desciscentis aut, si concordia et pax placeat, faciendum imperatorem: et minore discrimine sumi principem quam quaeri.

LVII. Proxima legionis primae hiberna erant et promptissimus e legatis Fabius Valens. Is die postero coloniam Agrippinensem cum equitibus legionis auxiliariorumque ingressus [1] imperatorem Vitellium consalutavit. Secutae ingenti certamine eiusdem provinciae legiones; et superior exercitus, speciosis senatus populique Romani nominibus relictis, tertium nonas Ianuarias Vitellio accessit: scires illum priore biduo non penes rem publicam fuisse. Ardorem exercituum Agrippinenses, Treviri, Lingones aequabant, auxilia equos, arma pecuniam offerentes, ut quisque corpore opibus ingenio validus.[2] Nec principes modo coloniarum aut castrorum, quibus praesentia ex affluenti et parta victoria magnae spes, sed manipuli quoque et gregarius miles viatica sua et balteos phalerasque, insignia armorum argento decora, loco pecuniae tradebant, instinctu et impetu et avaritia.

LVIII. Igitur laudata militum alacritate Vitellius ministeria principatus per libertos agi solita in equites Romanos disponit, vacationes centurionibus et fisco

[1] gressus *M*. [2] validis *M*.

---

[1] Corresponding to the medals of modern times.

announce that the Upper army had mutinied against Galba: therefore they must either fight against the mutineers or, if they preferred harmony and peace, must take an emperor. There was less danger, he added, in accepting an emperor than in looking for one.

LVII. The winter quarters of the First legion were nearest, and the most energetic of the commanders was Fabius Valens. The next day he entered Cologne with the horsemen of the legion and the auxiliary troops and saluted Vitellius as emperor. The legions of the same province showed the greatest rivalry in following this example; and the Upper army, abandoning the specious names of the senate and the Roman people, came over to Vitellius on the third of January, so that it was easy to realize that during the two preceding days it had never been faithful to the state. The citizens of Cologne, the Treviri, the Lingones, showed the same enthusiasm as the army. Individuals offered their personal services, horses, arms, or money, according to the physical strength, wealth, or talent that each possessed. Not only the chief men of the colonies and camps who had present wealth in abundance and great hopes should they secure a victory, but also whole companies and common soldiers, prompted by excitement and enthusiasm and also by greed, contributed their own spending money, or in place of money their belts and bosses, and the decorations of their armour[1] adorned with silver.

LVIII. Therefore Vitellius praised the eager spirit of the soldiers and then distributed the imperial offices which had been usually held by freedmen among Roman knights; he also paid the fees for

numerat, saevitiam militum plerosque ad poenam exposcentium saepius adprobat, raro[1] simulatione vinculorum frustratur. Pompeius Propinquus procurator Belgicae statim interfectus; Iulium Burdonem Germanicae classis praefectum astu subtraxit. Exarserat in eum iracundia exercitus tamquam crimen ac mox insidias Fonteio Capitoni struxisset. Grata erat memoria Capitonis, et apud saevientis occidere palam, ignoscere non nisi fallendo licebat: ita in custodia habitus et post victoriam demum, stratis[2] iam militum odiis, dimissus est. Interim ut piaculum obicitur centurio Crispinus. Sanguine Capitonis se[3] cruentaverat eoque et postulantibus manifestior et punienti vilior fuit.

LIX. Iulius deinde Civilis periculo exemptus, praepotens inter Batavos, ne supplicio eius ferox gens alienaretur. Et erant in civitate Lingonum octo Batavorum cohortes, quartae decimae legionis auxilia, tum discordia temporum a legione digressae, prout inclinassent, grande momentum sociae aut adversae. Nonium, Donatium, Romilium, Calpurnium centuriones, de quibus supra rettulimus, occidi

[1] raro *Jacob*: paro *M.* [2] statis *M.*
[3] se *add. I. Gronovius.*

---

[1] Cf. chap. 46. [2] Cf. chap. 12. [3] Cf. chap. 7.
[4] A few months later he raised a formidable revolt, as is narrated in Books IV and V below.
[5] These people lived chiefly on the island between the Rhine, the Maas, and the Waal; they had long furnished auxiliary troops.

furloughs to the centurions out of his own purse.[1] He frequently gave his approval to the savagery of the soldiers who demanded that many be given up to punishment; in some rare instances he evaded it by throwing the accused into chains. Pompeius Propinquus,[2] imperial agent in Belgian Gaul, was immediately put to death; Julius Burdo, commander of the German fleet, he saved by a clever ruse. The army's anger had blazed out against Burdo, because he had invented a charge against Fonteius Capito, and later had plotted against him.[3] The soldiers remembered Capito with gratitude, and while Vitellius might kill openly before the angry mob, he could not pardon except by deceit. And so Burdo was kept under guard and released only after the victory of Vitellius, when the hatred of the soldiers for him was now appeased. In the meantime the centurion Crispinus was offered as a scapegoat. Capito's blood was on his hands, and that made him the more obvious victim of the soldiers' demands and the cheaper sacrifice in the eyes of the executioner.

LIX. Next Julius Civilis was saved from danger.[4] He had great influence with the Batavians[5] so that Vitellius did not wish to alienate this savage people by punishing him. Moreover there were in the country of the Lingones eight cohorts of Batavians, auxiliaries belonging to the Fourteenth legion, who at that time, owing to the discord of the moment, had withdrawn from the legion; and, whichever way they inclined, these eight cohorts would have great weight as allies or opponents. The centurions Nonius, Donatius, Romilius, and Calpurnius, of whom we have spoken above, he ordered to be executed,

iussit, damnatos fidei crimine, gravissimo inter descicentis. Accessere partibus Valerius Asiaticus, Belgicae provinciae legatus, quem mox Vitellius generum adscivit, et Iunius Blaesus, Lugdunensis Galliae rector, cum Italica legione et ala Tauriana Lugduni tendentibus. Nec in Raeticis copiis mora quo minus statim adiungerentur: ne in Britannia quidem dubitatum.

LX. Praeerat Trebellius[1] Maximus, per avaritiam ac sordis[2] contemptus exercitui invisusque. Accendebat odium eius Roscius Coelius[3] legatus vicensimae legionis, olim discors, sed occasione civilium armorum atrocius proruperat. Trebellius seditionem et confusum ordinem disciplinae Coelio, spoliatas et inopes legiones Coelius Trebellio obiectabat, cum interim foedis[4] legatorum certaminibus modestia exercitus corrupta eoque discordiae ventum ut auxiliarium quoque militum conviciis proturbatus et adgregantibus se Coelio cohortibus alisque desertus Trebellius ad Vitellium perfugerit. Quies provinciae quamquam remoto consulari mansit: rexere legati legionum, pares iure, Coelius audendo potentior.

LXI. Adiuncto Britannico exercitu ingens viribus opibusque Vitellius duos duces, duo itinera bello

[1] trebellinus *M.* [2] sorde *M.*
[3] celius *M*: Caelius *vulgo, sed cf. Acta Arvalium a.* 81.
[4] faedus *M.*

---

[1] See iii. 38 f. for his alleged murder at Vitellius's orders.
[2] The *legio prima Italica.*
[3] Named from Statilius Taurus.

for they had been pronounced guilty of loyalty—the worst of charges among rebels. He also now gained the adherence of Valerius Asiaticus, governor of the Belgic Province, whom he later made his son-in-law; likewise of Junius Blaesus[1] who was in charge of Gallia Lugdunensis, together with the Italic legion[2] and the Taurian squadron of horse[3] who were stationed at Lyons. The forces in Raetia did not delay joining his side at once; nor was there any hesitation even in Britain.

LX. The governor of Britain was Trebellius Maximus, whose greed and meanness made him despised and hated by his soldiers. Their hostility towards him was increased by Roscius Coelius, the commander of the Twentieth legion, who had long been at odds with him; but now, on the occasion of civil war, the hostility between the two broke out with great violence. Trebellius charged Coelius with stirring up mutiny and destroying discipline; Coelius reproached Trebellius with robbing the legions and leaving them poor, while meantime the discipline of the army was broken down by this shameful quarrel between the commanders; and the trouble reached such a point that Trebellius was openly insulted by the auxiliary soldiers as well as by the legions, and when deserted by the auxiliary foot and horse who joined Coelius, fled to Vitellius. The province remained quiet, although the consular governor had been removed: control was in the hands of the commanders of the legions, who were equal in authority; but Coelius actually had the greater power because of his audacity.

LXI. Now that the army in Britain had joined his standard, Vitellius, who had enormous strength

destinavit: Fabius Valens adlicere vel, si abnuerent,[1] vastare Gallias et Cottianis Alpibus Italiam inrumpere, Caecina propiore transitu Poeninis[2] iugis degredi iussus. Valenti inferioris exercitus electi cum aquila quintae legionis et cohortibus alisque, ad quadraginta milia armatorum data; triginta milia Caecina e superiore Germania ducebat, quorum robur legio unaetvicensima[3] fuit. Addita utrique Germanorum auxilia, e quibus Vitellius suas quoque copias supplevit, tota mole belli secuturus.

LXII. Mira inter[4] exercitum imperatoremque diversitas: instare miles, arma poscere, dum Galliae trepident, dum Hispaniae cunctentur: non obstare hiemem neque ignavae pacis moras: invadendam Italiam, occupandam urbem; nihil in discordiis civilibus[5] festinatione tutius, ubi facto magis quam consulto opus esset. Torpebat Vitellius et fortunam principatus inerti luxu ac prodigis epulis praesumebat, medio diei temulentus et sagina gravis, cum tamen ardor et vis militum ultro ducis munia implebat, ut si adesset imperator et strenuis vel ignavis spem metumve adderet. Instructi intentique signum profectionis exposcunt. Nomen Germanici

[1] abnuerent *Rhenanus*: abnuerint *M.*
[2] Poeninus *Rhenanus*: paennis *M.*
[3] una et vicesima *codd. det. et ed. pr.*: una prima et vicensima *M.*
[4] mirante *M.* [5] vilibus *M.*

[1] By Mt. Genèvre. [2] The Great St. Bernard.

and resources at his command, selected two leaders and two lines of advance for the war. He ordered Fabius Valens to win over the Gallic provinces, or, if they refused his advances, to lay them waste and then break into Italy by the Cottian Alps.[1] Caecina was to descend by the nearer route over the Pennine range.[2] Valens was given picked soldiers from the Lower army together with the eagle of the Fifth legion and auxiliary foot and horse, the whole force numbering about 40,000 armed men. Caecina took from the Upper army 30,000; but his real strength lay in the Twenty-first legion. Both were given in addition German auxiliaries with whom Vitellius completed his own forces also, as he was prepared to follow with his whole strength.

LXII. There was a marked contrast between army and general. The soldiers were eager; they demanded battle, while the Gallic provinces were still timid and the Spanish hesitant. "Neither winter," they declared, "nor the delay caused by a peace which only a coward would make is an obstacle to us. We must invade Italy, seize Rome. In civil strife, where one must act rather than debate, nothing is more safe than haste." Vitellius, however, was sunk in sloth and was already enjoying a foretaste of his imperial fortune by indolent luxury and extravagant dinners; at midday he was tipsy and gorged with food. Still the soldiers in their eagerness and vigour actually performed the duties of a general, so that they inspired the energetic with hope or the indolent with fear, exactly as if the commander-in-chief were there in person. They were drawn up in line and eager for action; they demanded the signal for the start. Vitellius was at

Vitellio statim additum: Caesarem se appellari etiam victor prohibuit. Laetum augurium Fabio Valenti exercituique, quem in bellum agebat, ipso profectionis die aquila leni[1] meatu, prout agmen incederet, velut dux viae praevolavit, longumque per spatium is gaudentium militum clamor, ea quies interritae alitis fuit ut haud dubium magnae et prosperae rei omen[2] acciperetur.

LXIII. Et Treviros quidem ut socios securi adiere: Divoduri (Mediomatricorum id oppidum est) quamquam omni comitate exceptos subitus pavor terruit, raptis repente armis ad caedem innoxiae civitatis, non ob praedam aut spoliandi cupidine, sed furore et rabie et causis incertis eoque difficilioribus remediis, donec precibus ducis mitigati ab excidio civitatis temperavere; caesa tamen ad quattuor milia hominum. Isque terror Gallias invasit ut venienti mox agmini universae civitates cum magistratibus et precibus occurrerent, stratis per vias feminis puerisque: quaeque alia placamenta hostilis irae, non quidem in bello sed pro pace tendebantur.

LXIV. Nuntium de caede Galbae et imperio Othonis Fabius Valens in civitate Leucorum accepit. Nec militum animus in gaudium aut formidine permotus: bellum volvebat. Gallis cunctatio exempta est[3]: in Othonem ac Vitellium odium par,

[1] leni *Acidalius*: levi *M.* [2] nomen *M.*
[3] est *Halm*: et *M.*

---

[1] Metz.
[2] Living about the modern town of Toul.

once given the additional name of Germanicus; the appellation Caesar he forbade even after he was victorious. It was a happy augury to the mind of Fabius Valens and the army which he was leading to war that, on the very day they started, an eagle flew gently along before the advancing army apparently to guide their march; and for a long distance such were the exultant cries of the troops, such the undisturbed calm of the bird, that it was welcomed as a certain omen of a great and successful issue.

LXIII. The army approached the Treviri with a sense of security which they naturally felt among allies. But at Divodurum,[1] a town of the Mediomatrici, though received with all courtesy, the army was struck with sudden panic; the soldiers hurriedly seized their arms to massacre the innocent citizens, not for booty or from a desire to loot, but prompted by wild fury, the cause of which was uncertain and the remedies therefore more difficult. Finally, however, they were quieted by their general's appeals and refrained from completely destroying the community; still about 4,000 had been massacred, and such terror spread over the Gallic provinces that later on, as the army advanced, entire communities headed by their magistrates came out to meet it with appeals, women and children prostrating themselves along the roads, while everything else that can appease an enemy's wrath was offered to secure peace, although there was no war.

LXIV. Fabius Valens heard the news of Galba's death and the accession of Otho in the state of the Leuci.[2] The soldiers were neither moved to joy nor stirred by fear; they thought only of war. The Gauls no longer hesitated; though they hated Otho

ex Vitellio et metus. Proxima Lingonum civitas erat, fida partibus. Benigne excepti modestia certavere, sed brevis laetitia fuit cohortium intemperie, quas a legione quarta decima, ut supra memoravimus, digressas exercitui suo Fabius Valens adiunxerat. Iurgia primum, mox rixa inter Batavos et legionarios, dum his aut illis studia militum adgregantur, prope in proelium exarsere, ni Valens animadversione paucorum oblitos iam Batavos imperii admonuisset. Frustra adversus Aeduos quaesita belli causa: iussi pecuniam atque arma deferre[1] gratuitos insuper commeatus praebuere. Quod Aedui formidine Lugdunenses gaudio fecere. Sed legio Italica et ala Tauriana[2] abductae: cohortem duodevicensimam Lugduni, solitis sibi hibernis, relinqui placuit. Manlius Valens legatus Italicae legionis, quamquam bene de partibus meritus, nullo apud Vitellium honore fuit; secretis eum criminationibus infamaverat Fabius ignarum et, quo incautior deciperetur, palam laudatum.

LXV. Veterem inter Lugdunensis et Viennensis[3] discordiam proximum bellum accenderat. Multae

[1] deferret *M.* [2] taurina *M.*, *cf. c.* 59.
[3] et Viennensis *om. M*: Viennensesque *Puteolanus.*

---

[1] Apparently a *cohors civium Romanorum*, an auxiliary force.
[2] The rebellion of Vindex. See Introduction, p. xi.

and Vitellius equally, they also feared Vitellius. The next state was that of the Lingones, which was faithful to his party. There the Roman soldiers enjoyed a kindly reception and vied with one another in good behaviour. Yet the joy over this was short-lived, because of the violence of the auxiliary infantry, which, as we said above, had detached themselves from the Fourteenth legion and been incorporated by Fabius Valens in his force. At first a quarrel arose between the Batavians and the legionaries, and then a brawl. Finally, as the soldiers took sides with one or the other, they broke out almost into open battle, and in fact would have done so had not Valens, by the punishment of a few men, reminded the Batavians of the authority which they had forgotten. It was in vain that the Roman troops tried to find an excuse for war against the Aeduans; when ordered to furnish money and arms, the Aeduans went so far as to provide the army with supplies without cost, and what the Aeduans had done from fear the people of Lyons did from joy. The Italic legion and the Taurian squadron of horse were withdrawn from the city; it was decided, however, to leave the Eighteenth cohort there,[1] for that was their usual winter quarters. Manlius Valens, commander of the Italic legion, enjoyed no honour with Vitellius, though he had done good service to his party. Fabius had defamed him by secret charges of which Manlius knew nothing, but praised him openly that, being off his guard, he might be more easily deceived.

LXV. The old feud between the people of Lyons and Vienne had been inflamed by the last war.[2] They had inflicted many losses on each other and

in vicem clades, crebrius infestiusque quam ut tantum propter Neronem Galbamque pugnaretur. Et Galba reditus Lugdunensium occasione irae in fiscum verterat; multus contra in Viennensis honor: unde aemulatio et invidia et uno amne discretis conexum odium. Igitur Lugdunenses extimulare singulos militum et in eversionem Viennensium impellere, obsessam ab illis coloniam suam, adiutos Vindicis conatus, conscriptas nuper legiones in praesidium Galbae referendo. Et ubi causas odiorum praetenderant, magnitudinem praedae ostendebant, nec iam secreta exhortatio, sed publicae preces: irent ultores, excinderent sedem Gallici belli: cuncta illic externa et hostilia: se, coloniam Romanam et partem exercitus et prosperarum adversarumque rerum socios, si fortuna contra daret, iratis ne relinquerent.

LXVI. His et pluribus in eundem modum perpulerant ut ne[1] legati quidem ac duces partium restingui posse[2] iracundiam exercitus arbitrarentur, cum haud ignari discriminis sui Viennenses, velamenta et infulas praeferentes, ubi agmen incesserat, arma genua vestigia prensanda flexere militum animos; addidit Valens trecenos singulis militibus sestertios. Tum vestustas dignitasque coloniae valuit et verba Fabi salutem incolumitatemque Vien-

[1] ne *I. F. Gronovius*: nec *M.*
[2] posset *M.*

had done this too frequently and savagely for anyone to believe that they were fighting only for Nero or Galba. Galba too had taken advantage of his displeasure to divert the revenues of Lyons into his own treasury; on the other hand he had shown great honour to the people of Vienne. Hence arose rivalry and envy and a bond of hatred between the peoples who were separated only by a single river. Therefore the people of Lyons began to stir up individual soldiers and spur them on to destroy Vienne by reminding them that its inhabitants had besieged their own colony, aided Vindex in his attempts, and had lately enrolled legions for the defence of Galba. Moreover, after they had put forward these pretexts for hating Vienne, they began to point out the large booty to be obtained, no longer exhorting them in secret, but making public appeals. "Advance as avengers," they said; "destroy the home of war in Gaul. At Vienne there is nothing that is not foreign and hostile. We, a Roman colony and a part of your army, have shared your successes and reverses. Do not abandon us to an angry foe, should fortune prove adverse."

LXVI. By these and similar appeals, they had brought the soldiers to the point where not even the commanders and leaders of the party thought it possible to check the army's hostile fury, when the people of Vienne, well aware of their danger, diverted the soldiers from their purpose by coming out along the line of advance, bearing veils and fillets, and clasping the soldiers' weapons, knees, and feet. Valens too gave each soldier three hundred sesterces. The age also and the dignity of the colony prevailed; and the words of Fabius,

nensium commendantis aequis auribus[1] accepta; publice tamen armis multati, privatis et promiscis copiis iuvere militem. Sed fama constans fuit ipsum Valentem magna pecunia emptum. Is diu sordidus, repente dives mutationem fortunae male tegebat, accensis egestate longa cupidinibus immoderatus et inopi iuventa senex prodigus. Lento deinde agmine per finis Allobrogum ac Vocontiorum ductus exercitus, ipsa itinerum spatia et stativorum mutationes venditante duce, foedis pactionibus adversus possessores agrorum et magistratus civitatum, adeo minaciter ut Luco (municipium id Vocontiorum est) faces admoverit, donec pecunia mitigaretur. Quotiens pecuniae materia deesset, stupris et adulteriis exorabatur. Sic ad Alpis perventum.

LXVII. Plus praedae ac sanguinis Caecina hausit. Inritaverant turbidum ingenium Helvetii, Gallica gens olim[2] armis virisque, mox memoria nominis clara, de caede Galbae ignari et Vitellii imperium abnuentes. Initium bello fuit avaritia ac festinatio unaetvicensimae legionis; rapuerant pecuniam missam in stipendium castelli quod olim Helvetii suis militibus ac stipendiis tuebantur. Aegre id passi

[1] saxuribus *M.* [2] olim *Rhenanus*: solim *M.*

[1] The Allobroges lived in the districts known to-day as Savoy and northern Dauphiné; the southern part of Dauphiné and Provence were occupied by the Vocontii, whose chief town was Vasio (Vaison).

[2] Luc-en-Diois.

as he urged the soldiers to leave the Viennese in safety and unharmed, received a favourable hearing. Still the people were all deprived of their weapons, and they assisted the soldiers with private means of every sort. Yet report has always consistently said that Valens himself was bribed with a large sum. He had long been poor; now suddenly becoming rich, he hardly concealed his change of fortune. His desires had been increased by long poverty, so that he now put no restraint upon himself, and after a youth of poverty became a prodigal old man. Next he led his army slowly through the lands of the Allobroges and Vocontii,[1] the very length of each day's advance and the choice of encampment being sold by the general, who drove shameless bargains to the detriment of the owners of the land and the local magistrates. Indeed he acted so threateningly that he was on the point of applying the torch to Lucus,[2] a town of the Vocontii, until he was soothed by money. Whenever money was not available, he was appeased by sacrifices to his lust. In this way they reached the Alps.

LXVII. Caecina gained even more booty and shed more blood. His restless spirit had been provoked by the Helvetii, a Gallic people once famous for their deeds in arms and for their heroes, later only for the memory of their name. Of Galba's murder they knew nothing and they refused to recognize the authority of Vitellius. The origin of the war was due to the greed and haste of the Twenty-first legion, which had embezzled the money sent to pay the garrison of a fort once defended by the Helvetians with their own forces and at their own expense.

Helvetii, interceptis epistulis, quae nomine Germanici exercitus ad Pannonicas legiones ferebantur, centurionem et quosdam militum in custodia retinebant. Caecina belli avidus proximam quamque culpam, antequam paeniteret, ultum ibat: mota propere castra, vastati agri, direptus longa pace in modum municipii extructus locus, amoeno salubrium aquarum usu frequens; missi ad Raetica auxilia nuntii ut versos in legionem Helvetios a tergo adgrederentur.

LXVIII. Illi ante discrimen feroces, in periculo pavidi, quamquam primo tumultu Claudium Severum ducem legerant, non arma noscere, non ordines sequi, non in unum consulere. Exitiosum adversus veteranos proelium, intuta obsidio dilapsis vetustate moenibus; hinc Caecina cum valido exercitu, inde Raeticae alae cohortesque et ipsorum Raetorum iuventus, sueta armis et more militiae exercita. Undique populatio et caedes: ipsi medio vagi, abiectis armis, magna pars saucii aut palantes, in montem Vocetium perfugere. Ac statim immissa cohorte Thraecum depulsi et consectantibus Germanis Raetisque per silvas atque in ipsis latebris

---

[1] Subdued by Caesar in 58 B.C.
[2] Baden on the Limmat, north-west of Zurich.
[3] The Bötzberg in the Swiss Jura.

This angered the Helvetians, who intercepted some letters which were being carried in the name of the army in Germany to the legions in Pannonia,[1] and they kept the centurions and certain soldiers in custody. Caecina, eager for war, always moved to punish every fault instantly before there was a chance for repentance: he immediately shifted camp, devastated the fields, and ravaged a place that during the long peace had been built up into the semblance of a town and was much resorted to for its beauty and healthful waters.[2] Messages were sent to the auxiliaries in Raetia, directing them to attack in the rear the Helvetians who were facing the Roman legion.

LXVIII. The Helvetians were bold before the crisis came, but timid in the face of danger; and although at the beginning of the trouble they had chosen Claudius Severus leader, they had not learned the use of arms, did not keep their ranks, or consult together. Battle against veterans would be destructive to them; a siege would be dangerous, for their walls had fallen into ruin from lapse of time. On the one side was Caecina with a strong force, on the other the Raetian horse and foot, and the young men of Raetia itself, who were accustomed to arms and trained in warfare. Everywhere were rapine and slaughter. Wandering about between the two armies, the Helvetians threw away their arms and fled for life to Mt. Vocetius,[3] the majority of them wounded or straggling. A cohort of Thracian infantry was immediately dispatched against them and dislodged them. Then, pursued by Germans and Raetians through their forests, they were cut down even in their hiding places.

trucidati. Multa hominum milia caesa, multa sub corona venundata. Cumque dirutis omnibus Aventicum gentis caput infesto[1] agmine peteretur, missi qui dederent civitatem, et deditio accepta. In Iulium Alpinum e principibus ut concitorem belli Caecina animadvertit: ceteros veniae vel saevitiae Vitellii reliquit.

LXIX. Haud facile dictu est, legati Helvetiorum minus placabilem[2] imperatorem an militem invenerint. Civitatis[3] excidium poscunt, tela ac manus in ora legatorum intentant. Ne Vitellius quidem verbis et minis temperabat, cum Claudius Cossus, unus ex legatis, notae facundiae sed dicendi artem apta trepidatione occultans atque eo validior, militis animum mitigavit. Ut est mos, vulgus mutabile subitis et tam pronum in misericordiam[4] quam immodicum saevitia fuerat: effusis lacrimis et meliora constantius postulando impunitatem salutemque civitati impetravere.

LXX. Caecina paucos in Helvetiis moratus dies dum sententiae Vitellii certior fieret, simul transitum Alpium parans, laetum ex Italia nuntium accipit alam Silianam circa Padum agentem sacramento Vitellii accessisse. Pro consule Vitellium Siliani in Africa habuerant; mox a Nerone, ut in

[1] infesto *Andresen*: iusto *M*.

[2] *Verba quae sequuntur* [placa]bilem *usque ad* incertum (*c.* 75), *item* inopia (*c.* 86), *usque ad* Cyprum (II, 2) *desunt in Mediceo, bifolio iam ante a. MCCCCLII deperdito; lectiones discrepantes sunt codd. Florentinorum lxviii.* 4, *lxviii.* 5 (*a, b*), *ex Mediceo descriptorum.*

[3] novitatis *a b.*

[4] misericordia *a b.*

---

[1] Avenches near Freiburg.

[2] Probably named from C. Silius, governor of Upper Germany under Tiberius, who had raised the squadron.

Many thousands were massacred, many thousands sold into slavery. After all had been destroyed, when the Roman army was advancing to attack Aventicum,[1] the capital of the tribe, the people of that town sent envoys to offer surrender and this was accepted. Caecina punished Julius Alpinus, one of the leading men, as the promoter of the war: the rest he left to the mercy or the cruelty of Vitellius.

LXIX. It is not easy to say whether the envoys of the Helvetians found the general or the soldiers less merciful. The soldiers demanded the destruction of the state, shaking their weapons and fists in the faces of the envoys. Even Vitellius did not refrain from threatening words, till Claudius Cossus, one of the envoys, assuaged the anger of the soldiers; Cossus was a man of well-known eloquence, but at this time he concealed his skill as an orator under an appropriate trepidation which made him all the more effective. Like all mobs, the common soldiers were given to sudden change and were as ready to show pity as they had been extravagant in cruelty. By floods of tears and persistent prayers for a milder decision, the envoys obtained safety and protection for their state.

LXX. While Caecina delayed a few days among the Helvetians until he should learn the views of Vitellius, being engaged at the same time in preparations for the passage of the Alps, he received the joyful news from Italy that the Silian detachment[2] of horse that was operating along the Po had taken the oath of allegiance to Vitellius. This detachment had served under Vitellius when he was proconsul in Africa; later Nero had removed it to send it to Egypt,

Aegyptum praemitterentur, exciti et ob bellum Vindicis revocati[1] ac tum in Italia manentes, instinctu decurionum, qui Othonis ignari, Vitellio obstricti robur adventantium legionum et famam Germanici exercitus attollebant, transiere[2] in partis et ut donum aliquod novo principi firmissima transpadanae regionis municipia, Mediolanum ac Novariam et Eporediam et Vercellas, adiunxere. Id Caecinae per ipsos compertum. Et quia praesidio alae unius latissima Italiae pars defendi nequibat, praemissis Gallorum Lusitanorumque et Britannorum cohortibus et Germanorum vexillis cum ala Petriana,[3] ipse paulum cunctatus est num Raeticis iugis in Noricum flecteret adversus Petronium Urbicum[4] procuratorem, qui concitis et auxiliis interruptis fluminum pontibus fidus Othoni putabatur. Sed metu ne amitteret praemissas iam cohortis alasque, simul reputans plus gloriae retenta Italia et, ubicumque certatum foret, Noricos in cetera victoriae praemia cessuros, Poenino itinere subsignanum militem et grave legionum agmen hibernis adhuc Alpibus transduxit.

LXXI. Otho interim contra spem omnium non deliciis neque desidia torpescere: dilatae voluptates, dissimulata luxuria et cuncta ad decorem imperii

[1] provocati *a b*.
[2] transire *a b*.
[3] ala Petriana *Böcking*: alpe triaria *a b*.
[4] Urbicum *Freinsheim* : urbi *a b*.

---

[1] The commanders of the companies of horse.
[2] Milan, Novara, Ivrea, Vercelli.
[3] Named from a certain Petra who had organised the troop.
[4] The Arlberg.
[5] The Great St. Bernard.

but it had been recalled because of the war with Vindex and was at this time in Italy. Prompted by the decurions[1] who, being wholly unacquainted with Otho but bound to Vitellius, kept extolling the strength of the approaching legions and the reputation of the army in Germany, the members of the troop came over to the side of Vitellius, and as a kind of gift to the new emperor, they secured for him the strongest of the transpadane towns, Mediolanum, Novaria, Eporedia, and Vercellae.[2] This fact Caecina learned from the inhabitants of these towns, and since a single squadron of horse could not protect the broadest part of Italy, he sent in advance infantry, made up of Gauls, Lusitanians, and Britons, and some German detachments with the squadron of Petra's horse,[3] while he himself delayed a little to see whether he should turn aside over the Raetian range[4] to Noricum to oppose the imperial agent Petronius Urbicus, who was regarded as faithful to Otho since he had called out auxiliary troops and broken down the bridges over the stream. But Caecina was afraid that he might lose the infantry and cavalry which he had already dispatched before him, and, at the same time, he realized that there was more glory in securing Italy, and that wherever the decisive struggle took place, the people of Noricum would come with the other prizes of victory. He accordingly led his reserve troops and the heavy armed legions over the Pennine Pass[5] while the Alps were still covered with the winter's snow.

LXXI. Otho, meanwhile, contrary to everyone's expectation, made no dull surrender to luxury or ease: he put off his pleasures, concealed his profligacy, and ordered his whole life as befitted the

composita, eoque plus formidinis adferebant falsae virtutes et vitia reditura. Marium Celsum consulem designatum, per speciem vinculorum saevitiae militum subtractum, acciri in Capitolium iubet; clementiae titulus e viro claro et partibus inviso petebatur. Celsus constanter servatae erga Galbam fidei crimen confessus, exemplum ultro imputavit. Nec Otho quasi ignosceret sed, ne hostem metueret, conciliationes adhibens,[1] statim inter intimos amicos habuit et mox bello inter duces delegit, mansitque Celso velut fataliter etiam pro Othone fides integra et infelix. Laeta primoribus civitatis, celebrata in vulgus Celsi salus ne militibus quidem ingrata fuit, eandem virtutem admirantibus cui irascebantur.

LXXII. Par inde exultatio disparibus causis consecuta impetrato Tigellini exitio. Ofonius[2] Tigellinus obscuris parentibus, foeda pueritia, impudica senecta, praefecturam vigilum et praetorii et alia praemia virtutum, quia velocius erat, vitiis adeptus, crudelitatem mox, deinde avaritiam, virilia scelera, exercuit, corrupto ad omne facinus Nerone, quaedam ignaro ausus, ac postremo eiusdem desertor ac

[1] ne hostem metueret, conciliationes adhibens *Halm*: ne hostes metueret conciliationis *a b*.

[2] Ophonius *a b*, *sed cf. Dion. Cass.* lix. 23, *ed. Boissevain.*

imperial position; with the result that these simulated virtues and the sure return of his vices only inspired still greater dread. Marius Celsus, consul-elect, whom he had saved from the fury of the soldiers by pretending to imprison him, he had called to the Capitol, for he wished to obtain the credit of being merciful by his treatment of a distinguished man whom his party hated. Celsus boldly pleaded guilty of constant loyalty to Galba and went so far as to claim that his example was to Otho's advantage. Otho did not act toward him as if he were pardoning a criminal, but to avoid having to fear him as an enemy took steps to be reconciled to him and immediately began to treat him as one of his intimate friends; he later chose him as one of the leaders for the war. But Celsus, on his side, as by a fatal impulse, maintained a loyalty to Otho which was unbroken and ill-starred. His safety, which gave joy to the chief men of the state and which was commented on favourably by the common people, was not unpopular even with the soldiers, who admired the same virtue which roused their anger.

LXXII. Equal delight, but for different reasons, was felt when the destruction of Tigellinus was secured. Ofonius Tigellinus was of obscure parentage; his youth had been infamous and in his old age he was profligate. Command of the city watch and of the praetorians and other prizes which belong to virtue he had obtained by vices as the quicker course; then, afterwards, he practised cruelty and later greed, offences which belong to maturity. He also corrupted Nero so that he was ready for any wickedness; he dared certain acts without Nero's knowledge and finally deserted and betrayed him.

proditor: unde non alium pertinacius ad poenam flagitaverunt, diverso adfectu, quibus odium Neronis inerat et quibus desiderium. Apud Galbam Titi Vinii potentia defensus, praetexentis servatam ab eo filiam. Haud dubie servaverat, non clementia, quippe tot interfectis, sed effugium in futurum, quia pessimus quisque diffidentia praesentium mutationem pavens adversus publicum odium privatam gratiam praeparat: unde nulla innocentiae cura sed vices inpunitatis. Eo infensior populus, addita ad vetus Tigellini odium recenti Titi Vinii invidia, concurrere ex tota urbe in Palatium[1] ac fora et, ubi plurima vulgi licentia, in circum ac theatra effusi seditiosis vocibus strepere, donec Tigellinus accepto apud Sinuessanas aquas supremae necessitatis nuntio inter stupra concubinarum et oscula et deformis moras sectis novacula faucibus infamem vitam foedavit etiam exitu sero et inhonesto.

LXXIII. Per idem tempus expostulata ad supplicium Calvia Crispinilla variis frustrationibus et adversa dissimulantis principis fama periculo exempta est. Magistra libidinum Neronis, transgressa in Africam ad instigandum in arma Clodium Macrum, famem populo Romano haud obscure molita, totius

[1] in palatium et tota urbe *a b*: e tota *codd. dett.*

---

[1] The warm baths at Sinuessa in Campania were much visited. Cf. *Ann.* xii. 66.

[2] Cf. chap. 7.

So no one was more persistently demanded for punishment from different motives, both by those who hated Nero and by those who regretted him. Under Galba Tigellinus had been protected by the influence of Titus Vinius, who claimed that Tigellinus had saved his daughter. He undoubtedly had saved her, not, however, prompted by mercy (he had killed so many victims!) but to secure a refuge for the future, since the worst of rascals in their distrust of the present and fear of a change always try to secure private gratitude as an off-set to public detestation, having no regard for innocence, but wishing to obtain mutual impunity in wrong-doing. These facts made the people more hostile towards him, and their old hatred was increased by their recent dislike for Titus Vinius. They rushed from every part of the city to the Palatine and the fora, and, pouring into the circus and theatres where the common people have the greatest licence, they broke out into seditious cries, until finally Tigellinus, at the baths of Sinuessa,[1] receiving the message that the hour of his supreme necessity had come, amid the embraces and kisses of his mistresses, shamefully delaying his end, finally cut his throat with a razor, still further defiling a notorious life by a tardy and ignominious death.

LXXIII. At the same time the people demanded the punishment of Calvia Crispinilla. She was saved from danger, however, through various artifices on the part of the emperor, who brought ill-reputation upon himself by his duplicity. Crispinilla had taught Nero profligacy; then she had crossed to Africa to stir up Clodius Macer to rebellion,[2] and had openly tried to bring famine on the Roman people. Afterwards she secured popularity with

postea civitatis gratiam obtinuit, consulari matrimonio subnixa et apud Galbam Othonem Vitellium inlaesa, mox potens pecunia et orbitate, quae bonis malisque temporibus iuxta valent.

LXXIV. Crebrae interim et muliebribus blandimentis infectae ab Othone ad Vitellium epistulae [1] offerebant [2] pecuniam et gratiam et quemcumque [3] e [4] quietis locis prodigae vitae legisset. Paria Vitellius ostentabat, primo mollius, stulta utrimque et indecora simulatione, mox quasi rixantes stupra ac flagitia in vicem obiectavere, neuter falso. Otho, revocatis quos Galba miserat legatis, rursus ad utrumque Germanicum exercitum et ad legionem Italicam easque quae Lugduni agebant copias specie senatus misit. Legati apud Vitellium remansere, promptius quam ut retenti viderentur; praetoriani, quos per simulationem officii legatis Otho adiunxerat, remissi antequam legionibus miscerentur. Addidit epistulas [5] Fabius Valens nomine Germanici exercitus ad praetorias et urbanas cohortis de viribus partium magnificas et concordiam offerentis; increpabat ultro quod tanto ante traditum Vitellio imperium ad Othonem vertissent.

[1] epulae *a b*.
[2] offerebant *Rhenanus*: offerebantur *a b*.
[3] quaecunque *a b*. [4] e *add. Madvig*.
[5] epulas *a b*.

---

[1] The court paid by fortune-hunters to rich and childless men and women was one of the baser characteristics of this age and furnished a ready theme for the satirists. Cf. *e.g.* Horace, *Sat.* ii. 5; Juvenal 3. 126 ff.; 6. 548 ff.; and often.

the entire city by her marriage with a former consul, and so was unharmed under Galba, Otho, and Vitellius. Still later she became powerful through her wealth and childlessness, which have equal weight both in good and evil times.[1]

LXXIV. Meantime Otho sent Vitellius many letters, disfigured by unmanly flattery, offering him money and favour and granting him any quiet place he chose wherein to spend his profligate life.[2] Vitellius made similar proposals. At first both wrote in genial tones, resorting to pretence which was at once foolish and unbecoming: later, as if engaged in a common brawl, they each charged the other with debaucheries and low practices, neither of them falsely. Otho, after recalling the delegates that Galba had dispatched,[3] sent them again in the name of the senate to the two armies in Germany, to the Italic legion, and to the troops that were stationed at Lyons. The envoys remained with Vitellius, too readily for men to think they were detained. The praetorians that Otho had sent with the delegation to show it honour were sent back before they could mix with the legions. Fabius Valens also sent letters in the name of the army in Germany to the praetorian and city cohorts, boasting of the strength of his party and offering terms of agreement. He even reproached them for diverting to Otho the imperial power that had been given to Vitellius so long before.

[2] Suetonius (*Otho* 8) and Dio Cassius (lxiv. 10) say that Otho offered to share the imperial office with him; and Suetonius adds that he proposed to marry Vitellius's daughter.

[3] Cf. chap. 19.

LXXV. Ita promissis simul ac minis temptabantur, ut bello impares, in pace nihil amissuri ; neque ideo praetorianorum fides mutata. Sed insidiatores ab Othone in Germaniam, a Vitellio in urbem missi. Utrisque frustra fuit, Vitellianis inpune, per tantam hominum multitudinem mutua ignorantia fallentibus : Othoniani novitate vultus, omnibus in vicem gnaris,[1] prodebantur. Vitellius litteras ad Titianum fratrem Othonis composuit, exitium ipsi filioque eius minitans ni incolumes sibi mater ac liberi servarentur ; et stetit domus utraque, sub Othone incertum an metu : Vitellius victor clementiae gloriam tulit.

LXXVI. Primus Othoni fiduciam addidit ex Illyrico nuntius iurasse in eum Dalmatiae ac Pannoniae et Moesiae legiones. Idem ex Hispania adlatum laudatusque per edictum Cluvius Rufus : set[2] statim cognitum est conversam ad Vitellium Hispaniam. Ne Aquitania quidem, quamquam ab Iulio Cordo in verba Othonis obstricta, diu mansit. Nusquam fides aut amor : metu ac necessitate huc illuc mutabantur. Eadem formido provinciam Narbonensem ad Vitellium vertit, facili transitu ad proximos et validiores. Longinquae provinciae et

[1] gnaris *Rhenanus* : ignaris *a b*.
[2] set *Ritter* : et *M*.

LXXV. Thus the praetorians were plied at the same time with promises and threats. They were told that they were unequal to war but would lose nothing in peace; and yet they did not give up their loyalty. Otho sent secret agents to Germany, and Vitellius sent his agents to Rome. Neither accomplished anything, but the agents of Vitellius got off safely, since amid the great multitude they neither knew people nor were themselves known; Otho's agents, however, were betrayed by their strange faces, since in the army everyone knew everyone else. Vitellius wrote a letter to Otho's brother, Titianus, in which he threatened him and his son with death if his own mother and children were not kept unharmed. As a matter of fact both families were uninjured: under Otho this was probably due to fear; Vitellius, when victor, got the credit for mercy.

LXXVI. The first message that gave Otho confidence came from Illyricum, to the effect that the legions of Dalmatia and Pannonia and Moesia had sworn allegiance to him. The same news was brought from Spain, whereupon Otho extolled Cluvius Rufus in a proclamation; but immediately afterwards word was brought that Spain had gone over to Vitellius. Not even Aquitania long remained faithful, although it had been made to swear allegiance to Otho by Julius Cordus. Nowhere was there any loyalty or affection. Fear and necessity made men shift now to one side, now to the other. The same terror brought the province of Narbonensis over to Vitellius, it being easy to pass to the side of the nearest and the stronger. The distant provinces and all the armed forces across the sea

quidquid armorum mari dirimitur penes Othonem manebat, non partium studio, sed erat grande momentum in nomine urbis ac praetexto senatus, et occupaverat animos prior auditus. Iudaicum exercitum Vespasianus, Syriae legiones Mucianus sacramento Othonis adegere; simul Aegyptus omnesque versae in Orientem provinciae nomine eius tenebantur. Idem Africae obsequium, initio Carthagine orto neque expectata Vipstani[1] Aproniani proconsulis auctoritate; Crescens Neronis libertus (nam et hi malis temporibus partem se rei publicae faciunt) epulum plebi ob laetitiam recentis imperii obtulerat, et populus pleraque sine modo festinavit. Carthaginem ceterae civitates secutae.

LXXVII. Sic distractis exercitibus ac provinciis Vitellio quidem ad capessendam principatus fortunam bello opus erat, Otho ut in multa pace munia imperii obibat, quaedam ex dignitate rei publicae, pleraque contra decus ex praesenti usu properando. Consul cum Titiano fratre in kalendas Martias ipse; proximos mensis Verginio destinat ut aliquod exercitui Germanico delenimentum; iungitur Verginio Pompeius Vopiscus praetexto veteris amicitiae; plerique Viennensium honori datum interpretaban-

[1] Vipstani *Ryckius, cf. Acta Arvalium passim*: vipsani *M.*

---

[1] At the beginning of this year, 69 A.D., the thirty legions of the Roman army were distributed as follows: Spanish Provinces, 3; Gallic Provinces, 1; Upper Germany, 3; Lower Germany, 4; Britain, 3; Dalmatia, 2; Pannonia, 2; Moesia, 3; Syria, 3; Judea, 3; Egypt, 2; Africa, 1.

To these were attached auxiliary troops and cavalry of about the same strength as the legions, so that the total

remained on Otho's side, not from any enthusiasm for his party, but because the name of the city and the splendour of the senate had great weight; moreover the emperor of whom they first heard preëmpted their regard. The oath of allegiance to Otho was administered to the army in Judea by Vespasian, to the legions in Syria by Mucianus. At the same time Egypt and all the provinces to the East were governed in Otho's name. Africa showed the same ready obedience, led by Carthage, without waiting for the authority of Vipstanius Apronianus, the proconsul; Crescens, one of Nero's freedmen—for in evil times even freedmen take part in the government—had given the commonfolk a feast in honour of the recent accession; and the people hurried on with extravagant zeal the usual demonstrations. The rest of the communities followed Carthage.[1]

LXXVII. Since the armies and provinces were thus divided, Vitellius for his part needed to fight to gain the imperial fortune; but Otho was performing the duties of an emperor as if in profound peace. Some things he did in accordance with the dignity of the state, but often he acted contrary to its honour in the haste that was prompted by present need. He himself was consul with his brother Titianus until the first of March. The next months were allotted to Verginius as a sop to the army in Germany. With Verginius he associated Pompeius Vopiscus under the pretext of their ancient friendship; but most interpreted the act as an honour shown the people of Vienne. The

land forces of the Roman Empire at this time approximated 300,000 men.

tur. Ceteri consulatus ex destinatione Neronis aut Galbae mansere, Caelio ac Flavio Sabinis in Iulias, Arrio Antonino[1] et Mario Celso in Septembris, quorum honoribus[2] ne Vitellius quidem victor intercessit. Sed Otho pontificatus auguratusque honoratis iam senibus cumulum dignitatis addidit, aut recens ab exilio reversos nobilis adulescentulos avitis ac paternis sacerdotiis in solacium recoluit. Redditus Cadio Rufo, Pedio Blaeso, Saevino P . . .[3] senatorius locus. Repetundarum criminibus sub Claudio ac Nerone ceciderant: placuit ignoscentibus verso nomine, quod avaritia fuerat, videri maiestatem, cuius tum odio etiam bonae leges peribant.

LXXVIII. Eadem largitione civitatum quoque ac provinciarum animos adgressus Hispalensibus[4] et Emeritensibus familiarum adiectiones, Lingonibus universis civitatem Romanam, provinciae Baeticae Maurorum civitates dono dedit; nova iura Cappadociae, nova Africae, ostentata[5] magis quam mansura. Inter quae necessitate praesentium rerum et instantibus curis excusata ne tum quidem immemor amorum statuas Poppaeae per senatus consultum reposuit; creditus est etiam de celebranda Neronis memoria agitavisse spe vulgum adliciendi. Et fuere

[1] Antonino *Lipsius*: antonio *M.*
[2] honoribus *Haase*: honoris *M.*
[3] prom-se *M.*
[4] Hispalensibus *Faernus*: hispaniensibus *M.*
[5] ostentata *Ernesti*: ostentai *M.*

---

[1] Not the brother of Vespasian.
[2] The grandfather of the Emperor Antoninus Pius.
[3] The terms of these men were later shortened, and in fact there were fifteen consuls in the year 69.
[4] Seville and Merida.

rest of the consulships for the year remained as Nero or Galba had assigned them: Caelius Sabinus and Flavius Sabinus [1] until July; Arrius Antoninus [2] and Marius Celsus till September; their honours not even Vitellius vetoed when he became victor.[3] But Otho assigned pontificates and augurships as a crowning distinction to old men who had already gone through the list of offices, or solaced young nobles recently returned from exile with priesthoods which their fathers and ancestors had held. Cadius Rufus, Pedius Blaesus, and Saevinus P. . . were restored to senatorial rank, which they had lost under Claudius and Nero on account of charges of bribery made against them; those who pardoned them decided to shift the name so that what had really been greed should seem treason, which was now so odious that it made even good laws null and useless.

LXXVIII. With the same generosity Otho tried to win over the support of communities and provinces. To the colonies of Hispalis and Emerita [4] he sent additional families. To the whole people of the Lingones he gave Roman citizenship and presented the province Baetica with towns in Mauritania. New constitutions were given Cappadocia and Africa, more for display than to the lasting advantage of the provinces. Even while engaged in these acts, which found their excuse in the necessity of the situation and the anxieties that were forced upon him, he did not forget his loves and had the statues of Poppaea replaced by a vote of the senate. It was believed that he also brought up the question of celebrating Nero's memory with the hope of winning over the Roman people; and in fact some set

qui imagines Neronis proponerent: atque etiam Othoni quibusdam diebus populus et miles, tamquam nobilitatem ac decus adstruerent, Neroni Othoni adclamavit. Ipse in suspenso tenuit, vetandi metu vel agnoscendi pudore.

LXXIX. Conversis ad civile bellum animis externa sine cura habebantur. Eo audentius Rhoxolani,[1] Sarmatica gens, priore hieme caesis duabus cohortibus, magna spe Moesiam inruperant,[2] ad novem milia equitum, ex ferocia et successu praedae magis quam pugnae intenta. Igitur vagos et incuriosos tertia legio adiunctis auxiliis repente invasit. Apud Romanos omnia proelio apta: Sarmatae dispersi aut cupidine praedae graves onere sarcinarum et lubrico itinerum adempta equorum pernicitate velut vincti caedebantur. Namque mirum dictu ut sit omnis Sarmatarum virtus velut extra ipsos. Nihil ad pedestrem pugnam tam ignavum: ubi per turmas advenere vix ulla acies obstiterit. Sed tum umido die et soluto gelu neque conti neque gladii, quos praelongos utraque manu regunt, usui, lapsantibus equis et catafractarum pondere. Id principibus et nobilissimo cuique tegimen, ferreis laminis aut praeduro corio consertum, ut adversus ictus impene-

[1] Rhoxolani *Beroaldus*: rhosolanis *M*.
[2] ad Moesiam *M*: ad *ante* novem *posuit Acidalius*.

---

[1] Placed by Strabo, VII. iii. 17, between the Don and the Dneiper, but by some modern scholars located in Bessarabia.

up statues of Nero; moreover on certain days the people and soldiers, as if adding thereby to Otho's nobility and distinction, acclaimed him as Nero Otho; he himself remained undecided, from fear to forbid or shame to acknowledge the title.

LXXIX. While all men's thoughts were thus absorbed in civil war, there was no interest in foreign affairs. This inspired the Rhoxolani,[1] a people of Sarmatia who had massacred two cohorts the previous winter, to invade Moesia with great hopes. They numbered nine thousand horse, and their restive temper along with their success made them more intent on booty than on fighting. Consequently, when they were straggling and off their guard, the Third legion with some auxiliary troops suddenly attacked them. On the Roman side everything was ready for battle. The Sarmatians were scattered or in their greed for booty had weighted themselves down with heavy burdens, and since the slippery roads deprived them of the advantage of their horses' speed, they were cut down as if they were in fetters. For it is a strange fact that the whole courage of the Sarmatians is, so to speak, outside themselves. No people is so cowardly when it comes to fighting on foot, but when they attack the foe on horseback, hardly any line can resist them. On this occasion, however, the day was wet and the snow melting: they could not use their pikes or the long swords which they wield with both hands, for their horses fell and they were weighted down by their coats of mail. This armour is the defence of their princes and all the nobility: it is made of scales of iron or hard hide, and though impenetrable to blows, nevertheless it makes it difficult for the wearer to get up

trabile ita impetu hostium provolutis inhabile ad resurgendum; simul altitudine et mollitia nivis hauriebantur. Romanus miles facilis lorica et missili pilo aut lanceis adsultans, ubi res posceret, levi gladio inermem Sarmatam (neque enim scuto defendi mos est) comminus fodiebat, donec pauci qui proelio superfuerant paludibus abderentur. Ibi saevitia hiemis aut[1] vulnerum absumpti. Postquam id Romae compertum, M. Aponius Moesiam obtinens triumphali statua, Fulvus Aurelius et Iulianus Tettius ac Numisius Lupus, legati legionum, consularibus ornamentis donantur, laeto Othone et gloriam in se trahente, tamquam et ipse felix bello et suis ducibus suisque exercitibus rem publicam auxisset.

LXXX. Parvo interim initio, unde nihil timebatur, orta seditio prope urbi excidio fuit. Septimam decimam cohortem e colonia Ostiensi in urbem acciri Otho iusserat; armandae eius cura Vario Crispino tribuno e praetorianis data. Is quo magis vacuus quietis castris iussa exequeretur, vehicula cohortis incipiente nocte onerari aperto armamentario iubet. Tempus in suspicionem, causa in crimen, adfectatio quietis in tumultum evaluit, et visa inter temulentos

[1] hiemis aut *Schneider*: hic mīa *M.*

---

[1] Such armour was worn by many of Rome's enemies in both Europe and Asia. Cf. Tac. *Ann.* iii. 43; Livy xxxv. 48; xxxvii. 40; Curtius iv. 35, equitibus equisque tegumenta erant ex ferreis laminis serie inter se conexis (said with reference to the Scythians and Bactrians); and Amm. Mar. XVI. x. 8.

when overthrown by the enemy's charge;[1] at the same time they were continually sinking deep in the soft and heavy snow. The Roman soldier with his breast-plate moved readily about, attacking the enemy with his javelin, which he threw, or with his lances; when the situation required he used his short sword and cut down the helpless Sarmatians at close quarters, for they do not use the shield for defensive purposes. Finally the few who escaped battle hid themselves in the swamps, where they lost their lives from the cruel winter or the severity of their wounds. When the news of this reached Rome, Marcus Aponius, governor of Moesia, was given a triumphal statue; Fulvius Aurelius, Julianus Tettius, and Numisius Lupus, commanders of the legions, were presented with the decorations of a consul; for Otho was pleased and took the glory to himself, saying that he was lucky in war and had augmented the State through his generals and his armies.

LXXX. In the meantime, from a slight beginning which caused no fear, a mutiny arose which almost destroyed the city. Otho had given orders that the Seventeenth cohort be brought from the colony of Ostia to Rome. Varius Crispinus, one of the praetorian tribunes, had been charged with equipping these troops. That he might be the freer to carry out his orders, when the camp was quiet, he ordered the armoury to be opened and the wagons belonging to the cohort to be loaded at nightfall. The hour gave rise to suspicion; his motive became the basis of a charge against him; and his attempt to secure quiet resulted in an uproar, while the sight of arms in the hands of drunken men roused

arma cupidinem sui movere. Fremit miles et tribunos centurionesque proditionis arguit, tamquam familiae senatorum ad perniciem Othonis armarentur, pars ignari et vino graves, pessimus quisque in occasionem praedarum, vulgus, ut mos est, cuiuscumque motus novi cupidum; et obsequia meliorum nox abstulerat. Resistentem seditioni tribunum et severissimos centurionum obtruncant; rapta arma, nudati gladii; insidentes equis urbem ac Palatium petunt.

LXXXI. Erat Othoni celebre convivium primoribus feminis virisque; qui trepidi, fortuitusne militum furor an dolus imperatoris, manere ac deprehendi an fugere et dispergi periculosius foret, modo constantiam simulare, modo formidine detegi, simul Othonis vultum intueri; utque evenit inclinatis ad suspicionem mentibus, cum timeret Otho, timebatur. Sed haud secus discrimine senatus quam suo territus et praefectos praetorii ad mitigandas militum iras statim miserat et abire propere omnis e convivio iussit. Tum vero passim magistratus proiectis insignibus, vitata comitum et servorum frequentia senes feminaeque per tenebras diversa urbis itinera

a desire to use them. The soldiers began to murmur and charged the tribunes and centurions with treachery, saying that the slaves of the senators were being armed for Otho's destruction. A part of the soldiers were ignorant of the circumstances and heavy with wine; the worst of them wished to make this an opportunity for looting; the great mass, as is usual, were ready for any new movement, and the natural obedience of the better disposed was rendered ineffective by the night. When the tribune attempted to stay the mutiny, they killed him and the strictest of the centurions. Then they seized their arms, drew their swords, and jumping on their horses, hurried to Rome and to the Palace.

LXXXI. Otho was giving a great banquet to men and women of the nobility. In terror as to whether this was some chance frenzy on the part of the soldiers or some treachery on the part of the emperor, the guests did not know whether it was more dangerous to stay and be caught or to flee and scatter. Now they pretended courage, now they were unmasked by their fears; at the same time they watched Otho's face; and as generally happens when men's minds are inclined to suspicion, it was just when Otho felt fear that he made others fear him. Yet he was terrified as much by the danger to the senate as to himself; he had sent at once the prefects of the praetorian guard to calm the soldiers' anger and he told all to leave the banquet quickly. Then in every direction went officers of the state, throwing away their insignia of office and avoiding the attendance of their friends and slaves; old men and women stole in the darkness along different streets, few of them trying to

rari domos, plurimi amicorum tecta et ut cuique humillimus cliens, incertas latebras petivere.

LXXXII. Militum impetus ne foribus quidem Palatii coercitus quo minus convivium inrumperent, ostendi sibi Othonem expostulantes, vulnerato Iulio Martiale tribuno et Vitellio Saturnino praefecto legionis, dum ruentibus obsistunt. Undique arma et minae, modo in centuriones tribunosque, modo in senatum universum, lymphatis caeco pavore animis, et quia neminem unum destinare irae poterant, licentiam in omnis poscentibus, donec Otho contra decus imperii toro insistens precibus et lacrimis aegre cohibuit, redieruntque in castra inviti neque innocentes. Postera die velut capta urbe clausae domus, rarus per vias populus, maesta plebs; deiecti in terram militum vultus ac plus tristitiae quam paenitentiae. Manipulatim adlocuti sunt Licinius Proculus et Plotius Firmus praefecti, ex suo quisque ingenio mitius aut horridius. Finis sermonis in eo ut quina milia nummum singulis militibus numerarentur: tum Otho ingredi castra ausus. Atque illum tribuni centurionesque circumsistunt, abiectis militiae insignibus otium et salutem flagitantes.

reach their homes, but most of them hurrying to the houses of their friends and the obscurest hiding-place of the humblest dependent each had.

LXXXII. The excited soldiers were not kept even by the doors of the palace from bursting into the banquet. They demanded to be shown Otho, and they wounded Julius Martialis, the tribune, and Vitellius Saturninus, prefect of the legion, when they opposed their onrush. On every side were arms and threats directed now against the centurions and tribunes, now against the whole senate, for all were in a state of blind panic, and since they could not fix upon any individual as the object of their wrath, they claimed licence to proceed against all. Finally Otho, disregarding the dignity of his imperial position, stood on his couch and barely succeeded in restraining them with appeals and tears. Then they returned to camp neither willingly nor with guiltless hands. The next day private houses were closed as if the city were in the hands of the enemy; few respectable people were seen in the streets; the rabble was downcast. The soldiers turned their eyes to the ground, but were sorrowful rather than repentant. Licinius Proculus and Plotius Firmus, the prefects, addressed their companies, the one mildly, the other severely, each according to his nature. They ended with the statement that five thousand sesterces were to be paid to each soldier.[1] Only then did Otho dare to enter the camp. He was surrounded by tribunes and centurions, who tore away the insignia of their rank and demanded discharge and safety from their dangerous service.

[1] A sum equivalent to about $225 to-day; but its purchasing power was many times that sum.

Sensit invidiam miles et compositus in obsequium auctores seditionis ad supplicium ultro postulabat.

LXXXIII. Otho, quamquam turbidis rebus et diversis militum animis, cum optimus quisque remedium praesentis licentiae posceret, vulgus et plures seditionibus et ambitioso imperio laeti per turbas et raptus facilius ad civile bellum impellerentur, simul reputans non posse principatum scelere quaesitum subita modestia et prisca gravitate retineri, sed discrimine urbis et periculo senatus anxius, postremo ita disseruit: "Neque ut adfectus vestros in amorem mei accenderem, commilitones, neque ut animum ad virtutem cohortarer (utraque enim egregie supersunt), sed veni postulaturus a vobis temperamentum vestrae fortitudinis et erga me modum caritatis. Tumultus proximi initium non cupiditate vel odio, quae multos exercitus in discordiam egere, ac ne detrectatione quidem aut formidine periculorum: nimia pietas vestra acrius quam considerate[1] excitavit; nam saepe honestas rerum causas, ni iudicium adhibeas, perniciosi exitus consequuntur. Imus ad bellum. Num omnis nuntios palam audiri, omnia consilia cunctis praesentibus tractari ratio rerum aut occasionum velocitas patitur? Tam nescire quaedam milites quam scire oportet: ita se ducum

[1] considerate *Walther*: considerat *M.*

The common soldiers perceived the bad impression that their action had made and settled down to obedience, demanding of their own accord that the ringleaders of the mutiny should be punished.

LXXXIII. Otho was in a difficult position owing to the general disturbance and the divergences of sentiment among the soldiers; for the best of them demanded that some check be put on the present licence, while the larger mob delighted in mutinies and in an emperor whose power depended on popular favour, and were easily driven on to civil war by riots and rapine. He realized, however, that a throne gained by crime cannot be maintained by sudden moderation and old-fashioned dignity; but being distressed by the crisis that had befallen the city and the danger of the senate, he finally spoke as follows: "Fellow soldiers, I have not come to kindle your sentiments into love for me, nor to exhort your hearts to courage, for both these qualities you have in marked abundance; but I have come to ask you to put some check to your bravery and some limit to your regard for me. The recent disturbances owed their beginning not to any greed or hate, which are the sentiments that drive most armies to revolt, or even to any shirking or fear of danger; it was your excessive loyalty that spurred you to an action more violent than wise. Very often honourable motives have a fatal end, unless men employ judgment. We are proceeding to war. Do the exigencies of events or the rapid changes in the situation allow every report to be heard openly, every plan to be discussed in the presence of all? It is as proper that soldiers should not know certain things as that they should know them. The authority of the

auctoritas, sic rigor disciplinae habet, ut multa etiam centuriones tribunosque tantum iuberi expediat. Si cur[1] iubeantur quaerere singulis liceat, pereunte obsequio etiam imperium intercidit. An et illic nocte intempesta rapientur arma? Unus alterve perditus ac temulentus (neque enim pluris consternatione proxima insanisse crediderim) centurionis ac tribuni sanguine manus imbuet, imperatoris sui tentorium inrumpet?

LXXXIV. "Vos quidem istud pro me: sed in discursu ac tenebris et rerum omnium confusione patefieri occasio etiam adversus me potest. Si Vitellio et satellitibus eius eligendi facultas detur, quem[2] nobis animum, quas mentis imprecentur, quid aliud quam seditionem et discordiam optabunt? Ne miles centurioni, ne centurio tribuno obsequatur, ut confusi pedites equitesque in exitium ruamus. Parendo potius, commilitones, quam imperia ducum sciscitando res militares continentur, et fortissimus in ipso discrimine exercitus est qui ante discrimen quietissimus. Vobis arma et animus sit: mihi consilium et virtutis vestrae regimen relinquite. Paucorum culpa fuit, duorum poena erit: ceteri abolete memoriam foedissimae noctis. Nec illas adversus senatum voces ullus usquam exercitus audiat. Caput imperii et decora omnium provinciarum ad poenam

[1] si cur *Agricola*: sic ubi *M*.
[2] quae *M*.

leaders and strict discipline are maintained only by holding it wise that in many cases even centurions and tribunes should simply receive orders. For if individuals may inquire the reason for the orders given them, then discipline is at an end and authority also ceases. Suppose in the field you have to take your arms in the dead of night, shall one or two worthless and drunken men—for I cannot believe that the recent madness was due to the panic of more than that—stain their hands in the blood of a centurion or tribune? Shall they burst into the tent of their general?

LXXXIV. "You, it is true, did that for me. But in time of riot, in the darkness and general confusion, an opportunity may also be given for an attack on me. Suppose Vitellius and his satellites should have an opportunity to choose the spirit and sentiment with which they would pray you to be inspired, what will they prefer to mutiny and strife? Will they not wish that soldier should not obey centurion or centurion tribune, so that we may all, foot and horse, in utter confusion rush to ruin? It is rather by obedience, fellow-soldiers, than by questioning the commands of the leaders, that success in war is obtained, and that is the bravest army in time of crisis which has been most orderly before the crisis. Yours be the arms and spirit; leave to me the plan of campaign and the direction of your valour. Few were at fault; two shall pay the penalty: do all the rest of you blot out the memory of that awful night. And I pray that no army may ever hear such cries against the senate. That is the head of the empire and the glory of all the provinces; good heavens, not even those

vocare non hercule illi, quos cum maxime Vitellius in nos ciet, Germani audeant. Ulline Italiae alumni et Romana vere iuventus ad sanguinem et caedem depoposcerit ordinem, cuius splendore et gloria sordis et obscuritatem Vitellianarum partium praestringimus[1]? Nationes aliquas occupavit Vitellius, imaginem quandam exercitus habet, senatus nobiscum est: sic fit ut hinc res publica, inde[2] hostes rei publicae constiterint. Quid? Vos pulcherrimam hanc urbem domibus et tectis et congestu lapidum stare creditis? Muta[3] ista et inanima[4] intercidere ac reparari promisca sunt: aeternitas rerum et pax gentium et mea cum vestra salus incolumitate senatus firmatur. Hunc auspicato a parente et conditore urbis nostrae institutum et a regibus usque ad principes continuum et immortalem, sicut a maioribus[5] accepimus, sic posteris tradamus; nam ut ex vobis senatores, ita ex senatoribus principes nascuntur."

LXXXV. Et oratio apta ad[6] perstringendos mulcendosque militum animos et severitatis modus (neque enim in pluris quam in duos animadverti iusserat) grate accepta compositique ad praesens qui coerceri non poterant. Non tamen quies urbi redierat: strepitus telorum et facies belli, militibus ut nihil in commune turbantibus, ita sparsis per domos occulto habitu, et maligna cura in omnis, quos nobilitas aut opes aut aliqua insignis claritudo

[1] praestringimus *I. F. Gronovius*: perstringimus *M.*
[2] in *M.* [3] multa *M.* [4] inanima *Lipsius*: inania *M.*
[5] sicamatoribus *M.* [6] apta ad *Meiser*: perod *M.*

Germans whom Vitellius at this moment is stirring up against us would dare to call it to punishment. Shall any child of Italy, any true Roman youth, demand the blood and murder of that order through whose splendid glory we outshine the meanness and base birth of the partisans of Vitellius? Vitellius has won over some peoples; he has a certain shadow of an army, but the senate is with us. And so it is that on our side stands the state, on theirs the enemies of the state. Tell me, do you think that this fairest city consists of houses and buildings and heaps of stone? Those dumb and inanimate things can perish and readily be replaced. The eternity of our power, the peace of the world, my safety and yours, are secured by the welfare of the senate. This senate, which was established under auspices by the Father and Founder of our city and which has continued in unbroken line from the time of the kings even down to the time of the emperors, let us hand over to posterity even as we received it from our fathers. For as senators spring from your number, so emperors spring from senators."

LXXXV. Both this speech, well adapted as it was to reprove and quiet the soldiers, and also his moderation (for he had not ordered the punishment of more than two) were gratefully received, and in this way those who could not be checked by force were calmed for the present. But the city was not yet quiet; there was the din of weapons and the face of war, for while the troops did not engage in any general riot, they nevertheless distributed themselves in disguise among the houses and suspiciously kept watch on all whom high birth or wealth or some distinction had made the object of gossip.

rumoribus obiecerat: Vitellianos quoque milites venisse in urbem ad studia partium noscenda plerique credebant; unde plena omnia suspicionum et vix secreta domuum sine formidine. Sed plurimum trepidationis in publico, ut[1] quemque nuntium fama attulisset, animum vultumque conversis, ne diffidere dubiis ac parum gauderc prosperis viderentur. Coacto vero in curiam senatu arduus rerum omnium modus, ne contumax silentium, ne suspecta libertas; et privato Othoni nuper atque eadem dicenti[2] nota adulatio. Igitur versare sententias et huc atque illuc torquere, hostem et parricidam Vitellium vocantes, providentissimus quisque vulgaribus conviciis, quidam vera probra iacere, in clamore tamen et ubi plurimae voces, aut tumultu verborum sibi ipsi obstrepentes.

LXXXVI. Prodigia insuper terrebant diversis auctoribus vulgata: in vestibulo Capitolii omissas habenas bigae, cui Victoria institerat, erupisse cella Iunonis maiorem humana speciem, statuam divi Iulii in insula Tiberini amnis sereno et immoto die ab occidente in orientem conversam, prolocutum in Etruria bovem, insolitos animalium partus, et plura

[1] vim *M.* [2] dicenti *Lipsius*: dicendi *M.*

---

[1] That is in the temple of Jupiter Capitolinus, which had three *cellae*, one each for Jupiter, Juno, and Minerva.

Most of them believed that soldiers of Vitellius, too, had come to Rome to learn the sentiments of the different parties, so that there was suspicion everywhere, and the intimacy of the home was hardly free from fear. But there was the greatest terror in public, where men changed their spirit and looks according to the message that rumour brought at the moment, that they might not seem to lose heart over doubtful news or show too much joy over favourable report. Moreover, when the senate had assembled in the chamber, it was hard to maintain the proper measure in anything, that silence might not seem sullen or open speech suspicious; while Otho, who had so recently been a subject and had used the same terms, fully understood flattery. So the senators turned and twisted their proposals to mean this or that, many calling Vitellius an enemy and traitor; but the most foreseeing attacked him only with ordinary terms of abuse, although some made the truth the basis of their insults. Still they did this when there was an uproar and many speaking, or else they obscured their own meaning by a riot of words.

LXXXVI. Prodigies which were reported on various authorities also contributed to the general terror. It was said that in the vestibule of the Capitol the reins of the chariot in which Victory stood had fallen from the goddess's hands, that a superhuman form had rushed out of Juno's chapel,[1] that a statue of the deified Julius on the island of the Tiber had turned from west to east on a bright calm day, that an ox had spoken in Etruria, that animals had given birth to strange young, and that many other things had happened which in barbarous

alia rudibus saeculis etiam in pace observata, quae nunc tantum in metu audiuntur. Sed praecipuus et cum praesenti exitio etiam futuri pavor subita inundatione Tiberis, qui immenso auctu proruto[1] ponte sublicio ac strage obstantis molis refusus, non modo iacentia et plana urbis loca, sed secura eius modi casuum implevit: rapti e publico plerique, plures in tabernis et cubilibus intercepti. Fames in vulgus inopia quaestus et penuria alimentorum. Corrupta stagnantibus aquis insularum fundamenta, dein remeante flumine dilapsa. Utque primum vacuus a periculo animus fuit, id ipsum quod paranti expeditionem Othoni campus Martius et via Flaminia iter belli esset obstructum, a fortuitis vel naturalibus causis in prodigium et omen imminentium cladium vertebatur.

LXXXVII. Otho lustrata urbe et expensis bello consiliis, quando Poeninae Cottiaeque Alpes et ceteri Galliarum aditus Vitellianis exercitibus claudebantur, Narbonensem Galliam adgredi statuit classe valida et partibus fida, quod reliquos caesorum ad pontem Mulvium et saevitia Galbae in custodia habitos in numeros legionis composuerat, facta et ceteris spe[2] honoratae in posterum militiae. Addidit classi urba-

[1] proruto *I. F. Gronovius* : prorupto *M.*
[2] spe *I. F. Gronovius* : spes *M.*

---

[1] The famous Pons Sublicius, the oldest bridge across the Tiber.

[2] Cf. chaps. 6 and 37.

[3] Service in a legion was regarded as more honourable than that in the fleet, and so those who were still serving in the fleet looked forward to being treated as their comrades had been.

ages used to be noticed even during peace, but which now are only heard of in seasons of terror. Yet the chief anxiety which was connected with both present disaster and future danger was caused by a sudden overflow of the Tiber which, swollen to a great height, broke down the wooden bridge[1] and then was thrown back by the ruins of the bridge which dammed the stream, and overflowed not only the low-lying level parts of the city, but also parts which are normally free from such disasters. Many were swept away in the public streets, a larger number cut off in shops and in their beds. The common people were reduced to famine by lack of employment and failure of supplies. Apartment houses had their foundations undermined by the standing water and then collapsed when the flood withdrew. The moment people's minds were relieved of this danger, the very fact that when Otho was planning a military expedition, the Campus Martius and the Flaminian Way, over which he was to advance, were blocked against him was interpreted as a prodigy and an omen of impending disaster rather than as the result of chance or natural causes.

LXXXVII. Otho purified the city and then considered his plan for a campaign. Since the Pennine and Cottian Alps and the other passes into Gaul were closed by the forces of Vitellius, he decided to attack Narbonese Gaul with his fleet, which was strong and loyal, for he had enrolled as a legion those who had survived the massacre at the Mulvian Bridge and who had been kept in prison by Galba's cruelty;[2] and so he had given the rest reason to hope for an honourable service hereafter.[3] He

nas cohortis et plerosque e praetorianis, viris et robur exercitus atque ipsis ducibus consilium et custodes. Summa expeditionis Antonio Novello, Suedio Clementi primipilaribus, Aemilio Pacensi, cui ademptum a Galba tribunatum reddiderat, permissa. Curam navium Moschus libertus retinebat ad observandam honestiorum fidem immutatus. Peditum equitumque copiis Suetonius Paulinus, Marius Celsus, Annius Gallus rectores destinati, sed plurima fides Licinio Proculo praetorii praefecto. Is urbanae militiae impiger, bellorum insolens, auctoritatem Paulini, vigorem Celsi, maturitatem Galli, ut cuique erat, criminando, quod facillimum factu est, pravus et callidus bonos et modestos anteibat.

LXXXVIII. Sepositus per eos dies Cornelius Dolabella in coloniam Aquinatem, neque arta custodia neque obscura, nullum ob crimen, sed vetusto nomine et propinquitate Galbae monstratus. Multos e magistratibus, magnam consularium partem Otho non participes aut ministros bello, sed comitum specie secum expedire iubet, in quis et Lucium Vitellium, eodem quo ceteros cultu, nec ut imperatoris fratrem nec ut hostis. Igitur motae urbis curae; nullus ordo metu aut periculo vacuus. Primores senatus

---

[1] Moschus had held this office under Nero and Galba.
[2] Aquino.

added to the fleet the city cohorts and many of the praetorians to be the strength and back-bone of the army and also to advise and control the leaders themselves. At the head of the expedition he placed Antonius Novellus, Suedius Clemens, centurions of the first rank, and Aemilius Pacensis, to whom he had restored the tribunate which Galba had taken away. His freedman Moschus, however, retained command of the fleet, no change being made in his rank, that he might keep watch over the fidelity of men more honourable than himself.[1] As commanders of the foot and horse he named Suetonius Paulinus, Marius Celsus, Annius Gallus, but he trusted most in Licinius Proculus, prefect of the praetorian guard. Indefatigable on home service, inexperienced in war, Proculus, in strict accordance with their individual characters, made the "influence" of Paulinus, the "energy" of Celsus, the "proved ability" of Gallus the bases of his accusations, and thus—nothing is easier—by dishonesty and cunning outdid the virtuous and modest.

LXXXVIII. About this time Cornelius Dolabella was banished to the colony of Aquinum.[2] He was not kept under close or secret watch, and no charge was made against him; but he had been made prominent by his ancient name and his close relationship to Galba. Many of the magistrates and a large part of the ex-consuls Otho directed to join his expedition, not to share or help in the war but simply as a suite. Among these was Lucius Vitellius, who was treated in the same way as the others and not at all as the brother of an emperor or as an enemy. This action caused anxiety at Rome. No class was free from fear or danger. The leading men

aetate invalidi[1] et longa pace desides, segnis et oblita bellorum nobilitas, ignarus militiae eques, quanto magis occultare et abdere pavorem nitebantur, manifestius pavidi. Nec deerant e contrario qui ambitione stolida conspicua arma, insignis equos, quidam luxuriosos apparatus conviviorum et inritamenta libidinum ut instrumentum belli mercarentur. Sapientibus quietis et rei publicae cura; levissimus quisque et futuri improvidus spe vana tumens; multi[2] adflicta fide in pace anxii,[3] turbatis rebus alacres et per incerta tutissimi.

LXXXIX. Sed vulgus et magnitudine nimia communium curarum expers populus sentire paulatim belli mala, conversa in militum usum omni pecunia, intentis alimentorum pretiis, quae motu Vindicis haud perinde plebem attriverant, secura tum urbe et provinciali bello, quod inter legiones Galliasque velut externum fuit. Nam ex quo divus Augustus res Caesarum composuit, procul et in unius sollicitudinem aut decus populus Romanus bellaverat; sub Tiberio et Gaio tantum pacis adversa ad rem publicam pertinuere[4]; Scriboniani contra Claudium incepta simul audita et coercita; Nero nuntiis magis et rumoribus quam armis depulsus: tum legiones

[1] invalida *a b*. [2] multis *a b*.
[3] anxii *Nolte* : ac si *a b*. [4] ad r.p.p. *Halm* : r.p.p. *a b*.

---

[1] Cf. II, 75. M. Furius Camillus Scribonianus, governor of Dalmatia, had revolted in 42 A.D. but he had been crushed in five days.

of the senate were weak from old age and had grown inactive through a long peace; the nobility was indolent and had forgotten the art of war; the knights were ignorant of military service; the more all tried to hide and conceal their fear, the more evident they made their terror. Yet, on the other hand, there were some who with absurd ostentation bought splendid arms and fine horses; some made extravagant preparations for banquets and provided incentives to their lust as equipment for war. The wise had thought for peace and for the state; the foolish, careless of the future, were puffed up with idle hopes; many who had been distressed by loss of credit during peace were now enthusiastic in this time of disturbance and felt safest in uncertainty.

LXXXIX. But the mob and the mass of the people, whose vast numbers kept them aloof from cares of state, gradually began to feel the evils of war, for all money was now diverted to the use of the soldiers, and the prices of provisions rose. Such things had not affected the common people so much during the revolt of Vindex, because the city at that time was safe and the war was in a province; since it was between the legions and the Gauls, it was regarded as a foreign war. In fact, from the time when the deified Augustus had established the power of the Caesars, the wars of the Roman people had been far from Rome and had caused anxiety or brought honour to a single individual alone; under Tiberius and Gaius only the misfortunes of peace affected the state; the attempt of Scribonianus against Claudius was checked the moment it was known;[1] Nero had been driven from his throne rather by messages and rumours than by arms. But now,

classesque et, quod raro alias, praetorianus urbanusque miles in aciem deducti, Oriens Occidensque et quicquid utrimque virium est a tergo, si ducibus aliis bellatum foret, longo bello materia. Fuere qui proficiscenti Othoni moras religionemque nondum conditorum ancilium adferrent: aspernatus est omnem cunctationem ut Neroni quoque exitiosam; et Caecina iam Alpes transgressus extimulabat.

XC. Pridie idus Martias commendata patribus re publica reliquias Neronianarum sectionum nondum in fiscum conversas revocatis ab exilio concessit, iustissimum donum et in speciem magnificum, sed festinata iam pridem exactione usu sterile.[1] Mox vocata contione maiestatem urbis et consensum populi ac senatus pro se attollens, adversum Vitellianas partis modeste disseruit, inscitiam potius legionum quam audaciam increpans, nulla Vitellii mentione, sive ipsius ea moderatio, seu scriptor orationis sibi metuens contumeliis in Vitellium abstinuit, quando, ut in consiliis militiae Suetonio Paulino et Mario Celso, ita in rebus urbanis Galeri

[1] sterile *Lipsius*: sterili *a b*.

---

[1] The *ancilia*, that were used by the Salii throughout the month of March.

[2] Cf. chap. 20.

[3] Under Nero the confiscated properties of those who were sent into exile were hastily sold for what they would bring and the proceeds paid into the treasury, so that there was little left to be returned to the exiles.

[4] Galerius Trachalus, cos. 68, is praised by Quintilian for his impressive appearance and effective delivery.

legions and fleets and, by an act almost without precedent, the soldiers of the praetorian and city cohorts were led away to action; the East and the West and all the forces that both have behind them formed material for a long war had there been other leaders. There were some who attempted to delay Otho's departure by bringing forward the religious consideration that the sacred shields had not yet been restored to their place.[1] Yet he scorned every delay, for delay had proved ruinous to Nero also; and the fact that Caecina had already crossed the Alps spurred him on.

XC. On the fourteenth of March, after entrusting the interests of state to the senate, he granted to those who had been recalled from exile all that was left from the sales of property confiscated by Nero, so far as the monies had not yet been paid into the Imperial Treasury,[2]—a most just donation, and one that was generous in appearance; but it was worthless because the property had been hastily realized on long before.[3] Then he called an assembly, extolled the majesty of Rome, and praised the enthusiasm of the people and senate in his behalf. Against the party of Vitellius he spoke with moderation, blaming the legions for their ignorance rather than boldness, and making no mention of Vitellius. This omission may have been moderation on his part, or the man who wrote his speech may have omitted all insults towards Vitellius, fearing for himself. This is probable, because it was generally believed that Otho employed the ability of Galerius Trachalus in civil matters,[4] as he did that of Suetonius Paulinus and Marius Celsus in planning his military movements, and there were some who recognized the very

Trachali ingenio Othonem uti credebatur; et erant qui genus ipsum orandi noscerent, crebro fori usu celebre et[1] ad implendas populi aures latum et sonans. Clamor vocesque vulgi ex more adulandi nimiae et falsae: quasi dictatorem Caesarem aut imperatorem Augustum prosequerentur, ita studiis votisque certabant, nec metu aut amore, sed ex libidine servitii: ut in familiis, privata cuique stimulatio,[2] et vile iam decus publicum. Profectus Otho quietem urbis curasque imperii Salvio Titiano fratri permisit.

[1] et *om. a b.*

[2] simulatio *a b.*

style of Trachalus, which was well known, because he frequently appeared in court, and which was copious and sonorous in order to fill the ears of the people. The shouts and cries from the mob, according to their recognized fashion of flattering an emperor, were excessive and insincere. Men vied with one another in the expression of their enthusiasm and vows, as if they were applauding the Dictator Caesar or the Emperor Augustus. They did this, not from fear or affection, but from their passionate love of servitude. As happens in households of slaves, each one was spurred on by his private motive, and the honour of the state was held cheap. When Otho set out, he left the good order of the city and the cares of empire in the charge of his brother, Salvius Titianus.

BOOK II

LIBER II

I. Struebat iam fortuna in diversa parte terrarum initia causasque imperio, quod varia sorte[1] laetum rei publicae aut atrox, ipsis principibus prosperum vel exitio fuit. Titus Vespasianus, e Iudaea incolumi adhuc Galba missus a patre, causam profectionis officium erga principem et maturam petendis honoribus iuventam ferebat, sed vulgus fingendi avidum disperserat accitum in adoptionem. Materia sermonibus senium et orbitas principis et intemperantia civitatis, donec unus eligatur, multos destinandi. Augebat famam ipsius Titi ingenium quantaecumque fortunae capax, decor oris[2] cum quadam maiestate, prosperae Vespasiani res, praesaga responsa, et inclinatis ad credendum animis loco ominum etiam fortuita.[3] Ubi Corinthi, Achaiae urbe, certos nuntios accepit de interitu Galbae et aderant qui arma Vitellii bellumque adfirmarent, anxius animo paucis amicorum adhibitis cuncta utrimque perlustrat: si

[1] varia sorte *Lipsius*: varie ortum *a b*.
[2] decor oris *Rhenanus*: decoris *a b*.
[3] fortuita *Grotius*: fortuna *a b*.

---

[1] Vespasian and Titus were good emperors; but Domitian was a second Nero. He was assassinated at the instigation of the Empress Domitia.

[2] Titus was now twenty-nine years of age.

BOOK II

I. Fortune was already, in an opposite quarter of the world, founding and making ready for a new dynasty, which from its varying destinies brought to the state joy or misery, to the emperors themselves success or doom.[1] Titus Vespasianus had been dispatched by his father from Judea while Galba was still alive. The reason given out for his journey was a desire to pay his respects to the emperor, and the fact that Titus was now old enough to begin his political career.[2] But the common people, who are always ready to invent, had spread the report that he had been summoned to Rome to be adopted. This gossip was based on the emperor's age and childlessness, and was due also to the popular passion for designating many successors until one is chosen. The report gained a readier hearing from the nature of Titus himself, which was equal to the highest fortune, from his personal beauty and a certain majesty which he possessed, as well as from Vespasian's good fortune, from prophetic oracles, and even from chance occurrences which, amid the general credulity, were regarded as omens. When Titus received certain information with regard to Galba's death he was at Corinth, a city of Achaia, and met men there who positively declared that Vitellius had taken up arms and begun war; in his anxiety he called a few of his friends and reviewed fully the two possible courses of action: if he should go on

pergeret in urbem, nullam officii gratiam in alterius honorem suscepti, ac se Vitellio sive Othoni obsidem fore: sin rediret, offensam haud dubiam victoris, set[1] incerta adhuc victoria[2] et concedente in partis patre filium excusatum. Sin Vespasianus rem publicam susciperet, obliviscendum offensarum de bello agitantibus.

II. His ac talibus inter spem metumque iactatum spes vicit. Fuerunt qui accensum desiderio Berenices reginae vertisse iter crederent; neque abhorrebat a Berenice iuvenilis animus, sed gerendis rebus nullum ex eo impedimentum. Laetam voluptatibus adulescentiam egit, suo quam patris imperio moderatior. Igitur oram Achaiae et Asiae ac laeva maris praevectus, Rhodum et Cyprum insulas, inde Syriam audentioribus spatiis petebat. Atque illum cupido incessit adeundi visendique templum Paphiae Veneris, inclitum per indigenas advenasque. Haud fuerit longum initia religionis, templi ritum,[3] formam deae (neque enim alibi sic habetur) paucis disserere.

III. Conditorem templi regem Aeriam[4] vetus memoria, quidam ipsius deae nomen id perhibent. Fama recentior tradit a Cinyra sacratum templum

[1] set *Rhenanus*: et *a b*.
[2] incertam adhuc victoris *a b*.
[3] ritum *Dureau de Lamalle*: situm *M*.
[4] Aeriam *Rhenanus*: verian *M*.

---

[1] Berenice, daughter of Herodes Agrippa I and sister of Herodes Agrippa II, had been married first to her uncle Herodes, king of Chalcis, later to King Polemo of Pontus, whom she left. She supported the Flavian cause and later followed Titus to Rome. Cf. *Acts* 25, 13. 23; Suet. *Tit.* 7.

to Rome, he would enjoy no gratitude for an act of courtesy intended for another emperor, and he would be a hostage in the hands of either Vitellius or Otho; on the other hand, if he returned to his father, the victor would undoubtedly feel offence; yet, if his father joined the victor's party, while victory was still uncertain, the son would be excused; but if Vespasian should assume the imperial office, his rivals would be concerned with war and have to forget offences.

II. These considerations and others like them made him waver between hope and fear; but hope finally won. Some believed that he turned back because of his passionate longing to see again Queen Berenice; and the young man's heart was not insensible to Berenice, but his feelings towards her proved no obstacle to action.[1] He spent his youth in the delights of self-indulgence, but he showed more self-restraint in his own reign than in that of his father. So at this time he coasted along the shores of Achaia and Asia, leaving the land on the left, and made for the islands of Rhodes and Cyprus; from Cyprus he struck out boldly for Syria. While he was in Cyprus, he was overtaken by a desire to visit and examine the temple of Paphian Venus, which was famous both among natives and strangers. It may not prove a wearisome digression to discuss briefly the origin of this cult, the temple ritual, and the form under which the goddess is worshipped, for she is not so represented elsewhere.

III. The founder of the temple, according to ancient tradition, was King Aerias. Some, however, say that this was the name of the goddess herself. A more recent tradition reports that the temple was

deamque ipsam conceptam mari huc adpulsam; sed scientiam artemque haruspicum accitam et Cilicem Tamiram intulisse, atque ita pactum ut familiae utriusque posteri caerimoniis praesiderent. Mox, ne honore nullo regium genus peregrinam stirpem antecelleret, ipsa quam intulerant scientia hospites cessere: tantum Cinyrades sacerdos consulitur. Hostiae, ut quisque vovit, sed mares deliguntur: certissima fides haedorum fibris. Sanguinem arae obfundere vetitum: precibus et igne puro altaria adolentur, nec ullis imbribus quamquam in aperto madescunt. Simulacrum deae non effigie humana, continuus orbis latiore initio tenuem in ambitum metae modo exsurgens, set ratio in obscuro.

IV. Titus spectata opulentia donisque regum quaeque alia laetum antiquitatibus Graecorum genus incertae vetustati adfingit, de navigatione primum consuluit. Postquam pandi viam et mare prosperum accepit, de se per ambages[1] interrogat caesis compluribus hostiis. Sostratus (sacerdotis id nomen erat) ubi laeta et congruentia exta magnisque consultis adnuere deam videt, pauca in praesens et solita respondens, petito secreto futura aperit. Titus aucto

[1] perambales *M.*

---

[1] A mythical king, father of Adonis and Myrrha.

[2] *i.e.* the symbol of the goddess was a conical stone, not unlike the turning-posts (*metae*) in the circus. Cf. Servius on the *Aen.* i. 724 and Maxim. Tyr. viii. 8.

consecrated by Cinyras,[1] and that the goddess herself, after she sprang from the sea, was wafted hither; but that the science and method of divination were imported from abroad by the Cilician Tamiras, and so it was agreed that the descendants of both Tamiras and Cinyras should preside over the sacred rites. It is also said that in a later time the foreigners gave up the craft that they had introduced, that the royal family might have some prerogative over foreign stock. Only a descendant of Cinyras is now consulted as priest. Such victims are accepted as the individual vows, but male ones are preferred. The greatest confidence is put in the entrails of kids. Blood may not be shed upon the altar, but offering is made only with prayers and pure fire. The altar is never wet by any rain, although it is in the open air. The representation of the goddess is not in human form, but it is a circular mass that is broader at the base and rises like a turning-post to a small circumference at the top.[2] The reason for this is obscure.

IV. After Titus had examined the treasures, the gifts made by kings, and all those other things which the Greeks from their delight in ancient tales attribute to a dim antiquity, he asked the oracle first with regard to his voyage. On learning that his path was open and the sea favourable, he slew many victims and then questioned indirectly about himself. When Sostratus, for such was the priest's name, saw that the entrails were uniformly favourable and that the goddess favoured great undertakings, he made at the moment a brief reply in the usual fashion, but asked for a private interview in which he disclosed the future. Greatly en-

animo ad patrem pervectus suspensis provinciarum et exercituum mentibus ingens rerum fiducia accessit.

Profligaverat bellum Iudaicum Vespasianus, obpugnatione Hierosolymorum reliqua, duro magis et arduo opere ob ingenium montis et pervicaciam superstitionis quam quo satis virium obsessis ad tolerandas necessitates superesset. Tres, ut supra memoravimus, ipsi Vespasiano legiones erant, exercitae bello: quattuor Mucianus obtinebat in pace, sed aemulatio et proximi exercitus gloria depulerat segnitiam, quantumque illis roboris discrimina et labor, tantum his vigoris addiderat integra quies et inexperti belli amor.[1] Auxilia utrique cohortium alarumque et classes regesque ac nomen dispari fama celebre.

V. Vespasianus acer militiae anteire agmen, locum castris capere, noctu diuque consilio ac, si res posceret, manu hostibus obniti, cibo fortuito, veste habituque vix a gregario milite discrepans; prorsus, si avaritia abesset, antiquis ducibus par. Mucianum e contrario magnificentia et opes et cuncta privatum modum

[1] amor *Orelli*: labor *M.*

---

[1] Cf. i. 10 and 76.
[2] That is, Syria.
[3] The fleets of Egypt, Syria, and Pontus were at their disposal, while they could count on the active support of Antiochus of Commagene, Herodes Agrippa II of Peraea, and Sohaemus of Sophene.

couraged, Titus sailed on to his father; his arrival brought a great accession of confidence to the provincials and to the troops, who were in a state of anxious uncertainty.

Vespasian had almost put an end to the war with the Jews. The siege of Jerusalem, however, remained, a task rendered difficult and arduous by the character of the mountain-citadel and the obstinate superstition of the Jews rather than by any adequate resources which the besieged possessed to withstand the inevitable hardships of a siege. As we have stated above,[1] Vespasian himself had three legions experienced in war. Mucianus was in command of four in a peaceful province,[2] but a spirit of emulation and the glory won by the neighbouring army had banished from his troops all inclination to idleness, and just as dangers and toils had given Vespasian's troops power of resistance, so those of Mucianus had gained vigour from unbroken repose and that love of war which springs from inexperience. Both generals had auxiliary infantry and cavalry, as well as fleets and allied kings;[3] while each possessed a famous name, though a different reputation.

V. Vespasian was energetic in war. He used to march at the head of his troops, select a place for camp, oppose the enemy night and day with wise strategy and, if occasion demanded, with his own hands. His food was whatever chance offered; in his dress and bearing he hardly differed from the common soldier. He would have been quite equal to the generals of old if he had not been avaricious. Mucianus, on the other hand, was eminent for his magnificence and wealth and by the complete

supergressa extollebant; aptior sermone, dispositu provisuque civilium rerum peritus: egregium principatus temperamentum, si demptis utriusque vitiis solae virtutes miscerentur. Ceterum hic Syriae, ille Iudaeae praepositus, vicinis provinciarum administrationibus invidia discordes, exitu demum Neronis positis odiis in medium consuluere, primum per amicos, dein praecipua concordiae fides Titus prava certamina communi utilitate aboleverat, natura atque arte compositus adliciendis etiam Muciani moribus. Tribuni centurionesque et vulgus militum industria licentia, per virtutes per voluptates, ut cuique ingenium, adsciscebantur.

VI. Antequam Titus adventaret sacramentum Othonis acceperat uterque exercitus, praecipitibus, ut adsolet, nuntiis et tarda mole civilis belli, quod longa concordia quietus Oriens tunc primum parabat. Namque olim validissima inter se civium arma in Italia Galliave viribus Occidentis coepta; et Pompeio, Cassio, Bruto, Antonio, quos omnis trans mare secutum est civile bellum, haud prosperi exitus fuerant; auditique[1] saepius in Syria Iudaeaque Caesares quam inspecti. Nulla seditio legionum, tantum adversus Parthos minae, vario eventu; et

[1] aditique *M.*

superiority of his scale of life to that of a private citizen. He was the readier speaker, experienced in civil administration and in statesmanship. It would have been a rare combination for an emperor if the faults of the two could have been done away with and their virtues only combined in one man. But Mucianus was governor of Syria, Vespasian of Judea. They had quarrelled through jealousy because they governed neighbouring provinces. Finally at Nero's death they had laid aside their hostilities and consulted together, at first through friends as go-betweens; and then Titus, the chief bond of their concord, had ended their dangerous feud by pointing out their common interests; both by his nature and skill he was well calculated to win over even a person of the character of Mucianus. Tribunes, centurions, and the common soldiers were secured for the cause by industry or by licence, by virtues or by pleasures, according to the individual's character.

VI. Before Titus arrived, both armies had taken the oath of allegiance to Otho, for news came quickly as usual, while it was a slow and laborious task to set in motion civil war, for which the Orient, after its long period of quiet and peace, was then for the first time preparing. For in former times the most violent civil struggles had been begun in Italy or Gaul with the resources of the West, and Pompey, Cassius, Brutus, and Anthony, all of whom had been followed over-sea by civil strife, had come to no happy ends; and in Syria and Judea the Caesars had been oftener heard of than seen. There was no mutiny on the part of the legions, only some threatening demonstrations against the Parthians which met with varied success. In the last civil

proximo civili bello turbatis aliis inconcussa ibi pax, dein fides erga Galbam. Mox, ut Othonem ac Vitellium scelestis armis res Romanas raptum ire vulgatum est, ne penes ceteros imperii praemia, penes ipsos tantum servitii necessitas esset, fremere miles et viris suas circumspicere. Septem legiones statim et cum ingentibus auxiliis Syria Iudaeaque; inde continua Aegyptus duaeque legiones, hinc Cappadocia Pontusque et quicquid castrorum Armeniis praetenditur. Asia et ceterae provinciae nec virorum inopes et pecunia[1] opulentae. Quantum insularum mari cingitur, et parando interim bello secundum tutumque ipsum mare.

VII. Non fallebat duces impetus militum, sed bellantibus aliis placuit expectari. Bello civili[2] victores victosque numquam solida fide coalescere, nec referre Vitellium an Othonem superstitem fortuna faceret. Rebus secundis etiam egregios duces insolescere: discordia militis ignavia luxurie[3] et suismet vitiis alterum bello, alterum victoria periturum. Igitur arma in occasionem distulere, Vespasianus Mucianusque nuper, ceteri olim mixtis

[1] pecunia *Ritter*: pecuniae *M.*
[2] bello civili *Heinisch*: bellū cū /n *M.*
[3] discordiam militis ignavia luxurie *Madvig*: discordiam his ignaviam luxurię *M.*

struggle, while other provinces had been shaken, in the East peace was undisturbed, and then adhesion to Galba followed. Presently, when the news spread abroad that Otho and Vitellius were proceeding with their impious arms to make spoil of the imperial power, the soldiers began to murmur and examine their own resources, that the rewards of empire might not fall to the rest, to them only the necessity of servitude. They could count at once on seven legions, and they had besides Syria and Judea with the great auxiliary forces that they could furnish; immediately on the one side there was Egypt with two legions, on the other Cappadocia and Pontus and all the garrisons stationed along the Armenian border. Asia and the rest of the provinces were not poor in men of military age and were rich in money. Besides there were all the islands of the Mediterranean and the Mediterranean itself, which was convenient and a source of safety to them in the interval while they were preparing for war.

VII. The generals did not fail to notice the ardour of the soldiers, but they decided, while others fought, to await the issue. They knew that the victors and the vanquished in civil war never unite in any complete good faith, and that it made no difference whether it was Vitellius or Otho whom Fortune allowed to survive. In prosperity, they reflected, even great generals degenerate; here one of the contestants would perish in the field from the mutiny, sloth, and luxury of his soldiers, as well as from his own faults; the other contestant would meet his doom through success. Therefore Vespasian and Mucianus postponed the war until a more favourable opportunity, having recently agreed to act in concert,

consiliis; optimus quisque amore rei publicae, multos dulcedo praedarum stimulabat, alios ambiguae domi res: ita boni malique causis diversis, studio pari, bellum omnes cupiebant.

VIII. Sub idem tempus Achaia atque Asia falso exterritae velut Nero adventaret, vario super exitu eius rumore eoque pluribus vivere eum fingentibus credentibusque. Ceterorum casus conatusque in contextu operis dicemus: tunc servus e Ponto sive, ut alii tradidere, libertinus ex Italia, citharae et cantus peritus, unde illi super similitudinem oris propior ad fallendum fides, adiunctis desertoribus, quos inopia vagos ingentibus promissis corruperat, mare ingreditur; ac vi tempestatum Cythnum insulam detrusus et militum quosdam ex Oriente commeantium adscivit vel abnuentis interfici iussit, et spoliatis negotiatoribus mancipiorum valentissimum quemque armavit. Centurionemque Sisennam dextras, concordiae insignia, Syriaci exercitus nomine ad praetorianos ferentem variis artibus adgressus est, donec Sisenna clam relicta insula trepidus et vim metuens aufugeret. Inde late terror: multi ad celebritatem nominis erecti[1] rerum novarum cupidine et odio praesentium. Gliscentem in dies famam fors discussit.

[1] erecti *Weissenborn*: erectis *M*.

---

[1] The portions of the *Histories* referred to here are now lost.

[2] Cf. i. 54

while the others had come to an agreement long since: the best were moved by love for the state, many by the attractions of spoil, others by their private embarrassments. So all, both good and bad, were eager for war with equal zeal but for different reasons.

VIII. About this time Achaia and Asia were terrified by a false rumour of Nero's arrival. The reports with regard to his death had been varied, and therefore many people imagined and believed that he was alive. The fortunes and attempts of other pretenders we shall tell as we proceed;[1] but at this time, a slave from Pontus or, as others have reported, a freedman from Italy, who was skilled in playing on the cithara and in singing, gained the readier belief in his deceit through these accomplishments and his resemblance to Nero. He recruited some deserters, poor tramps whom he had bribed by great promises, and put to sea. A violent storm drove him to the island of Cythnus, where he called to his standard some soldiers who were returning from the East on leave, or ordered them to be killed if they refused. Then he robbed the merchants, and armed all the ablest-bodied of their slaves. A centurion, Sisenna, who was carrying clasped right hands,[2] the symbol of friendship, to the praetorians in the name of the army in Syria, the pretender approached with various artifices, until Sisenna in alarm and fearing violence secretly left the island and made his escape. Then the alarm spread far and wide. Many came eagerly forward at the famous name, prompted by their desire for a change and their hatred of the present situation. The fame of the pretender was increasing from day to day when a chance shattered it.

IX. Galatiam ac Pamphyliam provincias Calpurnio Asprenati regendas Galba permiserat. Datae e classe Misenensi duae triremes ad prosequendum, cum quibus Cythnum[1] insulam tenuit: nec defuere qui trierarchos nomine Neronis accirent. Is in maestitiam compositus et fidem suorum quondam militum invocans, ut eum in Syria aut Aegypto sisterent orabat. Trierarchi,[2] nutantes seu dolo, adloquendos sibi milites et paratis omnium animis reversuros firmaverunt. Sed Asprenati cuncta ex fide nuntiata, cuius cohortatione expugnata navis et interfectus quisquis ille erat. Corpus, insigne oculis comaque et torvitate vultus, in Asiam atque inde Romam pervectum est.

X. In civitate discordi et ob[3] crebras principum mutationes inter libertatem ac licentiam incerta parvae quoque res magnis motibus agebantur. Vibius Crispus, pecunia potentia ingenio inter claros magis quam inter bonos, Annium Faustum equestris ordinis, qui temporibus Neronis delationes factitaverat, ad cognitionem senatus vocabat; nam recens Galbae principatu censuerant patres, ut accusatorum causae noscerentur. Id senatus consultum varie iactatum et, prout potens vel inops reus inciderat, infirmum aut validum, retinebat adhuc aliquid[4] terroris. Et propria vi Crispus incubuerat delatorem fratris sui

[1] Cythnum *Frobenius*: scithinum *M.* [2] trierarchis *M.* [3] hoc *M.* [4] aliquid *suppl. Jacob.*

---

[1] Galatia, Pamphylia, and Lycia now formed one province.
[2] Vibius Secundus, who had been banished under Nero for extortion in Mauretania.

IX. The provinces of Galatia and Pamphylia[1] had been entrusted by Galba to Calpurnius Asprenas, who had been given as escort two triremes from the fleet at Misenum. With these Calpurnius reached the island of Cythnus, where there were many who tried to win over the captains in Nero's name. The pretender, assuming a look of sorrow and calling on the soldiers, once his own, for protection, begged them to land him in Syria or Egypt. The captains, either hesitating or acting with craft, declared that they must address their soldiers and that they would return after they had prepared the minds of all. But they faithfully reported everything to Asprenas, at whose bidding they captured the pretender's ship and killed him, whoever he was. His body, which was remarkable for its eyes, hair, and grim face, was carried to Asia and from there to Rome.

X. In a state distracted by civil strife and wavering between liberty and licence because of the frequent changes of emperors, even smaller matters caused excitement. Vibius Crispus, whose money, power, and ability caused him to be ranked with the prominent rather than among the good, summoned for trial before the senate Annius Faustus, a knight, who had been an informer under Nero; for the senate had voted recently in the reign of Galba that informers might be brought to trial. This vote of the senate had had various fortunes and had been weak or effective according to the power or poverty of the defendant; yet it still retained some of its terror. Moreover, Crispus had used his own power to the uttermost to ruin the man who had informed against his brother,[2] and had

pervertere, traxeratque magnam senatus partem, ut indefensum et inauditum dedi ad exitium postularent. Contra apud alios nihil aeque reo proderat quam nimia potentia accusatoris: dari tempus, edi crimina, quamvis invisum ac nocentem more tamen audiendum censebant. Et valuere primo dilataque in paucos dies cognitio: mox damnatus est Faustus, nequaquam eo adsensu civitatis quem pessimis moribus meruerat: quippe ipsum Crispum easdem accusationes cum praemio exercuisse meminerant, nec poena criminis sed ultor displicebat.

XI. Laeta interim Othoni principia belli, motis ad imperium eius e Dalmatia Pannoniaque exercitibus. Fuere quattuor legiones, e quibus bina milia praemissa; ipsae modicis intervallis sequebantur, septima a Galba conscripta, veteranae undecima ac tertia decima et praecipui fama quartadecumani, rebellione Britanniae compressa. Addiderat gloriam Nero eligendo ut potissimos, unde longa illis erga Neronem fides et erecta in Othonem studia. Sed quo plus virium ac roboris e fiducia tarditas inerat. Agmen legionum alae cohortesque praeveniebant; et ex ipsa urbe haud spernenda manus, quinque

---

[1] Brought by Galba with him from Spain. Cf. i. 6.

[2] The revolt of 61 A.D., led by Boudicca. Cf. *Ann.* xiv. 29 ff., and *Agricola* 15 ff.

prevailed upon a large part of the senate to demand that Annius should be given over for execution without defence and unheard. But, on the other hand, nothing helped the defendant with other senators so much as the excessive power of his accuser. They voted that time be allowed, the charges published, and that no matter how odious and guilty the defendant might be, yet he must be heard according to precedent. They prevailed at first and the case was put off for a few days. Later Faustus was condemned, but by no means with that unanimity of feeling on the part of the citizens which he had deserved by his infamous character; for they remembered that Crispus had likewise been an informer to his own profit, and they felt displeasure not at the penalty but at the would-be avenger.

XI. In the meantime the war had begun favourably for Otho. At his command the armies had moved from Dalmatia and Pannonia. There were four legions in all; two thousand of each were sent in advance of the main body. The legions proper followed at no long interval. The Seventh had been enrolled by Galba,[1] but the Eleventh, Thirteenth, and Fourteenth were veterans; the last enjoyed great reputation for crushing the revolt in Britain.[2] Nero had added to their fame by selecting them as his best soldiers, so that they had long been loyal towards him and were enthusiastic for Otho. But their power and strength were matched by a self-confidence that made their advance slow. The main line of the legion was preceded by allied cavalry and infantry. There was also a force drawn from Rome itself which was not to be despised, five

praetoriae cohortes et equitum vexilla cum legione prima, ac deforme insuper auxilium, duo milia gladiatorum, sed per civilia arma etiam severis ducibus usurpatum. His copiis rector additus Annius Gallus, cum Vestricio Spurinna ad occupandas Padi ripas praemissus, quoniam prima consiliorum frustra ceciderant, transgresso iam Alpis Caecina, quem sisti intra Gallias posse speraverat. Ipsum Othonem comitabantur speculatorum lecta corpora cum ceteris praetoriis cohortibus, veterani e praetorio, classicorum ingens numerus. Nec illi segne aut corruptum luxu iter, sed lorica ferrea usus est et ante signa pedes ire,[1] horridus, incomptus famaeque dissimilis.

XII. Blandiebatur coeptis fortuna, possessa per mare et navis maiore Italiae parte penitus usque ad initium maritimarum Alpium, quibus temptandis adgrediendaeque provinciae Narbonensi Suedium Clementem, Antonium Novellum, Aemilium Pacensem duces dederat. Sed Pacensis per licentiam militum vinctus, Antonio Novello nulla auctoritas: Suedius Clemens ambitioso imperio regebat, ut adversus modestiam disciplinae corruptus,[2] ita proeliorum avidus. Non Italia adiri nec loca sedesque patriae videbantur: tamquam externa litora et urbes

[1] pedes ire *Madvig*: pedestre *M.*
[2] corruptius *M.*

---

[1] Cf. i. 87.

praetorian cohorts and detachments of cavalry with the First legion. Besides these, there was a disreputable kind of auxiliary force—two thousand gladiators—but it was a means resorted to even by strict generals in civil war. Over these troops Annius Gallus was put in command. He had been sent on with Vestricius Spurinna to seize the banks of the Po, since Otho's first plans had come to naught, for Caecina had already crossed the Alps, whereas Otho had hoped he could be stopped in Gaul. Otho himself was accompanied by a selected bodyguard together with the rest of the praetorian cohorts, as well as by veteran praetorians and a great number of marines. He did not march slowly or disgrace his advance by luxury, but wearing an iron breastplate he preceded the standards on foot, rough, negligent of his person, and the opposite of his reputation.

XII. At first fortune smiled upon his undertaking. Since his fleets, which controlled the sea, made him master of the greater part of Italy up to the point where the maritime Alps begin, he had allotted the task of forcing the Alps and attacking the province of Narbonensis to the generals Suedius Clemens, Antonius Novellus, and Aemilius Pacensis.[1] But Pacensis was put in chains by his mutinous soldiers; Antonius Novellus had no authority; and Suedius Clemens used his office to secure popularity, being as reckless toward maintaining discipline as he was eager to fight. It did not seem as if it were Italy and the haunts and homes of their native land that Otho's troops were approaching. They burned, devastated, and looted, as if they were on foreign shores and in an enemy's cities;

hostium urere, vastare, rapere eo atrocius quod nihil usquam provisum adversum metus. Pleni agri, apertae domus; occursantes domini iuxta coniuges et liberos securitate pacis et belli malo circumveniebantur. Maritimas tum Alpis tenebat procurator Marius Maturus. Is concita gente (nec deest iuventus) arcere provinciae finibus Othonianos intendit: sed primo impetu caesi disiectique montani, ut quibus temere collectis, non castra, non ducem noscitantibus, neque in victoria decus esset neque in fuga flagitium.

XIII. Inritatus eo proelio Othonis miles vertit iras in municipium Albintimilium. Quippe in acie nihil praedae, inopes agrestes et vilia arma; nec capi poterant, pernix genus et gnari locorum: sed calamitatibus insontium expleta avaritia. Auxit invidiam praeclaro exemplo femina Ligus, quae filio abdito, cum simul pecuniam occultari milites credidissent eoque per cruciatus interrogarent ubi filium occuleret, uterum ostendens ibi[1] latere respondit, nec ullis deinde terroribus aut morte constantiam vocis egregiae mutavit.

[1] ibi *suppl. Ernesti.*

---

[1] Ventimiglia.

and their action was the more horrible, for no provision had been made anywhere to oppose their terrifying advance. The fields were filled with workers, the houses open. The owners of estates who hurried to meet them with their wives and children, in the security which peace warrants, were overwhelmed by the horrors of war. At this time the Maritime Alps were governed by the procurator Marius Maturus. Summoning to arms the people, among whom there is no lack of vigorous men, he proposed to keep Otho's troops from entering his province; but the mountaineers were cut to pieces and scattered at the first onset, as was natural with men who had been hastily collected and were not accustomed to a military camp or a regular leader, and so saw no glory in victory and no disgrace in flight.

XIII. Provoked by this battle, Otho's troops vented their rage on the town of Albintimilium,[1] for on the field of battle they had gained no booty, since the rustics were poor and their arms of no value; nor had they been able to make captives, since the people were fleet of foot and familiar with the locality. But the invaders satisfied their greed with the misfortunes of the innocent. The horror of their action was aggravated by the glorious example of a woman of Liguria, who had hidden her son. Since the soldiers believed that she had hidden money at the same time, they tortured her and asked where she had concealed her son; she pointed to her womb, answering, "Here is his hiding-place." Thereafter neither terrors nor death itself made her falter or change her noble reply.

XIV. Imminere provinciae Narbonensi, in verba Vitellii adactae, classem Othonis trepidi nuntii Fabio Valenti attulere; aderant legati coloniarum auxilium orantes. Duas Tungrorum cohortis, quattuor equitum turmas, universam Trevirorum alam[1] cum Iulio Classico praefecto misit, e quibus pars in colonia Foroiuliensi retenta, ne omnibus copiis in terrestre iter versis vacuo mari classis adceleraret. Duodecim equitum turmae et lecti e cohortibus adversus hostem iere, quibus adiuncta Ligurum cohors, vetus loci auxilium, et quingenti Pannonii, nondum sub signis. Nec mora proelio: sed acies[2] ita instructa ut pars classicorum mixtis paganis in collis mari propinquos exsurgeret, quantum inter collis ac litus aequi loci praetorianus miles expleret, in ipso mari ut adnexa classis et pugnae parata conversa et minaci fronte praetenderetur: Vitelliani, quibus minor peditum vis, in equite robur, Alpinos proximis iugis, cohortis densis ordinibus post equitem[3] locant. Trevirorum turmae obtulere se hosti incaute, cum exciperet contra veteranus miles, simul a latere saxis urgeret apta ad iaciendum etiam paganorum manus,

[1] universa mire virorum *M.*
[2] acies *Ruperti*: acie *M.*
[3] quietem *M.*

---

[1] Fréjus.
[2] The Ligurians just mentioned.

XIV. Meantime panic-stricken messengers brought news to Fabius Valens that Otho's fleet was threatening the province of Gallia Narbonensis, which had sworn allegiance to Vitellius; envoys from the colonies also came, asking help. He therefore despatched two cohorts of Tungrian infantry, four squadrons of cavalry, and the whole detachment of the cavalry of the Treviri with Julius Classicus as commander. A part of these troops were kept in the colony of Forum Julii[1] to prevent Otho's fleet from making a hasty descent on an unprotected coast, as it might do if all their forces were sent by an inland road. Twelve squadrons of cavalry and picked infantry advanced to meet the enemy. Their numbers were reinforced by a cohort of Ligurians, a local auxiliary force long existing, and by five hundred Pannonians not yet formally enrolled. The battle was begun without delay. But Otho's line was so drawn up that part of the marines with peasants in their ranks stood on the higher ground of the hills near the sea. The praetorians filled all the level ground between the hills and the shore, while on the sea itself, the fleet moved close to the shore; cleared for action, facing the land, it offered a threatening front. The Vitellians, who were less powerful in infantry but strong in cavalry, placed their Alpine troops[2] on the neighbouring heights, and ranged their infantry in close ranks behind the cavalry. The squadrons of the Treviri charged the enemy without due caution, for they were received in front by veteran troops and at the same time were hard pressed on the flank by showers of stones thrown by a company of peasants who were skilled in hurling. These peasants, being distributed among

qui sparsi inter milites, strenui ignavique, in victoria idem audebant. Additus perculsis terror invecta in terga pugnantium classe: ita undique clausi, deletaeque omnes copiae forent ni victorem exercitum attinuisset obscurum noctis, obtentui fugientibus.

XV. Nec Vitelliani quamquam victi quievere: accitis auxiliis securum hostem ac successu rerum socordius agentem invadunt. Caesi vigiles, perrupta castra, trepidatum apud navis, donec sidente paulatim metu, occupato iuxta colle defensi, mox inrupere. Atrox ibi caedes, et Tungrarum cohortium praefecti sustentata diu acie telis obruuntur. Ne Othonianis quidem incruenta victoria fuit, quorum improvide secutos conversi equites circumvenerunt. Ac velut pactis indutiis, ne hinc classis inde eques subitam formidinem inferrent, Vitelliani retro Antipolim Narbonensis Galliae municipium, Othoniani Albingaunum interioris Liguriae revertere.

XVI. Corsicam ac Sardiniam ceterasque proximi maris insulas fama victricis classis in partibus Otho-

---

[1] Antibes.
[2] Albenga.

the regular soldiers, showed, whether brave or cowardly, the same daring when victorious. The consternation of the Vitellians was increased by the alarm caused by the fleet which attacked their rear while they were in action. So they were shut in on all sides, and their entire force would have been wiped out if the obscurity of night had not checked the victorious army and given protection to the fugitives.

XV. Yet the Vitellians, though defeated, did not rest. They brought up auxiliary forces and attacked the enemy, who thought themselves secure and were less on their guard because of their success. The Vitellians cut down their opponents' pickets, broke into their camp, and caused alarm on the ships, until Otho's troops, as their fear gradually subsided, found defence on a neighbouring hill which they seized, and from which they presently assailed the Vitellians. Then there was terrible slaughter, and the prefects of the Tungrian infantry were overwhelmed by a shower of weapons after maintaining their line unbroken for a long time. Even Otho's troops did not find their victory a bloodless one, for when some of their number followed their enemy without due caution the Vitellian cavalry wheeled and surrounded them. Finally, as if they had completed an armistice to the effect that neither the fleet on the one side nor the cavalry on the other should cause any sudden panic, the Vitellians withdrew to Antipolis,[1] a town of Narbonese Gaul, while Otho's troops retired to Albingaunum [2] in the interior of Liguria.

XVI. Corsica, Sardinia, and the other islands in the neighbouring sea were kept faithful to Otho's

nis tenuit. Sed Corsicam prope adflixit Decumi Pacarii procuratoris temeritas, tanta mole belli nihil in summam[1] profutura, ipsi exitiosa. Namque Othonis odio iuvare Vitellium Corsorum viribus statuit, inani auxilio etiam si provenisset. Vocatis principibus insulae consilium aperit, et contra dicere ausos, Claudium Pyrrichum trierarchum Liburnicarum ibi navium, Quintium Certum equitem Romanum, interfici iubet: quorum morte exterriti qui aderant, simul ignara et alieni metus socia imperitorum[2] turba in verba Vitellii iuravere. Sed ubi dilectum agere Pacarius et inconditos homines fatigare militiae muneribus occepit, laborem insolitum perosi infirmitatem suam reputabant: insulam esse quam incolerent, et longe Germaniam virisque legionum; direptos vastatosque classe etiam quos cohortes alaeque protegerent. Et aversi repente animi, nec tamen aperta vi: aptum tempus insidiis legere. Digressis qui Pacarium frequentabant, nudus et auxilii inops balineis interficitur; trucidati et comites. Capita ut hostium ipsi interfectores ad Othonem tulere; neque eos aut Otho praemio adfecit aut puniit Vitellius, in multa conluvie rerum maioribus flagitiis permixtos.

[1] summam *Rhenanus*: summa *M.*
[2] imperatorum *M.*

---

[1] Light vessels modelled after those of the Liburni, an Illyrian people. Augustus made them an important part of his navy. Cf. Horace *Ep.* i. 1.

side by the report that his fleet was victorious. But Corsica was almost brought to disaster by the rash action of Decumus Pacarius, the procurator, an action which would have contributed nothing to the sum total in so great a war, and which was fatal to Decumus himself. For, hating Otho, he decided to use the strength of Corsica to help Vitellius—an assistance of no value even if he had succeeded. Accordingly he summoned the leading men of the island and disclosed his purpose; when Claudius Pyrrichus, commander of the Liburnian ships [1] there, and Quintius Certus, a Roman knight, dared to oppose him, he ordered them to be killed. This execution terrified those who were present; and along with them the uninstructed populace, sharing in its ignorance the fears of others, swore allegiance to Vitellius. But when Pacarius began to raise a levy and to put the exhausting burdens of military service on undisciplined men, disgusted with their unfamiliar labour, they thought of their own weakness; they realized that their land was an island and that Germany and the strength of its legions were far away, while even those who were protected by auxiliary infantry and cavalry had suffered rapine and robbery from the fleet. They suddenly repented their action, but yet did not resort to open violence; they selected a fitting time for treachery. When the attendants of Pacarius had left him, they killed him in his bath, naked and helpless. They slaughtered his attendants also. The murderers themselves carried the heads of the slain to Otho, as if they were the heads of enemies. Yet Otho did not reward them or Vitellius punish them, lost as they were in such a medley of foul acts and greater crimes.

XVII. Aperuerat iam Italiam bellumque transmiserat, ut supra memoravimus, ala Siliana, nullo apud quemquam Othonis favore, nec quia Vitellium mallent, sed longa pax ad omne servitium fregerat facilis occupantibus et melioribus incuriosos. Florentissimum Italiae latus, quantum inter Padum Alpisque camporum et urbium, armis Vitellii (namque et praemissae a Caecina cohortes advenerant) tenebatur. Capta Pannoniorum cohors apud Cremonam; intercepti centum equites ac mille classici inter Placentiam Ticinumque. Quo successu Vitellianus miles non iam flumine aut ripis arcebatur; inritabat quin etiam Batavos transrhenanosque Padus ipse, quem repente contra Placentiam transgressi raptis quibusdam exploratoribus ita ceteros terruere ut adesse omnem Caecinae exercitum trepidi ac falsi nuntiarent.

XVIII. Certum erat Spurinnae (is enim Placentiam optinebat) necdum venisse Caecinam et, si propinquaret, coercere intra munimenta militem nec tris praetorias cohortis et mille vexillarios cum paucis equitibus veterano exercitui obicere: sed indomitus miles et belli ignarus correptis signis vexillisque ruere et retinenti duci tela intentare,

[1] i. 70.
[2] Piacenza and Pavia.

XVII. The road into Italy had already been opened and the war transferred there by Silius's cavalry, as we have said above.[1] Although no one favoured Otho there, this success was not due to the preference of the people for Vitellius; but long peace had broken their spirits, so that they were ready for any kind of servitude, an easy prey to the first comer and careless as to who had the better cause. The richest district of Italy, all the plains and cities between the Po and the Alps, were now in the possession of the forces of Vitellius; for the auxiliary infantry which Caecina had sent on in advance had already arrived. A company of Pannonian infantry was captured at Cremona; a hundred horsemen and a thousand marines were intercepted between Placentia and Ticinum.[2] Encouraged by this success, the troops of Vitellius were no longer checked by the banks of a river. On the contrary the Po itself roused to fury the Batavians and those from beyond the Rhine; they suddenly crossed the stream by Placentia, captured some scouts, and so terrified the rest that, in their alarm, they spread the false report that Caecina's whole army was close at hand.

XVIII. Spurinna (for he was the commander at Placentia) was sure that Caecina had not yet come and had decided, in case he were approaching, to keep his soldiers within the fortifications and not to oppose to a veteran army three praetorian cohorts, a thousand reservists and a few cavalry. But the soldiers were not to be restrained, and in their ignorance of war they seized the standards and colours and rushed out. When their commander tried to restrain them, they threatened him with their

spretis centurionibus tribunisque[1]: quin[2] prodi[3] Othonem et accitum Caecinam clamitabant. Fit temeritatis alienae comes Spurinna, primo coactus, mox velle simulans, quo plus auctoritatis inesset consiliis si seditio mitesceret.

XIX. Postquam in conspectu Padus et nox adpe tebat vallari castra placuit. Is labor urbano militi insolitus contundit animos. Tum vetustissimus quisque castigare credulitatem suam, metum ac discrimen ostendere si cum exercitu Caecina patentibus campis tam paucas cohortis circumfudisset. Iamque totis castris modesti sermones, et inserentibus se centurionibus tribunisque laudari providentia[4] ducis quod coloniam virium et opum validam robur ac sedem bello legisset. Ipse postremo Spurinna, non tam culpam exprobrans quam rationem ostendens, relictis exploratoribus ceteros Placentiam reduxit minus turbidos et imperia accipientis. Solidati muri, propugnacula addita, auctae turres, provisa parataque non arma modo sed obsequium et parendi amor, quod solum illis partibus defuit, cum virtutis haud paeniteret.

XX. At Caecina, velut relicta post Alpis saevitia ac licentia, modesto agmine per Italiam incessit.

[1] tribunisque providentiam ducis laudari *M*: *tria postrema verba del. Madvig*: *cf.* 19.
[2] quin *Agricola*: qui *M.*
[3] prodi *Bekker*: pro *M.*
[4] providentia *I. F. Gronovius*: providentiam *M.*

weapons and scorned the centurions and tribunes. More than that, they kept shouting that Otho was being betrayed and that Caecina had been sent for. Spurinna joined the folly that others started, at first under compulsion, later pretending that it was his wish, for he desired to have his advice possess greater weight in case the mutiny subsided.

XIX. After the Po was in sight and night was at hand, Spurinna decided to entrench camp. The work involved was strange to the town troops and broke their spirit. Then all the older soldiers began to blame their own credulity and to point out their dangerous and critical situation if Caecina with his army should surround so few cohorts in the open country. Presently throughout the camp more temperate speech was heard, while the centurions and tribunes made their way among the common soldiers and praised the foresight of their general for selecting as a strong base of operations a colony which possessed great natural strength and resources. In the end Caecina himself, not so much reproving their faults as showing the reasons for his action, left some scouts and led the rest back to Placentia. They were now less mutinous and more ready to accept orders. The walls of the town were strengthened, battlements added, towers built higher, arms were provided and prepared, and steps were taken to secure good discipline and a ready obedience, which were the only things that side lacked, for there was no reason to be dissatisfied with the soldiers' bravery.

XX. But Caecina seemed to have left behind the Alps his cruelty and licence, and now advanced through Italy in well-disciplined order. His manner

Ornatum ipsius municipia et coloniae in superbiam trahebant, quod versicolori sagulo, bracas [barbarum tecgmen][1] indutus togatos adloqueretur. Uxorem quoque eius Saloninam, quamquam in nullius iniuriam insignis equo ostroque veheretur, tamquam laesi gravabantur, insita mortalibus natura recentem aliorum felicitatem acribus oculis introspicere modumque fortunae a nullis magis exigere quam quos in aequo[2] viderunt. Caecina Padum transgressus, temptata Othonianorum fide per conloquium et promissa, isdem petitus, postquam pax et concordia speciosis et inritis nominibus iactata sunt, consilia curasque in obpugnationem Placentiae magno terrore vertit, gnarus ut initia belli provenissent famam in cetera fore.

XXI. Sed primus dies impetu magis quam veterani exercitus artibus transactus: aperti incautique muros subiere, cibo vinoque praegraves. In eo certamine pulcherrimum amphitheatri opus, situm extra muros, conflagravit, sive ab obpugnatoribus incensum, dum faces et glandis et missilem ignem in obsessos iaculantur, sive ab obsessis, dum retorta ingerunt.[3] Municipale vulgus, pronum ad suspiciones, fraude inlata ignis alimenta credidit a quibusdam

[1] *secl. Ritter* [2] inequos *M.*

[3] retorta ingerunt *I. F. Gronovius*: reportans gerunt *M in rasura.*

---

[1] Gallic dress, considered inappropriate for a Roman.

of dress the towns and colonies interpreted as a mark of haughtiness, because he addressed civilians wearing a parti-coloured cloak and breeches.[1] They seemed to feel offence and annoyance over the fact that his wife Salonina also rode a fine horse with purple trappings, though it did no one any harm. But they were prompted by that inveterate trait of human nature, which makes men look with unfavourable eyes upon the recent good fortune of others and to demand moderation from none more than from those whom they have recently seen their equals. Caecina, having crossed the Po, tried to break down the loyalty of Otho's followers by a conference and promises, and was himself assailed by the same devices. Finally, when in vain and empty phrases they had bandied back and forth the words "peace and concord," he turned his purpose and thoughts to storming Placentia with terrific force, well aware that the success he made in the beginning of the war would determine his reputation thereafter.

XXI. The first day was spent in a furious onslaught rather than in skilful attacks appropriate to a veteran army. The troops, heavy with food and wine, came under the walls without protection and without caution. During the struggle the handsome amphitheatre, which was situated outside the walls, was burned, being set on fire either by the besiegers as they threw firebrands, hot bullets, and burning missiles against the besieged, or by the besieged themselves as they directed their return fire. The common people of the town, being given to suspicion, believed that inflammable material had been treacherously brought into the amphitheatre by some

ex[1] vicinis coloniis invidia et[2] aemulatione, quod nulla in Italia moles tam capax foret. Quocumque casu accidit, dum atrociora metuebantur, in levi habitum, reddita securitate, tamquam nihil gravius pati potuissent, maerebant. Ceterum multo suorum cruore pulsus Caecina, et nox parandis operibus absumpta. Vitelliani pluteos cratisque et vineas subfodiendis muris protegendisque obpugnatoribus, Othoniani sudis et immensas lapidum ac plumbi aerisque molis perfringendis obruendisque hostibus expediunt. Utrimque pudor, utrimque gloria et diversae exhortationes hinc legionum et Germanici exercitus robur, inde urbanae militiae et praetoriarum cohortium decus attollentium; illi ut segnem et desidem et circo ac theatris corruptum militem, hi peregrinum et externum increpabant. Simul Othonem ac Vitellium celebrantes culpantesve uberioribus inter se probris quam laudibus stimulabantur.

XXII. Vixdum orto die plena propugnatoribus moenia, fulgentes armis virisque campi: densum legionum agmen, sparsa auxiliorum manus altiora murorum sagittis aut saxis incessere, neglecta aut aevo fluxa comminus adgredi. Ingerunt desuper Othoniani pila librato magis et certo ictu adversus

[1] ex *Halm*: et *M.*
[2] invidia et *Muretus*: invidiae *M.*

persons from the neighbouring colonies, who looked on it with envy and jealousy, since no other building in Italy was so large. However it happened, the loss was regarded as slight, so long as they feared more awful disasters; but when a sense of security returned, they grieved as if they could have suffered nothing worse. Nevertheless Caecina was repulsed with great loss to his troops, and the night was spent in the preparation of siege-works. The Vitellians made ready mantlets, fascines, and sheds to undermine the walls and protect the assailants. Otho's followers prepared stakes and huge masses of stones and lead and bronze to break through and overwhelm the enemy. On both sides was a feeling of shame; on both an ambition for glory. Different exhortations were heard: one side exalted the strength of the legions and the army from Germany, while the other praised the high renown of the town soldiery and the praetorian cohorts. The Vitellians assailed their opponents as lazy and indolent, soldiers corrupted by the circus and the theatre; those within the town attacked the Vitellians as foreigners and barbarians. At the same time, while they thus lauded or blamed Otho and Vitellius, their mutual insults were more productive of enthusiasm than their praise.

XXII. Almost before dawn the walls were filled with defenders, the plains all agleam with armed men. The legionary forces in close array, the auxiliaries in open order, assailed the higher parts of the walls with arrows or stones and attacked at close quarters the parts of the walls that were neglected or weak from age. Otho's soldiers poured a shower of javelins from above with more deliberate

temere subeuntis cohortis Germanorum, cantu truci et more patrio nudis corporibus super umeros scuta quatientium. Legionarius pluteis et cratibus tectus subruit muros, instruit aggerem, molitur portas: contra praetoriani dispositos ad id ipsum molaris ingenti pondere ac fragore provolvunt. Pars subeuntium obruti, pars confixi et exsangues aut laceri: cum augeret stragem trepidatio eoque acrius e moenibus vulnerarentur, rediere[1] infracta partium fama. Et Caecina pudore coeptae temere obpugnationis, ne inrisus ac vanus isdem castris adsideret, traiecto rursus Pado Cremonam petere intendit. Tradidere sese abeunti Turullius Cerialis cum compluribus classicis et Iulius Briganticus cum paucis equitum, hic praefectus alae in Batavis genitus, ille primipilaris et Caecinae haud alienus, quod ordines in Germania duxerat.

XXIII. Spurinna comperto itinere hostium defensam Placentiam, quaeque acta et quid Caecina pararet, Annium Gallum per litteras docet. Gallus legionem primam in auxilium Placentiae ducebat, diffisus paucitati cohortium, ne longius obsidium et vim Germanici exercitus parum tolerarent. Ubi

[1] redire *M.*

---

[1] Cf. i. 87.

and certain aim upon the German infantry who approached with little caution, singing their wild songs and brandishing their shields above their shoulders, while their bodies, according to a native custom, were unprotected. The legionary soldiers, defended by mantlets and fascines, undermined the walls, built an earthwork, and assailed the gates, while the praetorians on their side rolled down upon them millstones of great weight, arranged for the purpose, which fell with a mighty crash. Many of the assailants under the walls were thus crushed, many were pierced and bleeding or mangled ; since their panic increased their demoralization, and the weapons rained upon them more fiercely from the walls, they began to withdraw, thus injuring the prestige of their side. Caecina, however, prompted by shame at his rash attempt to carry the town by storm and desiring to avoid appearing ridiculous and useless by remaining in the same camp, crossed the Po again and hurried to attack Cremona. As he was leaving, Turullius Cerialis, with a large number of marines, and Julius Briganticus, with a few horsemen, surrendered to him. Briganticus, a Batavian by birth, was commander of a squadron of cavalry ; Cerialis was a centurion of the first rank and no stranger to Caecina, for he had served in Germany.

XXIII. When Spurinna learned of the enemy's route, he informed Annius Gallus[1] of everything that had happened, of the defence of Placentia, and of Caecina's purpose. Gallus was at the time bringing the First legion to help Placentia, for he feared that the few cohorts there might not be able to withstand a long siege and the force of the German army.

pulsum Caecinam pergere Cremonam accepit, aegre coercitam legionem et pugnandi ardore usque ad seditionem progressam Bedriaci sistit. Inter Veronam Cremonamque situs est vicus, duabus iam Romanis cladibus notus infaustusque.[1]

Isdem diebus a Martio Macro haud procul Cremona prospere pugnatum; namque promptus[2] animi Martius transvectos navibus gladiatores in adversam Padi ripam repente effudit. Turbati ibi Vitellianorum auxilia, et ceteris Cremonam fugientibus caesi qui restiterant: sed repressus[3] vincentium impetus ne novis subsidiis firmati hostes fortunam proelii mutarent. Suspectum id Othonianis fuit, omnia ducum[4] facta prave aestimantibus. Certatim, ut quisque animo ignavus, procax ore, Annium Gallum et Suetonium Paulinum et Marium Celsum—nam eos quoque Otho praefecerat—variis criminibus incessebant.[5] Acerrima seditionum ac discordiae incitamenta, interfectores Galbae scelere et metu vaecordes miscere cuncta, modo palam turbidis vocibus, modo occultis ad Othonem litteris; qui humillimo cuique credulus, bonos metuens trepida-

[1] infastusque *M.* [2] promptius *M.*
[3] sed reprehensis *M.*
[4] ducum *Freinsheim*: quocum *M.*
[5] incessebant *Agricola*: incesserant *M.*

---

[1] At the juncture of the highroads leading from Hostilia and Mantua toward Cremona, near the present Calvatone.

When the news came that Caecina had been repulsed and was marching on Cremona, he had difficulty in restraining his legion which, in its enthusiasm for battle, had reached the point of mutiny, but he succeeded in stopping them at Bedriacum.[1] This is a village which lies between Verona and Cremona, and two Roman disasters have given it an unhappy celebrity.[2]

During these same days, Martius Macer had had a successful engagement not far from Cremona; for by a prompt decision he had transferred gladiators to the opposite bank of the Po, and suddenly hurled them at the enemy. This had thrown the auxiliaries of Vitellius into confusion and, while most fled to Cremona, those who resisted were cut down. But Macer checked the enthusiastic advance of his victorious troops, prompted by fear that the enemy might be reinforced and change the fortune of battle. This roused suspicion in the minds of Otho's troops, who put a bad construction upon every act of their leaders. Blustering in speech to match their cowardice at heart, they vied with one another in bringing various charges against Annius Gallus and Suetonius Paulinus and Marius Celsus, for Otho had appointed the latter two also as generals. The murderers of Galba were the most ardent promoters of mutiny and discord, for, driven mad by guilt and fear, they sought to cause utter confusion, now by openly seditious expressions, now by secret letters to Otho, who, between his readiness to trust the meanest and his fear of honest men, was in a state of

[2] Because here Vitellius defeated Otho (ii. 41 ff.), and Vespasian Vitellius (iii. 15 ff.).

bat, rebus prosperis incertus et inter adversa melior. Igitur Titianum fratrem accitum bello praeposuit.

XXIV. Interea Paulini et Celsi ductu res egregie gestae. Angebant Caecinam nequiquam omnia coepta et senescens exercitus sui fama. Pulsus Placentia, caesis nuper auxiliis, etiam per concursum exploratorum, crebra magis quam digna memoratu proelia, inferior, propinquante Fabio Valente, ne omne belli decus illuc concederet, reciperare gloriam avidius quam consultius properabat. Ad duodecimum a Cremona (locus Castorum[1] vocatur) ferocissimos auxiliarium imminentibus viae lucis occultos componit: equites procedere longius iussi[2] et inritato proelio sponte refugi festinationem sequentium elicere, donec insidiae coorerentur.[3] Proditum id Othonianis ducibus, et curam peditum Paulinus, equitum Celsus sumpsere. Tertiae decimae legionis vexillum, quattuor auxiliorum cohortes et quingenti equites in sinistro locantur; aggerem viae tres praetoriae cohortes altis ordinibus obtinuere; dextra fronte prima legio incessit cum duabus auxiliaribus[4] cohortibus et quingentis equitibus: super hos ex[5] praetorio auxiliisque mille equites, cumulus prosperis aut subsidium laborantibus, ducebantur.

[1] Castorum *Alciatus*: castrarum? *M*: castrorum *M*[1].
[2] iussi *Rhenanus*: iussit *M*.
[3] coorerentur *Rhenanus*: coercerentur *M*.
[4] auxiliaribus *Mercerus*: vexillaribus *M*.
[5] ex *Bach*: et *M*.

trepidation, hesitating in prosperity and yet showing himself the better man in adversity. Therefore he sent for his brother Titianus and appointed him to the chief command.

XXIV. In the meantime the generals Paulinus and Celsus had met with brilliant success. Caecina was distressed by the failure of all his efforts and by the waning reputation of his army. Driven from Placentia, he had lately had his auxiliaries cut to pieces, and, even when his scouts engaged in skirmishes which were frequent but not worth recording, he was worsted. Therefore, as Fabius Valens was approaching, he feared that all the honour in the campaign would fall to him, and hurried to recover his reputation with more impetuosity than wisdom. Twelve miles from Cremona, at a place called "The Castors'," he concealed the bravest of his auxiliary troops in some woods which overhung the road. His cavalry he ordered to advance and provoke battle, then to feign fright and draw the enemy into a hasty pursuit until the troops in ambuscade could assail them. This plan was betrayed to Otho's generals, and Paulinus took command of the foot, Celsus of the horse; they stationed a detachment of the Thirteenth legion, four auxiliary cohorts of infantry, and five hundred auxiliary cavalry on the left flank; the causeway three praetorian cohorts occupied in deep formation; on the right front the First legion advanced with two cohorts of auxiliary infantry and five hundred cavalry. In addition to these they were accompanied by a thousand praetorian and auxiliary horse to give them additional weight if victorious, or to act as a reserve if they were in difficulties.

XXV. Antequam miscerentur acies, terga vertentibus Vitellianis, Celsus doli prudens repressit suos; Vitelliani temere exsurgentes cedente sensim Celso longius secuti ultro in insidias praecipitantur; nam a lateribus cohortes, legionum adversa frons, et subito discursu terga cinxerant equites. Signum pugnae non statim a Suetonio Paulino pediti datum: cunctator natura et cui cauta potius consilia cum ratione quam prospera ex casu placerent, compleri fossas, aperiri campum, pandi aciem iubebat, satis cito incipi victoriam ratus ubi provisum foret ne vincerentur. Ea cunctatione spatium Vitellianis datum in vineas nexu traducum impeditas refugiendi; et modica silva adhaerebat, unde rursus ausi promptissimos praetorianorum equitum interfecere. Vulneratur rex Epiphanes, impigre pro Othone pugnam ciens.

XXVI. Tum Othonianus pedes erupit; protrita hostium acie versi in fugam etiam qui subveniebant; nam Caecina non simul cohortis sed singulas acciverat, quae res in proelio trepidationem auxit, cum dispersos nec usquam validos pavor fugientium abriperet. Orta et in castris seditio quod non universi ducerentur: vinctus praefectus castrorum Iulius

[1] Son of King Antiochus, king of Commagene.

XXV. Before the lines engaged the Vitellians fled; but Celsus, aware of the tricky stratagem, held his men back. The Vitellians rashly left their ambuscade, while Celsus gradually withdrew. They pursued too far and themselves fell into a trap; for the auxiliary infantry hemmed them in on the flanks, the legions opposed them in front, and their rear the cavalry cut off by a sudden manœuvre. Suetonius Paulinus did not at once give his infantry the signal to engage, for he was naturally inclined to delay, and a man who preferred cautious and well-reasoned plans to chance success. So he kept issuing orders to fill up the ditches, clear the fields, and extend the line, thinking that it was soon enough to begin to conquer when they had made provision against defeat. This delay gave the Vitellians time to retreat into some vineyards which were obstructed by the intertwining vines. There was a small wood also near at hand, from which they dared to issue again and killed the boldest of the praetorian horse. Prince Epiphanes[1] was wounded as he was enthusiastically cheering the soldiers on for Otho.

XXVI. Then Otho's soldiers charged; they crushed the enemy's line and routed also those who were coming to their assistance. For Caecina had not brought up his cohorts of auxiliary infantry all at once, but one by one, an action which increased the confusion while they were engaged, inasmuch as the bodies of troops which were thus scattered and nowhere strong were swept away by the panic of the fugitives. Even in the camp the soldiers mutinied because they were not all taken out together. They threw into chains Julius Gratus, the prefect of the camp, on the charge that he was having

Gratus, tamquam fratri apud Othonem militanti proditionem ageret, cum fratrem eius, Iulium Frontonem tribunum, Othoniani sub eodem crimine vinxissent. Ceterum ea ubique formido fuit apud fugientis occursantis, in acie pro vallo, ut deleri cum universo exercitu Caecinam potuisse, ni Suetonius Paulinus receptui cecinisset, utrisque in partibus percrebruerit.[1] Timuisse se Paulinus ferebat tantum insuper laboris atque itineris, ne Vitellianus miles recens e castris fessos adgrederetur et perculsis[2] nullum retro subsidium foret. Apud paucos ea ducis ratio probata, in vulgus adverso rumore fuit.

XXVII. Haud proinde id damnum Vitellianos in metum compulit quam ad modestiam composuit: nec solum apud Caecinam, qui culpam in militem conferebat seditioni magis quam proelio paratum: Fabii quoque Valentis copiae (iam enim Ticinum venerat) posito hostium contemptu et reciperandi decoris cupidine reverentius et aequalius duci parebant. Gravis alioquin seditio exarserat, quam altiore initio (neque enim rerum a Caecina gestarum ordinem interrumpi oportuerat) repetam. Cohortes Batavorum, quas bello Neronis a quarta decima legione digressas, cum

[1] percrebuerit *Beroaldus*: percrebuit *M.*
[2] periculosis *M.*

---

[1] That is, Paulinus, if successful here against Caecina, would then have to lead his troops some twelve miles to Cremona where Caecina's camp was situated.

[2] Tacitus here resumes his narrative from i. 66.

treacherous dealings with his brother who was serving under Otho, while Otho's troops had put that same brother, the tribune Julius Fronto, into fetters on the same charge. But there was universal panic both among the troops who were fleeing and those who were advancing, in the lines and in front of the camp, so that on both sides it was commonly said that Caecina could have been annihilated with his whole force if Suetonius Paulinus had not given the signal to retire. Paulinus offered as excuse that he had been afraid of the effect of such great additional effort and the long march,[1] lest the soldiers of Vitellius, fresh from camp, should attack his weary forces, and then, when they were demoralized, they should have no place of retreat. A few approved of the general's plan, but it caused adverse comment among the mass of the soldiers.

XXVII. Their disaster did not so much drive the Vitellians into a panic as bring them back to a state of obedience. This was true both among the troops with Caecina, who blamed the soldiers, saying that they were readier for mutiny than for battle; and likewise among the forces under Fabius Valens, who had now reached Ticinum. They gave up their scorn of their opponents, and, prompted by a desire to recover their former reputation, began to obey their commander with more respect and regularity. A serious mutiny had broken out among them on another occasion, the history of which I shall now trace from an early point, since before I could not properly interrupt my account of Caecina's operations. I have already related[2] how the Batavian cohorts that had withdrawn from the Fourteenth legion in the uprising against Nero, on hearing of

Britanniam peterent, audito Vitellii motu in civitate Lingonum Fabio Valenti adiunctas rettulimus, superbe agebant, ut cuiusque[1] legionis tentoria accessissent, coercitos a se quartadecimanos, ablatam Neroni Italiam atque omnem belli fortunam in ipsorum manu sitam iactantes. Contumeliosum id militibus, acerbum duci; corrupta iurgiis aut rixis disciplina; ad postremum Valens e petulantia etiam perfidiam suspectabat.

XXVIII. Igitur nuntio adlato pulsam Trevirorum[2] alam Tungrosque a classe Othonis et Narbonensem Galliam circumiri, simul cura socios tuendi et militari astu cohortis turbidas ac, si una forent, praevalidas dispergendi, partem Batavorum ire in subsidium iubet. Quod ubi auditum vulgatumque, maerere socii, fremere legiones. Orbari se fortissimorum virorum auxilio; veteres illos et tot bellorum victores, postquam in conspectu sit hostis, velut ex acie abduci. Si provincia urbe et salute imperii potior sit, omnes illuc sequerentur; sin victoriae columen[3] in Italia verteretur, non abrumpendos ut corpori validissimos artus.

XXIX. Haec ferociter iactando, postquam im-

[1] cuius *M*.
[2] ire virorum *M*.
[3] sanitas sustentaculum columen *M*: san. susten. *ut glossas agn. Nipperdey.*

---

[1] Cf. ii. 14f.

the revolt of Vitellius while they were on their way to Britain, had joined Fabius Valens in the country of the Lingones. These cohorts then began to be insolent, going up to the quarters of each legion and boasting that it was they who had checked the regulars of the Fourteenth legion, they who had taken Italy away from Nero, and that in their hands lay the whole fortune of the war. Such action was insulting to the legionaries, bitterly offensive to the commander; discipline was ruined by quarrels and brawls; finally their insolence began to make Valens suspect even their loyalty.

XXVIII. So when news came that the squadron of Treviran cavalry and the Tungrian foot had been defeated by Otho's fleet,[1] and that the province of Gallia Narbonensis was blockaded, Valens, prompted by his desire to protect the allies and, like a wise commander, to scatter the auxiliary cohorts which were now mutinous and which, if united, would prove too strong, ordered a part of the Batavians to march to the aid of the province. When the report of this action became common knowledge, the allied troops were dissatisfied, the legionaries angry. They declared that they were losing the help of their bravest troops; that it looked as if the Batavians, veterans in so many victorious campaigns, were being withdrawn from the line after the enemy was in sight. If the province was of more account than Rome and the safety of the empire, then all ought to follow thither; but if the main support of victory depended on Italy, the strongest limbs must not be torn, as it were, from the body of the army.

XXIX. While the soldiers were thus savagely

missis lictoribus Valens coercere seditionem coeptabat, ipsum invadunt, saxa iaciunt, fugientem sequuntur. Spolia Galliarum et Viennensium aurum, pretia[1] laborum suorum, occultare clamitantes, direptis sarcinis tabernacula ducis ipsamque humum pilis et lanceis rimabantur; nam Valens servili veste apud decurionem equitum tegebatur. Tum Alfenus Varus praefectus castrorum, deflagrante paulatim seditione, addit consilium, vetitis obire vigilias centurionibus, omisso tubae sono, quo miles ad belli munia cietur. Igitur torpere cuncti, circumspectare inter se attoniti et id ipsum quod nemo regeret paventes; silentio, patientia, postremo precibus ac lacrimis veniam quaerebant. Ut vero deformis et flens et praeter spem incolumis Valens processit, gaudium miseratio favor: versi in laetitiam, ut est vulgus utroque immodicum, laudantes gratantesque circumdatum aquilis signisque in tribunal ferunt. Ille utili moderatione non supplicium cuiusquam poposcit, ac ne dissimulans suspectior foret, paucos incusavit, gnarus civilibus bellis plus militibus quam ducibus licere.

[1] pretia *Classen*: et praetia *M.*

---

[1] Cf. i. 63–66.

[2] The eagles of the First and Fifth legions and the colours of auxiliary cohorts.

criticizing his action, Valens sent his lictors among them and tried to check the mutiny. Thereupon the troops attacked Valens himself, stoned him, and pursued him when he fled. Declaring that he was concealing the spoils of the Gallic provinces and the gold taken from the people of Vienne, the rewards of their own toil,[1] they began to ransack his baggage and explore the walls of his quarters and even the ground with their spears and javelins. Valens, disguised in a slave's clothes, hid in the quarters of a cavalry officer. Then, as the mutiny began gradually to lose its force, Alfenus Varus, prefect of the camp, helped the situation by the device of forbidding the centurions to make the rounds of the pickets and of omitting the usual trumpet call to summon the soldiers to their military duties. The result was that all were amazed, they began to look at one another in perplexity, frightened by the simple fact that no one issued orders. In silence and submission, finally with prayers and tears, they begged forgiveness. When Valens appeared in sorry plight and weeping, but unexpectedly safe, there came joy, pity, and even popularity. In their revulsion from anxiety to delight—mobs are always extravagant in both directions—they praised and congratulated him, surrounded him with the eagles and colours,[2] and carried him to the tribunal. Valens showed a wise moderation: he did not demand the punishment of any man; at the same time, that an assumption of ignorance might not arouse suspicion, he blamed a few severely. He was well aware that in civil wars the soldiers have more liberty than the leaders.

XXX. Munientibus castra apud Ticinum de adversa Caecinae pugna adlatum, et prope renovata seditio tamquam fraude et cunctationibus Valentis proelio defuissent: nolle requiem, non expectare ducem, anteire signa, urgere signiferos; rapido agmine Caecinae iunguntur. Improspera Valentis fama apud exercitum Caecinae erat: expositos se tanto pauciores integris hostium viribus querebantur, simul in suam excusationem et adventantium robur per adulationem attollentes, ne ut victi et ignavi despectarentur. Et quamquam plus virium, prope duplicatus legionum auxiliorumque numerus erat Valenti, studia tamen militum in Caecinam inclinabant, super benignitatem animi, qua promptior habebatur, etiam vigore aetatis, proceritate corporis et quodam inani favore. Hinc aemulatio ducibus: Caecina ut foedum ac maculosum, ille ut tumidum ac vanum inridebant. Sed condito odio eandem utilitatem fovere, crebris epistulis sine respectu veniae probra Othoni obiectantes, cum duces partium Othonis quamvis uberrima conviciorum in Vitellium materia abstinerent.

XXXI. Sane ante utriusque exitum, quo egregiam Otho famam, Vitellius flagitiosissimam meruere

XXX. While the soldiers were fortifying their camp at Ticinum, word of Caecina's defeat arrived; the troops almost mutinied again, for they suspected that their absence from the battle was due to treachery and delay on the part of Valens. They refused to rest; they would not wait for their general; they advanced before the standards, and spurred on the standard-bearers; and they quickly marched and joined Caecina. Valens did not enjoy a good reputation with Caecina's troops; they complained that in spite of their great inferiority in numbers Valens had exposed them to an enemy whose strength was unimpaired, and at the same time, to excuse themselves, they praised and flattered the strength of the troops that joined them, for they did not wish these to despise them as defeated and cowardly soldiers. Moreover, although Valens had the larger army, in fact almost twice as many legionaries and auxiliaries, the troops were inclined to favour Caecina, not only for his kindness of heart, which he was thought to display more readily than Valens, but also because of his vigorous youth, his tall person, and a certain unwarranted popularity. This caused rivalry between the generals. Caecina made sport of Valens as a shameful and disgraceful character; Valens ridiculed Caecina as a conceited and vain person. Yet they laid aside their hatred and devoted themselves to the common interest; in many communications, sacrificing all hope of pardon, they heaped insults on Otho, while the generals of Otho's party refrained from using the abundant material they had at hand for attacking Vitellius.

XXXI. In fact, before these two met their deaths, in which Otho won a glorious reputation while

minus Vitellii ignavae voluptates quam Othonis flagrantissimae libidines timebantur: addiderat huic terrorem atque odium caedes Galbae, contra illi initium belli nemo imputabat. Vitellius ventre et gula sibi inhonestus,[1] Otho luxu saevitia audacia rei publicae exitiosior ducebatur.

Coniunctis Caecinae ac Valentis copiis nulla ultra penes Vitellianos mora quin totis viribus certarent: Otho consultavit trahi bellum an fortunam experiri placeret.

XXXII. Tunc Suetonius Paulinus dignum fama sua ratus, qua nemo illa tempestate militaris rei callidior habebatur, de toto genere belli censere, festinationem hostibus, moram ipsis utilem disseruit: exercitum Vitellii universum advenisse, nec multum virium a tergo, quoniam Galliae tumeant et deserere Rheni ripam inrupturis tam infestis nationibus non conducat; Britannicum militem hoste et mari distineri:[2] Hispanias armis non ita redundare; provinciam Narbonensem incursu classis et adverso proelio contremuisse; clausam Alpibus et nullo maris subsidio transpadanam Italiam atque ipso transitu exercitus vastam; non frumentum usquam exercitui, nec exercitum sine copiis retineri posse: iam Germanos,

[1] inhonestus *Victorius*: inhostus *M*.
[2] destineri *M*.

---

[1] Paulinus had proved himself an able general in Africa as early as 42 A.D. (Dio Cass. lx. 4; Plin. *N.H.* v. 14), and in Britain during the years 59–61 (Tac. *Agric.* 14–16; *Ann.* xiv. 29–39; Dio Cass. lxii. 7–12). He was apparently consul in 42, and now was the senior among the ex-consuls (cf. ii 37).

'itellius gained infamy, the indolent pleasures of 'itellius were less feared than the fiery passions of)tho. Moreover the murder of Galba had made nen stand in terror of Otho and hate him; but no ne blamed Vitellius for beginning the war. The ensuality and gluttony of Vitellius were regarded s disgracing him alone; Otho's luxury, cruelty and laring seemed more dangerous to the state.

After Caecina and Valens had joined forces, the 'itellians no longer hesitated to engage with all heir forces. Otho, however, took counsel as to vhether it was better to protract the war or to try is fortune now.

XXXII. Then Suetonius Paulinus, who was re-;arded as the most skilful general of the time,[1] hought it consonant with his reputation to express is views with regard to the whole conduct of the var, maintaining that the enemy's advantage lay in aste, their own in delay. He spoke to this effect: 'The whole army of Vitellius has now arrived, and here are no strong reserves behind them, for the Gallic provinces are growing restless, and it would be nwise to abandon the bank of the Rhine when so nany hostile tribes are ready to rush across it. The roops in Britain are kept away by their enemies' ssaults and by the sea; the Spanish provinces have o forces to spare; Gallia Narbonensis has been adly frightened by the attacks of our fleet and by lefeat; Italy north of the Po, shut in by the Alps, an look to no relief by sea, and in fact has been levastated by the mere passage of an army. Our pponents have no supplies anywhere for their roops, and they cannot maintain their forces with-ut supplies; then the Germans, who are the fiercest

quod genus militum apud hostis atrocissimum sit, tracto in aestatem bello, fluxis corporibus, mutationem soli caelique haud toleraturos. Multa bella impetu valida per taedia et moras evanuisse. Contra ipsis omnia opulenta et fida, Pannoniam Moesiam Dalmatiam Orientem cum integris exercitibus, Italiam et caput rerum urbem senatumque et populum, nunquam obscura nomina, etiam si aliquando obumbrentur; publicas privatasque opes et immensam pecuniam, inter civilis discordias ferre validiorem; corpora militum aut Italiae sueta aut aestibus; obiacere flumen Padum, tutas viris murisque urbis, e quibus nullam hosti cessuram Placentiae defensione exploratum: proinde duceret bellum. Paucis diebus quartam decimam legionem, magna ipsam fama,[1] cum [2] Moesicis copiis adfore: tum rursus deliberaturum et, si proelium placuisset, auctis viribus certaturos.

XXXIII. Accedebat sententiae Paulini Mariu Celsus; idem placere Annio Gallo, paucos ante die lapsu equi adflicto, missi qui consilium eius sciscitarentur rettulerant. Otho pronus ad decertandum frater eius Titianus et praefectus praetorii Proculus imperitia properantes, fortunam et deos et numen Othonis adesse consiliis, adfore conatibus testaban

[1] magnam ipsam famam *M*. [2] cum *om*. *M*.

[1] This implies the withdrawal of Otho's troops to the sout of the Po.

[2] For the reputation of the Fourteenth legion, see above chap. 11; the troops from Moesia reached Aquilea at the time of the battle of Cremona. See below, chap. 46.

warriors in their army, if the war be protracted into summer, will soon lose their strength and be unable to endure the change of country and climate. Many wars, formidable in their first onset, have shrunk to nothing through the tedium caused by inaction. On the other hand, our own resources are rich and certain: Pannonia, Moesia, Dalmatia and the East are with us; their armies are undiminished; we have also Italy and Rome, the capital of the empire, the Senate and the People—names never insignificant, even if they be sometimes obscured. We have also on our side public and private resources and an enormous amount of money, which in time of civil strife is more powerful than the sword. Physically our soldiers are inured to Italy, or, at least, to heat. The Po is our defence;[1] our cities are well protected by their garrisons and walls, and we have learned from the defence of Placentia that none will surrender to the foe. Your policy therefore is to prolong the war. In a few days the Fourteenth legion itself, a force of great renown, will be here with troops from Moesia besides;[2] then you may again consider the question, and if we decide to fight we shall engage with increased strength."

XXXIII. Marius Celsus supported the opinion of Paulinus. Annius Gallus did likewise; he had been incapacitated a few days before by a fall from his horse, but a delegation which had been sent to consult him reported back his views. Otho was inclined to fight. His brother Titianus and the praetorian prefect, Proculus, impatient as they were through inexperience, declared that fortune, the gods, and Otho's good genius favoured his policy and would favour its execution; in fact they had

tur, neu quis obviam ire sententiae auderet, in adulationem concesserant. Postquam pugnari placitum, interesse pugnae imperatorem an seponi melius foret dubitavere. Paulino et Celso iam non adversantibus, ne principem obiectare periculis viderentur idem illi deterioris consilii auctores perpulere ut Brixellum concederet ac dubiis proeliorum exemptus summae[1] rerum et imperii se ipsum reservaret. Is primus dies Othonianas partis adflixit; namque et cum ipso praetoriarum cohortium et speculatorum equitumque valida manus discessit, et remanentium fractus animus, quando suspecti duces et Otho,[2] cui uni apud militem fides, dum et ipse non nisi militibus credit, imperia ducum in[3] incerto reliquerat.

XXXIV. Nihil eorum Vitellianos fallebat, crebris, ut in civili bello, transfugiis; et exploratores cura diversa sciscitandi sua non occultabant. Quieti intentique Caecina ac Valens, quando hostis imprudentia rueret, quod loco sapientiae est, alienam stultitiam opperiebantur, inchoato ponte transitum Padi simulantes adversus obpositam gladiatorum manum, ac ne ipsorum miles segne otium tereret. Naves pari inter se spatio, validis utrimque trabibus conexae, adversum in flumen dirigebantur, iactis super ancoris quae firmitatem pontis continerent, sed ancorarum funes

[1] summam *M.* [2] et ut Otho *M.* [3] in *om. M.*

[1] Brescello.

[2] See below, chap. 39. Otho's brother, Titianus, was apparently in nominal command, while Proculus possessed the real authority.

taken refuge in flattery to prevent anyone from daring to oppose their views. When they had decided on an engagement, they debated whether it was better for the emperor to take part in the battle in person or to withdraw. Paulinus and Celsus now offered no opposition for fear that they might seem to expose the emperor to danger; so the same councillors urged on him the baser course and persuaded him to withdraw to Brixellum[1] and there, safe from the risks of battle, to reserve himself for the supreme control of the empire. This day first brought doom to Otho's side, for with him went a strong force of praetorians, of his bodyguard, and of horse, and the spirit of those who remained was broken; they suspected their generals; and Otho, in whom alone the troops had confidence, while he trusted no one but his soldiers, had left the authority of his generals in doubt.[2]

XXXIV. None of these facts escaped the knowledge of the Vitellians, for there were many desertions, as is always the case in civil wars; and spies, in their anxiety to inquire into the purposes of the other side, failed to conceal their own. Caecina and Valens quietly watched for their enemy's imprudence to end in ruin, and, employing a common substitute for wisdom, waited to profit by their opponents' folly. They began a bridge and made a feint of crossing the Po in the face of a band of gladiators; they also wished to keep their own men from spending their time in idleness. They arranged some boats at equal intervals, heading upstream, and fastened them together with strong beams at prow and stern. They also cast out anchors to make the bridges more secure; the

non extenti fluitabant, ut augescente flumine inoffensus ordo navium attolleretur. Claudebat pontem imposita turris et in extremam navem educta, unde tormentis ac machinis hostes propulsarentur. Othoniani in ripa turrim struxerant saxaque et faces iaculabantur.

XXXV. Et erat insula amne medio, in quam gladiatores navibus molientes, Germani nando praelabebantur. Ac forte pluris transgressos completis Liburnicis per promptissimos gladiatorum Macer adgreditur: sed neque ea constantia gladiatoribus ad proelia quae militibus, nec proinde nutantes e navibus quam stabili gradu e ripa vulnera derigebant. Et cum[1] variis trepidantium inclinationibus mixti remiges propugnatoresque turbarentur, desilire in vada ultro Germani, retentare puppis, scandere foros aut comminus mergere: quae cuncta in oculis utriusque exercitus quanto laetiora Vitellianis, tanto acrius Othoniani causam auctoremque cladis detestabantur.

XXXVI. Et proelium quidem, abruptis quae supererant navibus, fuga diremptum: Macer ad[2] exitium poscebatur, iamque vulneratum eminus lancea strictis gladiis invaserant, cum intercursu tribunorum

[1] tum *M.* [2] ad *om. M.*

---

[1] Cf. ii. 16.

cables they did not draw taut, but let them hang loose, so that when the river rose the line of boats was lifted without being disturbed. At the end of the bridge a tower was built and raised aloft on the last boat, that they might repulse the enemy by artillery and machines. Otho's troops had built a tower on the opposite bank and kept shooting stones and firebrands at the Vitellians.

XXXV. In the middle of the river was an island, which the gladiators were trying to reach in boats, but the Germans swam across and anticipated them. When a considerable number of Germans had crossed, Macer filled some light Liburnian vessels [1] and attacked them with the bravest of his gladiators. But gladiators have not the same steadfast courage in battle as regular soldiers, and now in their unsteady boats they could not shoot so accurately as the Germans, who had firm footing on the shore; and when the gladiators in their fright began to move about in confusion so that rowers and fighters were commingled and got in one another's way, the Germans actually jumped into the shallow water, held back the boats, and boarded them, or sank them with their hands. All this went on under the eyes of both armies, and the keener the delight it gave the Vitellians, the greater the indignation which Otho's followers felt toward Macer, who was the cause and author of their defeat.

XXXVI. In fact the battle ended in flight, after the gladiators had succeeded in dragging off the boats that were left. Then they began to clamour for Macer's life. Wounded as he was by a lance thrown from a distance, they had already attacked him with drawn swords, when he was saved by the

centurionumque protegitur. Nec multo post Vestricius Spurinna iussu Othonis, relicto Placentiae modico praesidio, cum cohortibus subvenit. Dein Flavium Sabinum consulem designatum Otho rectorem copiis misit, quibus Macer praefuerat, laeto milite ad[1] mutationem ducum et ducibus ob crebras seditiones tam infestam militiam aspernantibus.

XXXVII. Invenio apud quosdam auctores pavore belli seu fastidio utriusque principis, quorum flagitia ac dedecus apertiore in dies fama noscebantur, dubitasse exercitus num posito certamine vel ipsi in medium consultarent, vel senatui permitterent legere imperatorem, atque eo duces Othonianos spatium ac moras suasisse, praecipua spe [2] Paulini, quod vetustissimus consularium[3] et militia clarus gloriam nomenque Britannicis expeditionibus meruisset. Ego ut concesserim apud paucos tacito voto quietem pro discordia, bonum et innocentem principem pro pessimis ac flagitiosissimis expetitum, ita neque Paulinum, qua prudentia fuit, sperasse corruptissimo saeculo tantam vulgi moderationem reor ut qui pacem belli amore turbaverant, bellum pacis caritate deponerent, neque aut exercitus linguis moribusque dissonos in hunc consensum potuisse coalescere, aut legatos ac duces magna ex parte luxus egestatis scelerum sibi conscios

[1] milite et ad *M.*
[2] praecipua spe *Bipontini*: praecipuas *M.*
[3] consularium b^2 *et Rhenanus*: consiliarium *M.*

---

[1] Cf. i. 77.

intervention of the tribunes and centurions. Shortly after, at Otho's orders, Vestricius Spurinna left a small garrison at Placentia and came with his cohorts of auxiliaries. Then Otho sent Flavius Sabinus,[1] consul designate, to take command of Macer's forces. The soldiers were delighted at the change of generals, but the numerous mutinies had made the generals dislike so troublesome a command.

XXXVII. In certain authorities I find it stated that, prompted by their fear of war or by their disgust with both emperors, whose shameful wickedness was becoming better known and more notorious every day, the armies debated whether they should not give up fighting and either consult together themselves or allow the senate to choose an emperor. This, it is urged, was the reason why the generals on Otho's side advised delay, and it is said that Paulinus had great hope of being chosen, since he was the senior ex-consul and by his distinguished service had won fame and reputation in his British campaigns. Now while I can grant that there were a few who silently prayed for peace instead of civil strife, and who wished a good and upright emperor instead of the worst rascals alive, still I do not believe that Paulinus, with his practical good sense, ever hoped for such moderation on the part of the people in that most corrupt age that the very men whose passion for war had destroyed peace would now abandon war from love of peace. Nor can I think that the two armies, whose habits and speech were so different, could ever have come to such an agreement or that the lieutenants and generals, most of whom were well aware of their own extravagance, poverty, and crimes, would ever have endured an

nisi pollutum obstrictumque meritis suis principem passuros.

XXXVIII. Vetus ac iam pridem insita mortalibus potentiae cupido cum imperii magnitudine adolevit erupitque ; nam rebus modicis aequalitas facile habebatur. Sed ubi subacto orbe et aemulis urbibus regibusve excisis securas opes concupiscere vacuum fuit, prima inter patres plebemque certamina exarsere. Modo turbulenti tribuni, modo consules praevalidi, et in urbe ac foro temptamenta civilium bellorum ; mox e plebe infima C. Marius et nobilium saevissimus L. Sulla victam armis libertatem in dominationem verterunt. Post quos Cn. Pompeius occultior non melior, et numquam postea nisi de principatu quaesitum. Non discessere ab armis in Pharsalia ac Philippis civium legiones, nedum Othonis ac Vitellii exercitus sponte posituri bellum fuerint: eadem illos deum ira, eadem hominum rabies, eaedem scelerum causae in discordiam egere. Quod singulis velut ictibus transacta sunt bella, ignavia principum factum est. Sed me veterum novorumque morum reputatio longius tulit: nunc ad rerum ordinem venio.

XXXIX. Profecto Brixellum Othone honor imperii penes Titianum fratrem, vis ac potestas penes

---

[1] The tribunes Tiberius and Gaius Gracchus, Saturninus, and Drusus, the consuls Appius Claudius and Lucius Opimius are probably meant.

emperor unless he was foul with vice and under obligations to them.

XXXVIII. The old greed for power, long ingrained in mankind, came to full growth and broke bounds as the empire became great. When resources were moderate, equality was easily maintained; but when the world had been subjugated and rival states or kings destroyed, so that men were free to covet wealth without anxiety, then the first quarrels between patricians and plebeians broke out. Now the tribunes made trouble, again the consuls usurped too much power;[1] in the city and forum the first essays at civil war were made. Later Gaius Marius, who had sprung from the dregs of the people, and that most cruel of nobles, Lucius Sulla, defeated liberty with arms and turned it into tyranny. After them came Gnaeus Pompey, no better man than they, but one who concealed his purpose more cleverly; and thenceforth there was never any aim but supreme power. The legions made up of Roman citizens did not lay down their arms at Pharsalia or Philippi; much less were the armies of Otho and Vitellius likely to abandon war voluntarily. The same divine wrath, the same human madness, the same motives to crime drove them on to strife. The fact that these wars were ended by a single blow, so to speak, was due to the worthlessness of the emperors. However, my reflections on the character of antiquity and of modern times have taken me too far afield; now I return to my narrative.

XXXIX. When Otho left for Brixellum the nominal command fell to his brother Titianus, but the real authority was in the hands of the prefect

Proculum praefectum; Celsus et Paulinus, cum prudentia eorum nemo uteretur, inani nomine ducum alienae culpae praetendebantur; tribuni centurionesque ambigui quod spretis melioribus deterrimi valebant; miles alacer, qui tamen iussa ducum interpretari quam exequi mallet. Promoveri ad quartum a Bedriaco castra placuit, adeo imperite ut quamquam verno tempore anni et tot circum amnibus[1] penuria aquae fatigarentur. Ibi de proelio dubitatum, Othone per litteras flagitante ut maturarent, militibus ut imperator pugnae adesset poscentibus: plerique copias trans Padum agentis acciri postulabant. Nec proinde diiudicari potest quid optimum factu fuerit, quam pessimum fuisse quod factum est.

XL. Non ut ad pugnam sed ad bellandum profecti confluentis Padi et Aduae fluminum, sedecim inde milium spatio distantis, petebant. Celso et Paulino abnuentibus militem itinere fessum, sarcinis gravem obicere hosti, non omissuro quo minus expeditus et vix quattuor milia passuum progressus aut incompositos in agmine aut dispersos et vallum molientis adgrederetur, Titianus et Proculus, ubi consiliis vincerentur, ad ius imperii transibant. Aderat sane

[1] manibus *M*.

[1] The Adda to-day. Since the march as here described would have exposed Otho's troops to a flank attack, Mommsen and others have doubted the accuracy of this account.

Proculus. As for Celsus and Paulinus, no one made any use of their practical knowledge; with the empty title of generals they only served to cloak the faults of others. The tribunes and centurions knew not what to do, because the better men were thrust aside and the worst held the power; the soldiers were enthusiastic, but they preferred to criticize their generals' orders rather than to execute them. It was decided to move camp to the fourth milestone from Bedriacum, but the advance was made in such ignorance that, in spite of the fact that it was spring and there were many rivers all about them, the troops were distressed by lack of water. There they discussed the question of a battle, for Otho kept sending dispatches urging them to hurry, while the soldiers kept demanding that the emperor take part in the engagement; many insisted that the troops operating across the Po be called in. It is not so easy to decide what they should have done as it is to be sure that the action they took was the worst possible.

XL. Setting out as if they were starting on a campaign and not going into battle, they aimed to reach the confluence of the Po and the Adua,[1] sixteen miles away. Celsus and Paulinus refused to expose their soldiers, weary as they were with their march and weighed down with baggage, to the enemy, who, unencumbered with baggage, after marching hardly four miles, would not lose the opportunity to attack them either while in disorder on the march or while scattered and engaged in fortifying camp. Thereupon Titianus and Proculus, being defeated in council, sought refuge in the imperial authority. And it is true that a Numidian arrived

citus equo Numida cum atrocibus mandatis, quibus Otho increpita ducum segnitia rem in discrimen mitti iubebat, aeger mora et spei impatiens.

XLI. Eodem die ad Caecinam operi pontis intentum duo praetoriarum cohortium tribuni, conloquium eius postulantes, venerunt: audire condiciones ac reddere parabat, cum praecipites exploratores[1] adesse hostem nuntiavere. Interruptus tribunorum sermo, eoque incertum fuit insidias an proditionem vel aliquod honestum consilium coeptaverint. Caecina dimissis tribunis revectus in castra datum iussu Fabii Valentis pugnae signum et militem in armis invenit. Dum legiones de ordine agminis sortiuntur, equites prorupere; et mirum dictu, a paucioribus Othonianis quo minus in vallum inpingerentur, Italicae legionis virtute deterriti sunt: ea strictis[2] mucronibus redire pulsos et pugnam resumere coegit. Disposita Vitellianarum legionum acies[3] sine trepidatione: etenim quamquam vicino hoste aspectus armorum densis arbustis prohibebatur. Apud Othonianos pavidi duces, miles ducibus infensus, mixta vehicula et lixae, et praeruptis utrimque fossis via quieto quoque agmini angusta. Circumsistere alii signa sua, quae-

[1] Explora | adesse *M.*
[2] ea strictis *Rhenanus*: et astrictis *M.*
[3] acies *Lipsius*: arte *M.*

---

[1] Cf. ii. 34 f.

post-haste with imperative commands from Otho, who, sick of delay and too impatient to rest on hope, rebuked his generals for their inaction and ordered them to bring matters to an issue.

XLI. On the same day, while Caecina was busy with the construction of his bridge,[1] two tribunes of the praetorian cohorts came to him and asked for an interview. Caecina was preparing to hear their proposals and to make counter propositions when suddenly scouts reported that the enemy was upon them. The conversation with the tribunes was broken off, and so it remained uncertain whether they were attempting some plot or treachery, or rather had in mind some honest purpose. Caecina, dismissing the tribunes, rode back to camp, where he found that Fabius Valens had ordered the signal for battle to be given and that the troops were under arms. While the legions were casting lot for positions in the line, the cavalry charged, but, strange to relate, they were kept from being driven back within their entrenchments by an inferior force of Otho's troops only through the courageous action of the Italian legion. This at the point of the sword compelled the beaten cavalry to wheel about and renew the battle. The legions of Vitellius formed in line without disorder, for although the enemy were close by, dense thickets made it impossible to see their arms. On Otho's side the generals were nervous, the soldiers disaffected towards the generals, wagons and camp-followers were mixed in confusion with the troops; moreover, the road, with deep ditches on either side, was narrow even for an army which was advancing quietly. Some of the troops were gathered about their proper

rere alii; incertus undique clamor adcurrentium, vocantium: ut cuique audacia vel formido, in primam postremamve aciem prorumpebant aut relabebantur.

XLII. Attonitas subito terrore mentis falsum gaudium in languorem vertit, repertis qui descivisse a Vitellio exercitum ementirentur. Is rumor ab exploratoribus Vitellii dispersus, an in ipsa Othonis parte seu dolo seu forte surrexerit, parum compertum. Omisso pugnae ardore Othoniani ultro salutavere; et hostili murmure excepti, plerisque suorum ignaris quae causa salutandi, metum proditionis fecere. Tum incubuit hostium acies, integris ordinibus, robore et numero praestantior: Othoniani, quamquam dispersi, pauciores, fessi, proelium tamen acriter sumpsere. Et per locos arboribus ac vineis impeditos non una pugnae facies: comminus eminus, catervis et cuneis concurrebant. In aggere viae conlato gradu corporibus et umbonibus niti, omisso pilorum iactu gladiis[1] et securibus galeas loricasque perrumpere: noscentes inter se, ceteris conspicui, in eventum totius belli certabant.

XLIII. Forte inter Padum viamque patenti campo

[1] gladibus *M*[1], cladibus *M*.

---

[1] That is, on the raised causeway of the Via Postumia, the high road on the left bank of the Po. Cf. ii. 24

standards, others were hunting to find theirs. From every side rose confused shouts of those running to their places or calling their comrades; soldiers rushed to the front or slunk to the rear as courage or fear prompted in each case.

XLII. The sudden consternation and fright of Otho's men were changed to indifference by an unwarranted joy, for some men were found who spread the false report that the army of Vitellius had deserted him. It was never discovered whether this rumour was spread by Vitellian scouts or whether it started on Otho's side through treachery or by chance. In any case Otho's men lost all enthusiasm for battle and actually cheered their foes; but the Vitellians received their cheers with hostile murmurings, and this made Otho's men fear treachery, for most of them did not know the reason for the cheering. Then the Vitellians charged: their lines were intact; they were superior in strength and in numbers. However, Otho's troops put up a brave resistance in spite of their disordered ranks, their inferior numbers, and their fatigue. The fact that in places the ground was encumbered by trees and vineyards gave the battle many aspects: the troops fought now hand to hand, again at a distance; they charged now in detachments, again in column. On the raised road[1] they struggled at close quarters, pressing with the weight of their bodies behind their shields; they threw no spears, but crashed swords and axes through helmets and breastplates. They could recognize one another, they could be seen by all the rest, and they were fighting to decide the issue of the whole war.

XLIII. In the open plain between the Po and

duae legiones congressae sunt, pro Vitellio unaetvicensima cui cognomen Rapaci, vetere gloria insignis, e parte Othonis prima Adiutrix, non ante in aciem deducta, sed ferox et novi decoris avida. Primani stratis unaetvicensimanorum[1] principiis aquilam abstulere; quo dolore accensa legio et impulit rursus primanos, interfecto Orfidio Benigno legato, et plurima signa vexillaque ex hostibus rapuit. A parte alia propulsa quintanorum impetu tertia decima legio, circumventi plurium adcursu quartadecimani. Et ducibus Othonis iam pridem profugis Caecina ac Valens subsidiis suos firmabant. Accessit recens auxilium, Varus[2] Alfenus cum Batavis, fusa gladiatorum manu, quam navibus transvectam obpositae cohortes in ipso flumine trucidaverant: ita victores latus hostium invecti.

XLIV. Et media acie perrupta fugere passim Othoniani, Bedriacum petentes. Immensum id spatium, obstructae strage corporum viae, quo plus caedis fuit; neque enim civilibus bellis capti in praedam vertuntur. Suetonius Paulinus et Licinius Proculus diversis itineribus castra vitavere. Vedium Aquilam tertiae decimae legionis legatum irae militum inconsultus pavor obtulit. Multo adhuc die vallum ingressus clamore seditiosorum et fugacium circum-

[1] unę et vicensimamorum *M*.
[2] Varus *Rhenanus*: varenus *M*.

---

[1] "The Invincibles," from Upper Germany.
[2] "The Helpers," made up of the marines. Cf. i. 6.
[3] From Lower Germany. Cf. i. 61.
[4] From Pannonia. Cf. ii. 24.
[5] Somewhere between twelve and sixteen Roman miles.
[6] Plutarch, *Otho* xiv. makes a similar remark. Dio Cassius (lxiv. 10) says that a total of over 40,000 fell in this battle.

the road two legions happened to engage. On the side of Vitellius was the Twenty-first, also called the Rapax,[1] a legion long renowned; on Otho's was the First Adjutrix[2] which had never been in an engagement before, but which was enthusiastic and eager to win its first success. The First cut down the front ranks of the Twenty-first and captured their eagle; thereupon shame at this loss so fired the Twenty-first that they drove back the First, killed their commander, Orfidius Benignus, and captured many colours and standards. In another part of the field the Fifth[3] charged and routed the Thirteenth[4] legion; the Fourteenth was surrounded by a superior force which attacked it. Otho's generals had long before fled. Caecina and Valens began to strengthen their forces by bringing up reserves; and a new reinforcement came when Varus Alfenus arrived with the Batavians. They had routed the gladiators who had crossed the river in boats, by meeting them with cohorts which cut them down while still in the water. So in the full flush of victory they assailed the enemy's flank.

XLIV. The Othonians' centre was now broken and they fled in disorder, making for Bedriacum. The distance to be covered was vast;[5] the roads were blocked with dead, and so the carnage was greater: for in civil wars captives are not turned to profit.[6] Suetonius Paulinus and Licinius Proculus took different roads and avoided the camp. Vedius Aquila, commander of the Thirteenth legion, was so terrified that he thoughtlessly exposed himself to the angry troops. It was still broad day when he entered camp and was surrounded by a shouting mob of mutinous fugitives. They spared no insult or

strepitur; non probris, non manibus abstinent; desertorem proditoremque increpant, nullo proprio crimine eius sed more vulgi suum quisque flagitium aliis obiectantes. Titianum et Celsum nox iuvit, dispositis iam excubiis conpressisque militibus, quos Annius Gallus consilio precibus auctoritate flexerat, ne super cladem adversae pugnae suismet ipsi caedibus saevirent: sive finis bello venisset seu resumere arma mallent, unicum victis in consensu levamentum. Ceteris fractus animus: praetorianus miles non virtute se sed proditione victum fremebat: ne Vitellianis quidem incruentam fuisse victoriam, pulso equite, rapta legionis aquila; superesse cum ipso Othone militum quod trans Padum fuerit, venire Moesicas legiones, magnam exercitus partem Bedriaci remansisse: hos certe nondum victos et, si ita ferret, honestius in acie perituros. His cogitationibus truces aut pavidi extrema desperatione ad iram saepius quam in formidinem stimulabantur.

XLV. At Vitellianus exercitus ad quintum a Bedriaco lapidem consedit, non ausis ducibus eadem die obpugnationem castrorum; simul voluntaria deditio sperabatur: sed expeditis et tantum ad proelium egressis munimentum fuere arma et

---

[1] Gallus had remained in camp (ii. 33), and therefore was not blamed by the soldiers.

[2] That is, without their trenching tools and stakes for building a rampart.

violence; they greeted him with cries of "deserter" and "traitor," not because of any crime of his own, but, after the habit of mobs, every man imputed to him his own shame. Night assisted Titianus and Celsus, for Annius Gallus[1] had already placed sentinels and got the soldiers under control. By advice, appeals, and commands he had induced the men not to add to the cruelty of their defeat by massacring their own leaders; he urged that whether the end of the war had come or whether they preferred to resume hostilities, their sole resource in defeat lay in concord. The spirit of the rest was broken; but the praetorians angrily declared that they had been defeated by treachery, not by the valour of their foes. "The troops of Vitellius," they maintained, "have not won a bloodless victory; we routed their cavalry, and captured the legion's eagle. Otho and the force with him on the other side of the Po are still left us; the legions from Moesia are on their way hither; a large part of the army is still at Bedriacum. These surely have not been defeated, and, if occasion require, they will consider it more honourable to die in open battle." Such reflections now roused them to exasperation, or again depressed them; in their utter despair they were more often goaded to fury than to fear.

XLV. But the army of Vitellius halted at the fifth milestone from Bedriacum, for the commanders did not dare to try to carry their opponents' camp by storm on the same day; and at the same time they hoped that Otho's troops would surrender voluntarily; but, although they had set out without their heavy equipment,[2] and with no other purpose than to give battle, their arms and their victory served

victoria. Postera die haud ambigua Othoniani exercitus voluntate et qui ferociores fuerant ad paenitentiam inclinantibus missa legatio; nec apud duces Vitellianos dubitatum quo minus pacem concederent. Legati paulisper retenti: ea res haesitationem attulit ignaris adhuc an impetrassent. Mox remissa legatione patuit vallum. Tum victi victoresque in lacrimas effusi, sortem civilium armorum misera laetitia detestantes; isdem tentoriis alii fratrum, alii propinquorum vulnera fovebant; spes et praemia in ambiguo, certa funera et luctus, nec quisquam adeo mali expers ut non aliquam mortem maereret. Requisitum Orfidii legati corpus honore solito crematur; paucos necessarii ipsorum sepelivere, ceterum vulgus super humum relictum.

XLVI. Opperiebatur Otho nuntium pugnae nequaquam trepidus et consilii certus. Maesta primum fama, dein profugi e proelio perditas res patefaciunt. Non expectavit militum ardor vocem imperatoris; bonum haberet animum iubebant: superesse adhuc novas viris, et ipsos extrema passuros ausurosque. Neque erat adulatio: ire in aciem, excitare partium fortunam furore quodam et instinctu flagrabant. Qui procul adstiterant,[1] tendere manus, et proximi

[1] astiterant *M.*

---

[1] At Brixellum. Cf. ii. 33 39.

them as a rampart. The next day the wishes of Otho's troops were clear beyond doubt; even those who had been most determined were inclined to change their views. Accordingly they sent a deputation, and the generals of Vitellius did not long hesitate to grant terms. But the deputation was detained for a time, and this action disturbed those who did not know whether they had secured terms or not; presently, however, the delegates were let go and the gates of the camp were opened. Then vanquished and victors alike burst into tears, cursing, amid their melancholy joy, the fate of civil war. In the same tents some nursed the wounds of brothers, others of relatives. Their hopes of reward were doubtful; but they knew for certainties the bereavements and sorrows that they suffered, and none of them was so free from misfortune as not to mourn some loss. The body of the legate Orfidius was discovered and burned with the usual honours, a few others were buried by their relatives, but the majority of the fallen were left lying on the ground.

XLVI. Otho was waiting[1] for a report of the battle without anxiety and with determined purpose. First there came a distressing rumour; then fugitives from the field showed clearly that the day was lost. But the troops in their zeal did not wait for the emperor to speak; they urged him to keep up his courage, for there were fresh troops left; and they declared that they were ready themselves to dare and suffer anything. Nor was this flattery: they were fired by an almost passionate desire to go into action and raise again the fortunes of their party. The soldiers who were not near him stretched out their hands to him appealingly, those near him

prensare genua, promptissimo Plotio Firmo. Is praetorii praefectus identidem orabat ne fidissimum exercitum, ne optime meritos milites desereret: maiore animo tolerari adversa quam relinqui; fortis et strenuos etiam contra fortunam insistere spei, timidos et ignavos ad desperationem formidine properare. Quas inter voces ut flexerat vultum aut induraverat Otho, clamor et gemitus. Nec praetoriani tantum, proprius[1] Othonis miles, sed praemissi e Moesia eandem obstinationem adventantis exercitus, legiones Aquileiam ingressas nuntiabant, ut nemo dubitet potuisse renovari bellum atrox, lugubre, incertum victis et victoribus.

XLVII. Ipse aversus a consiliis belli "hunc" inquit "animum, hanc virtutem vestram ultra periculis obicere nimis grande vitae meae pretium puto. Quanto plus spei ostenditis, si vivere placeret, tanto pulchrior mors erit. Experti in vicem sumus ego ac fortuna. Nec tempus conputaveritis: difficilius est temperare felicitati qua te non putes diu usurum. Civile bellum a Vitellio coepit, et ut de principatu certaremus armis initium illic fuit: ne plus quam semel certemus penes me exemplum erit; hinc

[1] propius *M*.

clasped his knees. The most zealous of all was Plotius Firmus, the prefect of the praetorian guard, who constantly begged him not to fail an army which was absolutely loyal, and soldiers who had served him so well. He reminded Otho that it called for greater courage to endure adversity than to yield to it; that brave and courageous men press on even against ill fortune to attain their hopes; the timid and cowardly are quickly moved to despair by fear. During these appeals the soldiers cheered or broke into groans as Otho's face showed signs of giving way to their appeals or grew hard. The praetorians, Otho's personal force, were not the only ones who encouraged him. The advance detachments from Moesia declared that the troops which were on their way were just as determined, and they reported that the legions had entered Aquileia, so that no one can doubt that it would have been quite possible to renew this cruel and awful war, with uncertain results for both the victors and the vanquished.

XLVII. Otho himself was opposed to the plan of continuing the war. "To expose such courageous and brave men as you to further dangers," he said, "I reckon too great a price for my life. The greater the hope you offer me, if it were my wish to live, so much the more glorious will be my death. Fortune and I know each other well. Do not reckon up the short duration of my rule; it is all the harder to make a moderate use of a good fortune which you do not expect to enjoy long. Vitellius began civil war; it was he who initiated the armed contest between us for the imperial power; but we shall not contend more than once, for it is in my power to set a precedent for that. I would have posterity thus

Othonem posteritas aestimet. Fruetur Vitellius fratre, coniuge, liberis: mihi non ultione neque solaciis opus est. Alii diutius imperium tenuerint, nemo tam fortiter reliquerit. An ego tantum Romanae pubis, tot egregios exercitus sterni rursus et rei publicae eripi patiar? Eat hic mecum animus, tamquam perituri pro me fueritis, set este superstites. Nec diu moremur, ego incolumitatem vestram, vos constantiam meam. Plura de extremis loqui pars ignaviae est. Praecipuum destinationis meae documentum habete quod de nemine queror; nam incusare deos vel homines eius est qui vivere velit."

XLVIII. Talia locutus, ut cuique aetas aut dignitas, comiter appellatos, irent propere neu remanendo iram victoris asperarent, iuvenes auctoritate, senes precibus movebat, placidus ore, intrepidus verbis, intempestivas suorum lacrimas coercens. Dari navis ac vehicula abeuntibus iubet; libellos epistulasque studio erga se aut in Vitellium contumeliis insignis abolet; pecunias distribuit parce nec ut[1] periturus. Mox Salvium Cocceianum, fratris filium, prima iuventa, trepidum et maerentem ultro solatus est, laudando pietatem eius, castigando formidinem: an Vitellium tam inmitis animi fore ut pro incolumi tota domo ne hanc quidem sibi gratiam redderet? Mereri se festinato exitu clementiam victoris; non

[1] ne cui *M*.

---

[1] Cocceianus was Titianus's son. He was later put to death by Domitian for celebrating Otho's birthday.

[2] Otho had left unharmed the mother and children of Vitellius. Cf. i. 75.

judge Otho. Vitellius shall enjoy his brother, his wife, and his children; I require neither vengeance nor solace. Others may hold the power longer than I; none shall give it up more bravely. Would you have me suffer so many of Rome's young men, such noble armies, to be again cut down and lost to the state? Let me carry with me the thought of your willingness to die for me; but you must live. Now there must be no more delay; let me not interfere with your safety, or you with my determination. To talk at length about the end is cowardice. Regard as the chief proof of my resolve the fact that I complain of no man. It is for him to blame gods or men who has the wish to live."

XLVIII. After Otho had spoken thus, he addressed all courteously as befitted the age or rank of the individual, and urged them to go quickly and not to incite the victor's wrath by remaining. The young men he persuaded by his authority, the older by his appeals; his face was calm, his words showed no fear; but he checked the unseasonable tears of his friends. He gave orders that boats and carriages should be furnished those who were leaving. Every document or letter which was marked by loyalty towards him or by abuse of Vitellius he destroyed. He distributed money, but sparingly and not as if he were about to die. Then he took pains to console his nephew, Salvius Cocceianus,[1] who was very young, frightened, and sad, praising his dutiful affection, but reproving his fear. He asked him if he thought Vitellius would prove so cruel as not to grant him even such a return as this for saving his whole house.[2] "By my quick end," said he, "I can earn the clemency of the victor. For it is not

enim ultima desperatione sed poscente proelium exercitu remisisse rei publicae novissimum casum. Satis sibi nominis, satis posteris suis nobilitatis quaesitum. Post Iulios Claudios Servios se primum in familiam novam imperium intulisse: proinde erecto animo capesseret vitam, neu patruum sibi Othonem fuisse aut oblivisceretur umquam aut nimium meminisset.

XLIX. Post quae dimotis omnibus paulum requievit. Atque illum supremas iam curas animo volutantem repens tumultus avertit, nuntiata consternatione ac licentia militum; namque abeuntibus exitium minitabantur, atrocissima in Verginium vi, quem clausa domo obsidebant. Increpitis seditionis auctoribus regressus vacavit abeuntium adloquiis, donec omnes inviolati digrederentur. Vesperascente die sitim haustu gelidae aquae sedavit. Tum adlatis pugionibus duobus, cum utrumque pertemptasset, alterum capiti subdidit. Et explorato iam profectos amicos, noctem quietam, utque adfirmatur, non insomnem egit: luce prima in ferrum pectore incubuit. Ad gemitum morientis ingressi liberti servique et Plotius Firmus praetorii praefectus unum vulnus invenere. Funus maturatum; ambitiosis id precibus petierat ne amputaretur caput ludibrio futurum. Tulere corpus praetoriae cohortes cum laudibus et

---

[1] Consul Suffectus at this time (cf. i. 77); he was later victorious over Vindex.

[2] The date was April 16.

in the extremity of despair, but while my army is still demanding battle that I have saved the state this last misfortune. I have won enough fame for myself, enough high rank for my descendants. After the Julii, the Claudii, and the Servii, I have been the first to confer the imperial rank on a new family. Therefore face life with a brave heart; never forget or too constantly remember that Otho was your uncle."

XLIX. After this he sent all away and rested for a time. As he was already pondering in his heart the last cares of life, he was interrupted by a sudden uproar and received word that the soldiers in their dismay had become mutinous and were out of control. In fact they were threatening with death all who wished to depart; they were most violent against Verginius,[1] whom they had shut up in his house and were now besieging. Otho reproved the ringleaders and then returned to his quarters, where he gave himself up to interviews with those who were departing, until all had left unharmed. As evening approached he slaked his thirst with a draught of cold water. Then two daggers were brought him; he tried the points of both and placed one beneath his head. After learning that his friends had gone, he passed a quiet night, and indeed, as is affirmed, he even slept somewhat. At dawn he fell on the steel.[2] At the sound of his dying groans his freedmen and slaves entered, and with them Plotius Firmus, the prefect of the praetorian guard; they found but a single wound. His funeral was hurriedly accomplished. He had earnestly begged that this be done, that his head might not be cut off to be an object of insult. Praetorians bore his body to the

lacrimis, vulnus manusque eius exosculantes. Quidam militum iuxta rogum interfecere se, non noxa neque ob metum, sed aemulatione decoris et caritate principis. Ac postea promisce Bedriaci, Placentiae aliisque in castris celebratum id genus mortis. Othoni sepulchrum extructum est modicum et mansurum. Hunc vitae finem habuit septimo et tricensimo aetatis anno.

L. Origo illi e municipio Ferentino,[1] pater consularis, avus praetorius; maternum genus impar nec tamen indecorum. Pueritia ac iuventa, qualem monstravimus. Duobus facinoribus, altero flagitiosissimo, altero egregio, tantundem apud posteros meruit bonae famae quantum malae. Ut conquirere fabulosa et fictis oblectare legentium animos procul gravitate coepti operis crediderim, ita vulgatis traditisque demere fidem non ausim. Die, quo Bedriaci certabatur, avem invisitata specie apud Regium Lepidum celebri luco consedisse incolae memorant, nec deinde coetu hominum aut circumvolitantium alitum territam pulsamve, donec Otho se ipse interficeret; tum ablatam ex oculis: et tempora reputantibus initium finemque miraculi cum Othonis exitu competisse.

LI. In funere eius novata luctu ac dolore militum

[1] Ferentino *Puteolanus:* ferentio *M.*

---

[1] In southern Etruria; Ferento to-day.

[2] His mother, Albia Ferentia, sprang from an equestrian family.

[3] The murder of Galba and his own suicide.

[4] Reggio, between Modena and Parma.

pyre, praising him amid their tears and kissing his wound and his hands. Some soldiers slew themselves near his pyre, not because of any fault or from fear, but prompted by a desire to imitate his glorious example and moved by affection for their emperor. Afterwards many of every rank chose this form of death at Bedriacum, Placentia, and in other camps as well. The tomb erected for Otho was modest, and therefore likely to endure. So he ended his life in the thirty-seventh year of his age.

L. Otho was born in the municipal town of Ferentinum[1]; his father had held the consulship, his grandfather had been praetor. His mother's family was not the equal of his father's, but still it was respectable.[2] His boyhood and youth were such as we have already described. By two bold deeds, the one most outrageous, the other glorious,[3] he gained with posterity as much fame as evil reputation. While I must hold it inconsistent with the dignity of the work I have undertaken to collect fabulous tales and to delight my readers with fictitious stories, I cannot, however, dare to deny the truth of common tradition. On the day of the battle at Bedriacum, according to the account given by the people of that district, a bird of unusual appearance settled in a much-frequented grove near Regium Lepidum,[4] and neither the concourse of people nor the other birds which flew about it frightened it or drove it away, until Otho had committed suicide; then it disappeared from view. And they add that when people reckoned up the time, they found that the beginning and end of this marvel coincided with Otho's death.

LI. At his funeral the soldiers' grief and sorrow

seditio, nec erat qui coerceret. Ad Verginium versi, modo ut reciperet imperium, nunc ut legatione apud Caecinam ac Valentem fungeretur, minitantes orabant: Verginius per aversam domus partem furtim digressus inrumpentis[1] frustratus est. Earum quae Brixelli egerant cohortium preces Rubrius Gallus tulit, et venia[2] statim impetrata, concedentibus ad victorem per Flavium Sabinum iis copiis quibus praefuerat.

LII. Posito ubique bello magna pars senatus extremum discrimen adiit, profecta cum Othone ab urbe, dein Mutinae relicta. Illuc adverso de proelio adlatum: sed milites ut falsum rumorem aspernantes, quod infensum Othoni senatum arbitrabantur, custodire sermones, vultum habitumque trahere in deterius; conviciis postremo ac probris causam et initium caedis quaerebant, cum alius insuper metus senatoribus instaret, ne praevalidis iam Vitellii partibus cunctanter excepisse victoriam crederentur. Ita trepidi et utrimque anxii coeunt, nemo privatim expedito consilio, inter multos societate culpae tutior. Onerabat paventium curas ordo Mutinensis arma et pecuniam offerendo, appellabatque patres conscriptos intempestivo honore.

[1] degressus inrumpente *M.* [2] veniam *M.*

---

[1] Modena.

caused the mutiny to break out afresh, and there was no one to check it. The soldiers turned to Verginius and threateningly besought him, now to accept the imperial office, again to act as their envoy to Caecina and Valens. Verginius slipped away by stealth through the rear of his house and so escaped them when they burst in the doors. Rubrius Gallus brought the appeals of the cohorts who had been quartered at Brixellum. They were at once forgiven, and the troops that Flavius Sabinus had commanded made known through him their adhesion to the victor.

LII. Although fighting had now ceased at every point, a large part of the senate, which had set out from Rome with Otho and then been left at Mutina,[1] encountered extreme danger. News of the defeat was brought to Mutina; but the soldiers treated the report with scorn, believing it false, and since they thought the senate hostile to Otho, they began to watch the senators' conversation and to put an unfavourable interpretation on their looks and bearing. Finally, resorting to abuse and insults, they looked for an excuse to start a massacre, while in addition the senators were weighed down by the further fear that, now the party of Vitellius was dominant, they might be held to have been slow in accepting the victory. Thus they assembled, frightened and distressed by a double anxiety; none was ready with any plan of his own, but each felt the safer in sharing his guilt with many. The local senate of Mutina added to the distress of the terrified company by offering them arms and money, and with an untimely compliment addressed them as "Conscript Fathers."

LIII. Notabile iurgium[1] fuit quo Licinius Caecina Marcellum Eprium ut ambigua disserentem invasit. Nec ceteri sententias aperiebant: sed invisum memoria delationum expositumque ad invidiam Marcelli nomen inritaverat Caecinam, ut novus adhuc et in senatum nuper adscitus magnis inimicitiis claresceret. Moderatione meliorum dirempti. Et rediere omnes Bononiam, rursus consiliaturi; simul medio temporis plures nuntii sperabantur. Bononiae, divisis per itinera qui recentissimum quemque percontarentur,[2] interrogatus Othonis libertus[3] causam digressus habere se suprema eius mandata respondit; ipsum viventem quidem relictum, sed sola posteritatis cura et abruptis vitae blandimentis. Hinc admiratio et plura interrogandi pudor, atque omnium animi in Vitellium inclinavere.

LIV. Intererat consiliis frater eius L. Vitellius seque iam adulantibus offerebat, cum repente Coenus libertus Neronis atroci mendacio universos perculit, adfirmans superventu quartae decimae legionis, iunctis a Brixello viribus, caesos victores; versam partium fortunam. Causa fingendi fuit ut diplomata Othonis, quae neglegebantur, laetiore nuntio revalescerent. Et Coenus quidem raptim in[4] urbem

[1] iurgium *Bekker*: virgenium *M*.
[2] percunctaretur *M*.
[3] Imbertus *M*.
[4] raptim in *I. Gronovius*: rapidum *M*.

---

[1] Eprius had laid information against Thrasea and gained 5,000,000 sesterces thereby. *Ann.* xvi. 22, 28, 33 and cf. *Hist.* iv. 6.
[2] Bologna.
[3] *Diplomata* that secured post-horses, lodging, etc.

LIII. There was a remarkable quarrel when Licinius Caecina attacked Marcellus Eprius for making ambiguous proposals. Yet the other senators did not disclose their opinions; but the name of Marcellus was hateful and exposed to odium, because men remembered that he had been an informer[1]; it consequently roused in Caecina, who was a new man, recently enrolled in the senate, a desire to win fame by making enemies of the great. The two were separated, however, by the moderate and wiser senators. They all returned to Bononia[2] to take counsel together again there; and they also hoped for fuller news in the meantime. At Bononia they posted men on the different roads to question every newcomer. One of Otho's freedmen who was asked why he had left, replied that he had Otho's last commands. He also said that Otho was still alive when he left, but that his sole anxiety was for posterity and that he had rejected all the allurements of life. This answer filled the senators with admiration and made them ashamed to question further; and then the hearts of all inclined toward Vitellius

LIV. His brother Lucius Vitellius was now sharing their councils and was already offering himself as an object of their flattery, when suddenly Coenus, one of Nero's freedmen, by a bold falsehood succeeded in terrifying them all. He declared that by the arrival of the Fourteenth legion and by its union with the forces from Brixellum, the victors had been crushed and the fortune of the two parties reversed. He had invented this tale to secure by such good news a renewed validity for Otho's passports[3] which were being disregarded. Now Coenus

vectus paucos post dies iussu Vitellii poenas luit: senatorum periculum auctum credentibus Othonianis militibus vera esse quae adferebantur. Intendebat formidinem quod publici consilii facie discessum Mutina desertaeque partes forent. Nec ultra in commune congressi sibi quisque consuluere, donec missae a Fabio Valente epistulae demerent metum. Et mors Othonis quo laudabilior eo velocius audita.

LV. At Romae nihil trepidationis; Ceriales ludi ex more spectabantur. Ut cessisse Othonem et a Flavio Sabino praefecto urbis quod erat in urbe militum sacramento Vitellii adactum certi auctores in theatrum attulerunt, Vitellio plausere; populus cum lauru ac floribus Galbae imagines circum templa tulit, congestis in modum tumuli coronis iuxta lacum Curtii, quem locum Galba moriens sanguine infecerat. In senatu cuncta longis aliorum principatibus composita statim decernuntur; additae erga Germanicum exercitum[1] laudes gratesque et missa legatio quae gaudio fungeretur. Recitatae Fabii Valentis epistulae ad consules scriptae haud immoderate: gratior Caecinae modestia fuit quod non scripsisset.

LVI. Ceterum Italia gravius atque atrocius quam bello adflictabatur. Dispersi per municipia et colonias

[1] exercitum *Ritter*: exercitus *M*.

---

[1] April 12–19.
[2] Vespasian's brother.
[3] Cf. i. 41.
[4] Only the highest officials were expected to address the consuls or the senate.

hurried to Rome, where a few days later, at the orders of Vitellius, he paid the penalty due; the senators, however, were in still greater danger, for Otho's soldiers believed that the story was the truth. Their alarm was increased also by the fact that their departure from Mutina and their abandonment of Otho's cause had the appearance of a formal and public act. They no longer met together, but each took thought for his own safety until letters from Fabius Valens did away with their fears. Moreover the laudable character of Otho's death made the news of it spread all the quicker.

LV. Yet at Rome there was no disorder. The festival of Ceres[1] was celebrated in the usual manner. When it was announced in the theatre on good authority that Otho was no more and that Flavius Sabinus,[2] the city prefect, had administered to all the soldiers in the city the oath of allegiance to Vitellius, the audience greeted the name of Vitellius with applause. The people, bearing laurel and flowers, carried busts of Galba from temple to temple, and piled garlands high in the form of a burial mound by the *Lacus Curtius*,[3] which the dying Galba had stained with his blood. The senate at once voted for Vitellius all the honours that had been devised during the long reigns of other emperors; besides they passed votes of praise and gratitude to the troops from Germany and dispatched a delegation to deliver this expression of their joy. Letters from Fabius Valens to the consuls were read, written in quite moderate style; but greater satisfaction was felt at Caecina's modesty in not writing at all.[4]

LVI. But the distress of Italy was now heavier and more terrible than that inflicted by war. The troops

Vitelliani spoliare, rapere, vi et stupris polluere: in omne fas[1] nefasque avidi aut venales non sacro, non profano abstinebant. Et fuere qui inimicos suos specie militum interficerent; ipsique milites regionum gnari refertos agros, ditis dominos in praedam aut, si repugnatum foret, ad exitium destinabant, obnoxiis ducibus et prohibere non ausis. Minus avaritiae in Caecina, plus ambitionis: Valens ob lucra et quaestus infamis eoque alienae etiam culpae dissimulator. Iam pridem attritis Italiae rebus tantum peditum equitumque, vis damnaque et iniuriae aegre tolerabantur.

LVII. Interim Vitellius victoriae suae nescius ut ad integrum bellum reliquas Germanici exercitus viris trahebat. Pauci veterum militum in hibernis relicti, festinatis per Gallias dilectibus, ut remanentium legionum nomina supplerentur. Cura ripae Hordeonio Flacco permissa; ipse e Britannico exercitu[2] delecta octo milia sibi adiunxit. Et paucorum dierum iter progressus prosperas apud Bedriacum res ac morte Othonis concidisse bellum accepit: vocata contione virtutem militum laudibus cumulat. Postulante exercitu ut libertum suum Asiaticum

[1] omnelas *M.*

[2] exercitu *add. Heraeus.*

of Vitellius, scattering among the municipalities and colonies, indulged in every kind of robbery, theft, violence and debauchery. Their greed and venality knew no distinction between right and wrong; they respected nothing, whether sacred or profane. There were cases too where, under the disguise of soldiers, men murdered their personal enemies; and the soldiers in their turn, being acquainted with the country, marked out the best-stocked farms and the richest owners for booty or destruction, in case any resistance was made. The generals were subject to their troops and did not dare to forbid them. Caecina was less avaricious, but more eager for popularity; Valens, notorious for his greed and sordid gains, was more inclined to overlook the crimes of others. Italy, whose wealth had long before been exhausted, now found all these troops, foot and horse, all this violence, loss, and suffering, an intolerable burden.

LVII. In the meantime, Vitellius, quite ignorant of his success, was bringing with him all the remaining forces from Germany, as if he had to face a war whose issue was undecided. He had left only a few veterans in the winter quarters and was now hurrying forward levies in the Gallic provinces to fill up the empty ranks of the legions that were left behind. The duty of guarding the Rhine he assigned to Hordeonius Flaccus. He supplemented his own forces with eight thousand men picked from the army in Britain. After he had advanced a few days, he heard of the success at Bedriacum and learned that at Otho's death the war had collapsed; then he assembled his troops and spoke in the highest praise of his brave army. When his soldiers demanded that

equestri dignitate donaret, inhonestam adulationem conpescit; dein mobilitate ingenii, quod palam abnuerat, inter secreta convivii largitur, honoravitque Asiaticum anulis, foedum mancipium et malis artibus ambitiosum.

LVIII. Isdem diebus accessisse partibus utramque Mauretaniam, interfecto procuratore Albino, nuntii venere. Lucceius Albinus a Nerone Mauretaniae Caesariensi praepositus, addita per Galbam Tingitanae provinciae administratione, haud spernendis viribus agebat. Decem novem cohortes, quinque alae, ingens Maurorum numerus aderat, per latrocinia et raptus apta bello manus. Caeso Galba in Othonem pronus nec Africa contentus Hispaniae angusto freto diremptae imminebat. Inde Cluvio Rufo metus, et decimam legionem propinquare litori ut transmissurus iussit; praemissi centuriones qui Maurorum animos Vitellio conciliarent. Neque arduum fuit, magna per provincias Germanici exercitus fama; spargebatur insuper spreto procuratoris vocabulo Albinum insigne regis et Iubae nomen usurpare.

LIX. Ita mutatis animis Asinius Pollio alae praefectus, e fidissimis[1] Albino, et Festus ac Scipio

[1] et fidissimis *M.*

---

[1] Cf. ii. 95, and iv. 11.

[2] The province of Mauretania Caesariensis corresponded roughly to the western half of Algeria and eastern Morocco Mauretania Tingitana to western Morocco.

he give his freedman Asiaticus the rank of knight, he checked this shameful adulation ; but later, prompted by his fickle nature, in the privacy of a dinner he granted that which he had refused in public, and honoured with the golden ring this Asiaticus, a servile, shameful creature, who owed his popularity to his wicked arts.[1]

LVIII. During these days word arrived that both Mauretanias[2] had come over to the side of Vitellius after the imperial governor Albinus had been killed. Lucceius Albinus, who had been appointed governor of Mauretania Caesariensis by Nero, had been charged by Galba with the administration of the province of Tingitana as well, and had forces at his command which were not to be despised. Nineteen cohorts of infantry, five squadrons of cavalry were at his disposal as well as a great number of Mauri, forming a band which robbery and brigandage had trained for war. After the assassination of Galba, Albinus had favoured Otho, and not satisfied with Africa, began preparations to threaten Spain, which is separated from Africa by only a narrow strait. This action frightened Cluvius Rufus, and he ordered the Tenth legion to advance towards the coast as if he planned to transport it across ; and he dispatched centurions ahead to win the Mauri to the cause of Vitellius. This was not hard, for the army from Germany enjoyed a great reputation in the provinces ; besides, gossip spread the report that Albinus, despising the name of imperial governor, was adopting the insignia of royalty and the name of Juba.

LIX. The sentiments of the Mauretanians were changed, and this reversal of feeling led to the assassination of the prefect of the cavalry, Asinius Pollio,

cohortium praefecti opprimuntur : ipse Albinus dum e Tingitana provincia Caesariensem Mauretaniam petit,[1] adpulsu litoris trucidatus; uxor eius cum se percussoribus obtulisset, simul interfecta est, nihil eorum quae fierent Vitellio anquirente: brevi auditu quamvis [2] magna transibat, impar curis gravioribus.

Exercitum itinere terrestri pergere iubet: ipse Arare flumine devehitur, nullo principali paratu, sed vetere egestate conspicuus, donec Iunius Blaesus Lugudunensis Galliae rector, genere inlustri, largus animo et par opibus, circumdaret principi ministeria, comitaretur liberaliter, eo ipso ingratus, quamvis odium Vitellius vernilibus blanditiis velaret. Praesto fuere Luguduni victricium victarumque partium duces. Valentem et Caecinam pro contione laudatos curuli suae circumposuit. Mox universum exercitum occurrere infanti filio iubet, perlatumque et paludamento opertum sinu retinens Germanicum appellavit cinxitque cunctis fortunae principalis insignibus. Nimius honos inter secunda rebus adversis in solacium cessit.

LX. Tum interfecti sunt [3] centuriones promptissimi Othonianorum, unde praecipua in Vitellium alienatio per Illyricos exercitus; simul ceterae legiones con-

[1] petiti *M*: petit, in *Halm*.
[2] breve auditu vi quamvis *M*.
[3] interfecti sunt *Ritter*: interfectis *M*.

---

[1] Now six years of age.

one of the most devoted friends of Albinus, and of the commanders of the cohorts, Festus and Scipio. Albinus, who was trying to reach Mauretania Caesariensis by sea from Tingitana, was killed as he disembarked; his wife offered herself to the assassins and was slain with him. Vitellius made no investigation of all these acts; however important matters were, he dismissed them after a brief hearing; he was quite unequal to serious business.

His army he ordered to advance by land; but he himself sailed down the Arar, distinguished by no imperial show, but rather by the same poverty that he had displayed of old; until finally Junius Blaesus, governor of Gallia Lugudunensis—a man of illustrious family, whose wealth matched his liberal spirit,—surrounded him with all the service that an emperor should have and gave him generous escort, earning dislike by that very act, although the emperor concealed his hatred under servile flattery. At Lugudunum the generals of both sides, the victors and the defeated, awaited him. Vitellius spoke in praise of Valens and Caecina in public assembly and placed them on either side of his own curule chair. Then he ordered the entire army to parade before his infant son,[1] whom he brought out and, wrapping him in a general's cloak, held in his arms; he called him Germanicus, and surrounded him with all the attributes of imperial rank. These excessive honours in prosperity presently became a solace in misfortune.

LX. Then the centurions who had been most active in supporting Otho were put to death, an action which more than anything else turned the forces in Illyricum against Vitellius; at the same time the contagion spread to the rest of the legions,

tactu et adversus Germanicos milites invidia bellum meditabantur. Suetonium Paulinum ac Licinium Proculum tristi mora squalidos tenuit, donec auditi necessariis magis defensionibus quam honestis uterentur. Proditionem ultro imputabant, spatium longi ante proelium itineris, fatigationem Othonianorum, permixtum vehiculis agmen ac pleraque fortuita fraudi suae adsignantes. Et Vitellius credidit de perfidia et fidem absolvit. Salvius Titianus Othonis frater nullum discrimen adiit, pietate et ignavia excusatus. Mario Celso consulatus servatur: sed creditum fama obiectumque mox in senatu Caecilio Simplici, quod eum honorem[1] pecunia mercari, nec sine exitio Celsi, voluisset: restitit Vitellius deditque postea consulatum Simplici innoxium et inemptum. Trachalum adversus criminantis Galeria uxor Vitellii protexit.

LXI. Inter magnorum virorum discrimina, pudendum dictu, Mariccus quidam, e plebe Boiorum, inserere sese fortunae et provocare arma Romana simulatione numinum ausus est. Iamque adsertor Galliarum et deus (nam id sibi indiderat) concitis octo milibus hominum proximos Aeduorum pagos

[1] cum honore *M.*

---

[1] Cf. i. 77. [2] Cf. i. 90.
[3] The Boii lived between the Loire and the Allier.

who were jealous of the forces from Germany, and they began to think of war. Suetonius Paulinus and Licinius Proculus were kept in anxiety and distress by a long delay, until at last, when admitted to audience, they resorted to a defence which necessity rather than honour dictated: they actually charged themselves with treachery towards Otho, declaring that their own bad faith was responsible for the long march before the battle, for the exhaustion of his forces, for the baggage train becoming involved with the marching troops and the resulting confusion, and finally for many things which were due to mere chance. Vitellius believed in their treachery and acquitted them of the crime of loyalty towards Otho. Salvius Titianus, Otho's brother, was in no danger, being forgiven because of his duty towards his brother and his own incapacity. Marius Celsus did not lose his consulship.[1] But gossip, which was widely believed, gave rise to the charge made later in the senate against Caecilius Simplex to the effect that he had wished to purchase the consulship, even at the cost of the life of Celsus. Vitellius opposed this rumour and later gave Simplex a consulship which cost neither crime nor money. Trachalus was protected against his accusers by Galeria, the wife of Vitellius.[2]

LXI. While men of high distinction were thus endangered, it raises a blush to record how a certain Mariccus, a common Boian,[3] dared to take a hand in Fortune's game, and, pretending the authority of heaven, to challenge the Roman arms. And this liberator of the Gallic provinces, this god—for he had given himself that honour—after collecting eight thousand men, was already plundering the

trahebat, cum gravissima civitas electa iuventute, adiectis a Vitellio cohortibus, fanaticam multitudinem disiecit. Captus in eo proelio Mariccus; ac mox feris obiectus quia non laniabatur, stolidum vulgus inviolabilem credebat, donec spectante Vitellio interfectus est.

LXII. Nec ultra in defectores aut bona cuiusquam saevitum: rata fuere eorum qui acie Othoniana ceciderant, testamenta aut lex intestatis: prorsus, si luxuriae temperaret, avaritiam non timeres. Epularum foeda et inexplebilis libido: ex urbe atque Italia inritamenta gulae gestabantur, strepentibus ab utroque mari itineribus; exhausti conviviorum apparatibus principes civitatum; vastabantur ipsae civitates; degenerabat a labore ac virtute miles adsuetudine voluptatum et contemptu ducis. Praemisit in urbem edictum quo vocabulum Augusti differret, Caesaris non reciperet, cum de potestate nihil detraheret. Pulsi Italia mathematici; cautum severe ne equites Romani ludo et harena polluerentur. Priores id principes pecunia et saepius vi perpulerant, ac

---

[1] The capital was Augustodunum (Autun).
[2] Cf. i. 22.

Aeduan cantons nearest him, when that most important state,[1] with the best of its youth and the cohorts which Vitellius gave, dispersed the fanatic crowd. Mariccus was taken prisoner in the battle. Later, when he was exposed to the beasts and the animals did not rend him, the stupid rabble believed him inviolable, until he was executed before the eyes of Vitellius.

LXII. No other severe measures were taken against the rebels; there were no further confiscations. The wills of those who fell in Otho's ranks were allowed to stand, and if the soldiers died intestate, the law took its regular course. In fact, if Vitellius had only moderated his luxurious mode of life, there would have been no occasion to fear his avarice. But his passion for elaborate banquets was shameful and insatiate. Dainties to tempt his palate were constantly brought from Rome and all Italy, while the roads from both the Adriatic and Tyrrhenian seas hummed with hurrying vehicles. The preparation of banquets for him ruined the leading citizens of the communities through which he passed; the communities themselves were devastated; and his soldiers lost their energy and their valour as they became accustomed to pleasure and learned to despise their leader. Vitellius sent a proclamation to Rome in advance of his arrival, deferring the title *Augustus* and declining the name *Caesar,* although he rejected none of an emperor's powers. The astrologers[2] were banished from Italy; strict measures were taken to prevent Roman knights from degrading themselves in gladiatorial schools and the arena. Former emperors had driven knights to such actions by money or more often by

pleraque municipia et coloniae aemulabantur corruptissimum quemque adulescentium pretio inlicere.

LXIII. Sed Vitellius adventu fratris et inrepentibus dominationis magistris superbior et atrocior occidi Dolabellam iussit, quem in coloniam Aquinatem sepositum ab Othone rettulimus. Dolabella audita morte Othonis urbem introierat: id ei Plancius Varus praetura functus, ex intimis Dolabellae amicis, apud Flavium Sabinum praefectum urbis obiecit, tamquam rupta custodia ducem se victis partibus ostentasset; addidit temptatam cohortem quae Ostiae ageret; nec ullis tantorum criminum probationibus in paenitentiam versus seram veniam post scelus quaerebat. Cunctantem super tanta[1] re Flavium Sabinum Triaria L. Vitellii uxor, ultra feminam ferox, terruit ne[2] periculo principis famam clementia adfectaret. Sabinus suopte ingenio mitis, ubi formido incessisset, facilis mutatu et in alieno discrimine sibi pavens, ne adlevasse videretur, impulit ruentem.

LXIV. Igitur Vitellius metu et odio quod Petroniam uxorem eius mox Dolabella in matrimonium accepisset, vocatum per epistulas vitata Flaminiae

[1] supertēntare *M*. [2] e *M*.

---

[1] i. 88. [2] Cf. i. 80.

force; and most municipal towns and colonies were in the habit of rivalling the emperors in bribing the worst of their young men to take up these disgraceful pursuits.

LXIII. But Vitellius was moved to greater arrogance and cruelty by the arrival of his brother and by the cunning approaches of his teachers in the imperial art; he ordered the execution of Dolabella, whose banishment by Otho to the colony of Aquinum we have previously related.[1] Dolabella, on hearing of Otho's death, had entered Rome. For this he was accused before the city-prefect, Flavius Sabinus, by Plancius Varus, an ex-praetor, one of Dolabella's most intimate friends. To the charge of escaping from custody and offering himself as leader to the defeated party Varus added that Dolabella had tampered with the cohort stationed at Ostia,[2] but being unable to present any proofs for his grave charges, he repented of his action and sought pardon for his friend—too late, for the outrage had been done. While Flavius Sabinus was hesitating—for the matter was serious—Triaria, the wife of Lucius Vitellius, violent beyond her sex, frightened Sabinus from any attempt to secure a reputation for clemency at the expense of the emperor. Sabinus was by nature gentle, but ready to change his decision when alarmed, and now being afraid for himself when the danger was another's, and wishing to avoid seeming to have helped him, he precipitated Dolabella's fall.

LXIV. So Vitellius, who not only feared but also hated Dolabella, because Dolabella had married his former wife, Petronia, summoned him by letter, directing him to avoid the crowded Flaminian Road

viae celebritate devertere Interamnium atque ibi interfici iussit. Longum interfectori visum: in itinere ac taberna proiectum humi iugulavit, magna cum invidia novi principatus, cuius hoc primum specimen noscebatur. Et Triariae licentiam modestum e proximo exemplum onerabat, Galeria imperatoris uxor non immixta[1] tristibus; et pari probitate mater Vitelliorum Sextilia, antiqui moris: dixisse quin etiam ad primas filii sui epistulas ferebatur, non Germanicum a se sed Vitellium genitum. Nec ullis postea fortunae inlecebris aut ambitu civitatis in gaudium evicta domus suae tantum adversa sensit.

LXV. Digressum a Luguduno Vitellium Cluvius Rufus adsequitur omissa Hispania, laetitiam et gratulationem vultu ferens, animo anxius et petitum se criminationibus gnarus. Hilarus Caesaris libertus detulerat tamquam audito Vitellii et Othonis principatu propriam ipse potentiam et possessionem Hispaniarum temptasset, eoque diplomatibus nullum principem praescripsisset; et[2] interpretabatur quaedam ex orationibus[3] eius contumeliosa in Vitellium et pro se ipso popularia. Auctoritas Cluvii praevaluit ut puniri ultro libertum suum Vitellius iuberet. Cluvius

[1] inmixta *I. F. Gronovius*: Inmix *M.*
[2] et *add. Ernesti.*
[3] ex orationibus *Rhenanus*: exortationibus *M.*

---

[1] Terni. [2] Cf chap. 58 above.

and go to Interamnium,[1] where he ordered that he should be killed. The executioner thought the journey too long; at a tavern on the way he struck Dolabella to the ground and cut his throat, to the great discredit of the new principate, of whose character this was regarded as the first indication. The bold nature of Triaria was made odious by comparison with an example of modesty within her own family, for the Emperor's wife Galeria never took a hand in such horrors, while Sextilla, the mother of the two Vitellii, showed herself a woman of the same high character, an example of ancient ways. Indeed it was said that when she received the first letter from her son, she declared that she had borne a Vitellius, not a Germanicus. And never later was she moved to joy by the allurements of fortune or by popular favour: it was only the misfortunes of her house that she felt.

LXV. After Vitellius left Lugdunum, he was overtaken by Cluvius Rufus, who had left Spain.[2] Rufus had an air of joy and congratulation, but in his heart he was anxious, for he knew that charges had been laid against him. Hilarus, one of the imperial freedmen, had denounced him, claiming that when Rufus had heard of the elevation of Vitellius and of Otho, he had made an attempt to gain power and possession of the Spanish provinces for himself, and for that reason had not prefixed the name of any emperor to his public documents; moreover, Hilarus interpreted some parts of his public speeches as derogatory to Vitellius and calculated to win popularity for himself. The influence of Cluvius was strong enough to move Vitellius so far as to order the punishment of his own freedman. Cluvius was

comitatui principis adiectus, non adempta Hispania, quam rexit absens exemplo L. Arrunti. Sed Arruntium[1] Tiberius Caesar ob metum, Vitellius Cluvium nulla formidine retinebat. Non idem Trebellio Maximo honos: profugerat Britannia ob iracundiam militum; missus est in locum eius Vettius Bolanus e praesentibus.

LXVI. Angebat Vitellium victarum legionum haudquaquam fractus animus. Sparsae per Italiam et victoribus permixtae hostilia loquebantur, praecipua quartadecimanorum ferocia, qui se victos abnuebant: quippe Bedriacensi acie vexillariis tantum pulsis viris legionis non adfuisse. Remitti eos in Britanniam, unde a Nerone exciti erant, placuit atque interim Batavorum cohortis una tendere ob veterem adversus quartadecimanos discordiam. Nec diu in tantis armatorum odiis quies fuit: Augustae Taurinorum, dum opificem quendam Batavus ut fraudatorem insectatur, legionarius ut hospitem tuetur, sui cuique commilitones adgregati a conviciis ad caedem transiere. Et proelium atrox arsisset, ni duae praetoriae cohortes causam quartadecimanorum secutae his fiduciam et metum Batavis fecissent:

[1] Arrunti sed Arruntium *Haase*: arruntium *M*.

---

[1] Cf. *Ann.* vi. 27. [2] Cf. i. 60.

added to the emperor's train but not deprived of his province of Spain; he continued to govern it from a distance, after the precedent of Lucius Arruntius. But the emperor Tiberius had kept Arruntius with him because he was afraid of him;[1] Vitellius had no fear of Cluvius. Trebellius Maximus did not receive the same honour.[2] He had fled from Britain to escape the resentment of his army; Vettius Bolanus, one of the suite of Vitellius, was sent out in his place.

LXVI. Vitellius found cause for anxiety in the spirit of the defeated legions, which was by no means conquered. Scattered about Italy and mingling with the victorious troops, their talk was constantly hostile; the soldiers of the Fourteenth legion were particularly bold, declaring that they never had been defeated, for in the battle at Bedriacum it was only some veterans who had been beaten; the strength of the legion had not been there at all. Vitellius decided to send them back to Britain, from which Nero had withdrawn them, and in the meantime to have the Batavian cohorts camp with them, because the Batavians had had a difference of long standing with the Fourteenth. Peace did not last long among armed men who hated one another so violently. At Turin a Batavian charged a workman with being a thief, while a legionary defended the workman as his host; thereupon their fellow-soldiers rallied to the support of each and matters soon passed from words to blows. In fact there would have been a bloody battle if two Praetorian cohorts had not taken the side of the soldiers of the Fourteenth and inspired them with courage while they frightened the Batavians. Vitellius directed that

quos Vitellius agmini suo iungi ut fidos, legionem Grais Alpibus traductam eo flexu itineris ire iubet quo Viennam vitarent; namque et Viennenses timebantur. Nocte, qua proficiscebatur legio, relictis passim ignibus pars Taurinae coloniae ambusta, quod damnum, ut pleraque belli mala, maioribus aliarum urbium cladibus oblitteratum. Quartadecimani postquam Alpibus degressi[1] sunt, seditiosissimus quisque signa Viennam ferebant: consensu meliorum conpressi et legio in Britanniam transvecta.

LXVII. Proximus Vitellio e praetoriis cohortibus metus erat. Separati primum, deinde addito honestae missionis lenimento, arma ad tribunos suos deferebant, donec motum a Vespasiano bellum crebresceret: tum resumpta militia robur Flavianarum partium fuere. Prima classicorum legio in Hispaniam missa ut pace et otio mitesceret, undecima ac septima suis hibernis redditae, tertiadecimani struere amphitheatra iussi; nam Caecina Cremonae, Valens Bononiae spectaculum gladiatorum edere parabant, numquam ita ad curas intento Vitellio ut voluptatum oblivisceretur.

LXVIII. Et victas[2] quidem partis modeste distraxerat: apud victores orta seditio, ludicro initio ni[3]

[1] degressi *Pichena*: digressi *M.*
[2] victas *add. Haase.*
[3] ni *add.* Agricola.

---

[1] The Little St. Bernard.
[2] Vienne.
[3] Normally the praetorians received 5000 denarii (about $900) with their discharge after completing sixteen years of service. Cf. Dio Cass. lv. 23.
[4] To Dalmatia and Pannonia respectively.

the Batavians, as being trustworthy, should join his train, while the Fourteenth was to be conducted over the Graian Alps[1] by a circuitous route to avoid Vienna,[2] for the people of Vienna also gave him alarm. On the night in which the legion set out, the soldiers left fires burning everywhere, and a part of the colony of the Taurini was consumed; but this loss, like most of the misfortunes of war, was obscured by the greater disasters that befell other cities. After the Fourteenth had descended the Alps, the most mutinous were for advancing on Vienna, but they were restrained by the common action of the better soldiers, and the legion was got over to Britain.

LXVII. The next alarm of Vitellius arose from the praetorian cohorts. At first they had been kept apart; later the offer of an honourable discharge was employed to soothe their feelings,[3] and they started to turn their arms over to their tribunes, until the report that Vespasian had begun war became common; then they resumed their service and formed the backbone of the Flavian party. The First legion of marines was sent to Spain to have their savage temper softened by peace and quiet; the Eleventh and Seventh legions[4] were sent back to winter quarters, while the members of the Thirteenth were ordered to build amphitheatres, for Caecina was preparing to exhibit gladiators at Cremona, Valens at Bononia. Vitellius was never so absorbed in serious business that he forgot his pleasures.

LXVIII. The conquered party Vitellius had thus succeeded in scattering without an outbreak. But among the victors a mutiny broke out; the mutiny

numerus caesorum invidiam Vitellio[1] auxisset. Discubuerat Vitellius Ticini adhibito ad epulas Verginio. Legati tribunique ex moribus imperatorum severitatem aemulantur vel tempestivis conviviis gaudent; proinde miles intentus aut licenter agit. Apud Vitellium omnia indisposita, temulenta, pervigiliis ac bacchanalibus quam disciplinae et castris propiora. Igitur duobus militibus, altero legionis quintae, altero e Gallis auxiliaribus, per lasciviam ad certamen luctandi accensis, postquam legionarius prociderat, insultante Gallo et iis qui ad spectandum convenerant in studia diductis, erupere legionarii in perniciem auxiliorum ac duae cohortes interfectae. Remedium tumultus fuit alius tumultus. Pulvis procul et arma aspiciebantur: conclamatum repente quartam decimam legionem verso itinere ad proelium venire; sed erant agminis coactores: agniti dempsere sollicitudinem. Interim Verginii servus forte obvius ut percussor Vitellii insimulatur: et ruebat ad convivium miles, mortem Verginii exposcens. Ne Vitellius quidem, quamquam ad omnis suspiciones pavidus, de innocentia eius dubitavit: aegre tamen cohibiti qui exitium consularis et quondam ducis sui flagitabant. Nec quemquam saepius quam Verginium omnis seditio

[1] Vitellio *Döderlein*: bello *M.*

---

[1] That is, in dinners that began unseasonably early that they might last the longer.

originated in sport; only, the number of the slain aggravated the unpopularity of Vitellius. The emperor was dining at Ticinum, and Verginius was his guest. According to the character of their commanders, legati and tribuni either imitate their strictness or find pleasure in extravagant dinners;[1] and in the same way the soldiers exhibit devotion or licence. In the army of Vitellius complete disorder and drunkenness prevailed—things which belong rather to night revels and bacchanalian routs than to the discipline appropriate to an armed camp. So it happened that two soldiers, one from the Fifth legion and the other a Gallic auxiliary, in sport challenged each other to a wrestling match. When the legionary was thrown and the Gaul began to mock him, the crowd of spectators that had gathered took sides and the legionaries suddenly started to kill the auxiliaries, and in fact two cohorts were wiped out. The remedy for this disturbance was a second riot. A cloud of dust and arms were seen in the distance. A general cry was at once raised that the Fourteenth legion was retracing its steps and coming to fight; but in fact it was the rear-guard, and when they were recognized the general panic ceased. In the meantime the soldiers accused a slave of Verginius who happened to be passing with being an assassin of Vitellius; they rushed to the dinner, demanding that Verginius be put to death. Even Vitellius, who was timid and ready to entertain any suspicion, had no doubt of his innocence. Still it was with difficulty that the troops were kept from insisting on the execution of this ex-consul who had once been their own general. In fact no man was endangered by every riot so often as Verginius.

infestavit: manebat admiratio viri et fama, set oderant ut fastiditi.

LXIX. Postero die Vitellius senatus legatione, quam ibi opperiri iusserat, audita transgressus in castra ultro pietatem militum conlaudavit, frementibus auxiliis tantum impunitatis atque adrogantiae legionariis accessisse. Batavorum cohortes, ne quid truculentius auderent,[1] in Germaniam remissae, principium interno simul externoque bello parantibus fatis. Reddita civitatibus Gallorum auxilia, ingens numerus et prima statim defectione inter inania belli adsumptus. Ceterum ut largitionibus adfectae iam[2] imperii opes sufficerent, amputari legionum auxiliorumque numeros iubet vetitis supplementis; et promiscae missiones offerebantur. Exitiabile id rei publicae, ingratum militi, cui eadem munia inter paucos periculaque ac labor crebrius redibant: et vires luxu corrumpebantur, contra veterem disciplinam et instituta maiorum apud quos virtute quam pecunia res Romana melius stetit.

LXX. Inde Vitellius Cremonam flexit et spectato

[1] audirent *M.*
[2] iam *Agricola*: tam *M.*

---

[1] Verginius had refused the imperial power. Cf. i. 8, 52; ii. 51.

[2] Referring to the revolt of Civilis described in Books IV and V.

Admiration for him and his reputation continued unimpaired; but the troops hated him, for he had despised their offer.[1]

LXIX. The next day Vitellius first received the delegation from the senate, which he had directed to wait for him here; then he went to the camp and took occasion to praise the loyal devotion of the soldiers. This action made the auxiliaries complain that the legionaries were allowed to enjoy such impunity and to display such impudence. Then, to keep the Batavian cohorts from undertaking some bold deed of vengeance, he sent them back to Germany, for the Fates were already preparing the sources from which both civil and foreign war was to spring.[2] The Gallic auxiliaries were dismissed to their homes. Their number was enormous, for at the very outbreak of the rebellion they had been taken into the army as part of the empty parade of war. Furthermore, that the resources of the empire, which had been impaired by donatives, might be sufficient for the needs of the state, Vitellius ordered that the legionary and auxiliary troops should be reduced and forbade further recruiting, besides offering discharges freely. This policy was destructive to the state and unpopular with the soldiers, for the same tasks were now distributed among fewer men, so that dangers and toil fell more often on the individual. Their strength also was corrupted by luxury in contrast to the ancient discipline and maxims of our forefathers, in whose day valour formed a better foundation for the Roman state than money.

LXX. Vitellius next turned aside to Cremona, and after witnessing the exhibition of gladiators provided

munere Caecinae insistere Bedriacensibus campis ac vestigia recentis victoriae lustrare oculis concupivit. foedum atque atrox spectaculum: intra quadragensimum pugnae diem lacera corpora, trunci artus, putres virorum equorumque formae, infecta tabo humus, protritis arboribus ac frugibus dira vastitas. Nec minus inhumana pars viae quam Cremonenses lauru rosaque constraverant, extructis altaribus caesisque victimis regium in morem; quae laeta in praesens mox perniciem ipsis fecere. Aderant Valens et Caecina, monstrabantque pugnae locos: hinc inrupisse legionum agmen, hinc equites coortos, inde circumfusas auxiliorum manus: iam tribuni praefectique, sua quisque facta extollentes, falsa vera aut maiora vero miscebant. Vulgus quoque militum clamore et gaudio deflectere via, spatia certaminum recognoscere, aggerem armorum, strues corporum intueri mirari; et erant quos varia sors[1] rerum lacrimaeque et misericordia subiret. At non Vitellius flexit oculos nec tot milia insepultorum civium exhorruit: laetus ultro et tam propinquae sortis ignarus instaurabat sacrum dis loci.

LXXI. Exim Bononiae a Fabio Valente gladiatorum spectaculum editur, advecto ex urbe cultu. Quan-

[1] fors *M*.

by Caecina, conceived a desire to tread the plains of Bedriacum and to see with his own eyes the traces of his recent victory. It was a revolting and ghastly sight: not forty days had passed since the battle, and on every side were mutilated corpses, severed limbs, rotting bodies of men and horses, the ground soaked with filth and gore, trees overthrown and crops trampled down in appalling devastation. No less barbarous was the sight presented by that part of the road which the people of Cremona strewed with laurel and roses, while they erected altars and slew victims as if they were greeting an eastern king; but their present joy was later the cause of their ruin. Valens and Caecina attended Vitellius and explained the scene of the battle; they showed that at this point the legions had rushed to the attack; there the cavalry had charged; and there the auxiliary forces had surrounded the foe. Tribunes too and prefects, each extolling his own deeds, mingled truth with falsehood or at least with exaggeration of the truth. The common soldiers also with shouts of joy turned from the road, recognized the stretches over which the battle had raged, and looked with wonder on the heaps of arms and the piles of bodies. Some among them were moved to tears and pity by the vicissitudes of fortune on which they gazed. But Vitellius never turned away his eyes or showed horror at the sight of so many citizens deprived of the rites of burial. Indeed he was filled with joy, and, ignorant of his own fate which was so near, he offered sacrifice to the local divinities.

LXXI. Thereafter at Bononia Fabius Valens presented his gladiatorial exhibition for which the equip-

toque magis propinquabat, tanto corruptius iter immixtis histrionibus et spadonum gregibus et cetero Neronianae aulae ingenio; namque et Neronem ipsum Vitellius admiratione celebrabat, sectari cantantem solitus, non necessitate, qua honestissimus quisque, sed luxu et saginae mancipatus emptusque. Ut Valenti et Caecinae vacuos honoris mensis aperiret, coartati aliorum consulatus, dissimulatus Marci Macri tamquam Othonianarum partium ducis; et Valerium Marinum destinatum a Galba consulem distulit, nulla offensa, sed mitem et iniuriam segniter laturum. Pedanius Costa omittitur, ingratus principi ut adversus Neronem ausus et Verginii extimulator, sed alias protulit causas; actaeque insuper Vitellio gratiae consuetudine servitii.

LXXII. Non ultra paucos dies quamquam acribus initiis coeptum mendacium valuit. Extiterat quidam Scribonianum se Camerinum ferens, Neronianorum temporum metu in Histria occultatum, quod illic clientelae et agri veterum Crassorum ac nominis favor manebat. Igitur deterrimo quoque in argumentum fabulae adsumpto vulgus credulum et quidam militum, errore veri seu turbarum studio,

---

[1] Cf. i. 77.

[2] Scribonianus and his father had been murdered by Helios, Nero's slave, according to Dio Cass. lxiii. 18 Cf. Plin. *Epist.* I. 5. 3. The Scriboniani were a family of the Crassi.

ment had been brought from Rome. As Vitellius drew nearer to the capital, his train exhibited the greater corruption; actors, crowds of eunuchs, and every other kind of creature that belonged to Nero's court mixed with his soldiers. For Vitellius cherished great admiration for Nero himself, whom he had been in the habit of accompanying on his singing tours, not under compulsion, as so many honourable men were forced to do, but because he was the slave and chattel of luxury and gluttony. To secure free months in which to honour Valens and Caecina with consulships, he shortened the terms of others[1] and passed over Marcus Macer in silence as having been a leader of Otho's party. He put off the consulship of Valerius Marinus, who had been selected by Galba, not because of any offence, but because Marinus was of a mild nature and would put up with the injury. Pedanius Costa was omitted from the list; he was unpopular with the emperor because he had dared to move against Nero and to urge Verginius to action, although other reasons were alleged. Vitellius received the usual thanks, for the habit of servility was well established.

LXXII. A deception, which had a lively success at first, prevailed for only a few days. A man appeared who gave himself out as Scribonianus Camerinus, alleging that he had remained concealed in Istria during Nero's reign, for there the ancient Crassi still possessed clients, lands, and popularity.[2] He accordingly associated with himself, to develop this comedy, a company made up of the dregs of mankind; the credulous common people and some of the soldiers, either deceived by the falsehood or led

certatim adgregabantur, cum pertractus ad Vitellium interrogatusque quisnam mortalium esset. Postquam nulla dictis fides et a domino noscebatur condicione fugitivus, nomine Geta, sumptum de eo supplicium in servilem modum.

LXXIII. Vix credibile memoratu est quantum superbiae socordiaeque Vitellio adoleverit, postquam speculatores e Syria Iudaeaque adactum in verba eius Orientem nuntiavere. Nam etsi vagis adhuc et incertis auctoribus erat tamen in ore famaque Vespasianus ac plerumque ad nomen eius Vitellius excitabatur: tum ipse exercitusque, ut nullo aemulo, saevitia libidine raptu in externos mores proruperant.

LXXIV. At Vespasianus bellum armaque et procul vel iuxta sitas viris circumspectabat. Miles ipsi adeo paratus ut praeeuntem sacramentum et fausta Vitellio omnia precantem per silentium audierint; Muciani animus nec Vespasiano alienus et in Titum pronior; praefectus Aegypti Ti.[1] Alexander consilia sociaverat; tertiam legionem, quod e[2] Syria in Moesiam transisset, suam numerabat; ceterae Illyrici legiones secuturae sperabantur; namque omnis exercitus flammaverat adrogantia venientium a Vitellio militum, quod truces corpore, horridi sermone ceteros

[1] Ti. *add. Ursinus.*
[2] e *Lipsius*: de *M.*

---

[1] Cf. ii. 5.

on by a desire for trouble, were rapidly rallying about him, when he was dragged before Vitellius and questioned as to his identity. No faith was put in his answers; and after he had been recognized by his master as a runaway slave, Geta by name, he suffered the punishment usually inflicted on slaves.

LXXIII. The degree to which the insolent pride of Vitellius increased after couriers arrived from Syria and Judea and reported that the East had sworn allegiance to him is almost past belief. For although the grounds for the gossip were as yet vague and uncertain, rumour had much to say of Vespasian, and his name frequently excited Vitellius. But now both emperor and army, believing that they had no rival, broke out into cruelty, lust, and rapine, equalling all the excesses of barbarians.

LXXIV. As for Vespasian, he now began to reflect on the possibilities of war and armed combat and to review the strength of the forces near and far. His own soldiers were so ready that when he administered the oath and made vows for the success of Vitellius, they listened in complete silence. The sentiments of Mucianus were not hostile to him and indeed were favourable to Titus[1]; Tiberius Alexander, the prefect of Egypt, had already cast his lot with his side; he could count on the loyalty of the Third legion, which had been transferred from Syria to Moesia; and he had hopes that the legions in Illyricum would follow the Third. There was reason for this expectation, for all the eastern forces had been fired with rage over the arrogance of the soldiers of Vitellius who came to them, because though savage in appearance and barbarous in speech, they constantly mocked at all the others as

ut imparis inridebant. Sed in tanta mole[1] belli plerumque cunctatio; et Vespasianus modo in spem erectus, aliquando adversa reputabat: quis ille dies foret quo sexaginta aetatis annos et duos filios iuvenes bello permitteret? Esse privatis cogitationibus progressum et, prout velint, plus minusve sumi ex fortuna: imperium cupientibus nihil medium inter summa aut praecipitia.

LXXV. Versabatur ante oculos Germanici exercitus robur, notum viro militari: suas legiones civili bello inexpertas, Vitellii victrices, et apud victos plus querimoniarum quam virium. Fluxam per discordias militum fidem et periculum ex singulis: quid enim profuturas cohortis alasque, si unus alterve praesenti facinore paratum ex diverso praemium petat? Sic Scribonianum sub Claudio interfectum, sic percussorem eius Volaginium e gregario ad summa militiae provectum: facilius universos impelli quam singulos vitari.

LXXVI. His pavoribus nutantem et alii legati amicique firmabant et Mucianus, post multos secretosque sermones iam et coram ita locutus: "Omnes, qui magnarum rerum consilia suscipiunt, aestimare debent an quod inchoatur rei publicae utile, ipsis

[1] sed iniant amole *M*.

---

[1] Cf. i. 89.

their inferiors. But a war of such scope can never be undertaken without hesitation; and Vespasian, at one moment inspired with hope, would at times ponder over the obstacles—what could that day be on which he should entrust his sixty years and his two young sons to the fortune of war? He reflected that private plans allow one to advance or retreat and permit the individual to take that measure of Fortune's gifts that he will; but when a man aims at the imperial power, there is no mean between the heights and the abyss.

LXXV. He pictured to himself the strength of the army from Germany, which as a soldier he well understood. He realized that his own legions were untried in civil war, that the troops of Vitellius knew the joy of victory, and that there was more discontent than strength in the ranks of the defeated. In time of discord the fidelity of an army is uncertain and danger may come from individuals. "For what will cohorts and squadrons avail me," he asked himself, "if some one or two assassins go red-handed to demand the reward which my opponents will always be ready to pay? Thus Scribonianus was killed under Claudius;[1] thus his assassin Volaginius won advancement from the lowest to the highest rank. It is easier to move whole armies than to avoid individuals."

LXXVI. While he was hesitating, moved by such fears as these, his mind was confirmed by his officers and friends and especially by Mucianus, who first had long private conversations with him and then spoke openly before the rest: "All who are debating high emprises ought to consider whether their purpose is useful to the state, glorious for them-

gloriosum, promptum[1] effectu aut certe non[2] arduum sit; simul ipse qui suadet considerandus est, adiciatne consilio periculum suum, et, si fortuna coeptis adfuerit, cui summum decus adquiratur. Ego te, Vespasiane, ad imperium voco, quam[3] salutare rei publicae, quam tibi magnificum, iuxta deos in tua manu positum est. Nec speciem adulantis expaveris: a contumelia quam a laude propius fuerit post Vitellium eligi. Non adversus divi Augusti acerrimam mentem nec adversus cautissimam Tiberii senectutem, ne contra Gai quidem aut Claudii vel Neronis fundatam longo imperio domum exsurgimus; cessisti etiam Galbae imaginibus: torpere ultra et polluendam perdendamque rem publicam relinquere sopor et ignavia videretur, etiam si tibi quam inhonesta, tam tuta servitus esset. Abiit iam et transvectum est tempus quo posses videri non cupisse[4]: confugiendum est ad imperium. An excidit trucidatus Corbulo? Splendidior origine quam nos sumus, fateor, sed et Nero nobilitate natalium Vitellium anteibat. Satis clarus est apud timentem quisquis timetur. Et posse ab exercitu principem fieri sibi ipse Vitellius documento, nullis stipendiis, nulla militari fama, Galbae odio provectus. Ne Othonem quidem ducis arte aut exercitus vi,[5] sed

[1] promptum *Nipperdey*: aut promptum *M.*
[2] non certe non *M.*
[3] quam *Müller*: tanquam *M.*
[4] non cupisse *Ruperti et Madvig*: concupisse *M.*
[5] exercitus vi *Rhenanus*: exercitu sui *M.*

---

[1] Cn. Domitius Corbulo, who had distinguished himself in the war against the Parthians, aroused Nero's jealousy and was put to death by him. Cf. Dio Cass. lxiii. 17.

selves, easy of accomplishment, or at least not difficult. At the same time they must take into account the character of their adviser. Is he ready to share the risks involved as well as to give advice? If Fortune favours the undertaking, who is the man for whom the highest honour is sought? I call you, Vespasian, to the throne. How advantageous to the state, how glorious for you this may prove, are questions which depend, after the gods, on your own acts. Have no fear that I may appear to flatter you. It is rather a disgrace than a glory to be chosen emperor after Vitellius. It is not against the keen mind of the deified Augustus, nor the cautious nature of the aged Tiberius, nor against the long-established imperial house of even a Gaius or a Claudius, or, if you like, of a Nero, that we are rising. You respected the ancestry even of Galba. But to remain longer inactive and to leave the state to corruption and ruin would appear nothing but sloth and cowardice on your part, even if subservience should prove as safe for you as it certainly would be disgraceful. The time is already past and gone when you could seem to have no desires for supreme power. Your only refuge is the throne. Have you forgotten the murder of Corbulo? [1] He was of more splendid family than I am, I grant you, but Nero also was superior to Vitellius in point of noble birth. Anyone who is feared is noble enough in the eyes of the man who fears him. Moreover you have proof in the case of Vitellius himself that an army can make an emperor, for Vitellius owes his elevation to no campaigns or reputation as a soldier, but solely to men's hatred of Galba. Even Otho, who owed his defeat, not to his rival's skill as general

praepropera ipsius desperatione victum, iam desiderabilem et magnum principem fecit, cum interim spargit legiones, exarmat cohortis, nova cotidie bello semina ministrat. Si quid ardoris ac ferociae miles habuit, popinis et comissationibus et principis imitatione deteritur: tibi e Iudaea et Syria et Aegypto novem legiones integrae, nulla acie exhaustae, non discordia corruptae, sed firmatus usu miles et belli domitor externi: classium alarum cohortium robora et fidissimi reges et tua ante omnis experientia.

LXXVII. "Nobis nihil ultra adrogabo quam ne post Valentem et Caecinam numeremur: ne tamen Mucianum socium spreveris, quia aemulum non experiris. Me Vitellio antepono, te mihi. tuae domui triumphale nomen, duo iuvenes, capax iam imperii alter et primis militiae annis apud Germanicos quoque exercitus clarus. Absurdum fuerit non cedere imperio ei cuius filium adoptaturus essem, si ipse imperarem. Ceterum inter nos non idem prosperarum adversarumque rerum ordo erit: nam si vincimus, honorem quem dederis habebo: discrimen ac pericula ex aequo patiemur. Immo, ut melius est, tu[1] tuos exercitus rege, mihi bellum et

[1] tu *add. Kiessling.*

---

[1] The Jews.

[2] Cf. ii. 4 and 81.

[3] Vespasian had won this distinction by his services in Britain in 43 A.D. Cf. iii. 44; Suet. *Vesp.* 4.

[4] Titus had served in Germany and Britain with credit. Cf. Suet. *Titus*, 4.

or to the force of the opposing army, but to his own hasty despair, Vitellius has already made seem a great emperor whom men regret; and in the meantime he is scattering his legions, disarming his cohorts, and every day sowing new seeds of war. All the enthusiasm and courage that his soldiers ever had is being dissipated in taverns, in debauches, and in imitation of their emperor. You have in Syria, Judea, and Egypt nine legions at their full strength, not worn out by fighting, not infected by mutiny, but troops who have gained strength by experience and proved themselves victorious over a foreign foe.[1] You have strong fleets, cavalry, and cohorts, princes wholly loyal to you,[2] and an experience greater than all others.

LXXVII. "For myself I shall make no claim save not to be reckoned second to Valens and Caecina; yet I beg you not to despise Mucianus as partner in your enterprise because you do not find in him a rival. I count myself superior to Vitellius and you superior to me. Your house has the honour of a triumphal name;[3] it possesses two young men, one of whom is already equal to ruling the empire; he also enjoys a high reputation with the forces in Germany because his first years of service were spent there.[4] It would be absurd for me not to bow before the throne of a man whose son I should adopt if I myself held it. Besides, you and I shall not stand on the same footing in success as in failure, for if we win, I shall have simply the position you choose to give; but risks and dangers we shall share alike. Rather—and this is better—do you command your forces here; leave to me the conduct of the actual war and the risks of battle.

proeliorum incerta trade. Acriore hodie disciplina victi quam victores agunt. Hos ira, odium, ultionis cupiditas ad virtutem accendit: illi per fastidium et contumacia hebescunt. Aperiet et recludet contecta et tumescentia victricium partium vulnera bellum ipsum; nec mihi maior in tua vigilantia parsimonia sapientia fiducia est quam in Vitellii torpore inscitia saevitia. Sed meliorem in bello causam quam in pace habemus; nam qui deliberant, desciverunt."

LXXVIII. Post Muciani orationem ceteri audentius circumsistere, hortari, responsa vatum et siderum motus referre. Nec erat intactus tali superstitione, ut qui mox rerum dominus Seleucum quendam mathematicum rectorem et praescium palam habuerit. Recursabant animo vetera omina[1]: cupressus arbor in agris eius conspicua altitudine repente prociderat ac postera die eodem vestigio resurgens procera et latior virebat. Grande id prosperumque consensu haruspicum et summa claritudo iuveni admodum Vespasiano promissa, sed primo triumphalia et consulatus et Iudaicae victoriae decus implesse fidem ominis videbatur: ut haec adeptus est, portendi sibi imperium credebat. Est Iudaeam inter Syriamque Carmelus: ita vocant montem deumque.

[1] omina *Rhenanus*: omnia *M*.

There is stricter discipline to-day in the ranks of the defeated than among the victors. The former are fired to brave action by rage, hatred, and eager desire for revenge; the latter are losing their vigour because they scorn and disdain their opponents. War will inevitably open and lay bare the angry wounds which the victorious party now conceals; nor is the confidence that I have in your vigilance, frugality, and wisdom greater than that I feel in the sloth, ignorance, and cruelty of Vitellius. Besides, our situation is better in war than in peace, for they who plan revolt have already revolted."

LXXVIII. After Mucianus had spoken, the rest became bolder; they gathered about Vespasian, encouraged him, and recalled the prophecies of seers and the movements of the stars. Nor indeed was he wholly free from such superstitious belief, as was evident later when he had obtained supreme power, for he openly kept at court an astrologer named Seleucus, whom he regarded as his guide and oracle. Old omens came back to his mind: once on his country estate a cypress of conspicuous height suddenly fell, but the next day it rose again on the selfsame spot fresh, tall, and with wider expanse than before. This occurrence was a favourable omen of great significance, as the haruspices all agreed, and promised the highest distinctions for Vespasian, who was then still a young man. At first, however, the insignia of a triumph, his consulship, and his victory over Judea appeared to have fulfilled the promise given by the omen; yet after he had gained these honours, he began to think that it was the imperial throne that was foretold. Between Judea and Syria lies Carmel: this is the name given to both

Nec simulacrum deo aut templum—sic tradidere maiores—: ara tantum et reverentia.[1] Illic sacrificanti Vespasiano, cum spes occultas versaret animo, Basilides sacerdos inspectis identidem extis "Quicquid est" inquit, "Vespasiane, quod paras, seu domum extruere seu prolatare agros sive ampliare servitia, datur tibi magna sedes, ingentes termini, multum hominum." Has ambages et statim exceperat fama et tunc aperiebat; nec quicquam magis in ore vulgi. Crebriores apud ipsum sermones, quanto sperantibus plura dicuntur. Haud dubia destinatione discessere Mucianus Antiochiam, Vespasianus Caesaream: illa Syriae, hoc Iudaeae caput est.

LXXIX. Initium ferendi ad Vespasianum imperii Alexandriae coeptum, festinante Tiberio Alexandro, qui kalendis Iuliis sacramento eius legiones adegit. Isque primus principatus dies in posterum celebratus, quamvis Iudaicus exercitus quinto nonas Iulias apud ipsum iurasset, eo ardore ut ne Titus quidem filius expectaretur, Syria remeans et consiliorum inter Mucianum ac patrem nuntius. Cuncta impetu militum acta non parata contione,[2] non coniunctis legionibus.

[1] ara . . reverentia *Agricola*: aram . . reverentiam *M.*
[2] contione *Agricola*: cognitione *M.*

---

[1] The Roman procurator resided at Caesarea; but naturally Jerusalem was the only capital in the eyes of the Jews.

the mountain and the divinity. The god has no image or temple—such is the rule handed down by the fathers; there is only an altar and the worship of the god. When Vespasian was sacrificing there and thinking over his secret hopes in his heart, the priest Basilides, after repeated inspection of the victim's vitals, said to him: "Whatever you are planning, Vespasian, whether to build a house, or to enlarge your holdings, or to increase the number of your slaves, the god grants you a mighty home, limitless bounds, and a multitude of men." This obscure oracle rumour had caught up at the time, and now was trying to interpret; nothing indeed was more often on men's lips. It was discussed even more in Vespasian's presence—for men have the more to say to those who are filled with hope. The two leaders now separated with clear purposes before them, Mucianus going to Antioch, Vespasian to Caesarea. Antioch is the capital of Syria, Caesarea of Judea.[1]

LXXIX. The transfer of the imperial power to Vespasian began at Alexandria, where Tiberius Alexander acted quickly, administering to his troops the oath of allegiance on the first of July. This day has been celebrated in later times as the first of Vespasian's reign, although it was on the third of July that the army in Judea took the oath before Vespasian himself, and did it with such enthusiasm that they did not wait even for his son Titus, who was on his way back from Syria and was the medium of communication between Mucianus and his father. The whole act was carried through by the enthusiastic soldiery without any formal speech or regular parade of the legions.

LXXX. Dum quaeritur tempus locus quodque in re tali difficillimum est, prima vox, dum animo spes timor, ratio casus obversantur, egressum cubiculo Vespasianum pauci milites, solito adsistentes[1] ordine ut legatum salutaturi, imperatorem salutavere: tum ceteri adcurrere, Caesarem et Augustum et omnia principatus vocabula cumulare. Mens a metu ad fortunam transierat: in ipso nihil tumidum, adrogans aut in rebus novis novum fuit. Ut primum tantae altitudinis[2] obfusam oculis caliginem disiecit, militariter locutus laeta omnia et affluentia excepit; namque id ipsum opperiens Mucianus alacrem militem in verba Vespasiani adegit. Tum Antiochensium theatrum ingressus, ubi illis[3] consultare mos est, concurrentis et in adulationem effusos adloquitur, satis decorus etiam Graeca facundia, omniumque quae diceret atque ageret arte quadam ostentator. Nihil aeque provinciam exercitumque accendit quam quod adseverabat Mucianus statuisse Vitellium ut Germanicas legiones in Syriam ad militiam opulentam quietamque transferret, contra Syriacis legionibus Germanica hiberna[4] caelo ac laboribus dura mutarentur; quippe et provinciales sueto militum contubernio gaudebant, plerique necessitudinibus et

[1] adsistentes *Pichena*: adsistent *M.*
[2] altitudinis *Triller*: multitudinis *M.* [3] illi *M.*
[4] hiberna *Rhenanus*: hiberno *M.*

LXXX. While the time, the place, and—what is in such case the most difficult thing—the person to speak the first word were being discussed, while hope and fear, plans and possibilities filled every mind, as Vespasian stepped from his quarters, a few soldiers who were drawn up in their usual order to salute him as their Legate, saluted him as Emperor. Then the rest ran up and began to call him Caesar and Augustus; they heaped on him all the titles of an emperor. Their minds suddenly turned from fears to confidence in Fortune's favour. In Vespasian himself there was no arrogance or pride, no novelty of conduct in his new estate. The moment that he had dispelled the mist which his elevation to such a height spread before his eyes, he spoke as befitted a soldier; then he began to receive favourable reports from every quarter; for Mucianus, who was waiting only for this action, now administered to his own eager troops the oath of allegiance to Vespasian. Then he entered the theatre at Antioch, where the people regularly hold their public assemblies, and addressed the crowd which hurried there, and expressed itself in extravagant adulation. His speech was graceful although he spoke in Greek, for he knew how to give a certain air to all he said and did. There was nothing that angered the province and the army so much as the assertion of Mucianus that Vitellius had decided to transfer the legions of Germany to Syria, where they could enjoy a profitable and easy service, while in exchange he would assign to the troops in Syria the wintry climate and the laborious duties of Germany. For the provincials were accustomed to live with the soldiers, and enjoyed association with them; in fact,

propinquitatibus mixti, et militibus vetustate stipendiorum nota et familiaria castra in modum penatium diligebantur.

LXXXI. Ante idus Iulias Syria omnis in eodem sacramento fuit. Accessere cum regno Sohaemus haud spernendis viribus, Antiochus vetustis opibus ingens et inservientium regum ditissimus. Mox per occultos suorum nuntios excitus[1] ab urbe Agrippa, ignaro adhuc Vitellio, celeri navigatione properaverat. Nec minore animo regina Berenice partis iuvabat, florens aetate formaque et seni quoque Vespasiano magnificentia munerum grata. Quidquid provinciarum adluitur mari Asia atque Achaia tenus, quantumque introrsus in Pontum et Armenios patescit, iuravere; sed inermes legati regebant, nondum additis Cappadociae legionibus. Consilium de summa rerum Beryti habitum. Illuc Mucianus cum legatis tribunisque et splendidissimo quoque centurionum ac militum venit, et e Iudaico exercitu lecta decora: tantum simul peditum equitumque et aemulantium inter se regum paratus speciem fortunae principalis effecerant.

[1] exercitus *M.*

---

[1] Sohaemus, a prince of the house of Emesa, had been set up by Nero in 54 A.D. as king of Sophene, a district on the east of the upper Euphrates. Cf. ii, 4; *Ann.* xiii. 7.

[2] Antiochus, of the Seleucid family, was at this time king of Commagene and of a part of Cilicia; three years later Vespasian deposed him and changed his kingdom into a Roman province. Cf. ii. 4; *Ann.* xii. 55.

[3] The son of Herod Agrippa, who died in 44 A.D., and the brother of Berenice; at this time he was governor of the district east of the Jordan. Cf. ii. 4.

[4] Cf. ii. 2.

[5] Cappadocia was now governed by a procurator of eques-

many civilians were bound to the soldiers by ties of friendship and of marriage, and the soldiers from their long service had come to love their old familiar camps as their very hearths and homes.

LXXXI. Before the fifteenth of July all Syria had sworn the same allegiance. Vespasian's cause was now joined also by Sohaemus [1] with his entire kingdom, whose strength was not to be despised, and by Antiochus [2] who had enormous ancestral wealth, and was in fact the richest of the subject princes. Presently Agrippa,[3] summoned from Rome by private messages from his friends, while Vitellius was still unaware of his action, quickly crossed the sea and joined the cause. Queen Berenice showed equal spirit in helping Vespasian's party: she had great youthful beauty, and commended herself to Vespasian for all his years by the splendid gifts she made him.[4] All the provinces on the coast to the frontiers of Achaia and Asia, as well as all the inland provinces as far as Pontus and Armenia, took the oath of allegiance; but their governors had no armed forces, since Cappadocia had as yet no legions.[5] A grand council was held at Berytus.[6] Mucianus came there with all his lieutenants and tribunes, as well as his most distinguished centurions and soldiers; the army in Judea also sent its best representatives. This great concourse of foot and horse, with princes who rivalled one another in splendid display, made a gathering that befitted the high fortune of an emperor.

trian rank; later Vespasian was forced by the frequent inroads on the province to put it in charge of an ex-consul supported by troops. Suet. *Vesp.* 8.

[6] Beyrout.

LXXXII. Prima belli cura agere dilectus, revocare veteranos; destinantur validae civitates exercendis armorum officinis; apud Antiochensis aurum argentumque signatur, eaque cuncta per idoneos ministros suis quaeque locis festinabantur. Ipse Vespasianus adire, hortari, bonos laude, segnis exemplo incitare saepius quam coercere, vitia magis amicorum quam virtutes dissimulans. Multos praefecturis et procurationibus, plerosque senatorii ordinis honore percoluit, egregios viros et mox summa adeptos; quibusdam fortuna pro virtutibus fuit. Donativum militi neque Mucianus prima contione nisi modice ostenderat, ne Vespasianus quidem plus civili bello obtulit quam alii in pace, egregie firmus adversus militarem largitionem eoque exercitu meliore. Missi ad Parthum Armeniumque legati, provisumque ne versis ad civile bellum legionibus terga nudarentur. Titum instare Iudaeae, Vespasianum obtinere claustra Aegypti placuit: sufficere videbantur adversus Vitellium pars copiarum et dux Mucianus et Vespasiani nomen ac nihil arduum fatis. Ad omnis exercitus legatosque scriptae epistulae praeceptumque ut praetorianos Vitellio infensos reciperandae militiae premio invitarent.

LXXXIII. Mucianus cum expedita manu, socium

---

[1] Their diplomacy was so successful that Vologaeses, king of the Parthians, offered Vespasian forty thousand cavalry, which, however, Vespasian prudently refused. Cf. iv. 51.

[2] Alexandria and Pelusium.

LXXXII. The first business of the war was to hold levies and to recall the veterans to the colours. The strong towns were selected to manufacture arms; gold and silver were minted at Antioch; and all these preparations, each in its proper place, were quickly carried forward by expert agents. Vespasian visited each place in person, encouraged the workmen, spurring on the industrious by praise and the slow by his example, concealing his friends' faults rather than their virtues. Many he rewarded with prefectures and procuratorships; large numbers of excellent men who later attained the highest positions he raised to senatorial rank; in the case of some good fortune took the place of merit. In his first speech Mucianus had held out hopes of only a moderate donative to the soldiers; even Vespasian did not offer more for civil war than others did in time of peace. He was firmly opposed to extravagant gifts to the soldiers and therefore had a better army. Embassies were dispatched to the Parthians and Armenians, and provision made to avoid leaving their rear exposed when the legions were drawn off to civil war.[1] It was decided that Titus should follow up the war in Judea, Vespasian hold the keys to Egypt;[2] and it was agreed that a part of the troops, if led by Mucianus, would be enough to deal with Vitellius, aided as they would be by the prestige of Vespasian's name and by the fact that all things are easy for Fate. Letters were addressed to all the armies and to all their commanders, directing them to try to win over the praetorians, who hated Vitellius, by holding out to them the hope of re-entering the service.

LXXXIII. Mucianus, bearing himself rather as a

magis imperii quam ministrum agens, non lento itinere, ne cunctari videretur, neque tamen properans, gliscere famam ipso spatio sinebat, gnarus modicas viris sibi et maiora credi de absentibus; sed legio sexta et tredecim vexillariorum milia ingenti agmine sequebantur. Classem e Ponto Byzantium adigi iusserat, ambiguus consilii num omissa Moesia Dyrrachium pedite atque equite, simul longis navibus versum in Italiam mare clauderet, tuta pone tergum Achaia Asiaque, quas[1] inermis exponi Vitellio, ni praesidiis firmarentur; atque ipsum Vitellium in incerto fore quam partem Italiae protegeret, si sibi Brundisium Tarentumque et Calabriae Lucaniaeque litora infestis classibus peterentur.

LXXXIV. Igitur navium militum armorum paratu strepere provinciae, sed nihil aeque fatigabat quam pecuniarum conquisitio: eos esse belli civilis nervos dictitans Mucianus non ius aut verum in cognitionibus, sed solam magnitudinem opum spectabat. Passim delationes, et locupletissimus quisque in praedam correpti. Quae gravia atque intoleranda, sed necessitate armorum excusata etiam in pace mansere, ipso Vespasiano inter initia imperii ad obtinendas

[1] quasi *M.*

partner in empire than as a subordinate, advanced with a force in light marching order, not indeed slowly, for fear of seeming to hesitate, nor yet in haste, for he wished to let distance increase his renown, being well aware that he had only moderate forces at his disposal and conscious that men magnify what is far away. Yet the Sixth legion and thirteen thousand veterans followed after him in imposing array. He had directed the fleet in the Black Sea to concentrate at Byzantium, for he was undecided whether he should not leave Moesia to one side and occupy Dyrrachium with his foot and horse, establishing meantime a blockade in the waters around Italy with his ships-of-war. In that way he would protect Achaia and Asia in his rear, whereas they would be without protection and exposed to Vitellius, unless he left forces to guard them. He believed also that Vitellius himself would be at a loss what part of Italy to protect if he prepared to attack with his fleet Brundisium, Tarentum, and the coasts of Calabria and Lucania.

LXXXIV. So then the provinces were filled with din as ships, soldiers, and arms were made ready for their needs; but nothing troubled them so much as the exaction of money. "Money," Mucianus kept saying, "is the sinews of civil war." And in deciding cases which came before him as judge he had an eye not for justice or truth, but only for the size of the defendants' fortunes. Delation was rife, and all wealthy men were seized as prey. Such proceedings are an intolerable burden; nevertheless, though at the time excused by the necessities of war, they continued later in time of peace. It is true that Vespasian for his part at the beginning of his reign

iniquitates haud perinde obstinante, donec indulgentia fortunae et pravis magistris didicit[1] aususque est. Propriis quoque opibus Mucianus bellum iuvit, largus privatim, quod avidius de re publica sumeret. Ceteri conferendarum pecuniarum[2] exemplum secuti, rarissimus quisque eandem in reciperando licentiam habuerunt.

LXXXV. Adcelerata interim Vespasiani coepta Illyrici exercitus studio transgressi in partis; tertia legio exemplum ceteris Moesiae legionibus praebuit; octava erat ac septima Claudiana, imbutae favore Othonis, quamvis proelio non interfuissent. Aquileiam progressae, proturbatis qui de Othone nuntiabant laceratisque vexillis nomen Vitellii praeferentibus, rapta postremo pecunia et inter se divisa, hostiliter egerant. Unde metus et ex metu consilium, posse imputari Vespasiano quae apud Vitellium excusanda erant. Ita tres Moesicae legiones per epistulas adliciebant Pannonicum exercitum aut abnuenti vim parabant. In eo motu Aponius Saturninus Moesiae rector pessimum facinus audet, misso centurione ad interficiendum Tettium Iulianum septimae legionis legatum ob simultates, quibus

[1] dicit *M*. [2] pucuniam *M*.

was not so insistent on carrying through such unjust actions; but finally, schooled by an indulgent fortune and wicked teachers, he learned and dared the like. Mucianus contributed generously to the war from his own fortune also; his liberality with his private means corresponding, as men remarked, to the excessive greed he showed in taking from the state. The rest of the leaders followed his example in making contributions; but only the fewest enjoyed the same licence in recovering them.

LXXXV. Meantime Vespasian's enterprise received a favourable impulse from the enthusiasm with which the army in Illyricum came over to his side. The Third legion set a precedent for the other legions in Moesia: these were the Eighth and the Seventh Claudiana, both loyal to the memory of Otho, although they had not taken part in the battle of Bedriacum. Having advanced as far as Aquileia, by driving off with violence the messengers who brought the news of Otho's defeat, tearing in pieces the standards that displayed the name of Vitellius, and finally seizing the camp treasury and dividing it among themselves, they had acted like enemies. Their conduct filled them with fear, and then fear brought the reflection that acts might win them credit with Vespasian for which they would have to apologize to Vitellius. So the three legions in Moesia tried to win over the army in Pannonia by letter; at the same time they prepared to use force if the Pannonian troops refused. In this undertaking Aponius Saturninus, the governor of Moesia, tried a bold and shameful act: prompted by private hatred which he tried to conceal behind political motives, he sent a centurion to murder Tettius

causam partium praetendebat. Iulianus comperto discrimine et gnaris locorum adscitis per avia Moesiae ultra montem Haemum profugit; nec deinde civili bello interfuit, per varias moras susceptum ad Vespasianum iter trahens et ex nuntiis cunctabundus aut properans.

LXXXVI. At in Pannonia tertia decima legio ac septima Galbiana, dolorem iramque Bedriacensis pugnae retinentes, haud cunctanter Vespasiano accessere, praecipua vi Primi Antonii. Is legibus nocens et tempore Neronis falsi damnatus inter alia belli[1] mala senatorium ordinem reciperaverat. Praepositus a Galba septimae legioni scriptitasse Othoni credebatur, ducem se partibus offerens; a quo neglectus in nullo Othoniani belli usu fuit. Labantibus Vitellii rebus Vespasianum secutus grande momentum addidit, strenuus manu, sermone promptus, serendae in alios invidiae artifex, discordiis et seditionibus potens, raptor, largitor, pace pessimus, bello non spernendus. Iuncti inde Moesici ac Pannonici exercitus Dalmaticum militem traxere, quamquam consularibus legatis nihil turbantibus. Tampius[2] Flavianus Pannoniam, Pompeius Silvanus Dalmatiam tenebant, divites senes; sed procurator

[1] bellum *M.*
[2] Tampius *Faernus*: titus amplius *M.*

---

[1] The Balkan Mountains.

Julianus, legate of the Seventh legion. Julianus, however, learning of his danger, took some men who knew the country and escaped through the pathless stretches of Moesia to the district beyond Mt. Haemus.[1] Thereafter he took no part in civil war, for although he started to join Vespasian, he kept hesitating or hurrying according to the news he received, and found various pretexts for delay.

LXXXVI. But in Pannonia the Thirteenth legion and the Seventh Galbiana, which still felt deep resentment over the battle at Bedriacum, did not delay to join Vespasian's cause, influenced by the conspicuous violence of Primus Antonius. He had been found guilty and condemned for fraud in Nero's reign, but, as one of the evil effects of the war, he had recovered his senatorial rank. Although Galba had put him in command of the Seventh legion, it was believed that he had written to Otho, offering his services as a leader of his cause. Since Otho paid no attention to him, he rendered no service in the war. Now that the fortunes of Vitellius began to totter, Primus followed Vespasian and gave his cause a great impulse; for he was vigorous in action, ready of speech, skilful in sowing differences among his enemies, powerful in stirring up discord and strife, ever ready to rob or to bribe—in short he was the worst of mortals in peace, but in war a man not to be despised. Then the union of the forces in Moesia and Pannonia drew the troops in Dalmatia to follow their example, although the ex-consuls who governed the provinces took no lead in the revolt. Tampius Flavianus was the governor of Pannonia, Pompeius Silvanus of Dalmatia, both rich and old. But with them was the imperial

aderat Cornelius Fuscus, vigens aetate, claris natalibus. Prima iuventa quietis cupidine senatorium ordinem exuerat; idem pro Galba dux coloniae suae, eaque opera procurationem adeptus, susceptis Vespasiani partibus acerrimam bello facem praetulit: non tam praemiis periculorum quam ipsis periculis laetus pro certis et olim partis nova ambigua ancipitia malebat. Igitur movere et quatere, quidquid usquam aegrum foret, adgrediuntur. Scriptae in Britanniam ad quartadecimanos, in Hispaniam ad primanos epistulae, quod utraque legio pro Othone, adversa Vitellio fuerat; sparguntur per Gallias litterae; momentoque temporis flagrabat ingens bellum, Illyricis exercitibus palam desciscentibus, ceteris fortunam secuturis.

LXXXVII. Dum haec per provincias a Vespasiano ducibusque partium geruntur, Vitellius contemptior in dies segniorque, ad omnis municipiorum villarumque amoenitates resistens, gravi urbem agmine petebat. Sexaginta milia armatorum sequebantur, licentia corrupta; calonum numerus amplior, procacissimis etiam inter servos lixarum ingeniis; tot legatorum amicorumque comitatus inhabilis ad parendum, etiam si summa modestia regeretur.[1] Onerabant

[1] regetur *M*.

---

[1] The name of the colony is unknown.

agent Cornelius Fuscus, who was in the full vigour of life and of high birth. In his youth his desire to lead a quiet life had led him to give up his senatorial rank. Yet he had brought his own colony [1] over to Galba's side, and by this service had secured a procuratorship. He now adopted Vespasian's cause and contributed all the fire of his enthusiasm to the war; he found his satisfaction in danger itself rather than in the rewards of danger, and preferred to certainty and advantages long secured whatever was new, uncertain, and in doubt. Therefore the leaders set to work to stir up the discontented throughout the entire empire. They addressed communications to the Fourteenth legion in Britain and to the First in Spain, for both these legions had been for Otho and opposed to Vitellius; letters were scattered broadcast through the Gallic provinces, and in a moment a great war burst into flame, as the armies in Illyricium openly revolted and all the rest prepared to follow Fortune's lead.

LXXXVII. While Vespasian and the leaders of his party were accomplishing this in the provinces, Vitellius became from day to day the more despised as he grew the more indolent. He stopped at every attractive town and villa on his way, and so gradually approached Rome with his cumbrous army. Sixty thousand armed men were in his train, all corrupted by lack of discipline; still greater was the number of camp-followers, and even among the slaves the soldiers' servants were the most unruly. There was also a great train of officers and courtiers, a company incapable of obedience even if they had been subject to the strictest discipline. The unwieldiness of this great crowd

multitudinem obvii ex urbe senatores equitesque, quidam metu, multi per adulationem, ceteri ac paulatim omnes ne aliis proficiscentibus ipsi remanerent. Adgregabantur e plebe flagitiosa per obsequia Vitellio cogniti, scurrae, histriones, aurigae, quibus ille amicitiarum dehonestamentis mire gaudebat. Nec coloniae modo aut municipia congestu copiarum, sed ipsi cultores arvaque maturis iam frugibus ut hostile solum vastabantur.

LXXXVIII. Multae et atroces inter se militum caedes, post seditionem Ticini coeptam manente legionum auxiliorumque discordia; ubi adversus paganos certandum foret,[1] consensu. Sed plurima strages ad septimum ab urbe lapidem. Singulis ibi militibus Vitellius paratos cibos ut gladiatoriam saginam dividebat; et effusa plebes totis se castris miscuerat. Incuriosos milites—vernacula utebantur urbanitate—quidam spoliavere, abscisis furtim balteis an accincti forent rogitantes. Non tulit ludibrium insolens contumeliarum animus: inermem populum gladiis invasere. Caesus inter alios pater militis, cum filium comitaretur; deinde agnitus et vulgata

[1] fore *M.*

---

[1] ii. 68.

was increased by senators and knights who came out from Rome to meet him, some moved by fear, many from a desire to flatter, the majority, and then gradually everyone, prompted by a desire not to stay behind while others went. From the dregs of the people came hordes, well known to Vitellius by their shameful and obsequious services—buffoons, actors, jockeys, in whose disgraceful friendship he took extraordinary pleasure. Not only the colonies and municipal towns with their stores of supplies, but the very farmers and their fields in which the grain stood ready for the harvest, were despoiled as if the land were an enemy's.

LXXXVIII. The soldiers often fought among themselves with sad and fatal effect, for after the outbreak at Ticinum the differences between the legionaries and the auxiliaries had continued.[1] When, however, they had to deal with the country people, there was complete unanimity. But the worst massacre was perpetrated seven miles from Rome. There Vitellius was distributing cooked rations to each soldier, as if he were fattening gladiators; and crowds of people pouring out from Rome had filled the whole camp. While the soldiers were off their guard, some of the civilians, indulging in a servile pleasantry, disarmed them by cutting their belts without their knowledge; then they asked them if they had their swords. The soldiers were not accustomed to ridicule, so that their tempers could not brook the insult; they drew their weapons and attacked the civilians, who were unarmed. Among others, the father of one of the soldiers was killed while with his son; later on he was recognized, and, the news of his death

caede temperatum ab innoxiis. In urbe tamen trepidatum praecurrentibus passim militibus; forum maxime petebant, cupidine visendi locum in quo Galba iacuisset. Nec minus saevum[1] spectaculum erant ipsi, tergis ferarum et ingentibus telis horrentes, cum turbam populi per inscitiam parum vitarent, aut ubi lubrico viae vel occursu alicuius procidissent, ad iurgium, mox ad manus et ferrum transirent. Quin et tribuni praefectique cum terrore et armatorum catervis volitabant.

LXXXIX. Ipse Vitellius a ponte Mulvio insigni equo, paludatus accinctusque, senatum et populum ante se agens, quo minus ut captam urbem ingrederetur, amicorum consilio deterritus, sumpta praetexta et composito agmine incessit. Quattuor legionum aquilae per frontem totidemque circa e legionibus aliis vexilla, mox duodecim alarum signa et post peditum ordines eques; dein quattuor et triginta cohortes, ut nomina gentium aut species armorum forent, discretae. Ante aquilas praefecti castrorum tribunique et primi centurionum candida veste, ceteri iuxta suam quisque centuriam, armis donisque fulgentes; et militum phalerae torquesque

[1] scaevum *M.*

spreading, this slaughter of the innocent ceased. Yet in Rome no less alarm was caused by the soldiers who everywhere preceded the main army; these tried to find the forum first of all, for they wanted to see the place where Galba's body had lain. They themselves presented a sight that was equally savage, dressed as they were in shaggy skins of wild beasts and armed with enormous spears; while, in their ignorance, they failed to avoid the crowds, or, when they got a fall from the slippery streets or ran into a civilian, broke out in curses and soon went on to use their fists and swords. Even tribunes and prefects hurried up and down the streets spreading terror with their armed bands.

LXXXIX. Vitellius, mounted on a handsome horse and wearing a general's cloak and arms, had set out from the Mulvian bridge, driving the senate and people before him; but he was dissuaded by his courtiers from entering Rome as if it were a captured city, and so he changed to a senator's toga, ranged his troops in good order, and made his entry on foot. The eagles of four legions were at the head of the line, while the colours of four other legions were to be seen on either side; then came the standards of twelve troops of cavalry, and after them foot and horse; next marched thirty-four cohorts distinguished by the names of their countries or by their arms. Before the eagles marched the prefects of camp, the tribunes, and the chief centurions, dressed in white; the other centurions, with polished arms and decorations gleaming, marched each with his century. The common soldiers' medals and collars were likewise bright and shining. It was an imposing sight and

splendebant: decora facies et non Vitellio principe dignus exercitus. Sic Capitolium ingressus atque ibi matrem complexus Augustae nomine honoravit.

XC. Postera die tamquam apud alterius civitatis senatum populumque magnificam orationem de semet ipso prompsit, industriam temperantiamque suam laudibus attollens, consciis flagitiorum ipsis qui aderant omnique Italia, per quam somno et luxu pudendus incesserat. Vulgus tamen vacuum curis et sine falsi verique discrimine solitas adulationes edoctum clamore et vocibus adstrepebat; abnuentique nomen Augusti expressere ut adsumeret, tam frustra quam recusaverat.

XCI. Apud civitatem cuncta interpretantem funesti ominis[1] loco acceptum est quod maximum pontificatum adeptus Vitellius de caerimoniis publicis xv kalendas Augustas edixisset, antiquitus infausto die Cremerensi Alliensique cladibus: adeo omnis humani divinique iuris expers, pari libertorum amicorum socordia, velut inter temulentos agebat. Sed comitia consulum cum candidatis civiliter celebrans omnem infimae plebis rumorem in theatro ut spectator, in circo ut fautor adfectavit: quae grata sane et popularia, si a virtutibus proficiscerentur, memoria

[1] omīs *M*.

---

[1] At the Cremera the Fabii had died to a man in 477 B.C.; and at the Allia the Gauls had defeated the Romans in 390. No work, public or private, was undertaken on this dies Alliensis. Cf. Livy vi. 1 ff.; Suet. *Vitell.* 11.

an army which deserved a better emperor than Vitellius. With this array he mounted the Capitol, where he embraced his mother and bestowed on her the name of Augusta.

XC. The next day, as if he were speaking to the senate and people of an alien state, Vitellius made a boastful speech about himself, extolling his own industry and restraint, although his crimes were well known to his hearers and indeed to all Italy, through which he had come in shameful sloth and luxury. Yet the populace, careless and unable to distinguish between truth and falsehood, shouted loud the usual flattery, as it had been taught to do; in spite of his refusal they forced him to take the name of Augustus—but his acceptance proved as useless as his refusal.

XCI. A city which found a meaning in everything naturally regarded as an evil omen the fact that on becoming pontifex maximus Vitellius issued a proclamation concerning public religious ceremonies on the eighteenth of July, a day which for centuries had been held to be a day of ill-omen because of the disasters suffered at the Cremera and Allia:[1] thus, wholly ignorant of law both divine and human, his freedmen and courtiers as stupid as himself, he lived as if among a set of drunkards. Yet at the time of the consular elections he canvassed with his candidates like an ordinary citizen; he eagerly caught at every murmur of the lowest orders in the theatre where he merely looked on, but in the circus he openly favoured his colours. All this no doubt gave pleasure and would have won him popularity, if it had been prompted by virtue; but as it was, the memory of his former life made men regard these acts as un-

vitae prioris indecora et vilia accipiebantur. Ventitabat in senatum, etiam cum parvis de rebus patres consulerentur. Ac forte Priscus Helvidius praetor designatus contra studium eius censuerat. Commotus primo Vitellius, non tamen ultra quam tribunos plebis in auxilium spretae potestatis advocavit; mox mitigantibus amicis, qui altiorem iracundiam eius verebantur, nihil novi accidisse respondit quod duo senatores in re publica dissentirent; solitum se etiam Thraseae contra dicere. Inrisere plerique impudentiam aemulationis; aliis id ipsum placebat quod neminem ex praepotentibus, sed Thraseam ad exemplar verae gloriae legisset.

XCII. Praeposuerat praetorianis Publilium[1] Sabinum a[2] praefectura cohortis, Iulium Priscum tum centurionem:[3] Priscus Valentis, Sabinus Caecinae gratia pollebant; inter discordis Vitellio nihil auctoritas. Munia imperii Caecina ac Valens obibant, olim anxii odiis, quae bello et castris male dissimulata pravitas amicorum et fecunda gignendis inimicitiis civitas auxerat, dum ambitu comitatu et immensis salutantium agminibus contendunt comparanturque, variis in hunc aut illum Vitellii inclinationibus; nec umquam satis fida potentia, ubi nimia est: simul ipsum Vitellium, subitis offensis aut

[1] Publilium *Halm*: publium *M.*
[2] a *Mercerus*: ad *M.*
[3] tum centurionem *Lipsius*: dum centurio ē *M.*

---

[1] Thrasea had been the father-in-law of Helvidius. He was a leader of the Stoic opposition under Nero, by whose orders the senate condemned Thrasea to death in 66 A.D. Helvidius was banished from Italy at the same time. Cf. *Ann.* xvi. 21-35.

becoming and base. He frequently came to the senate, even when the senators were discussing trivial matters. Once it happened that Helvidius Priscus, being then praetor-elect, expressed a view which was opposed to his wishes. Vitellius was at first excited, but he did nothing more than call the tribunes of the people to support his authority that had been slighted. Later, when his friends, fearing that his anger might be deep-seated, tried to calm him, he replied that it was nothing strange for two senators to hold different views in the state; indeed he had usually opposed even Thrasea.[1] Many regarded this impudent comparison as absurd; others were pleased with the very fact that he had selected, not one of the most influential, but Thrasea, to serve as a model of true glory.

XCII. Vitellius had appointed as prefects of the praetorian guard Publilius Sabinus, who was prefect of a cohort, and Julius Priscus, a centurion at the time. Priscus owed his position to the favour of Valens, Sabinus to that of Caecina. When these two disagreed Vitellius had no authority. The emperor's duties were actually performed by Caecina and Valens. These had long hated each other with a hatred which had been hardly concealed during the war and in camp, and which was now increased by base friends and by civic life, always prolific in breeding enmities. In their efforts to have a great entourage, many courtiers, and long lines at their receptions they rivalled each other and provoked comparison, while the favour of Vitellius inclined now to one and again to the other; when a man has excessive power, he never can have complete trust: at the same time Vitellius himself, with his fickle readiness to take

intempestivis blanditiis mutabilem, contemnebant metuebantque. Nec eo segnius invaserant domos hortos opesque imperii, cum flebilis et egens nobilium turba, quos ipsos liberosque patriae Galba reddiderat, nulla principis misericordia iuvarentur. Gratum primoribus civitatis etiam plebs adprobavit, quod reversis ab exilio iura libertorum concessisset, quamquam id omni modo servilia ingenia corrumpebant, abditis pecuniis per occultos aut ambitiosos sinus, et quidam in domum Caesaris transgressi atque ipsis dominis potentiores.

XCIII. Sed miles, plenis castris et redundante multitudine, in porticibus aut delubris et urbe tota vagus, non principia noscere, non servare vigilias neque labore firmari: per inlecebras urbis et inhonesta dictu corpus otio, animum libidinibus imminuebant. Postremo ne salutis quidem cura infamibus Vaticani locis magna pars tetendit, unde crebrae in vulgus mortes; et adiacente Tiberi Germanorum Gallorumque[1] obnoxia morbis corpora fluminis aviditas[2] et aestus impatientia labefecit. Insuper confusus pravitate vel ambitu ordo militiae: sedecim

[1] gavorumque *M.*
[2] aviditas *Puteolanus*: aviditate *M.*

sudden offence or to resort to unseasonable flattery, was the object of their contempt and fears. This had not, however, made them slow to seize houses, gardens, and the wealth of the empire, while a pathetic and poverty-stricken crowd of nobles, whom with their children Galba had restored to their native city, received no pity or help from the emperor. An act which pleased the great and found approval even among the plebeians was that which gave those who returned from exile the rights of patrons over their freedmen; yet the freedmen by their servile cunning avoided the consequences of this act in every way, concealing their money by depositing it with obscure friends or with people of high position; some of them passed into Caesar's household and became more powerful even than their masters.

XCIII. But the soldiers, whose number was far too great for the crowded camp, wandered about in the colonnades, the temples, and in fact throughout the city; they did no guard-duty and were not kept in condition by service. Giving themselves up to the allurements of the capital and to excesses too shameful to name, they constantly weakened their physical strength by inactivity, their courage by debaucheries. Finally, with no regard even for their very lives, a large proportion camped in the unhealthy districts of the Vatican, which resulted in many deaths among the common soldiery; and the Tiber being close by, the inability of the Gauls and Germans to bear the heat and the consequent greed with which they drank from the stream weakened their bodies, which were already an easy prey to disease. Besides this, the different classes of service were thrown into confusion by corruption and self-

praetoriae, quattuor urbanae cohortes scribebantur, quis singula milia inessent. Plus in eo dilectu Valens audebat, tamquam ipsum Caecinam periculo exemisset. Sane adventu eius partes convaluerant, et sinistrum lenti itineris rumorem prospero proelio verterat. Omnisque inferioris Germaniae miles Valentem adsectabatur, unde primum creditur Caecinae fides fluitasse.

XCIV. Ceterum non ita ducibus indulsit Vitellius ut non plus militi liceret. Sibi quisque militiam sumpsere: quamvis indignus, si ita maluerat, urbanae militiae adscribebatur; rursus bonis remanere inter legionarios aut alaris volentibus permissum. Nec deerant qui vellent, fessi morbis et intemperiem caeli incusantes; robora tamen legionibus alisque subtracta, convulsum castrorum decus, viginti milibus e toto exercitu permixtis magis quam electis.

Contionante Vitellio postulantur ad supplicium Asiaticus et Flavus et Rufinus duces Galliarum, quod pro Vindice bellassent. Nec coercebat eius modi voces Vitellius: super insitam animo ignaviam con-

---

[1] The nine praetorian cohorts, which had formed the backbone of Otho's army, Vitellius had disbanded (ii. 67); in their place he now enrolled sixteen praetorian cohorts, and apparently increased the usual three City cohorts to four. This increase was probably due to the number volunteering for these advantageous services (chap. 94).

[2] Cf. i. 66; ii. 27, 31–44.

[3] Cf. i. 6. Of these chiefs nothing more is known.

seeking: sixteen praetorian, four city cohorts were enrolled with a quota of a thousand men each.[1] In organizing these bodies Valens put himself forward as having rescued Caecina himself from peril. It was true that his arrival had enabled the party of Vitellius to prevail, and that by the victory[2] he had got rid of the ugly rumour that he had delayed his advance; and all the troops of lower Germany were his enthusiastic followers, which gives us reason to think that this was the moment when Caecina's fidelity to Vitellius began to waver.

XCIV. However, the indulgences of Vitellius to his generals did not equal the licence he granted to his soldiers. Everyone selected the branch of the service he desired: no matter how unworthy a soldier might be, he was enrolled for service at Rome, if he preferred it. On the other hand, the good soldiers were allowed to remain with the legions or the cavalry if they wished; and there were some who did so desire, for they were exhausted by disease and cursed the climate of Rome. Nevertheless the strength was drawn off from the legions and cavalry, and the high prestige of the praetorian camp was shaken, for these twenty thousand men were not a picked body but only a confused mob taken from the whole army.

When Vitellius was addressing his troops, the soldiers demanded the punishment of Asiaticus, Flavius, and Rufinus, Gallic chiefs who had fought for Vindex.[3] Vitellius did not try to check demands of this sort, for not only was he naturally without energy, but he was well aware that the time was close at hand when he must pay his soldiers a

scius sibi instare donativum et deesse pecuniam omnia alia militi largiebatur. Liberti principum conferre pro numero mancipiorum ut tributum iussi; ipse sola perdendi cura stabula aurigis extruere, circum gladiatorum ferarumque spectaculis opplere, tamquam in summa abundantia[1] pecuniae inludere.

XCV. Quin et natalem Vitellii diem Caecina ac Valens editis tota urbe vicatim gladiatoribus celebravere, ingenti paratu et ante illum diem insolito. Laetum foedissimo cuique apud bonos invidiae fuit quod extructis in campo Martio aris inferias Neroni fecisset.[2] Caesae publice victimae cremataeque; facem Augustales subdidere,[3] quod sacerdotium, ut Romulus Tatio regi, ita Caesar Tiberius Iuliae genti sacravit. Nondum quartus a victoria mensis, et libertus Vitellii Asiaticus Polyclitos Patrobios et vetera odiorum nomina aequabat. Nemo in illa aula probitate aut industria certavit: unum ad potentiam iter, prodigis epulis et sumptu ganeaque[4] satiare inexplebilis Vitellii libidines. Ipse abunde ratus si praesentibus frueretur, nec in longius consultans, noviens miliens sestertium paucissimis mensibus intervertisse creditur.[5] Magna et misera civitas,

[1] abundantiae *M.*
[2] fecisset *Lipsius*: lecisset *M.*
[3] subdidere *Rhenanus*: subdere *M.*
[4] ganeaque *Palmerius*: galane: aque *M.*
[5] crederetur sagina *M.*

---

[1] Cf. i. 37, 49, and ii. 57.
[2] Equivalent to over $40,000,000. But the sum may have been exaggerated.

donative and that he had not the necessary money: therefore he indulged his troops in everything else. The freedmen of the imperial house were ordered to pay a tribute proportionate to the number of their slaves; but the emperor, whose only care was to spend money, kept building stables for jockeys, filling the arena with exhibitions of gladiators and wild beasts, and fooling away money as if his treasuries were filled to overflowing.

XCV. Moreover, Caecina and Valens celebrated his birthday by giving gladiatorial shows in every precinct of the city on an enormous scale unheard of up to that time. The worst element were delighted but the best citizens were scandalized by the act of Vitellius in erecting altars on the Campus Martius and sacrificing to the shades of Nero. The victims were killed and burned in the name of the state. The torch was applied to the sacrifices by the Augustales, a sacred college which Tiberius Caesar had dedicated to the Julian *gens*, as Romulus had dedicated a college to King Tatius. Four months had not yet passed since his victory, and yet Asiaticus, a freedman of Vitellius, already equalled a Polyclitus, a Patrobius, and the other detested names of the past.[1] In his court no one tried to win a reputation through honesty or industry: there was one single road to power, and that was by satisfying the emperor's boundless greed with extravagant banquets and expensive orgies. He himself was more than content to enjoy the present hour with no thought beyond: and he is believed to have squandered nine hundred million sesterces in a very few months.[2] At once great and wretched, the state was forced to endure within a single year an

eodem anno Othonem Vitellium passa, inter Vinios Fabios Icelos Asiaticos varia et pudenda sorte agebat, donec successere Mucianus et Marcellus et magis alii homines quam alii mores.

XCVI. Prima Vitellio tertiae legionis defectio nuntiatur, missis ab Aponio Saturnino epistulis, antequam is quoque Vespasiani partibus adgregaretur; sed neque Aponius cuncta, ut trepidans re subita, perscripserat, et amici adulantes mollius interpretabantur: unius legionis eam seditionem, ceteris exercitibus constare fidem. In hunc modum etiam Vitellius apud milites disseruit, praetorianos nuper exauctoratos[1] insectatus, a quibus falsos rumores dispergi, nec ullum civilis belli metum adseverabat, suppresso Vespasiani nomine et vagis per urbem militibus qui sermones populi coercerent. Id praecipuum alimentum famae erat.

XCVII. Auxilia tamen e Germania Britanniaque et Hispaniis excivit, segniter et necessitatem dissimulans. Perinde legati provinciaeque cunctabantur, Hordeonius Flaccus suspectis iam Batavis anxius proprio bello, Vettius Bolanus numquam satis quieta Britannia, et uterque ambigui. Neque ex Hispaniis properabatur, nullo tum ibi consulari: trium legionum legati, pares iure et prosperis Vitellii rebus

[1] exaucto rato *M.*

---

[1] Governor of Moesia. [2] Cf. ii. 57.
[3] Cf. ii. 65.

Otho and a Vitellius, and to suffer all the vicissitudes of a shameful fate at the hands of a Vinius, a Fabius, an Icelus, and an Asiaticus, until at last they were succeeded by a Mucianus and a Marcellus—other men rather than other characters.

XCVI. The first defection reported to Vitellius was that of the Third legion. The news came in a letter sent by Aponius Saturninus [1] before he also joined Vespasian's side. But Aponius, in his excitement over the sudden change, had not written the whole truth, and the flattery of courtiers gave a less serious interpretation to the news. They said that this was the mutiny of only one legion; that the rest of the troops were faithful. It was to the same effect that Vitellius himself spoke to the soldiers: he attacked the praetorians who had lately been discharged, blaming them for spreading false rumours, and declared that there was no occasion to fear civil war, keeping back Vespasian's name and sending soldiers round through the city to check the people's talk. Nothing furnished rumour with more food.

XCVII. Nevertheless he summoned auxiliaries from Germany, Britain, and the Spains; but he did this slowly and tried to conceal the necessity of his action. The governors and the provinces moved as slowly as he. Hordeonius Rufus already suspected the Batavians and was disturbed by the possibility of having a war of his own [2]; Vettius Bolanus never enjoyed entire peace in Britain,[3] and both of them were wavering in their allegiance. Nor did troops hurry from the Spains, for at that moment there was no governor there. The commanders of the three legions, who were equal in authority and who would have vied with each other in obedience to Vitellius

certaturi ad obsequium, adversam eius fortunam ex aequo detrectabant. In Africa legio cohortesque delectae a Clodio Macro, mox a Galba dimissae, rursus iussu Vitellii militiam cepere; simul cetera iuventus dabat impigre nomina. Quippe integrum illic ac favorabilem proconsulatum Vitellius, famosum invisumque Vespasianus egerat: proinde socii de imperio utriusque coniectabant, sed experimentum contra fuit.

XCVIII. Ac primo Valerius Festus legatus studia provincialium cum fide iuvit; mox nutabat, palam epistulis edictisque Vitellium, occultis nuntiis Vespasianum fovens et haec illave defensurus, prout invaluissent. Deprehensi cum litteris edictisque Vespasiani per Raetiam et Gallias militum et centurionum quidam ad Vitellium missi necantur: plures fefellere, fide amicorum aut suomet astu[1] occultati. Ita Vitellii paratus noscebantur, Vespasiani consiliorum pleraque ignota, primum socordia Vitellii, dein Pannonicae Alpes praesidiis insessae nuntios retinebant. Mare quoque etesiarum[2] flatu in Orientem navigantibus secundum, inde adversum erat.

XCIX. Tandem inruptione hostium atrocibus un-

[1] suomet astu *Agricola*: suo mestatu *M.*
[2] etesiarum *Rhenanus*: et esi flabra aquilonis arum *M.*

---

[1] Cf. i. 7 and 11.
[2] Valerius Festus was commander of the Third legion in Africa, placed there apparently to keep watch on the proconsul Lucius Piso. Cf. iv. 48, 49.

if his affairs had been prosperous, now all alike shrank from sharing his adversity. In Africa the legion and the cohorts raised by Clodius Macer, but afterwards dismissed by Galba,[1] resumed their service by order of Vitellius; at the same time the young civilians as well enlisted with enthusiasm. For the government of Vitellius as proconsul had been honest and popular, while that of Vespasian had been notorious and hated; from such memories the allies formed their conjectures as to what each would be as emperor; but experience proved exactly the opposite.

XCVIII. At first the commander, Valerius Festus, loyally supported the wishes of the provincials.[2] But presently he began to waver; in his public letters and documents he favoured Vitellius, but by secret messages he fostered Vespasian's interest and was ready to take whichever side prevailed. Some soldiers and centurions who had been dispatched through Rhaetia and the Gallic provinces were arrested with letters and proclamations of Vespasian on their persons, sent to Vitellius, and put to death. The majority of the messengers, however, escaped arrest, being concealed by faithful friends or escaping by their own wits. In this way the preparations of Vitellius became known while most of Vespasian's plans remained secret. This was due first of all to the stupidity of Vitellius, and secondly to the fact that the guards stationed in the Pannonian Alps blocked the messengers. Moreover, as this was the season of the etesian winds, the sea was favourable for vessels sailing to the East, but unfavourable to those coming from that quarter.

XCIX. Finally Vitellius became alarmed by the oncoming of the enemy and by the terrifying messages

dique nuntiis exterritus Caecinam ac Valentem expedire[1] ad bellum iubet. Praemissus Caecina, Valentem e gravi corporis morbo tum primum adsurgentem infirmitas tardabat. Longe alia proficiscentis ex urbe Germanici exercitus species: non vigor corporibus, non ardor animis; lentum et rarum agmen, fluxa arma, segnes equi; impatiens solis pulveris tempestatum, quantumque hebes ad sustinendum laborem miles, tanto ad discordias promptior. Accedebat huc Caecinae ambitio vetus, torpor recens, nimia fortunae indulgentia soluti in luxum, seu perfidiam meditanti[2] infringere exercitus virtutem inter artes erat. Credidere plerique Flavii Sabini consiliis concussam Caecinae mentem, ministro sermonum Rubrio Gallo: rata apud Vespasianum fore pacta transitionis. Simul odiorum invidiaeque erga Fabium Valentem admonebatur ut impar apud Vitellium gratiam virisque apud novum principem pararet.

C. Caecina e complexu Vitellii multo cum honore digressus partem equitum ad occupandam Cremonam praemisit. Mox vexilla primae, quartae, quintaedecimae, sextaedecimae[3] legionum, dein quinta et duoetvicensima secutae; postremo agmine unaetvi-

[1] expedire *Acidalius*: expediri *M*.
[2] meditanti *Rhenanus*: meditatio *M*.
[3] primae . . . sextaedecimae *Ferletus et Nipperdey*: in quattuor decum XVI *M*.

which reached him from every side, and ordered Caecina and Valens to prepare for war. Caecina was sent on in advance; Valens, who was at that moment just getting up from a serious sickness, was delayed by physical weakness. As the army from Germany left the city it presented a very different appearance from that which it had displayed on entering Rome: the soldiers had no vigour, no enthusiasm; they marched in a slow and ragged column, dragging their weapons, while their horses were without spirit; but the troops who could not endure sun, dust, or storm and who had no heart to face toil, were all the more ready to quarrel. Another factor in the situation was furnished by Caecina's old ambition and his newly acquired sloth, for an excess of Fortune's favours had made him give way to luxury; or he may have been already planning to turn traitor and so have made it part of his plan to break the morale of his army. It has been generally believed that it was the arguments of Flavius Sabinus that made Caecina's loyalty waver, and that the go-between was Rubrius Gallus, who assured him that Vespasian would approve the conditions on which Caecina was to come over. At the same time he was reminded of his hatred and jealousy towards Fabius Valens and was urged, since his influence with Vitellius was not equal to that of his rival, to seek favour and support from the new emperor.

C. Caecina, departing from the embraces of Vitellius with great honours, sent a part of his horse ahead to occupy Cremona. Presently detachments of the First, Fourth, Fifteenth and Sixteenth legions followed; then the Fifth and Twenty-second; in the rear marched the Twenty-first Rapax and the

censima Rapax et prima Italica incessere cum vexillariis trium Britannicarum legionum et electis auxiliis. Profecto Caecina scripsit Fabius Valens exercitui, quem ipse ductaverat, ut in itinere opperiretur: sic sibi cum Caecina convenisse. Qui praesens eoque validior mutatum id consilium finxit ut ingruenti bello tota mole occurreretur. Ita adcelerare legiones Cremonam, pars Hostiliam petere iussae: ipse Ravennam devertit praetexto classem adloquendi; mox Patavii[1] secretum componendae proditionis quaesitum. Namque Lucilius Bassus[2] post praefecturam alae Ravennati simul ac Misenensi classibus a Vitellio praepositus, quod non statim praefecturam praetorii adeptus foret, iniquam iracundiam flagitiosa perfidia ulciscebatur. Nec sciri potest traxeritne Caecinam, an, quod evenit inter malos ut et similes sint, eadem illos pravitas impulerit. CI. Scriptores temporum, qui potiente rerum Flavia domo monimenta belli huiusce composuerunt, curam pacis et amorem rei publicae, corruptas in adulationem causas, tradidere: nobis super insitam levitatem et prodito Galba vilem mox fidem aemulatione etiam invidiaque, ne ab

[1] patvi *M.* [2] Bassus *Rhenanus*: blaessus *M.*

---

[1] When in Lower Germany.

First Italic with detachments from the three legions in Britain and with picked auxiliary troops. After Caecina had gone, Fabius Valens wrote to the troops which he had earlier commanded,[1] and ordered them to wait for him on the way, saying that he and Caecina had agreed to this effect. But Caecina, being with the troops and therefore having the advantage over Valens, pretended that the plan had been changed that they might meet the rising tide of war with their whole strength. So the legions were ordered to press on, part to Cremona, part to Hostilia; he himself turned aside to Ravenna under the pretext of addressing the fleet; but presently he retired to the secrecy of Padua to arrange the conditions of betrayal. For Lucilius Bassus, who had previously been only a prefect of a squadron of cavalry, had been placed by Vitellius in command of the fleet of Ravenna along with that of Misenum; but his failure to receive promptly the prefecture of the praetorian guard had roused in him an unjust resentment, which he was now satisfying by a shameful and treacherous act of vengeance. It is impossible to determine whether Bassus drew Caecina on, or whether, since it often happens that there is a likeness between bad men, the same villainy impelled them both. CI. The contemporary historians, who wrote their accounts of this war while the Flavian house occupied the throne, have indeed recorded their anxiety for peace and devotion to the State, falsifying motives in order to flatter; but to me it seems that both men, in addition to their natural fickleness and the fact that after betraying Galba they then held their honour cheap, were moved by mutual rivalry and a jealous fear

aliis apud Vitellium anteirentur, pervertisse ipsum Vitellium videntur. Caecina legiones adsecutus centurionum militumque animos obstinatos pro Vitellio variis artibus subruebat: Basso eadem molienti minor difficultas erat, lubrica ad mutandam fidem classe ob memoriam recentis pro Othone militiae.

that they would be surpassed by others in the imperial favour, and so overthrew Vitellius himself. Caecina caught up with his legions and began by various devices to undermine the unshaken loyalty of the centurions and soldiers towards Vitellius; Bassus found less difficulty when he attempted the same with the fleet, for the sailors, remembering their recent service to Otho, were ready to shift their allegiance.

BOOK III

LIBER III

I. Meliore fato fideque partium Flavianarum duces consilia belli tractabant. Poetovionem in hiberna tertiae decimae legionis convenerant. Illic agitavere placeretne obstrui Pannoniae Alpes, donec a tergo vires universae consurgerent, an ire comminus et certare pro Italia constantius foret. Quibus opperiri auxilia et trahere bellum videbatur, Germanicarum legionum vim famamque extollebant, et advenisse mox cum Vitellio Britannici exercitus robora: ipsis nec numerum parem pulsarum nuper legionum, et quamquam atrociter loquerentur, minorem esse apud victos animum. Sed insessis interim Alpibus venturum cum copiis Orientis Mucianum; superesse Vespasiano mare, classis, studia provinciarum, per quas velut alterius belli molem cieret. Ita salubri mora novas viris adfore, ex[1] praesentibus nihil periturum.

[1] ex *Urlichs*: et *M.*

---

[1] Pettau on the Drave in Styria.
[2] Cf. ii. 57. Eight thousand had come from Britain.
[3] At Bedriacum. Cf. ii. 41–45.

BOOK III

I. The generals of the Flavian party were planning their campaign with better fortune and greater loyalty. They had come together at Poetovio,[1] the winter quarters of the Thirteenth legion. There they discussed whether they should guard the passes of the Pannonian Alps until the whole mass of their forces could be raised behind them, or whether it would not be a bolder stroke to engage the enemy at once and struggle with him for the possession of Italy. Those who favoured waiting for the auxiliaries and prolonging the war, emphasized the strength and reputation of the German legions and dwelt on the fact that the flower of the army in Britain had recently arrived with Vitellius;[2] they pointed out that they had on their side an inferior number of legions, and at best legions which had lately been beaten,[3] and that although the soldiers talked boldly enough, the defeated always have less courage. But while they meantime held the Alps, Mucianus, they said, would arrive with the troops from the east; Vespasian had besides full control of the sea and his fleets, and he could count on the enthusiastic support of the provinces, through whose aid he could raise the storm of almost a second war. Therefore they declared that delay would favour them, that new forces would join them, and that they would lose none of their present advantages.

II. Ad ea Antonius Primus (is acerrimus belli concitator[1]) festinationem ipsis utilem, Vitellio exitiosam disseruit. Plus socordiae quam fiduciae accessisse victoribus; neque enim in procinctu et castris habitos: per omnia Italiae municipia desides, tantum hospitibus metuendos, quanto ferocius ante se egerint, tanto cupidius insolitas voluptates hausisse. Circo quoque ac theatris et amoenitate urbis emollitos aut valetudinibus fessos; sed addito spatio rediturum et his robur meditatione belli; nec procul Germaniam, unde vires; Britanniam freto dirimi, iuxta Gallias Hispaniasque, utrimque viros equos tributa, ipsamque Italiam et opes urbis; ac si inferre arma ultro velint, duas classis vacuumque Illyricum mare. Quid tum claustra montium profutura? Quid tractum in aestatem aliam bellum? Unde interim pecuniam et commeatus? Quin potius eo ipso uterentur quod Pannonicae legiones deceptae magis quam victae resurgere in ultionem properent, Moesici exercitus integras viris attulerint. Si numerus militum potius quam legionum putetur, plus hinc roboris, nihil libidinum; et profuisse disciplinae ipsum pudorem: equites vero ne tum quidem victos,

[1] conciator *M.*

---

[1] Commander of the Seventh legion, Galbiana. Cf. ii. 86.

[2] The large fleets stationed at Misenum and Ravenna.

[3] Cf. ii. 42.

II. In answer Antonius Primus,[1] the most enthusiastic partisan of war, argued that haste was helpful to them, ruinous to Vitellius. "The victorious side," he said, "has gained a spirit of sloth rather than confidence, for their soldiers have not been kept within the bounds of camp; they have been loafing about all the municipal towns of Italy, fearful only to their hosts; the savagery that they once displayed has been matched by the greed with which they have drunk deep of their new pleasures. They have been weakened, too, by the circus, by the theatres, and by the delights of Rome, or else exhausted by disease; but if they are given time, even they will recover their strength by preparing for war; Germany, from which they draw their strength, is not far away; Britain is separated only by a strait; the provinces of Gaul and Spain are near: from both they receive men, horses, and tribute; they hold Italy itself and the wealth of Rome; and if they wish to attack they have two fleets[2] and the Illyrian Sea is open. In that case, what will the mountain barriers avail us? What profit shall we find in prolonging the war into another summer? Where shall we meantime find money and supplies? Rather let us take advantage of the fact that the Pannonian legions, which were deceived rather than defeated,[3] are eager to rise in revenge; that the troops in Moesia have contributed their strength, which is quite unimpaired. If we reckon the number of soldiers rather than of legions, we see that we have on our side the greater force and no debauchery; the very shame of the defeat at Bedriacum has helped our discipline. Moreover, the cavalry were not beaten even then,

sed quamquam rebus adversis disiectam Vitellii aciem. "Duae tunc Pannonicae ac Moesicae alae perrupere hostem: nunc sedecim alarum coniuncta signa pulsu sonituque et nube ipsa operient ac superfundent oblitos proeliorum equites equosque. Nisi quis retinet, idem suasor auctorque consilii ero. Vos, quibus fortuna in integro est, legiones continete: mihi expeditae cohortes sufficient. Iam reseratam Italiam,[1] impulsas Vitellii res audietis. Iuvabit sequi et vestigiis vincentis insistere."

III. Haec ac talia flagrans oculis, truci voce, quo latius audiretur (etenim se centuriones et quidam militum consilio miscuerant), ita effudit ut cautos quoque ac providos permoveret, vulgus et ceteri unum virum ducemque, spreta aliorum segnitia, laudibus ferrent. Hanc sui famam ea statim contione commoverat, qua recitatis Vespasiani epistulis non ut plerique incerta disseruit, huc illuc tracturus interpretatione,[2] prout conduxisset: aperte descendisse in causam videbatur, eoque gravior militibus erat culpae vel gloriae socius.

IV. Proxima Cornelii Fusci procuratoris auctoritas.

[1] reseratam Italiam *Pichena*: reserata militiam *M.*
[2] interpretatione *Acidalius*: interpraetationem *M.*

---

[1] Cf. ii. 41. [2] Cf. ii. 82.
[3] Cf. ii. 86.

but in spite of disaster they broke the forces of Vitellius.[1] On that day two squadrons from Pannonia and Moesia pierced the enemy's line; now sixteen squadrons charging in a body, by the very noise they make and the cloud of dust they raise, will overwhelm and bury the horsemen and horses of our foes, for they have forgotten what a battle is. Unless someone restrains me, I who advise will also perform. Do you, whose fortune is still unblemished, hold back your legions, if you will; for me light cohorts will be enough. Presently you shall hear that the gates of Italy are open, that the power of Vitellius is overthrown. Yours will be the delight of following the victor and of treading in his footsteps."

III. Thus and in like strain, with flashing eyes and in fierce tones that he might be more widely heard (for the centurions and some of the common soldiers had made their way into the council) did he pour forth his words so that he moved even men of caution and foresight, while the general throng, and after them the rest, scorning the cowardly inaction of the other officers, extolled him as the one man and the one leader. This reputation Primus had won in that assembly from the moment in his harangue when, after reading out the letter of Vespasian,[2] he did not talk in equivocal terms, ready to put this or that interpretation on Vespasian's words to his own advantage, as the others had done; but he seemed to have openly joined Vespasian's cause; therefore he carried the greater weight with the soldiers, for he was now an accomplice in their fault or a partner in their glory.

IV. After Primus the procurator Cornelius Fuscus[3]

Is quoque inclementer in Vitellium invehi solitus nihil spei sibi inter adversa reliquerat. Tampius Flavianus, natura ac senecta cunctantior,[1] suspiciones militum inritabat, tamquam adfinitatis cum Vitellio meminisset; idemque,[2] quod coeptante legionum motu profugus, dein sponte remeaverat, perfidiae locum quaesisse credebatur. Nam Flavianum, omissa Pannonia ingressum Italiam et discrimini exemptum, rerum novarum cupido legati nomen resumere et misceri civilibus armis impulerat, suadente Cornelio Fusco, non quia industria Flaviani egebat, sed ut consulare nomen surgentibus cum maxime partibus honesta specie praetenderetur.

V. Ceterum ut transmittere in Italiam impune et usui foret, scriptum Aponio Saturnino,[3] cum exercitu Moesico celeraret. Ac ne inermes provinciae barbaris nationibus exponerentur, principes Sarmatarum Iazugum, penes quos civitatis regimen, in commilitium adsciti. Plebem quoque et vim equitum, qua sola valent, offerebant: remissum id munus, ne inter discordias externa molirentur aut maiore ex diverso mercede ius fasque exuerent. Trahuntur in partis

[1] cunctantior *Halm*: cunctatior *M.* [2] idque *M.*

[3] aponio satiū *post quae sequitur* (7) revirescere . . . ut inimici (9), *deinde* ninocū exercitum moesico (5); *verum ordinem restituit Pichena.*

---

[1] The governor of Pannonia. [2] *i.e.* against Vespasian.

[3] Governor of Moesia.

[4] A people living between the Danube and the Theiss.

[5] They also served as hostages for the good behaviour of their people.

had the greatest influence. He also had been in the habit of assailing Vitellius violently and so had left himself no hope in case of failure. Tampius Flavianus,[1] whose nature and years made him more hesitant, roused the suspicions of the soldiers; they thought that he still remembered the family ties that bound him to Vitellius. Furthermore, since he had fled at the first movement of the legions and then had come back of his own accord, the troops believed that he had treacherous designs.[2] There was some basis for this suspicion, since Flavianus had abandoned Pannonia and withdrawn to Italy, where he was not involved in the crisis; but later his desire for a revolution had impelled him to resume his title of governor and to bear a hand in civil war. Cornelius Fuscus urged him to take this present step, not because he needed the assistance of Flavianus, but because he wished to display a consular name to give credit and prestige to his party which was just then rising to view.

V. But in order to be able to enter Italy without danger and with advantage, word was sent Aponius Saturninus[3] to hurry with the army then in Moesia. To avoid exposing the provinces in their unprotected condition to barbarous nations, the ruling chiefs of the Sarmatian Iazuges[4] were called into service with the army.[5] These chiefs offered their people also and their force of cavalry, which constitutes their sole effective strength; but this offer was declined for fear that in the midst of civil troubles they might undertake some hostile enterprise, or that, if a larger reward should be offered by the other side, they might abandon all sense of right and justice. Vespasian's officers further drew to their side Sido

Sido atque Italicus reges Sueborum, quis vetus obsequium erga Romanos et gens fidei quam iussorum[1] patientior. Opposita[2] in latus auxilia, infesta Raetia, cui Porcius Septiminus procurator erat, incorruptae erga Vitellium fidei. Igitur Sextilius Felix cum ala Auriana et octo cohortibus ac Noricorum iuventute ad occupandam ripam Aeni[3] fluminis, quod Raetos Noricosque interfluit, missus. Nec his aut illis proelium temptantibus, fortuna partium alibi transacta.

VI. Antonio vexillarios e cohortibus et partem equitum ad invadendam Italiam rapienti comes fuit Arrius Varus, strenuus bello, quam gloriam et dux Corbulo et prosperae in Armenia res addiderant. Idem secretis apud Neronem sermonibus ferebatur Corbulonis virtutes criminatus; unde infami gratia primum pilum adepto laeta ad praesens male parta mox in perniciem vertere. Sed Primus ac Varus occupata Aquileia per[4] proxima quaeque et Opitergii et Altini laetis animis accipiuntur. Relictum Altini praesidium adversus classis Ravennatis conatus,[5] nondum defectione eius audita. Inde Patavium et Ateste partibus adiunxere. Illuc cognitum tris Vi-

[1] quam iussorum *Scheffer*: commissior *M.*
[2] opposita *Rhenanus*: posita *M.*
[3] Aeni *Rhenanus*: rheni *M.*
[4] per *add. Baiter.*
[5] conatus *suppl. Heinisch.*

---

[1] These Suebi had been established by the younger Drusus Caesar north of the Danube, between the March and the Waag, in 19 A.D.

[2] Raetia lay west of Noricum and north of Italy, so that the party of Vespasian had to protect their right flank from possible attack by Septiminus.

[3] Antonius Primus was commander of the Seventh Legion

and Italicus, princes of the Suebi, who had long been loyal to the Romans and whose people were more inclined to remain faithful to Rome than to take orders from others.[1] They protected their flank with auxiliary troops, for Raetia was hostile to Vespasian's party, its procurator Porcius Septiminus being unshaken in his loyalty to Vitellius.[2] This was the reason that Sextilius Felix with the Aurian squadron of horse and eight cohorts of infantry was despatched to occupy the bank of the river Inn, which flows between Raetia and Noricum. Neither side wished to test the fortunes of battle, and the fate of the parties was decided elsewhere.

VI. As Antonius[3] hurried forward some detachments from the cohorts and part of the cavalry to invade Italy, he was accompanied by Arrius Varus,[4] a vigorous fighter, whose fame had been increased by his service under Corbulo and by his successes in Armenia. This same Varus, according to common report, had in secret conference with Nero brought serious charges against Corbulo's good character; by this means he had won, as a reward of shame, the rank of chief centurion, and this ill gain, which delighted him at the time, later proved to be his ruin. However, Antonius and Varus occupied Aquileia, and then advancing through the adjacent districts were received with joy at Opitergium and Altinum.[5] A force was left at Altinum to block any attempt on the part of the fleet at Ravenna, of whose defection they had not yet heard. Next they drew Padua and Ateste[6] to their side. At Ateste they heard

Galbiana in Pannonia. Cf. ii. 86; *Ann.* xiv. 40; Suetonius *Vitellius* 18.

[4] Cf. *Ann.* xiii. 9. [5] Oderzo and Altino. [6] Este.

tellianas cohortis et alam, cui Sebosianae nomen, ad Forum Alieni ponte iuncto consedisse. Placuit occasio invadendi incuriosos; nam id quoque nuntiabatur. Luce prima inermos plerosque oppressere. Praedictum ut paucis interfectis ceteros pavore ad mutandam fidem cogerent. Et fuere qui se statim dederent: plures abrupto ponte instanti hosti viam abstulerunt. Principia belli secundum Flavianos data.[1]

VII. Vulgata victoria legiones septima Galbiana, tertia decima Gemina cum Vedio Aquila legato Patavium alacres veniunt. Ibi pauci dies ad requiem sumpti, et Minicius Iustus praefectus castrorum legionis septimae, quia adductius quam civili bello imperitabat, subtractus militum irae ad Vespasianum missus est. Desiderata diu res interpretatione gloriaque in[2] maius accipitur, postquam Galbae imagines discordia temporum subversas in omnibus municipiis recoli iussit Antonius, decorum pro causa ratus, si placere Galbae principatus et partes revirescere crederentur.

VIII. Quaesitum inde quae sedes bello legeretur.

[1] Principia (p'rincipia) . . . data (datae) *huc transtulit Nipperdey ex c.* 7 *ubi haec verba* vulgata victoria *sequuntur.*
[2] in *om. M.*

---

[1] Probably the present Legnago; the bridge there was over the Adige.

that three cohorts of the Vitellian forces and the squadron of cavalry called Sebosian had occupied Forum Alieni[1] and built a bridge over the stream there. Primus and Varus decided that this was a good opportunity to attack the Vitellians, who were wholly off their guard; for this fact also had been reported. At daybreak they cut down many of them quite unarmed. They had been advised that if they killed a few, they could force the rest by fear to change their allegiance; and there were some who surrendered at once. The larger part, however, broke down the bridge and so, by cutting off the road, blocked their foes' advance. The opening of the campaign was favourable to Vespasian's side.

VII. When the news of the victory was noised abroad, two legions, the Seventh Galbiana and the Tenth Gemina, marched with all speed to Padua under their commander Vedius Aquila. There they rested for a few days during which Minicius Justus, prefect of the camp of the Seventh legion, whose discipline had been somewhat too strict for civil war, was withdrawn from the soldiers' resentment by being sent to Vespasian. An act long desired was now received with delight and given a flattering interpretation beyond its deserts, when Antonius gave orders that in all the towns Galba's statues, which had been thrown down in the disorders of the times, should again be honoured. His real motive was that he believed that it would dignify Vespasian's cause if this were accounted an approval of Galba's principate and a revival of his party.

VIII. Then Vespasian's commanders considered what place they should select as the seat of war.

Verona potior visa, patentibus circum campis ad pugnam equestrem, qua praevalebant: simul coloniam copiis validam auferre Vitellio in rem famamque videbatur. Possessa ipso transitu Vicetia; quod per se parvum[1] (etenim modicae municipio vires) magni momenti locum obtinuit reputantibus illic Caecinam genitum et patriam hostium duci ereptam. In Veronensibus pretium fuit: exemplo opibusque partis iuvere; et interiectus exercitus Raetiam Iuliasque Alpis, [ac][2] ne pervium illa Germanicis exercitibus foret, obsaepserat. Quae ignara Vespasiano aut vetita: quippe Aquileiae sisti bellum expectarique Mucianum iubebat, adiciebatque imperio consilium, quando Aegyptus, claustra annonae, vectigalia opulentissimarum provinciarum obtinerentur, posse Vitellii exercitum egestate stipendii frumentique ad deditionem subigi. Eadem Mucianus crebris epistulis monebat, incruentam et sine luctu victoriam et alia huiusce modi praetexendo, sed gloriae avidus atque omne belli decus sibi retinens. Ceterum ex distantibus terrarum spatiis consilia post res adferebantur.

IX. Igitur repentino incurso Antonius stationes hostium inrupit; temptatisque levi proelio animis

[1] parvum *Halm*: parum *M*. [2] *secl. Lipsius.*

---

[1] Vicenza. [2] Over the Brenner Pass.
[3] Egypt, Syria, and Asia.

They decided on Verona because there are open plains about it suited to the operations of cavalry, in which their chief strength lay; and at the same time to take away from Vitellius so strong a colony seemed likely to contribute to their own cause and reputation. As they advanced they seized Vicetia.[1] This was no great thing in itself, for the town had but moderate resources, yet its capture had great significance in the minds of those who considered that it was Caecina's birthplace and that the enemy's general had seen his native town snatched from him. But Verona was a real gain: the example and resources of its inhabitants were helpful, and the army's position between Raetia and the Julian Alps blocked the entrance at that point of the forces from Germany.[2] All these operations were unknown to Vespasian or had been forbidden by him. He had directed that his forces should not carry their operations beyond Aquileia, but should wait there for Mucianus; and he had also given the reasons for his orders, pointing out that since they held Egypt, controlled the grain supply of Italy, and possessed the revenues of the richest provinces,[3] the army of Vitellius could be forced to surrender by lack of pay and food. Mucianus wrote frequent warnings to the same effect, giving as his reason his desire for a victory which would cost no blood or sorrow; in reality he was ambitious for personal fame and wished to keep for himself all the glory of the war. However, the distances were so great that the advice arrived after the events.

IX. So then Antonius suddenly attacked the enemy's posts; but after testing his foe's courage in a trifling skirmish, he withdrew his troops with

ex aequo discessum. Mox Caecina inter Hostiliam, vicum Veronensium, et paludes Tartari fluminis castra permuniit, tutus loco, cum terga flumine, latera obiectu paludis tegerentur. Quod si adfuisset fides, aut opprimi universis Vitellianorum viribus duae legiones, nondum coniuncto Moesico exercitu, potuere, aut retro actae deserta Italia turpem fugam conscivissent. Sed Caecina per varias moras prima hostibus prodidit tempora belli, dum quos armis pellere promptum erat, epistulis increpat, donec per nuntios pacta perfidiae firmaret. Interim Aponius Saturninus cum legione septima Claudiana advenit. Legioni tribunus Vipstanus Messala praeerat, claris maioribus, egregius ipse et qui solus ad id bellum artis bonas attulisset. Has ad copias nequaquam Vitellianis paris (quippe tres adhuc legiones erant) misit epistulas Caecina, temeritatem victa arma tractantium incusans. Simul virtus Germanici exercitus laudibus attollebatur, Vitellii modica et vulgari mentione, nulla in Vespasianum contumelia nihil prorsus quod aut corrumperet hostem aut terreret. Flavianarum partium duces omissa prioris fortunae defensione pro Vespasiano magnifice, pro

[1] Ostiglia. [2] Tartaro.

[3] From Moesia. Cf. chap. 5.

[4] For the legate Tettius Julianus had fled. Cf. ii. 85.

[5] Vipstanus Messala wrote a history of this war which Tacitus employed (iii. 25, 28); he is also one of the participants in the *Dialogus de Oratoribus*.

no advantage to either side. Presently Caecina established his camp between Hostilia,[1] a village in the district of the Veronese, and the marshes of the river Tartarus.[2] Here he was protected by the situation itself, his rear being covered by the river and his flanks by the marshes. If he had only been loyal to Vitellius, with the combined forces of the Vitellians he might have crushed the two legions at Verona, for the troops from Moesia had not yet joined them; or at least he could have driven them back and made them abandon Italy in disgraceful flight. But as it was, by various delays he betrayed to his opponents the first advantages of the campaign, spending his time in writing letters, reproving those whom he might easily have routed with his arms, until he could through messengers conclude the terms of his own treason. In the meantime Aponius Saturninus arrived with the Seventh or Claudian legion.[3] This legion was commanded[4] by the tribune Vipstanus Messala,[5] a man of eminent family and of personal distinction; indeed he was the only one who had brought with him to the war some honourable pursuits. To these forces, which were by no means a match for those of Vitellius, since thus far only three legions had concentrated at Verona, Caecina now wrote, reproving them for their rashness in taking up arms after defeat. At the same time he praised the valour of the German army, but made only slight and casual reference to Vitellius, with no derogatory mention of Vespasian; and he said nothing that was calculated to win over or frighten his opponents. The chiefs of the Flavian party in reply made no apology for their past misfortunes, but they spoke out boldly for Vespasian;

causa fidenter, de exercitu securi, in Vitellium ut inimici praesumpsere, facta tribunis centurionibusque retinendi quae Vitellius indulsisset spe; atque ipsum Caecinam non obscure ad transitionem hortabantur. Recitatae pro contione epistulae addidere fiduciam, quod submisse[1] Caecina, velut offendere Vespasianum timens, ipsorum duces contemptim tamquam insultantes Vitellio scripsissent.

X. Adventu deinde duarum legionum, e quibus tertiam Dillius Aponianus,[2] octavam Numisius Lupus ducebant, ostentare viris et militari vallo Veronam circumdare placuit. Forte Galbianae legioni in adversa fronte valli opus cesserat, et visi procul sociorum equites vanam formidinem ut hostes fecere. Rapiuntur arma metu[3] proditionis. Ira militum in Tampium Flavianum incubuit, nullo criminis argumento, sed iam pridem invisus turbine quodam ad exitium poscebatur: propinquum Vitellii, proditorem Othonis, interceptorem donativi clamitabant. Nec defensioni locus, quamquam supplicis manus tenderet, humi plerumque stratus, lacera veste, pectus atque ora singultu quatiens. Id ipsum apud infensos

[1] summisisse *M.*
[2] Aponianus *Rhenanus*: apontanus *M.*
[3] arma metu *Faernus*: armā et ut *M.*

---

[1] Governor of Pannonia, iii. 4.

displaying confidence in their cause and faith in the security of their army, they assailed Vitellius as if they were his personal enemies, and gave the tribunes and centurions reason to hope that they might keep the indulgences that Vitellius had granted them. Caecina himself they urged in no ambiguous terms to come over to their side. This correspondence the Flavian leaders read to their soldiers in assembly and thereby inspired their troops with additional confidence; for Caecina had written in humble terms, as if afraid of offending Vespasian, while their generals had written in scorn and with the evident desire to insult Vitellius.

X. Then two other legions arrived, the Third in command of Dillius Aponianus, the Eighth under Numisius Lupus. The Flavian party now decided to show their strength and to surround Verona with a rampart. It happened that the Galbian legion was assigned to work on that part of the lines that faced the enemy; seeing in the distance some allied cavalry, they became panic-stricken, for they thought that the enemy was coming. They seized their arms, fearing that they had been betrayed. The soldiers' wrath fell on Tampius Flavianus,[1] of whose guilt there was not the slightest proof; but the troops already hated him and now in a whirlwind of rage demanded his death. They cried out that he was a kinsman of Vitellius, that he had betrayed Otho, and had diverted the donative intended for them. Flavianus had no opportunity to defend himself, although he raised his hands in supplication, grovelled repeatedly on the ground, tore his garments, while the tears ran down his face and his breast was convulsed with sobs. These very acts

incitamentum erat, tamquam nimius pavor conscientiam argueret. Obturbabatur militum vocibus Aponius, cum loqui coeptaret; fremitu et clamore ceteros aspernantur. Uni Antonio apertae militum aures; namque et facundia aderat mulcendique vulgum artes et auctoritas. Ubi crudescere seditio et a conviciis ac probris ad tela et manus transibant, inici catenas Flaviano iubet. Sensit ludibrium miles, disiectisque qui tribunal tuebantur extrema vis parabatur. Opposuit sinum Antonius stricto ferro, aut militum se manibus aut suis moriturum obtestans, ut quemque notum et aliquo militari decore insignem aspexerat, ad ferendam opem nomine ciens. Mox conversus ad signa et bellorum deos, hostium potius exercitibus illum furorem, illam discordiam inicerent orabat, donec fatisceret seditio et extremo iam die sua quisque in tentoria dilaberentur. Profectus eadem nocte Flavianus obviis Vespasiani litteris discrimini exemptus est.

XI. Legiones velut tabe infectae Aponium Saturninum Moesici exercitus legatum eo atrocius adgrediuntur, quod non, ut prius, labore et opere fessae, sed medio diei exarserant, vulgatis epistulis,

---

[1] Aponius Saturninus, the governor of Moesia (ii. 85; iii. 5) naturally took the lead, but without avail.

[2] The eagles were regarded as sacred and were kept with images of the gods in a kind of chapel at headquarters.

[3] The letter from Vespasian absolved Flavianus from any disloyalty toward him.

increased the rage of the soldiers, for they regarded his excessive terror as proof of his guilt. When Aponius[1] began to speak, he was interrupted by the soldiers' cries; they expressed their scorn of the other commanders by groans and howls. Antonius was the only one to whom they would lend an ear, for he was eloquent, had influence, and possessed the art of quieting a mob. When he saw that the mutiny was gaining strength and the soldiers were about to pass from reproaches and insults to armed force, he ordered Flavianus to be put in chains. But the troops saw through the ruse, thrust aside those who guarded the tribunal, and prepared to use extreme violence. Antonius drew his sword and pointed it at his breast, declaring that he would die by his soldiers' hands or by his own; at the same time he called by name to his assistance every soldier in sight whom he knew or who had some military decoration. Presently he turned toward the standards and the gods of war,[2] praying them to inspire rather the enemy's forces with this madness and this discord. At last the mutiny gradually spent itself, and as the day was now near its end, the soldiers slipped away, each to his quarters. The same night Flavianus set out from camp, but was met by a letter from Vespasian which saved him from danger.[3]

XI Then the legions, as if smitten with a mad contagion, assailed Aponius Saturninus, the commander of the army from Moesia. They attacked him with the greater violence, for they were not as before tired by severe labour, but their anger blazed up suddenly in the middle of the day on the publication of some letters which Saturninus was believed

quas Saturninus ad Vitellium scripsisse credebatur. Ut olim virtutis modestiaeque, tunc procacitatis et petulantiae certamen erat, ne minus violenter Aponium quam Flavianum ad supplicium deposcerent. Quippe Moesicae legiones adiutam a se Pannonicorum ultionem referentes, et Pannonici, velut absolverentur aliorum seditione, iterare culpam gaudebant. In hortos, in quibus devertebatur Saturninus, pergunt. Nec tam Primus et Aponianus et Messala, quamquam omni modo nisi, eripuere Saturninum quam obscuritas latebrarum, quibus occulebatur, vacantium forte balnearum fornacibus abditus; mox omissis lictoribus Patavium concessit: digressu consularium uni Antonio vis ac potestas in utrumque exercitum fuit, cedentibus collegis et obversis militum[1] studiis. Nec deerant qui crederent utramque seditionem fraude Antonii coeptam, ut solus bello frueretur.

XII. Ne in Vitellii quidem partibus quietae mentes: exitiosiore discordia non suspicionibus vulgi, sed perfidia ducum turbabantur. Lucilius Bassus classis Ravennatis praefectus ambiguos militum animos, quod magna pars Dalmatae Pannoniique erant, quae provinciae Vespasiano tenebantur, partibus eius adgregaverat. Nox proditioni electa, ut

[1] militibus *M.*

---

[1] Here Tacitus picks up the story from the end of the second book.

to have written to Vitellius. While once the soldiers had vied with one another in bravery and good discipline, they now strove to excel in insolence and audacity, for they did not wish to be less violent in the demands for the punishment of Aponius than they had been for that of Flavianus. The legions from Moesia remembered that they had supported the troops from Pannonia in the vengeance that they had taken, and the latter, as if freed from guilt by the mutiny of others, found delight in repeating their fault. They hurried to the gardens where Saturninus had his quarters; and in spite of all their efforts, it was not so much Primus and Aponianus and Messala who saved Saturninus as it was the obscurity of his hiding-place. He concealed himself in the furnace of a bath that happened to be unused. Presently he dismissed his lictors and fled to Padua. Now that the ex-consuls had gone, all power and authority over both armies fell into the hands of Antonius alone, for his fellow-officers gave way to him, and the soldiers had regard only for him. There were some who believed that he had treacherously fostered both mutinies that he alone might profit by the war.

XII. Nor on the side of Vitellius were men's minds at ease;[1] their distress, however, arose from more fatal discord, due not to the suspicions of the common soldiers, but to the treachery of the commanders. Lucilius Bassus, prefect of the fleet at Ravenna, taking advantage of the irresolution of his forces caused by the fact that most of them came from the provinces of Dalmatia and Pannonia, which were then in Vespasian's hands, had won them to his side. Night was selected as the time to con-

ceteris ignaris soli in principia defectores coirent. Bassus pudore seu metu, quisnam exitus foret, intra domum opperiebatur. Trierarchi magno tumultu Vitellii imagines invadunt; et paucis resistentium obtruncatis[1] ceterum vulgus rerum novarum studio in Vespasianum inclinabat. Tum progressus Lucilius auctorem se palam praebet. Classis Cornelium Fuscum praefectum sibi destinat, qui propere adcucurrit. Bassus honorata custodia Liburnicis navibus Atriam pervectus a praefecto alae Vibennio Rufino, praesidium illic agitante, vincitur, sed exsoluta statim vincula interventu Hormi Caesaris liberti: is quoque inter duces habebatur.

XIII. At Caecina, defectione classis vulgata, primores centurionum et paucos militum, ceteris per militiae munera dispersis, secretum castrorum adfectans in principia vocat. Ibi Vespasiani virtutem virisque partium extollit: transfugisse classem, in arto commeatum, adversas Gallias Hispaniasque, nihil in urbe fidum; atque omnia de Vitellio in deterius. Mox incipientibus qui conscii aderant, ceteros re nova attonitos in verba Vespasiani adigit;

[1] obtruncatis *cod. det.*: obumbratis *M.*

---

[1] Cf. ii. 86. [2] Atri.

summate the treason, in order that the accomplices might meet at headquarters alone without the knowledge of the rest. Bassus waited in his quarters, prompted by shame or by fear as to the outcome. The trierarchs with loud shouts attacked the statues of Vitellius; and after a few of those who resisted had been killed, the rest of the crowd, eager for a change, began to favour Vespasian. Then Lucilius appeared and showed himself openly as the ringleader. But the fleet chose Cornelius Fuscus [1] as their prefect, who came to Ravenna with all speed. Bassus was taken to Adria [2] with an escort of light vessels under an honourable guard. He was put in chains by the prefect of cavalry, Vibennius Rufinus, who was on garrison duty there; but he was at once released through the intervention of Hormus, a freedman of Vespasian. Hormus also was counted among the leaders of the Flavian party.

XIII. But as soon as the revolt of the fleet was known, Caecina sent away most of his troops on various military duties, and then, taking advantage of the empty camp, called the leading centurions and a few of the common soldiers to headquarters. There he spoke in high terms of Vespasian's courage and the strength of his party. "The fleet has revolted," he said, "we are hard pressed for supplies, the Gallic and Spanish provinces are hostile, and no dependence can be put on Rome." All that he had to say concerning Vitellius was derogatory to his cause. Then while the majority of those present were still dazed by this sudden turn of affairs, he administered to them the oath of allegiance to Vespasian, those who were privy to the plan being the first to take it. At the same time they tore down the statues of

simul Vitellii imagines dereptae et missi qui Antonio nuntiarent. Sed ubi totis castris in fama proditio, recurrens in principia miles praescriptum Vespasiani nomen, proiectas Vitellii effigies aspexit, vastum primo silentium, mox cuncta simul erumpunt. Huc cecidisse Germanici exercitus gloriam ut sine proelio, sine vulnere vinctas manus et capta traderent arma? Quas enim ex diverso legiones? Nempe victas; et abesse unicum Othoniani exercitus robur, primanos quartadecimanosque, quos tamen isdem illis campis fuderint straverintque. Ut tot armatorum milia, velut grex venalium, exuli Antonio donum darentur? Octo nimirum legiones unius classis accessionem fore. Id Basso, id Caecinae visum, postquam domos hortos opes principi abstulerint, etiam auferre militem.[1] Integros incruentosque, Flavianis quoque partibus vilis, quid dicturos reposcentibus aut prospera aut adversa?

XIV. Haec singuli, haec universi, ut quemque dolor impulerat, vociferantes, initio a quinta legione orto, repositis Vitellii imaginibus vincla Caecinae iniciunt; Fabium Fabullum quintae legionis legatum et Cassium Longum praefectum castrorum duces deligunt; forte oblatos trium Liburnicarum milites, ignaros et insontis, trucidant; relictis castris, ab-

[1] etiam auferre militem *Halm*: etiam militibus principem auferre litem *M*.

---

[1] Cf. ii. 86.

Vitellius and sent a committee to inform Antonius of what they had done. But when the news of the treason spread through the whole camp, the soldiers ran to headquarters, where they saw Vespasian's name put up on the standards and the statues of Vitellius overthrown; at first there was utter silence, and then all their rage burst out. "Has the glory of the German troops sunk to this," they cried, "that without a struggle and without a wound they will offer their hands to fetters and surrender their weapons to the foe? What are these legions that are opposed to us? Those we defeated! And yet the chief strength of Otho's army, the First and Fourteenth legions, are not here; still those legions too we routed and overthrew on the same fields. Shall all these thousands of armed men be presented to that exile Antonius,[1] as if they were a herd of slaves on the block? No doubt eight legions are to go over to one poor fleet! Bassus and Caecina have now decided, after having robbed the emperor of palaces, gardens, and treasure, to take away his soldiers also. Uninjured and with no mark of blood upon us, we shall be cheap in the eyes even of the Flavian party; and what shall we say to those who ask us about our successes and defeats?"

XIV. With such cries, now separately, now in a body, as indignation moved each, the Fifth legion taking the lead, they replaced the statues of Vitellius and threw Caecina into chains. They chose as their commanders Fabius Fabullus, legate of the Fifth legion, and Cassius Longus, prefect of the camp. Happening to meet the marines from three light galleys who had no knowledge or complicity in what had happened, they slew them. Leaving their

rupto ponte Hostiliam rursus, inde Cremonam pergunt, ut legionibus primae Italicae et unietvicensimae Rapaci iungerentur, quas Caecina ad obtinendam Cremonam cum parte equitum praemiserat.

XV. Ubi haec comperta Antonio, discordis animis, discretos viribus hostium exercitus adgredi statuit, antequam ducibus auctoritas, militi obsequium et iunctis legionibus fiducia rediret. Namque Fabium Valentem profectum ab urbe adceleraturumque cognita Caecinae proditione coniectabat; et fidus Vitellio Fabius nec militiae ignarus. Simul ingens Germanorum vis per Raetiam timebatur. Ex[1] Britannia Galliaque et Hispania auxilia Vitellius acciverat, immensam belli luem, ni Antonius id ipsum metuens festinato proelio victoriam praecepisset. Universo cum exercitu secundis[2] a Verona castris Bedriacum venit. Postero die legionibus ad muniendum retentis, auxiliares cohortes in Cremonensem agrum missae ut specie parandarum copiarum civili praeda miles imbueretur: ipse cum quattuor milibus equitum ad octavum a Bedriaco progressus quo licentius popularentur. Exploratores, ut mos est, longius curabant.

XVI. Quinta ferme hora diei erat, cum citus eques

[1] ex *Agricola*: et *M.*
[2] secundi *M.*

---

[1] Cf. ii. 100.
[2] Something over thirty miles.

camp, they broke down the bridge and hurried back to Hostilia, and then moved toward Cremona to join the two legions that Caecina had despatched with part of the cavalry to occupy the town. These were the First Italian and the Twenty-first Rapax.[1]

XV. When Antonius heard of this, he decided to attack his opponents' troops while they were still distracted in purpose and while their strength was divided, and not to give time for the leaders to recover their authority, the troops their spirit of obedience, and the legions the confidence that they would feel when once more united. For he suspected that Fabius Valens had already left Rome and would make all haste when he heard of Caecina's treachery; and in fact Fabius was both faithful to Vitellius and not ignorant of war. At the same time Antonius feared a great invasion of Germans through Raetia. Moreover, Vitellius had summoned auxiliaries from Britain, Gaul, and Spain, who would indeed have been utter ruin to the war, if Antonius, fearing this very thing, had not precipitated an engagement and gained the victory before their arrival. He now moved in two days with his entire army from Verona to Bedriacum.[2] The next day, keeping his legionaries to fortify his position, he sent his cohorts of auxiliaries into the district around Cremona to let the soldiers have a taste of the booty to be gained from civilians, although his pretext was to secure supplies. Antonius himself with four thousand horse advanced eight miles beyond Bedriacum that they might pillage with greater freedom. His scouts, as usual, watched the country still further from camp.

XVI. About eleven o'clock a horseman rode up

adventare hostis, praegredi paucos, motum fremitumque late audiri nuntiavit. Dum Antonius quidnam agendum consultat, aviditate navandae operae Arrius Varus cum promptissimis equitum prorupit impulitque Vitellianos modica caede; nam plurium adcursu versa fortuna, et acerrimus quisque sequentium fugae ultimus erat. Nec sponte Antonii properatum, et fore quae acciderunt[1] rebatur. Hortatus suos ut magno animo capesserent pugnam, diductis in latera turmis vacuum medio relinquit iter quo Varum equitesque eius reciperet; iussae armari legiones: datum per agros signum ut, qua cuique proximum, omissa praeda proelio occurreret. Pavidus interim Varus turbae suorum miscetur intulitque formidinem. Pulsi cum sauciis integri suomet ipsi metu et angustiis viarum conflictabantur.

XVII. Nullum in illa trepidatione Antonius constantis ducis aut fortis[2] militis officium omisit. Occursare paventibus, retinere cedentis, ubi plurimus labor, unde aliqua spes, consilio manu voce insignis hosti, conspicuus suis. Eo postremo ardoris pro-

[1] acciderunt *Madvig*: acciderant *M.*
[2] fortis *Acidalius*: fortissimi *M.*

---

[1] That is, those who had been most eager in pursuit were also the most stubborn in retreat.

at full speed and reported that the enemy was coming; that a small number preceded the main body, but that the movement and noise of their advance could be heard over a wide area. While Antonius was considering what course to pursue, Arrius Varus, prompted by his eagerness to do something important, rushed forward with the boldest of the cavalry and drove back the Vitellians; but he inflicted only a slight loss, for when larger forces came up, the fortune of battle was reversed; and those who had been pursuing the Vitellians most vigorously now were the last to retreat.[1] Antonius had not desired this hasty attack and he expected the result to be what it actually proved. He now urged his men to engage with all courage and withdrew his squadrons to the flanks, leaving an open path in the centre for the reception of Varus and his cavalry. He directed the legions to arm, and gave the signal through the fields for his men to leave their booty and quickly form for battle, each joining the company nearest him. In the meantime Varus in a panic regained the main body of his comrades and communicated his terror to them. The uninjured and the wounded alike were forced back in the confusion caused by their own fright and the narrow roads.

XVII. In this panic Antonius failed in no duty that a determined general or a brave soldier should perform. He ran to those who were terrified, held back those who were fleeing; wherever there was the greatest danger, wherever there was some hope, there his counsel, his action, and his words of encouragement made him a mark for the enemy and conspicuous before his men. Finally, he was

vectus est ut vexillarium fugientem hasta transverberaret; mox raptum vexillum in hostem vertit. Quo pudore haud plures quam centum equites restitere:[1] iuvit locus, artiore illic via et fracto interfluentis rivi ponte, qui incerto alveo et praecipitibus ripis fugam impediebat. Ea necessitas seu fortuna lapsas iam partis restituit. Firmati inter se densis ordinibus excipiunt Vitellianos temere effusos, atque illi[2] consternantur. Antonius instare perculsis, sternere obvios, simul ceteri, ut cuique ingenium, spoliare, capere, arma equosque abripere. Et exciti prospero clamore, qui modo per agros fuga palabantur, victoriae se miscebant.

XVIII. Ad quartum a Cremona lapidem fulsere legionum signa Rapacis atque Italicae, laeto inter initia equitum suorum proelio illuc usque provecta. Sed[3] ubi fortuna contra fuit, non laxare ordines, non recipere turbatos, non obviam ire ultroque adgredi hostem tantum per spatium cursu et pugnando fessum. Forte ducti[4] haud perinde rebus prosperis ducem desideraverant atque in adversis deesse intellegebant. Nutantem aciem victor equitatus incursat; et Vipstanus Messala tribunus cum

[1] resistere *M.*
[2] illi *Rhenanus*: illic *M.*
[3] provectas. et *M.*
[4] ducti *Halm*: victi *M.*

carried to such a pitch of excitement that he transfixed with a spear a colour-bearer who was running away, then seized the standard, and turned it towards the foe. Struck with shame some horsemen—not over one hundred in all—made a stand against the enemy. The character of the ground favoured them, the road at this point being narrower and the bridge broken down across a stream which came in the way and with its unknown depths and steep banks made flight difficult. It was such necessity or good luck that restored the fortunes of a side that was already well nigh lost. The troops reformed in firm and solid ranks and received the Vitellians, who, coming on in disorder, were thrown back in confusion. Antonius pursued those who were panic-stricken, cut down those who resisted, while the rest of his troops, each following his own nature, robbed the dead, took prisoners, or carried off arms and horses. The soldiers, who a moment before were fleeing through the open fields, were attracted by the shouts of success and joined in the victory.

XVIII. Four miles from Cremona the gleam of the standards of the legions Rapax and Italica was suddenly seen; for, hearing of the early success of their cavalry, they had hurried on to this point. But when fortune opposed them, they did not open out their lines, receive the fugitives, or advance and take the initiative in attacking their opponents, who were exhausted with their long advance and with fighting. Being now guided by chance, in their adversity they realized their lack of a leader as they had never missed him in success. When their line wavered, the enemy's victorious horse suddenly attacked; the tribune Vipstanus Messala also came

Moesicis auxiliaribus adsequitur, quos multi e[1] legionariis quamquam raptim ductos aequabant: ita mixtus pedes equesque rupere legionum agmen. Et propinqua Cremonensium moenia quanto plus spei ad effugium minorem ad resistendum animum dabant. Nec Antonius ultra institit, memor laboris ac vulnerum, quibus tam anceps proelii fortuna, quamvis prospero fine, equites equosque adflictaverat.

XIX. Inumbrante vespera universum Flaviani exercitus robur advenit. Utque cumulos super et recentia caede vestigia incessere, quasi debellatum foret, pergere Cremonam et victos in deditionem accipere aut expugnare deposcunt. Haec in medio, pulchra dictu: illa sibi quisque, posse coloniam plano sitam impetu capi. Idem audaciae per tenebras inrumpentibus et maiorem rapiendi licentiam. Quod si lucem opperiantur, iam pacem, iam preces, et pro labore ac vulneribus clementiam et gloriam, inania, laturos, sed opes Cremonensium in sinu praefectorum legatorumque fore. Expugnatae urbis praedam ad militem, deditae ad duces pertinere. Spernuntur centuriones tribunique, ac ne vox cuiusquam

[1] multi e *Dübner*: militiae *M.*

up bringing some auxiliary troops from Moesia with whom many legionaries had kept pace in spite of their rapid advance; and so the Flavian foot and horse combined broke through the line of the two legions. The neighbouring walls of Verona, while offering hope of a refuge, gave them less courage for resistance. Still Antonius did not press on further, for he realized that his soldiers were exhausted by their efforts and by the wounds with which the struggle, so long uncertain in spite of its successful end, had afflicted both horsemen and horses.

XIX. As evening fell, the great mass of the Flavian troops arrived in a body. As they marched over the heaps of the dead where the signs of the bloody conflict were still fresh, imagining that the war was over, they demanded to go on to Cremona and receive the surrender of their defeated opponents, or else to storm the town. Thus they spoke openly—fine words indeed; but what each said to himself was that the colony situated in a plain could be carried by storm; they would have as much courage if they broke in during the dark, and they would have a greater licence to plunder. But if they waited for the light, there would be at once appeals and prayers for peace, and in return for toil and wounds the common soldiers would bear off such empty prizes as clemency and glory, while the wealth of Cremona would fill the purses of the prefects and commanders. "The booty of a city," they said, "always falls to the soldiers if it is captured, to the officers if it surrenders." They treated with scorn their centurions and tribunes, rattling their arms to avoid hearing

audiatur, quatiunt[1] arma, rupturi imperium ni ducantur.

XX. Tum Antonius inserens se manipulis, ubi aspectu et auctoritate silentium fecerat, non se decus neque pretium eripere tam bene meritis adfirmabat, sed divisa inter exercitum ducesque munia: militibus cupidinem pugnandi convenire, duces providendo, consultando, cunctatione saepius quam temeritate prodesse. Ut pro virili portione armis ac manu victoriam iuverit, ratione et consilio, propriis ducis artibus, profuturum; neque enim ambigua esse quae occurrant, noctem et ignotae situm urbis, intus hostis et cuncta insidiis opportuna. Non si pateant portae, nisi explorato, nisi die intrandum. An obpugnationem inchoaturos adempto omni prospectu, quis aequus locus, quanta altitudo moenium, tormentisne et telis an operibus et vineis adgredienda urbs foret? Mox conversus ad singulos, num securis dolabrasque et cetera expugnandis urbibus secum attulissent, rogitabat. Et cum abnuerent, "Gladiisne" inquit "et pilis perfringere ac subruere muros ullae manus possunt? Si aggerem struere, si pluteis cratibusve protegi necesse fuerit, ut vulgus improvidum inriti stabimus, altitudinem turrium et aliena munimenta mirantes? Quin potius

[1] quatiuntur *M*.

anyone's words, and they were ready to defy their officers if not led to the assault.

XX. Then Antonius made his way among the companies, and when by his appearance and influence he had secured silence, he addressed them to this effect: "I have no desire to take away either honour or reward from soldiers who have deserved so well, but there is a division of duties between soldiers and generals: to soldiers belongs the eager enthusiasm for battle, but generals must help by foresight, by counsel, and more often by delay than by rash action. As I have done my full part to secure victory with my arms and my personal efforts, I will now help by wise counsel, which is the quality proper to a leader. For there can be no question as to the obstacles before us—night and the situation of this strange city, the fact that the enemy is within, and that everything is favourable for an ambuscade. Even if the gates were open, we ought not to enter except after reconnaissance and by day. Or will you begin a siege when wholly cut off from seeing what ground is level, how high the walls, whether to attack with artillery and weapons or with siege works and protecting sheds?" Then turning to one and another, he asked them whether they had brought with them axes, picks, and the other implements for storming cities. When they said that they had not, he asked: "Can any troops break through walls and undermine them with swords and javelins? If we need to build a mound, or protect ourselves with mantlets and fascines, shall we stand here useless like an improvident mob, gaping with wonder at the lofty towers and fortifications of others? Shall we not rather

mora noctis unius, advectis tormentis machinisque, vim victoriamque nobiscum ferimus?" Simul lixas calonesque cum recentissimis equitum Bedriacum mittit, copias ceteraque usui adlaturos.

XXI. Id vero aegre tolerante milite prope seditionem ventum, cum progressi equites sub ipsa moenia vagos e Cremonensibus corripiunt, quorum indicio noscitur sex Vitellianas legiones omnemque exercitum, qui Hostiliae egerat, eo ipso die triginta milia passuum emensum, comperta suorum clade in proelium accingi ac iam adfore. Is terror obstructas mentis consiliis ducis aperuit. Sistere tertiam decimam legionem in ipso viae[1] Postumiae aggere iubet, cui iuncta a laevo septima Galbiana patenti campo stetit, dein septima Claudiana, agresti fossa (ita locus erat) praemunita; dextro octava per apertum limitem, mox tertia[2] densis arbustis intersepta. Hic aquilarum signorumque ordo: milites mixti per tenebras, ut fors tulerat; praetorianum vexillum proximum tertianis, cohortes auxiliorum in cornibus, latera ac terga equite circumdata; Sido atque Italicus Suebi cum delectis popularium primori in acie versabantur.

XXII. At Vitellianus exercitus, cui adquiescere Cremonae et reciperatis cibo somnoque viribus

[1] in alae vo *M*.
[2] tertia *Pichena*: tertia decima *M*.

---

[1] The Postumian Road, which ran from Cremona to Verona, was here carried on a raised causeway because of the marshy character of the ground.

at the expense of a single night fetch up artillery and engines, and so bring with us the force to secure victory?" At the same time he sent the sutlers, servants, and the freshest of the cavalry to Bedriacum to fetch supplies and all else they needed.

XXI. But the soldiers found inaction hard; in fact they were near a mutiny when a body of horsemen who had ridden up under the very walls of Cremona caught some stragglers from the town and learned from them that six Vitellian legions and all the force that had been stationed at Hostilia, after marching thirty miles that day, had heard of the losses that their associates had suffered, and that they were now preparing for battle—in fact would soon be there. This alarming danger opened their obstinate ears to the plans of their general. He ordered the Thirteenth legion to take its position on the actual causeway of the Postumian Road.[1] Immediately on the Thirteenth's left the Seventh Galbian stood in open country, next the Seventh Claudian, protected, as the ground ran, by a ditch. On the right was the Eighth legion on an open cross-road, and then the Third, distributed among dense thickets. This was the order of the eagles and standards; the soldiers took their places in the darkness without order, wherever chance set them. The praetorians' standard was next the Third legion; the cohorts of auxiliaries were on the wings; and the cavalry covered their flanks and rear. The Suebian princes Sido and Italicus with picked troops from their tribes were in the front ranks.

XXII. The wise policy for the troops of Vitellius was to revive their strength by food and sleep at Cremona and then to put to flight and crush their

confectum algore atque inedia hostem postera die profligare ac proruere ratio fuit, indigus rectoris, inops consilii, tertia ferme noctis hora paratis iam dispositisque Flavianis impingitur. Ordinem agminis disiecti per iram ac tenebras adseverare non ausim, quamquam alii tradiderint quartam Macedonicam dextrum[1] suorum cornu, quintam et quintam decimam cum vexillis nonae secundaeque et vicensimae Britannicarum legionum mediam aciem, sextadecimanos duoetvicensimanosque et primanos laevum cornu complesse. Rapaces atque Italici omnibus se manipulis miscuerant; eques auxiliaque sibi ipsi locum legere. Proelium tota nocte varium, anceps, atrox, his, rursus illis exitiabile. Nihil animus aut manus, ne oculi quidem provisu iuvabant. Eadem utraque acie arma, crebris interrogationibus notum pugnae signum, permixta vexilla, ut quisque globus capta ex hostibus huc vel illuc raptabat. Urguebatur maxime septima legio, nuper a Galba conscripta. Occisi sex primorum ordinum centuriones, abrepta quaedam signa: ipsam aquilam Atilius Verus primi pili centurio multa cum hostium strage et ad extremum moriens servaverat.

XXIII. Sustinuit labentem aciem Antonius accitis

[1] dextrum *Faernus*: dextro *M.*

opponents, who would be exhausted by cold and lack of food. But being without a leader, destitute of a plan, at about nine o'clock in the evening they flung themselves on the Flavian troops, who were ready and in their stations. I should not dare to state definitely the order in which they advanced, for their line was thrown into confusion by the soldiers' fury and by the darkness. Some writers, however, have said that the Fourth Macedonian legion was on their extreme right, the Fifth and Fifteenth with detachments from the Ninth, Second, and Twentieth British formed their centre, while the Sixteenth, Twenty-second, and First constituted their left. The troops of the two legions known as the Rapax and the Italica had joined companies in every part of the line; the cavalry and auxiliaries selected their own positions. The battle lasted the entire night with varied fortune, uncertain as to its outcome, savage, and fatal now to one side, now to the other. Neither courage nor arms, nor even their eyes, which might have foreseen danger, were of any avail. The weapons in both lines were the same, the watchwords for battle became known, for they were constantly asked; the standards were confused as some band or other carried off in this direction or that those they had captured from their foes. The Seventh legion, lately enrolled by Galba, was hardest pressed: it lost six centurions of the first rank; some of its standards were captured; its eagle was finally saved by Atilius Verus, a centurion of the first rank, who in his efforts killed many of the enemy, only finally to fall dying himself.

XXIII. Antonius strengthened his wavering line

praetorianis. Qui ubi excepere pugnam, pellunt hostem, dein pelluntur. Namque Vitelliani tormenta in aggerem viae contulerant ut tela vacuo atque aperto excuterentur, dispersa primo et arbustis sine hostium noxa inlisa. Magnitudine eximia quintae[1] decimae legionis ballista ingentibus saxis hostilem aciem proruebat. Lateque cladem intulisset ni duo milites praeclarum facinus ausi, arreptis e strage scutis ignorati, vincla ac libramenta tormentorum abscidissent. Statim confossi sunt eoque intercidere nomina: de facto haud ambigitur. Neutro inclinaverat fortuna donec adulta nocte luna surgens ostenderet acies falleretque. Sed Flavianis aequior a tergo; hinc maiores equorum virorumque umbrae, et falso, ut in corpora, ictu tela hostium citra cadebant: Vitelliani adverso lumine conlucentes velut ex occulto iaculantibus incauti offerebantur.

XXIV. Igitur Antonius, ubi noscere suos noscique poterat, alios pudore et probris, multos laude et hortatu, omnis spe promissisque accendens, cur resumpsissent[2] arma, Pannonicas legiones interro-

[1] quintae *Lipsius*: quartae *M*.
[2] cur resumpsissent *Lipsius*: currari sumpsissent *M*.

by bringing up the praetorians. On engaging they drove back the enemy, only to be driven back themselves, for the Vitellians had concentrated their artillery on the raised road that they might have free and open ground from which to fire; their earlier shots had been scattered and had struck the trees without injuring the enemy. A ballista of enormous size belonging to the Fifteenth legion began to do great harm to the Flavians' line with the huge stones that it hurled; and it would have caused wide destruction if it had not been for the splendid bravery of two soldiers, who, taking some shields from the dead and so disguising themselves, cut the ropes and springs of the machine. They were at once run through and thus their names were lost; but there is no doubt about their deed. Fortune inclined to neither side until, as the night wore on, the rising moon illuminated the lines with its deceptive light. But this was more favourable to the Flavian forces, for the moon was behind them and so magnified the shadows of horses and men; while their opponents, deceived by the shadows, aimed at them as if they were the actual bodies, and therefore their spears fell short; but the Vitellians, having the moonlight in their faces and thus being clearly seen, unconsciously presented a mark to their enemies, who shot, so to speak, from concealment.

XXIV. When Antonius could recognize his soldiers and be recognized by them, he began to urge them on, some by shame and reproaches, more by praise and encouragement, but all by hope and promises. He asked the Pannonian legions why they had taken up their arms again; he reminded them that

gabat: illos esse campos, in quibus abolere labem prioris ignominiae, ubi reciperare gloriam possent. Tum ad Moesicos conversus principes auctoresque belli ciebat: frustra minis[1] et verbis provocatos Vitellianos, si manus eorum oculosque non tolerent.[2] Haec, ut quosque accesserat; plura ad tertianos, veterum recentiumque admonens, ut sub M. Antonio Parthos, sub Corbulone Armenios, nuper Sarmatas pepulissent. Mox infensus praetorianis "Vos" inquit, "nisi vincitis, pagani, quis alius imperator, quae castra alia excipient? Illic signa armaque vestra sunt, et mors victis; nam ignominiam[3] consumpsistis." Undique clamor, et orientem solem (ita in Syria mos est) tertiani salutavere.

XXV. Vagus inde an consilio ducis subditus rumor, advenisse Mucianum, exercitus in vicem salutasse. Gradum inferunt quasi recentibus auxiliis aucti, rariore iam Vitellianorum acie, ut quos nullo rectore suus quemque impetus vel pavor contraheret diduceretve.[4] Postquam impulsos[5] sensit Antonius denso agmine obturbabat. Laxati ordines abrum-

[1] frustrā Inisset *M*. [2] tollerent *M*. [3] ignominia *M*.
[4] diduceretve *Lipsius*: duceretve *M*.
[5] inpulsos *Bipontini*: pulsos *M*.

---

[1] In 36 B.C. [2] 63 A.D. [3] Cf. i. 79.
[4] That is, the action of the Third legion in saluting the rising sun.

this was the field on which they could blot out the stain of their earlier disgrace, where they could regain their former glory. Then turning to the soldiers from Moesia he appealed to them as the authors and promoters of this war. He told them that it had been useless to challenge the Vitellians with threats and words, if they could not endure their hands and looks. This he said as he came to each division; but he spoke at greater length to the troops of the Third legion, reminding them of their ancient glory as well as of their later achievements, of their victory over the Parthians when Mark Antony was their leader,[1] over the Armenians when Corbulo commanded,[2] and of their recent defeat of the Sarmatians.[3] Then he indignantly said to the praetorians: "As for you, clowns that you are, if you do not win to-day, what other general or other camp will take you in? Yonder are your standards and your arms, and, if defeated, death; for dishonour you have exhausted." A shout arose from the entire army; and the soldiers of the Third legion, according to the Syrian custom, hailed the rising sun.

XXV. This action[4] gave rise to a vague rumour, which perhaps the general started with intention, to the effect that Mucianus had arrived and that the two armies had greeted each other. The Flavian forces then advanced as if reinforced by fresh troops; the Vitellian line was now more ragged, as was natural with troops who had no commander, but closed or opened out their ranks as courage or fear moved individuals. After Antonius saw that they were shaken, he assailed them in mass formation. Their weakened lines were broken and could not be

puntur, nec restitui quivere impedientibus vehiculis tormentisque. Per limitem viae sparguntur festinatione consectandi victores. Eo notabilior caedes fuit, quia filius patrem interfecit. Rem nominaque auctore Vipstano Messala tradam. Iulius Mansuetus ex Hispania, Rapaci legioni additus, impubem filium domi liquerat. Is mox adultus, inter septimanos a Galba conscriptus, oblatum forte patrem et vulnere stratum dum semianimem scrutatur, agnitus agnoscensque et exsanguem amplexus, voce flebili precabatur placatos patris manis, neve se ut parricidam aversarentur: publicum id facinus; et unum militem quotam civilium armorum partem? Simul attollere corpus, aperire humum, supremo erga parentem officio fungi. Advertere proximi, deinde plures: hinc per omnem aciem miraculum et questus et saevissimi belli exsecratio. Nec eo segnius propinquos adfinis fratres trucidant[1] spoliant: factum esse scelus loquuntur faciuntque.

XXVI. Ut Cremonam venere, novum immensumque opus occurrit. Othoniano bello Germanicus miles moenibus Cremonensium castra sua, castris vallum circumiecerat eaque munimenta rursus auxerat. Quorum aspectu haesere victores, incertis ducibus

[1] trucidant *I. Gronovius*: trucidati *M.*

[1] In April of this year, at the time of the first battle of Bedriacum.

eformed, because they were entangled among the upply-wagons and artillery. The victorious troops n their hasty pursuit were strung out along the ides of the road. The carnage was peculiarly narked by the fact that in it a son killed his own ather. The story and the names I shall give on he authority of Vipstanus Messala. Julius Manuetus of Spain, when enrolled with the legion nown as Rapax, had left behind him a young son. Later, when this son had grown up, he had been onscripted into the Seventh legion by Galba. Now e happened to meet his father, whom he wounded nd struck down; then, as he looked closely at he dying man, the father and son recognized each ther; the son embraced his expiring father and rayed with tears in his voice that his father's spirit vould forgive him and not abhor him as a patricide. "The crime," he cried, "is the State's; and what loes a single soldier count for in civil war?" At he same time he lifted up the body and began to lig a grave, performing the last duties toward a ather. The soldiers near first noticed it, presently nore; then through the whole line were heard ries of wonder, of pity, and of cursing against this nost horrible war. Yet not one whit did they lacken their murder of relatives, kinsmen, and rothers. They called the deed a crime but did it.

XXVI. When they reached Cremona they found new task of enormous difficulty before them. In he war against Otho[1] the troops from Germany had itched their camp around the walls of Cremona and hen had built a rampart around their camp; these lefences they had later strengthened. At the sight f the fortifications the victorious troops hesitated,

quid iuberent. Incipere obpugnationem fesso[1] pe
diem noctemque exercitu arduum et nullo iuxt
subsidio anceps: sin Bedriacum redirent, intoleran
dus tam longi itineris labor, et victoria ad inritum
revolvebatur: munire castra, id quoque propinqui
hostibus formidolosum, ne dispersos et opus molienti
subita eruptione[2] turbarent. Quae super cunct
terrebat ipsorum miles periculi quam morae patien
tior: quippe ingrata quae tuta, ex temeritate spes
omnisque caedes et vulnera et sanguis aviditat
praedae pensabantur.

XXVII. Huc inclinavit Antonius cingique vallum
corona iussit. Primo sagittis saxisque eminus certa
bant, maiore Flavianorum pernicie, in quos tel
desuper librabantur; mox vallum portasque legioni
bus attribuit, ut discretus labor fortis ignavosque
distingueret atque ipsa contentione decoris accende
rentur. Proxima Bedriacensi viae tertiani septi
manique sumpsere, dexteriora valli octava ac septim
Claudiana; tertiadecimanos ad Brixianam portam
impetus tulit. Paulum inde morae, dum ex[3] proximi
agris ligones[4] dolabras et alii falcis scalasque con

[1] fessos *M.*
[2] subite ruptione *M.*
[3] et *M.*
[4] ligones *Rhenanus*: legionem *M.*

for their leaders were in doubt what orders to give. To begin an attack on the town with troops that were exhausted by fighting an entire day and night was a difficult undertaking and one of doubtful issue, when there were no reserves at hand; but if they returned to Bedriacum, their victory shrank to nothing, not to speak of the intolerable burden of such a long march. To fortify a camp even, with the enemy close at hand, involved the danger that the foe might by a sudden sortie cause them serious difficulty while their troops were scattered and busy with the work. But beyond all these things the Flavian leaders feared their own soldiers, who were more ready to face danger than delay; the troops detested safe measures and put all their hope in rash action. Every disaster, all wounds and blood, were outweighed by their greed for booty.

XXVII. Antonius inclined to meet his troops' desires and ordered the investment of the enemy's camp. At first they fought at a distance with arrows and stones; but in this contest the Flavians suffered the greater loss, for their opponent shot down upon them. Then Antonius assigned to each legion a gate or a part of the wall, that the division of labour might show who was brave and who cowardly, and thus fire the enthusiasm of his troops by making them rivals for glory. The sections next the road to Bedriacum the Third and Seventh legions took, the fortification farther to the right the Eighth and the Seventh Claudiana; the Thirteenth assailed the gate toward Brixia. Then there followed a brief delay while some of the soldiers gathered from the neighbouring fields mattocks and picks and others brought hooks and ladders. Then the soldiers,

vectant: tum elatis super capita scutis densa testu dine succedunt. Romanae utrimque artes: ponder saxorum Vitelliani provolvunt, disiectam fluitantem que[1] testudinem lanceis contisque[2] scrutantur, done soluta compage scutorum exsanguis aut lacero prosternerent multa cum strage. Incesserat cuncta tio, ni duces fesso militi et velut inritas exhortatione abnuenti Cremonam monstrassent.

XXVIII. Hormine id ingenium, ut Messala tra dit, an potior auctor sit C. Plinius, qui Antoniun incusat, haud facile discreverim, nisi quod nequ Antonius neque Hormus a fama vitaque sua quamvi pessimo flagitio degeneravere. Non iam . sangui neque vulnera morabantur quin subruerent vallun quaterentque portas, innixi umeris et super iteratan testudinem scandentes prensarent hostium tela bra chiaque. Integri cum sauciis, semineces cum exspi rantibus volvuntur, varia pereuntium forma et omn imagine mortium.

XXIX. Acerrimum tertiae septimaeque legionur certamen; et dux Antonius cum delectis auxiliaribu eodem incubuerat. Obstinatos inter se cum susti nere Vitelliani nequirent et superiacta tela de testudine laberentur, ipsam postremo ballistam i subeuntis propulere, quae ut ad praesens disieci

[1] fluvitantemque *M.*
[2] concitisque *M.*
[3] *add. Halm.*

---

[1] In this formation—the testudo—the soldiers held thei shields over their heads with the edges overlapping, and the were so skilful in this that the roof thus formed was no easily broken through.

[2] Cf. Verg. *Aen.* ii. 369, plurima mortis imago.

raising their shields above their heads, advanced under the wall in a close "tortoise" formation.[1] Both sides used the familar artifices of Roman warfare: the Vitellians rolled down heavy stones, and when they had separated and loosened the cover of compact shields, they searched its joints with lances and pikes until they broke up the close structure of the "tortoise," and hurled their dead and mangled foes to the ground with great slaughter. The soldiers would have slackened their assault, for they were weary and ready to reject exhortations as idle, had not the leaders pointed to Cremona.

XXVIII. Whether this was the inspiration of Hormus, as Messala says, or whether Gaius Pliny, who blames Antonius, is the better authority, I cannot easily decide; all I can say is that whether it was Antonius or Hormus, this most monstrous crime was not unworthy of the life and reputation of either. Blood and wounds no longer delayed the soldiers in their attempts to undermine the wall and shatter the gates; they renewed the "tortoise," and climbing on their comrades' shoulders, they mounted on it and seized their foes' weapons and arms. The unharmed and the wounded, the half-dead and the dying all rolled in one mass; men perished in many ways and death took every form.[2]

XXIX. The Third and Seventh legions made the most violent assault; and their general, Antonius, attacked at the same point with picked auxiliaries. When the Vitellian troops could no longer sustain this combined and persistent attack, finding that their shots slipped off the "tortoise" without doing harm, they finally pushed over their ballista itself on the heads of their assailants beneath. This for the

obruitque[1] quos inciderat, ita pinnas ac summa valli ruina sua traxit; simul iuncta turris ictibus saxorum cessit, qua septimani dum nituntur cuneis, tertianus securibus gladiisque portam perfregit. Primum inrupisse C. Volusium tertiae legionis militem inter omnis auctores constat. Is in vallum egressus, deturbatis qui restiterant,[2] conspicuus manu ac voce capta castra conclamavit; ceteri trepidis iam Vitellianis seque e vallo praecipitantibus perrupere. Completur caede quantum inter castra murosque vacui fuit.

XXX. Ac rursus nova laborum facies: ardua urbis moenia, saxeae turres, ferrati portarum obices, vibrans tela miles, frequens obstrictusque Vitellianis partibus Cremonensis populus, magna pars Italiae stato in eosdem dies mercatu congregata, quod defensoribus auxilium ob multitudinem, obpugnantibus incitamentum ob praedam erat. Rapi ignis Antonius inferrique amoenissimis extra urbem aedificiis iubet, si damno rerum suarum Cremonenses ad mutandam fidem traherentur. Propinqua muris tecta et altitudinem moenium egressa fortissimo quoque militum complet; illi trabibus tegulisque et facibus propugnatores deturbant.

[1] disiecto bruitque *M.*
[2] resisterant *M.*

moment scattered and crushed those on whom it fell, but in its fall it dragged down the parapet and the upper part of the rampart; at the same time a neighbouring tower gave way before the volleys of stones. While men of the Seventh legion pressed forward in wedge formation, the Third broke down a gate with axes and swords. All authorities agree that the first man to rush in was Gaius Volusius, a private of the Third legion. He mounted the rampart, flung down those who resisted, and before the eyes of all, with uplifted hand and voice, cried that the camp had been captured; thereupon the rest burst in, while the Vitellians, already in a panic, threw themselves from the rampart. All the open space between the camp and the walls of Cremona was covered with the dead.

XXX. Now a new difficulty again confronted the Flavian troops in the city's high walls, its towers of masonry, its iron-barred gates, and the soldiers who were brandishing their weapons. Furthermore the civil population of Cremona was large and attached to the party of Vitellius, while a great part of Italy had gathered there to attend a market which fell at this time. This great number strengthened the defenders, but the possible booty encouraged the assailants. Antonius ordered his troops quickly to set fire to the finest buildings outside the town, in the hope that the people of Cremona might be moved by the loss of their property to change their allegiance. The roofs of the houses near the walls, and particularly those which rose above the city ramparts, he filled with his bravest troops; these dislodged the defenders with beams, tiles, and firebrands.

XXXI. Iam legiones in testudinem glomerabantur, et alii tela saxaque incutiebant, cum languescere paulatim Vitellianorum animi. Ut quis ordine anteibat, cedere fortunae, ne Cremona quoque excisa nulla ultra venia omnisque ira victoris non in vulgus inops, sed in tribunos centurionesque, ubi pretium caedis erat, reverteretur. Gregarius miles futuri socors et ignobilitate tutior perstabat: vagi per vias, in domibus abditi pacem ne tum quidem orabant, cum bellum posuissent. Primores castrorum nomen atque imagines Vitellii amoliuntur; catenas Caecinae (nam etiam tunc vinctus erat) exsolvunt orantque ut causae suae deprecator adsistat. Aspernantem tumentemque lacrimis fatigant, extremum malorum, tot fortissimi viri proditoris opem invocantes; mox velamenta et infulas pro muris ostentant. Cum Antonius inhiberi tela iussisset, signa aquilasque extulere; maestum inermium agmen deiectis in terram oculis sequebatur. Circumstiterant victores et primo ingerebant probra, intentabant ictus: mox, ut praeberi ora contumeliis et posita omni ferocia cuncta victi patiebantur, subit recordatio illos esse quid nuper

[1] Cf. i. 66.

XXXI. The legions were already forming a "tortoise," while others were beginning to hurl spears and stones, when the spirit of the Vitellians gradually slackened. The higher a man's rank, the readier he was to yield to fortune for fear that if Cremona also were captured by assault, there would be no more pardon, but that the whole rage of the victors would fall not on the penniless mob, but on the tribunes and centurions, whose murder meant gain. The common soldiers, however, having no thought for the future and being better protected by their humble position, continued their resistance. They wandered through the streets or concealed themselves in houses, but did not beg for peace even when they had given up fighting. The chief officers removed the name and statues of Vitellius from headquarters; they took off Caecina's fetters—for even at that time he was kept a prisoner—and begged him to plead their cause. When he haughtily refused they besought him with tears; all these brave men, and this was the uttermost of their ills, invoked the aid of a traitor. Presently they displayed hangings and fillets on the walls as signs of their submission.[1] After Antonius had ordered his men to cease firing, they brought out their standards and eagles; a sad line of unarmed men followed, their eyes cast upon the ground. The victorious troops stood about, heaping insults upon them and threatening them with blows; later when the defeated troops offered their faces to every indignity, and without a spark of courage left in them were ready to suffer anything, the victors began to remember that these were the troops who had recently shown moderation after they had won

Bedriaci victoriae temperassent. Sed ubi Caecina praetexta lictoribusque insignis, dimota turba, consul incessit, exarsere victores: superbiam saevitiamque (adeo invisa scelera sunt), etiam perfidiam obiectabant. Obstitit Antonius datisque defensoribus ad Vespasianum dimisit.

XXXII. Plebs interim Cremonensium inter armatos conflictabatur; nec procul caede aberant, cum precibus ducum mitigatus est miles. Et vocatos ad contionem Antonius adloquitur, magnifice victores, victos clementer, de Cremona in neutrum. Exercitus praeter insitam praedandi cupidinem vetere odio ad excidium Cremonensium incubuit. Iuvisse partis Vitellianas Othonis quoque bello credebantur; mox tertiadecimanos ad extruendum amphitheatrum relictos, ut sunt procacia urbanae plebis ingenia, petulantibus iurgiis inluserant. Auxit invidiam editum illic a Caecina gladiatorum spectaculum eademque rursus belli sedes et praebiti in acie Vitellianis cibi, caesae quaedam feminae studio partium ad proelium progressae; tempus quoque mercatus ditem alioqui coloniam maiore opum specie complebat. Ceteri duces in obscuro: Antonium fortuna

---

[1] That is, in his robes of office.
[2] Cf. ii. 67.

at Bedriacum. Yet when Caecina appeared, in the rôle of consul, dressed in the toga praetexta[1] and escorted by his lictors who put aside the crowd before him, the victors' rage blazed forth: they taunted him with arrogance, cruelty, and—so hateful are crimes—even with perfidy. Antonius interposed, gave him a guard, and sent him to Vespasian.

XXXII. In the meantime the people of Cremona were buffeted about among the troops, and there came near being a massacre, when the commanders by their appeals succeeded in calming the soldiers. Then Antonius called them together and spoke in warmest eulogy of the victors; the conquered he addressed in kindly terms; but he said nothing for or against Cremona. The troops, prompted not only by their ingrained desire for plunder, but also by their old hatred, were bent on destroying the people of the town. They believed that they had helped the party of Vitellius in the war with Otho as well; and later the common people of the town (for the mob always has an insolent nature) had insulted and taunted the soldiers of the Thirteenth legion who had been left behind to finish the amphitheatre.[2] The troops' anger was increased by other causes as well: Caecina had given an exhibition of gladiators there; the town had twice been the seat of war; the townspeople had provided food for the Vitellians when they were actually in battle-line; and some women had been killed who had been carried by their zeal for Vitellius's side into the very battle; besides this the market season had filled the colony, always rich, with a greater show of wealth. Now the other commanders were little noticed; but fame and fortune had made Antonius conspicuous to

famaque omnium oculis exposuerat. Is balineas abluendo cruori propere petit. Excepta vox est, cum teporem incusaret, statim futurum ut incalescerent[1]: vernile dictum omnem invidiam in eum vertit, tamquam signum incendendae Cremonae dedisset, quae iam flagrabat.

XXXIII. Quadraginta armatorum milia inrupere, calonum lixarumque amplior numerus et in libidinem ac saevitiam corruptior. Non dignitas, non aetas protegebat quo minus stupra caedibus, caedes stupris miscerentur. Grandaevos senes, exacta aetate feminas, vilis ad praedam, in ludibrium trahebant: ubi adulta virgo aut quis forma conspicuus incidisset, vi manibusque rapientium divulsus ipsos postremo direptores in mutuam perniciem agebat. Dum pecuniam vel gravia auro templorum dona sibi quisque trahunt, maiore aliorum vi truncabantur. Quidam obvia aspernati verberibus tormentisque dominorum abdita scrutari, defossa eruere: faces in manibus, quas, ubi praedam egesserant, in vacuas domos et inania templa per lasciviam iaculabantur; utque exercitu vario linguis moribus, cui cives socii externi interessent, diversae cupidines et aliud cuique fas nec quicquam inlicitum. Per quadriduum

[1] incalescerent *ed. Spirensis*: inalesceret *M.*

the eyes of all. He hurried to some baths to wash away the blood with which he was covered. When he complained of the temperature, a voice was heard saying that they would soon be hot enough. This answer of some slave turned all the odium of what followed on Antonius, as if he had given the signal to burn Cremona, which was indeed at that moment in flames.

XXXIII. Forty thousand armed men burst into the town; the number of camp-followers and servants was even greater, and they were more ready to indulge in lust and cruelty. Neither rank nor years protected anyone; their assailants debauched and killed without distinction. Aged men and women near the end of life, though despised as booty, were dragged off to be the soldiers' sport. Whenever a young woman or a handsome youth fell into their hands, they were torn to pieces by the violent struggles of those who tried to secure them, and this in the end drove the despoilers to kill one another. Individuals tried to carry off for themselves money or the masses of gold dedicated in the temples, but they were assailed and slain by others stronger than themselves. Some, scorning the booty before their eyes, flogged and tortured the owners to discover hidden wealth and dug up buried treasure. They carried firebrands in their hands, and when they had secured their loot, in utter wantonness they threw these into the vacant houses and empty temples. In this army there were many passions corresponding to the variety of speech and customs, for it was made up of citizens, allies, and foreigners; no two held the same thing sacred and there was no crime which was held unlawful. For four days did Cremona

Cremona suffecit. Cum omnia sacra profanaque in ignem[1] considerent, solum Mefitis templum stetit ante moenia, loco seu numine defensum.

XXXIV. Hic exitus Cremonae anno ducentesimo octogesimo sexto a primordio sui. Condita erat Ti.[2] Sempronio P. Cornelio consulibus, ingruente in Italiam Annibale, propugnaculum adversus Gallos trans Padum agentis et si qua alia vis per Alpis rueret. Igitur numero colonorum, opportunitate fluminum, ubere agri, adnexu conubiisque gentium adolevit floruitque, bellis externis intacta, civilibus infelix. Antonius pudore flagitii, crebrescente invidia, edixit ne quis Cremonensem captivum detineret. Inritamque praedam militibus effecerat consensus Italiae, emptionem talium mancipiorum aspernantis: occidi coepere; quod ubi enotuit, a propinquis adfinibusque occulte redemptabantur. Mox rediit Cremonam reliquus populus: reposita fora templaque magnificentia municipum; et Vespasianus hortabatur.

XXXV. Ceterum adsidere sepultae urbis ruinis noxia tabo humus haud diu permisit. Ad tertium lapidem progressi vagos paventisque Vitellianos, sua

[1] ignem *Heinsius*: igne *M.*
[2] Ti. *Lipsius*: T. *M.*

---

[1] The goddess of malaria, whose ravages in the valley of the Po must have been serious in antiquity.
[2] 218 B.C.

supply food for destruction. When everything sacred and profane sank into the flames, there stood solitary outside the walls the temple of Mefitis,[1] protected by either its position or its deity.

XXXIV. Such was the fate of Cremona in the two hundred and eighty-sixth year after its foundation. It was established in the consulship of Tiberius Sempronius and Publius Cornelius,[2] at the time when Hannibal was threatening Italy, to be a bulwark of defence against the Transpadane Gauls and to prevent any possible invasion over the Alps. The large number of colonists sent there, the advantages given by its navigable streams, the fertility of its land, as well as the connections established with other peoples by intermarriage and alliance, all combined to make the colony increase and prosper; untouched in foreign wars, it found misfortune in civil strife. Antonius, ashamed of his atrocious crime, as public indignation grew, issued a proclamation forbidding anyone to keep a citizen of Cremona captive. In fact, the common feeling of all Italy had already made the soldiers' booty valueless, for all Italians loathed the idea of buying slaves like these. The soldiers then began to kill their captives; when this became known, they were secretly ransomed by their relatives and kin. Later the remnant of the people returned to Cremona; the fora and the temples were restored by the munificence of its citizens; and Vespasian encouraged such action.

XXXV. However, the infection that pervaded the bloodstained ground did not allow the army to encamp long by the ruins of this dead city. The Flavian forces moved to the third milestone; the straggling and terrified Vitellians were reorganized,

quemque apud signa, componunt; et victae legiones, ne manente adhuc civili bello ambigue agerent, per Illyricum dispersae. In Britanniam inde et Hispanias nuntios famamque, in Galliam Iulium Calenum tribunum, in Germaniam Alpinium Montanum praefectum cohortis, quod hic Trevir, Calenus Aeduus, uterque Vitelliani fuerant, ostentui misere. Simul transitus Alpium praesidiis occupati, suspecta Germania, tamquam in auxilium Vitellii accingeretur.

XXXVI. At Vitellius profecto Caecina, cum Fabium Valentem paucis post diebus ad bellum impulisset, curis luxum obtendebat; non parare arma, non adloquio exercitioque militem firmare, non in ore vulgi agere, sed umbraculis hortorum abditus, ut ignava animalia, quibus si cibum suggeras, iacent torpentque, praeterita instantia futura pari oblivione dimiserat. Atque illum in nemore Aricino desidem et marcentem proditio Lucilii Bassi ac defectio classis Ravennatis perculit; nec multo post de Caecina adfertur mixtus gaudio dolor et descivisse et ab exercitu vinctum. Plus apud socordem animum laetitia quam cura valuit. Multa cum exultatione in urbem revectus frequenti contione pietatem militum

[1] Tacitus resumes his narrative from ii. 101.

each man under his own colours; and the defeated legions were distributed through Illyricum to keep them from any doubtful action, for civil war was not yet over. The Flavian leaders then despatched messengers to carry the news to Britain and to Spain; to Gaul they sent Julius Calenus, a tribune, and to Germany Apinius Montanus, a prefect of a cohort. The latter being a Trevir and Calenus an Aeduan, but both Vitellians, they were despatched to advertise the Flavians' victory. At the same time the Flavian forces occupied the passes of the Alps, for they suspected Germany of preparing to help Vitellius.

XXXVI. A few days after Caecina had left Rome,[1] Vitellius, having succeeded in driving Fabius Valens to the war, began to conceal his anxieties by giving himself up to pleasures. He took no steps to provide weapons, he did not try to inspire his troops by addressing them or by having them drilled, nor did he appear before the people. He kept hidden in the shade of his gardens, like those lazy animals that lie inactive and never move so long as you give them abundant food. The past, the present, and the future alike he had dismissed completely from his mind. He was actually lounging in indolence in the woods at Aricia when he was startled by the report of the treachery of Lucilius Bassus and of the revolt of the fleet at Ravenna. Shortly afterwards the report that Caecina had gone over to Vespasian but had been arrested by his troops caused Vitellius both delight and sorrow. It was the joy rather than the anxiety that had the greater influence on his sluggish spirit. In high exultation he rode back to the city, and in a crowded assembly extolled to the

laudibus cumulat; Publilium Sabinum praetorii praefectum ob amicitiam Caecinae vinciri iubet, substituto in locum eius Alfeno Varo.

XXXVII. Mox senatum composita in magnificentiam oratione adlocutus, exquisitis patrum adulationibus attollitur. Initium atrocis in Caecinam sententiae a L. Vitellio factum; dein ceteri composita indignatione, quod consul rem publicam, dux imperatorem, tantis opibus tot honoribus cumulatus amicum prodidisset, velut pro Vitellio conquerentes, suum dolorem proferebant. Nulla in oratione cuiusquam erga Flavianos duces obtrectatio: errorem imprudentiamque exercituum culpantes, Vespasiani nomen suspensi et vitabundi circumibant, nec defuit qui unum consulatus diem (is enim in locum Caecinae supererat) magno cum inrisu tribuentis accipientisque eblandiretur.[1] Pridie kalendas Novembris Rosius Regulus iniit eiuravitque. Adnotabant periti numquam antea non abrogato magistratu neque lege lata alium suffectum; nam consul uno die et ante fuerat Caninius Rebilus C. Caesare dictatore, cum belli civilis praemia festinarentur.

XXXVIII. Nota per eos dies Iunii Blaesi mors et

[1] eblandiretur *Rhenanus*: blandiretur *M*.

---

[1] Varus had been hitherto prefect of the camp. Cf. ii. 29.

[2] Caecina had been appointed consul for September and October, and evidently the news of his defection reached Rome about October 29 or 30. He was not removed from office, but his treacherous act was apparently regarded as vacating the office.

skies the devoted loyalty of his soldiers; then he ordered the arrest of Publilius Sabinus, prefect of the Praetorian guard, because he was Caecina's friend, appointing Alfenus Varus[1] in his place.

XXXVII. Later he addressed the senate in a grandiloquent speech, and was himself extolled by the senate with most elaborate flattery. Lucius Vitellius took the lead in proposing severe measures directed against Caecina; then the rest with feigned indignation, because, "as consul he had betrayed the State, as general his emperor, as a friend the one who had loaded him with wealth and honours," under the form of complaints in behalf of Vitellius expressed their own resentment. But in no speech was there any attack on the Flavian leaders. While the senators blamed the troops for their errors and lack of wisdom, they carefully and cautiously avoided mentioning Vespasian's name; and indeed there was one senator found to wheedle from Vitellius the one day of Caecina's consulship that was left[2]—a thing which brought many a sneer on both giver and receiver. On the thirty-first of October Rosius Regulus entered and gave up his office. The learned noted that never before had one consul succeeded another unless the office had first been declared vacant or a law duly passed. There had indeed been a consul for a single day once before: that was the case of Caninius Rebilus in the dictatorship of Gaius Caesar, when Caesar was in haste to pay the rewards of civil war.[3]

XXXVIII. The death of Junius Blaesus, becoming

[3] When Caninius Rebilus was made consul on the afternoon of the last day of 45 B.C. See Cicero, *ad. Fam.* vii. 30. 1.

famosa fuit, de qua sic accepimus. Gravi corporis morbo aeger Vitellius Servilianis hortis turrim vicino sitam conlucere per noctem crebris luminibus animadvertit. Sciscitanti causam apud Caecinam Tuscum epulari multos, praecipuum honore Iunium Blaesum nuntiatur; cetera in maius, de apparatu et solutis in lasciviam animis. Nec defuere qui ipsum Tuscum et alios, sed criminosius Blaesum incusarent, quod aegro principe laetos dies ageret. Ubi asperatum Vitellium et posse Blaesum perverti satis patuit iis qui principum offensas acriter speculantur, datae L. Vitellio delationis partes. Ille infensus Blaeso aemulatione prava, quod eum omni dedecore maculosum egregia fama anteibat, cubiculum imperatoris reserat, filium eius sinu complexus et genibus accidens. Causam confusionis quaerenti, non se proprio metu nec sui anxium, sed pro fratre, pro liberis fratris preces lacrimasque attulisse. Frustra Vespasianum timeri, quem tot Germanicae legiones, tot provinciae virtute ac fide, tantum denique terrarum ac maris immensis spatiis arceat: in urbe ac sinu cavendum hostem, Iunios Antoniosque avos iactantem, qui se stirpe imperatoria comem ac magnificum mili-

[1] Cf. ii. 59.

known at the time, caused much gossip.[1] The story, as we learn it, is this. When Vitellius was seriously ill in the gardens of Servilius, he noticed that a tower near by was brilliantly lighted at night. On asking the reason he was told that Caecina Tuscus was giving a large dinner at which Junius Blaesus was the guest of honour; and his informants went on to exaggerate the elaborate preparations made for this dinner and to speak of the guests' extravagant enjoyment. There was no lack of men ready to accuse Tuscus and others; but they blamed Blaesus most severely because he spent his days in pleasure while his emperor was sick. When the people, who have a keen eye for the angry moods of princes, saw that Vitellius was exasperated and that Blaesus could be destroyed, Lucius Vitellius was assigned the rôle of informant. His hatred for Blaesus sprang from base jealousy, for, stained as he was by every infamy, Blaesus surpassed him by his eminent reputation. So now, bursting into the emperor's bedroom, Lucius embraced the son of Vitellius and fell on his knees. When Vitellius asked the reason for his trepidation, Lucius replied that he had no personal fear and was not anxious for himself, but that it was on behalf of his brother and his brother's children that he brought his prayers and tears. "There is no point," he said, "in fearing Vespasian, whose approach is blocked by all the German legions, by all the brave and loyal provinces, and in short by boundless stretches of sea and land. The enemy against whom you must be on your guard is in the city, in your own bosom: he boasts that the Junii and Antonii are his ancestors; and, claiming imperial descent, he parades before the

tibus ostentet. Versas illuc omnium mentis, dum Vitellius amicorum inimicorumque neglegens fovet aemulum principis labores e convivio prospectantem. Reddendam pro intempestiva laetitia maestam et funebrem noctem, qua sciat et sentiat vivere Vitellium et imperare et, si quid fato accidat, filium habere.

XXXIX. Trepidanti inter scelus metumque, ne dilata Blaesi mors maturam perniciem, palam iussa atrocem invidiam ferret, placuit veneno grassari; addidit facinori fidem notabili[1] gaudio, Blaesum visendo. Quin et audita est saevissima Vitellii vox qua se (ipsa enim verba referam) pavisse oculos spectata inimici morte iactavit. Blaeso super claritatem natalium et elegantiam morum fidei obstinatio fuit. Integris quoque rebus a Caecina et primoribus partium iam Vitellium aspernantibus ambitus abnuere perseveravit. Sanctus, inturbidus, nullius repentini honoris, adeo non principatus adpetens, parum effugerat ne dignus crederetur.

XL. Fabius interim Valens multo ac molli concubinarum spadonumque agmine segnius quam ad bellum incedens, proditam a Lucilio Basso Ravennatem classem pernicibus nuntiis accepit. Et si coep-

[1] notabili *Faernus*: nobili *M*.

soldiers his courtesy and magnificence. Everyone's thoughts are attracted to him, while you, failing to distinguish between friend and foe, cherish a rival who watches his emperor's distress from a dinner-table. To pay him for his unseasonable joy, he should suffer a night of sorrow and doom, that he may know and feel that Vitellius is alive and emperor, and furthermore that, if any misfortune happens to him, he still has a son."

XXXIX. Anxiously hesitating between crime and the fear that, if delayed, the death of Blaesus might bring prompt ruin or, if openly ordered, a storm of hate, Vitellius decided to resort to poison. He gave the public reason to believe in his guilt by his evident joy when he went to see Blaesus. Moreover, he was heard to make a brutal remark, boasting—and I shall quote his very words—that he had "feasted his eyes on the sight of his enemy's death-bed." Blaesus was a man not only of distinguished family and of refinement, but also of resolute loyalty. Even while the position of Vitellius was still unshaken, he had been solicited by Caecina and the party leaders who already despised the emperor, but he persisted in rejecting their advances. Honourable, opposed to revolution, moved by no desire for sudden honours, least of all for the principate, he could not escape being regarded as worthy of it.

XL. Fabius Valens in the meantime, with his long effeminate train of concubines and eunuchs, moved on too slowly for a general going out to war. On his way he heard from messengers who came in haste, that Lucius Bassus had betrayed the fleet at Ravenna to the Flavians. Yet if he had hurried, he

tum iter properasset, nutantem Caecinam praevenire aut ante discrimen pugnae adsequi legiones potuisset. Nec deerant qui monerent ut cum fidissimis per occultos tramites vitata Ravenna Hostiliam Cremonamve pergeret; aliis placebat accitis ex urbe praetoriis cohortibus valida manu perrumpere. Ipse inutili cunctatione agendi tempora consultando consumpsit; mox utrumque consilium aspernatus, quod inter ancipitia deterrimum est, dum media sequitur, nec ausus est satis nec providit.

XLI. Missis ad Vitellium litteris auxilium postulat. Venere tres cohortes cum ala Britannica, neque ad fallendum aptus numerus neque ad penetrandum. Sed Valens ne in tanto quidem discrimine infamia caruit, quo minus rapere inlicitas voluptates adulterisque ac stupris polluere hospitum domus crederetur: aderant vis et pecunia et ruentis fortunae novissima libido. Adventu demum peditum equitumque pravitas consilii patuit, quia nec vadere per hostis tam parva manu poterat, etiam si fidissima foret, nec integram fidem attulerant; pudor tamen et praesentis ducis reverentia morabatur, haud diuturna vincla apud pavidos[1] periculorum et dedecoris securos. Eo metu cohortes Ariminum praemittit, alam tueri terga iubet: ipse paucis, quos adversa non mutaverant,

[1] pavidos *Faernus*: avidos *M*.

---

[1] Rimini.

might have stopped Caecina, who was still wavering; or at least he could have reached the legions before the decisive battle. Some advised him to take his most trusty men and, avoiding Ravenna, to push on by secret roads to Hostilia or Cremona; others favoured summoning the praetorian cohorts from Rome and then breaking through with a strong force. But Valens by useless delay wasted in discussion the time for action; later he rejected both the plans proposed, and in following a middle course —the worst of all policies in times of doubt—he showed neither adequate courage nor foresight.

XLI. He wrote to Vitellius asking for help. Three cohorts and a squadron of cavalry from Britain came in response, a force whose size was ill-suited either to escape observation or to force a passage. But even in such a crisis Valens did not avoid the infamy of snatching illicit pleasures and polluting with adulteries and debaucheries the homes of those who entertained him: he had power, money, and, as fortune failed, the lust of the last hour. When the foot and horse finally arrived, the folly of his plan became evident, because he could not make his way through the enemy's lines with so small a band, no matter how faithful, and, in fact, they did not bring a loyalty that was wholly unshaken. Still shame and awe in the presence of their commander held them back; but these are weak restraints over men who are fearful of danger and regardless of disgrace. Accordingly, in his alarm, he sent the cohorts on to Ariminum,[1] and ordered the squadron of cavalry to protect his rear. He himself turned aside into Umbria with a few companions whose loyalty had not been changed by

comitantibus flexit[1] in Umbriam atque inde Etruriam, ubi cognito pugnae Cremonensis eventu non ignavum et, si provenisset, atrox consilium iniit, ut arreptis navibus in quamcumque partem Narbonensis provinciae egressus Gallias et exercitus et Germaniae gentis novumque bellum cieret.

XLII. Digresso Valente trepidos, qui Ariminum tenebant, Cornelius Fuscus, admoto exercitu et missis per proxima litorum Liburnicis, terra marique circumvenit: occupantur plana Umbriae et qua Picenus ager Hadria adluitur, omnisque Italia inter Vespasianum ac Vitellium Appennini[2] iugis dividebatur. Fabius Valens e sinu Pisano segnitia maris aut adversante vento portum Herculis Monoeci depellitur. Haud procul inde agebat Marius Maturus Alpium maritimarum procurator, fidus Vitellio, cuius sacramentum cunctis circa hostilibus nondum exuerat. Is Valentem comiter exceptum, ne Galliam Narbonensem temere ingrederetur, monendo terruit; simul ceterorum fides metu infracta.

XLIII. Namque circumiectas civitates procurator Valerius Paulinus, strenuus militiae et Vespasiano ante fortunam amicus, in verba eius adegerat; concitisque omnibus, qui exauctorati a Vitellio bellum

[1] eo metu et paucis . . . comitantibus cohortes . . . ipse flexit *M*: *verum ordinem rest. Acidalius.*
[2] Appennini *Puteolanus*: appenninis *M.*

---

[1] Now in command of the fleet at Ravenna. Cf. iii. 12.
[2] Monaco.

adversity, and from Umbria he moved into Etruria. There, hearing the result of the battle at Cremona, he formed a plan which was not cowardly and which would have been formidable if it had only succeeded: he proposed to seize some ships, land somewhere on the coast of the province of Narbonne, and then rouse the Gallic provinces, the armies, and the tribes of Germany—in fact to begin a new war.

XLII. Valens' departure made the troops at Ariminum anxious and timid. Cornelius Fuscus[1] brought up his land forces and sent light men-of-war along the neighbouring coast and thereby cut the garrison off by land and sea. The Flavians now held the plains of Umbria and that part of Picenum that is washed by the Adriatic; in fact, all Italy was divided between Vespasian and Vitellius by the range of the Apennines. Fabius Valens sailed from the harbour of Pisa, but was forced by calm or by head winds to put in at the port of Hercules Monoecus.[2] Marius Maturus, procurator of the Maritime Alps, was not far from here; he was still faithful to Vitellius, not having yet abandoned his oath of allegiance to him although all the districts round about were hostile. He received Valens kindly, and persuaded him by his advice not to risk entering Narbonese Gaul. At the same time the fidelity of the rest was shaken by their fears.

XLIII. There was reason for this, since the imperial agent, Valerius Paulinus, a vigorous soldier and a friend of Vespasian even before his great fortune befell him, had bound the neighbouring communities by an oath of allegiance to him. Paulinus had also called out all the veterans who had been discharged by Vitellius, but now freely took up

sponte sumebant, Foroiuliensem coloniam, claustra maris, praesidio tuebatur, eo gravior auctor, quod Paulino patria Forum Iulii et honos apud praetorianos, quorum quondam tribunus fuerat, ipsique pagani favore municipali et futurae potentiae spe iuvare partis adnitebantur. Quae ut[1] paratu firma et aucta rumore apud varios Vitellianorum animos increbruere, Fabius Valens cum quattuor speculatoribus et tribus amicis, totidem centurionibus, ad navis regreditur; Maturo ceterisque remanere et in verba Vespasiani adigi volentibus fuit. Ceterum ut mare tutius Valenti quam litora aut urbes, ita futuri ambiguus et magis quid vitaret quam cui fideret certus, adversa tempestate Stoechadas Massiliensium insulas defertur.[2] Ibi eum missae a Paulino Liburnicae oppressere.

XLIV. Capto Valente cuncta ad victoris opes conversa, initio per Hispaniam a prima[3] Adiutrice legione orto, quae memoria Othonis infensa Vitellio decimam quoque ac sextam traxit. Nec Galliae cunctabantur. Et Britanniam inclinatus[4] erga Vespasianum favor, quod illic secundae legioni a Claudio praepositus et bello clarus egerat, non sine motu adiunxit ceterarum, in quibus plerique centuriones

[1] ut *Jacob* : vi *M.*
[2] defertur *Ernesti* : adfertur *M.*
[3] hispania adprima *M.*
[4] inclinatus *Schütz* : inditus *M.*

---

[1] Cf. ii. 67. [2] Fréjus.
[3] Les îles d'Hyères, near Toulon.

arms again;[1] and he kept a garrison in Forum Julii,[2] which controls the sea here, while his authority was increased by the fact that Forum Julii was his native city and that he was esteemed by the praetorians, whose tribune he had once been. Also the people of the district, moved by zeal for a fellow-townsman and by hope of his future power, did their best to help his party. When these preparations, which were effective and were exaggerated by rumour, were reported again and again to the Vitellians, whose minds were already in doubt, Fabius Valens returned to his ships with four soldiers of the body-guard, three friends, and three centurions; Maturus and the rest chose to remain and take the oath of fidelity to Vespasian. But while the sea seemed to Valens safer than shores or cities, he was still doubtful of the future and saw more clearly what to avoid than what to trust. An adverse storm drove him to the Stoechadae islands belonging to the Massilians,[3] where he was captured by some light galleys which Paulinus sent after him.

XLIV. Now that Valens was captured everything turned to the victor's advantage. The movement in Spain was begun by the First legion Adjutrix, which was devoted to the memory of Otho and so hostile to Vitellius. This legion drew the Tenth and Sixth after it. The Gallic provinces did not hesitate. In Britain a favourable sentiment inclined toward Vespasian, because he had been put in command of the Second legion there by Claudius and had distinguished himself in the field. This secured the island for him, but only after some resistance on the part of the other legions, in which there were many centurions and soldiers who owed their promotions to

ac milites a Vitellio provecti expertum iam principem anxii mutabant.

XLV. Ea discordia et crebris belli civilis rumoribus Britanni sustulere animos auctore Venutio, qui super insitam ferociam et Romani nominis odium propriis in Cartimanduam reginam stimulis accendebatur. Cartimandua Brigantibus imperitabat, pollens nobilitate; et auxerat potentiam, postquam capto per dolum rege Carataco instruxisse triumphum Claudii Caesaris videbatur. Inde opes et rerum secundarum luxus: spreto Venutio (is fuit maritus) armigerum eius Vellocatum in matrimonium regnumque accepit. Concussa statim flagitio domus: pro marito studia civitatis, pro adultero libido reginae et saevitia. Igitur Venutius accitis auxiliis, simul ipsorum Brigantum defectione in extremum discrimen Cartimanduam adduxit. Tum petita a Romanis praesidia. Et cohortes alaeque nostrae variis proeliis, exemere tamen periculo reginam; regnum Venutio, bellum nobis relictum.

XLVI. Turbata per eosdem dies Germania, et socordia ducum, seditione legionum, externa vi,

---

[1] Celebrated in 51 A.D. See Tacitus, *Ann.* xii. 33–37; *CIL.* vi. 920.

Vitellius, and so hesitated to change from an emperor of whom they had already had some experience.

XLV. Inspired by these differences between the Roman forces and by the many rumours of civil war that reached them, the Britons plucked up courage under the leadership of Venutius, who, in addition to his natural spirit and hatred of the Roman name, was fired by his personal resentment toward Queen Cartimandua. She was ruler over the Brigantes, having the influence that belongs to high birth, and she had later strengthened her power when she was credited with having captured King Caratacus by treachery and so furnished an adornment for the triumph of Claudius Caesar.[1] From this came her wealth and the wanton spirit which success breeds. She grew to despise her husband Venutius, and took as her consort his squire Vellocatus, whom she admitted to share the throne with her. Her house was at once shaken by this scandalous act. Her husband was favoured by the sentiments of all the citizens; the adulterer was supported by the queen's passion for him and by her savage spirit. So Venutius, calling in aid from outside and at the same time assisted by a revolt of the Brigantes themselves, put Cartimandua into an extremely dangerous position. Then she asked the Romans for protection, and in fact some companies of our foot and horse, after meeting with indifferent success in a number of engagements, finally succeeded in rescuing the queen from danger. The throne was left to Venutius; the war to us.

XLVI. At the same time there was trouble in Germany. Indeed the Roman cause almost suffered disaster because of the negligence of the generals,

perfidia sociali prope adflicta Romana res. Id bellum cum causis et eventibus (etenim longius provectum est) mox memorabimus. Mota et Dacorum gens numquam fida, tunc sine metu, abducto e Moesia exercitu. Sed prima rerum quieti speculabantur: ubi flagrare Italiam bello, cuncta in vicem hostilia accepere, expugnatis cohortium alarumque hibernis utraque Danuvii ripa potiebantur. Iamque castra legionum excindere parabant, ni Mucianus sextam legionem opposuisset, Cremonensis victoriae gnarus, ac ne externa moles utrimque ingrueret, si Dacus Germanusque diversi inrupissent. Adfuit, ut saepe alias, fortuna populi Romani, quae Mucianum virisque Orientis illuc tulit, et quod Cremonae interim transegimus. Fonteius Agrippa ex Asia (pro consule eam provinciam annuo imperio tenuerat) Moesiae praepositus est, additis copiis e Vitelliano exercitu, quem spargi per provincias et externo bello inligari pars consilii pacisque erat.

XLVII. Nec ceterae nationes silebant. Subita per Pontum arma barbarum mancipium, regiae

---

[1] Tacitus fulfils his promise in iv. 12–37, 54–79, and in v. 14–26.

[2] Living in what is now Rumania.

[3] The legionaries having been withdrawn from the bank of the Danube, it was now defended by the auxiliaries alone.

the mutinous spirit of the legions, the assaults from without the empire, and the treachery of our allies. The history of this war with its causes and results we shall give later, for the struggle was a long one.[1] The Dacians [2] also, never trustworthy, became uneasy and now had no fear, for our army had been withdrawn from Moesia. They watched the first events without stirring; but when they heard that Italy was aflame with war and that the whole empire was divided into hostile camps, they stormed the winter quarters of our auxiliary foot and horse [3] and put themselves in possession of both banks of the Danube. They were already preparing to destroy the camps of the legions, and would have succeeded in their purpose if Mucianus had not placed the Sixth legion across their path. He took this step because he had learned of the victory at Cremona, and he also feared that two hordes of foreigners might come down upon the empire, if the Dacians and the Germans should succeed in breaking in at different points. As so often before, the fortune of the Roman people attended them, bringing, as it had, Mucianus and the forces of the East to that point and securing meantime the success at Cremona. Fonteius Agrippa was transferred from Asia, where, as proconsul, he had governed the province for a year, and put in charge of Moesia; there he was given additional troops from the army of Vitellius, which it was wise from the point of view of both policy and peace to distribute in the provinces and to involve in war with a foreign foe.

XLVII. Nor were the other nations quiet. There was a sudden armed uprising in Pontus led by a barbarian slave who had once been prefect of the

quondam classis praefectus, moverat. Is fuit Anicetus Polemonis libertus,[1] praepotens olim, et postquam regnum in formam provinciae verterat, mutationis impatiens. Igitur Vitellii nomine adscitis gentibus, quae Pontum accolunt, corrupto in spem rapinarum egentissimo quoque, haud temnendae manus ductor, Trapezuntem vetusta fama civitatem, a Graecis in extremo Ponticae orae conditam, subitus inrupit. Caesa ibi cohors, regium auxilium olim; mox donati civitate Romana signa armaque in nostrum modum, desidiam licentiamque Graecorum retinebant. Classi quoque faces intulit, vacuo mari eludens, quia lectissimas Liburnicarum omnemque militem Mucianus Byzantium adegerat: quin et barbari contemptim [2] vagabantur, fabricatis repente navibus. Camaras vocant, artis lateribus latam alvum sine vinculo aeris aut ferri conexam; et tumido mari, prout fluctus attollitur, summa navium tabulis augent, donec in modum tecti claudantur. Sic inter undas volvuntur, pari utrimque prora et mutabili remigio, quando hinc vel illinc adpellere [3] indiscretum et innoxium est.

XLVIII. Advertit ea res Vespasiani animum ut vexillarios e legionibus ducemque Virdium Geminum spectatae militiae deligeret. Ille incompositum et

[1] libertus prepotens libertus, *M.*
[2] contempti *M.* [3] appellare *M.*

---

[1] Polemo II., who at his death in 63 A.D. left the kingdom of Pontus to the Romans.
[2] Trebizond.

royal fleet. This was a certain Anicetus, a freedman of Polemo,[1] who, having been once very powerful, was impatient of the change after the kingdom was transformed into a province. So he stirred up the people of Pontus in the name of Vitellius, bribing the poorest among them with hope of plunder. Then at the head of a band, which was far from being negligible, he suddenly attacked Trapezus,[1] a city of ancient fame, founded by Greeks at the extreme end of the coast of Pontus. There he massacred a cohort, which originally consisted of auxiliaries furnished by the king; later its members had been granted Roman citizenship and had adopted Roman standards and arms, but retained the indolence and licence of the Greeks. He also set fire to the fleet and escaped by sea, which was unpatrolled since Mucianus had concentrated the best light galleys and all the marines at Byzantium. Moreover, the barbarians had hastily built vessels and now roamed the sea at will, despising the power of Rome. Their boats they call *camarae;* they have a low freeboard but are broad of beam, and are fastened together without spikes of bronze or iron. When the sea is rough the sailors build up the bulwarks with planks to match the height of the waves, until they close in the hull like the roof of a house. Thus protected these vessels roll about amid the waves. They have a prow at both ends and their arrangement of oars may be shifted, so that they can be safely propelled in either direction at will.

XLVIII. These events attracted Vespasian's attention, so that he sent detachments from his legions under the command of Virdius Geminus, whose military skill had been well tested. He attacked

praedae cupidine vagum hostem adortus coegit in navis; effectisque raptim Liburnicis adsequitur Anicetum in ostio fluminis Chobi, tutum sub Sedochezorum regis auxilio, quem pecunia donisque ad societatem perpulerat. Ac primo rex minis armisque supplicem tueri: postquam merces proditionis aut bellum ostendebatur, fluxa, ut est barbaris, fide pactus Aniceti exitium perfugas tradidit, belloque servili finis impositus.

Laetum ea victoria Vespasianum, cunctis super vota fluentibus, Cremonensis proelii nuntius in Aegypto adsequitur. eo properantius Alexandriam pergit, ut fractos Vitellii exercitus urbemque externae opis indigam fame urgeret. Namque et Africam, eodem latere sitam, terra marique invadere parabat, clausis annonae subsidiis inopiam ac discordiam hosti facturus.

XLIX. Dum hac totius orbis nutatione fortuna imperii transit, Primus Antonius nequaquam pari innocentia post Cremonam agebat, satis factum bello ratus et cetera ex facili, seu felicitas in tali ingenio avaritiam superbiam ceteraque occulta mala patefecit.

---

[1] The Khopi.
[2] Tacitus here returns to the matter of iii. 35.

the enemy's troops when they were off their guard and were scattered in their greed for booty, and forced them to their boats; afterwards he quickly built some light galleys and caught up with Anicetus at the mouth of the river Chobus,[1] where hc had sought shelter under the protection of the king of the Sedochezi, whose alliance he had secured by bribes and gifts. At first the king sheltered his suppliant with the aid of threats and arms; but after the reward for treachery and the alternative of war were set before him, with the unstable loyalty of a barbarian he bargained away the life of Anicetus, gave up the refugees, and so an end was put to this servile war.

While Vespasian was rejoicing over this victory, for everything was succeeding beyond his hopes and prayers, the news of the battle at Cremona reached him in Egypt. He moved with all the more speed to Alexandria, that he might impose the burden of famine on the broken armies of Vitellius and on Rome, which always needs help from outside. For he was now preparing to invade Africa also by land and sea, situated as it is in the same quarter of the world, his purpose being to shut off Italy's supplies of grain and so cause need and discord among his foes.

XLIX. While the imperial power was shifting with these world-wide convulsions,[2] Primus Antonius did not behave so blamelessly after the battle of Cremona as before, whether it was that he thought that he had done enough for the war and that everything else would easily follow, or whether success in the case of a nature like his brought to the surface the avarice, arrogance, and other evils that had remained hidden hitherto. He stalked

Ut captam Italiam persultare, ut suas legiones colere; omnibus dictis factisque viam[1] sibi ad potentiam struere. Utque licentia militem imbueret interfectorum centurionum ordines legionibus offerebat. Eo suffragio turbidissimus quisque delecti; nec miles in arbitrio ducum, sed duces militari violentia trahebantur. Quae seditiosa et corrumpendae disciplinae mox in praedam vertebat, nihil adventantem Mucianum veritus, quod exitiosius erat quam Vespasianum sprevisse.

L. Ceterum propinqua hieme et umentibus Pado campis expeditum agmen incedere. Signa aquilaeque victricium legionum, milites vulneribus aut aetate graves, plerique etiam integri Veronae relicti; sufficere cohortes alaeque et e legionibus lecti profligato iam bello videbantur. Undecima legio sese adiunxerat, initio cunctata, sed prosperis rebus anxia quod defuisset; sex milia Dalmatarum, recens dilectus, comitabantur; ducebat Pompeius Silvanus consularis; vis consiliorum penes Annium Bassum legionis legatum. Is Silvanum socordem bello et dies rerum verbis terentem specie obsequii regebat et[2] ad omnia quae agenda forent quieta cum industria

[1] viam *Lipsius*: vim *M*.
[2] et ad omnia *Halm*: omniaque *M*.

---

[1] That is, by extorting or accepting money from soldiers in return for his support.
[2] It was now November.
[3] From Dalmatia. Cf. ii. 67.

through Italy as if it were captured territory; he courted the legions as if they were his own; he used his every word and act to pave his way to power. To inspire the soldiers with a spirit of licence, he offered to the rank and file the places of the centurions who had fallen. The soldiers chose the most turbulent of their number. The ranks were no longer directed by the will of their leaders, but the leaders were at the mercy of the common soldiers' whims. These acts, which made for mutinies and the ruin of discipline, Antonius presently turned to his own profit.[1] He had no fear of the arrival of Mucianus, although in the event this was more fatal for him than the fact that he had treated Vespasian with little respect.

L. Meantime, since winter was approaching and the plains were inundated by the Po,[2] the Flavian troops moved without their heavy baggage. They left at Verona the eagles and standards of the victorious legions, such soldiers as were incapacitated by wounds or years, and also a number who were in good condition; the auxiliary foot and horse with selected legionaries seemed sufficient now that the worst of the war was over. The Eleventh legion [3] had joined them; at first it had hesitated, but, now that the Flavians were succeeding, it became apprehensive because it had not joined them before. Six thousand Dalmatians, a new levy, accompanied them, led by Pompeius Silvanus, an ex-consul. The actual guiding spirit was Annius Bassus, the legionary legate. Silvanus displayed no energy in war, but wasted in mere talk the days for action. Bassus directed him by pretending to defer to him, and continually attended to all necessary operations

aderat. Ad has copias e classicis Ravennatibus, legionariam militiam poscentibus, optimus quisque adsciti: classem Dalmatae supplevere. Exercitus ducesque ad Fanum Fortunae iter sistunt, de summa rerum cunctantes, quod motas ex urbe praetorias cohortis audierant et teneri praesidiis Appenninum rebantur; et ipsos in regione[1] bello attrita inopia et seditiosae militum voces terrebant, clavarium (donativi nomen est) flagitantium. Nec pecuniam aut frumentum providerant, et festinatio atque aviditas praepediebant, dum quae accipi poterant rapiuntur.

LI. Celeberrimos auctores habeo tantam victoribus adversus fas nefasque inreverentiam fuisse ut gregarius eques occisum a se proxima acie fratrem professus praemium a ducibus petierit. Nec illis aut honorare eam caedem ius hominum aut ulcisci ratio belli permittebat. Distulerant tamquam maiora meritum quam quae[2] statim exsolverentur; nec quidquam ultra traditur. Ceterum et prioribus civium bellis par scelus inciderat. Nam proelio, quo apud Ianiculum adversus Cinnam pugnatum est, Pompeianus miles fratrem suum, dein cognito facinore se ipsum interfecit, ut Sisenna memorat: tanto acrior apud maiores, sicut virtutibus gloria, ita flagitiis

[1] regione *Faernus*: legione *M.*
[2] quam quae *Puteolanus*: quanquam *M.*

---

[1] Fano.
[2] A piece of soldiers' slang; literally, "hob-nail (*clavus*) money."
[3] In 87 B.C.

with unobtrusive activity. The marines at Ravenna now demanded service with the legions, and the best of them were enrolled among them; Dalmatians replaced them in the fleet. The troops and commanders halted at Fanum Fortunae,[1] being uncertain as to the proper course of action, for they had received a report that six praetorian cohorts had left Rome, and they supposed that the passes in the Apennines were guarded. The commanders, too, were alarmed by the lack of supplies, being now in a district completely devastated by the war, as well as by the mutinous demands of the soldiers for the *clavarium*,[2] as they call the donative. They had provided neither money nor provisions; moreover, their haste and greed in seizing as private booty what might have been stores to draw upon now proved embarrassing.

LI. I have it from the best authorities that the victors had come to disregard the difference between right and wrong so completely that a common soldier declared that he had killed his brother in the last battle and actually asked the generals for a reward. The common dictates of humanity did not permit them to honour such a murder or military policy to punish it. They put off the soldier on the ground that he deserved a reward greater than could be repaid at once; nor is anything further told concerning the case. And yet a similar crime had happened in civil war before. In the struggle against Cinna on the Janiculum,[3] as Sisenna relates, one of Pompey's soldiers killed his own brother and then, on realizing his crime, committed suicide. So much livelier among our ancestors was repentance for guilt as well as glory in virtuous action. Such

paenitentia fuit. Sed haec aliaque ex vetere memoria petita, quotiens res locusque exempla recti aut solacia mali poscet, haud absurde memorabimus.

LII. Antonio ducibusque partium praemitti equites omnemque Umbriam explorari placuit, si qua Appennini iuga clementius adirentur; acciri aquilas signaque et quidquid Veronae militum foret, Padumque et mare commeatibus compleri. Erant inter duces qui necterent moras: quippe nimius iam Antonius, et certiora ex Muciano sperabantur. Namque Mucianus tam celeri victoria anxius et, ni praesens urbe potiretur, expertem se belli gloriaeque ratus, ad Primum et Varum media scriptitabat, instandum coeptis aut rursus cunctandi utilitates edisserens atque ita compositus ut ex eventu rerum adversa abnueret vel prospera agnosceret. Plotium Grypum, nuper a Vespasiano in senatorium ordinem adscitum [1] ac legioni praepositum, ceterosque sibi fidos apertius monuit, hique omnes de festinatione Primi ac Vari sinistre et Muciano volentia rescripsere. Quibus epistulis Vespasiano missis effecerat ut non pro spe Antonii consilia factaque eius aestimarentur.

[1] adscitum *Ritter*: additum *M.*

deeds as this and others like them, drawn from our earlier history, I shall not improperly insert in my work whenever the theme or situation demands examples of the right or solace for the wrong.

LII. Antonius and the other Flavian commanders decided to send their cavalry on ahead and to reconnoitre throughout Umbria, to see if they could approach the Apennines at any point without danger; they proposed also to bring up the eagles and standards with all the soldiers then at Verona, and to fill the Po and the sea with convoys of provisions. There were some among the commanders who devised reasons for delay; they felt that Antonius was becoming too pretentious, and they hoped to get more certain advantages from Mucianus. For Mucianus, disturbed by the speed with which the victory had been won, and believing that he would have no share in the glory to be gained by the war unless he took Rome in person, kept writing to Primus and Varus in ambiguous terms, saying in one letter that they must follow up their successes and in another dwelling on the advantages of proceeding slowly, so trimming his course that according to the event he might at will repudiate all responsibility for failure or take the credit for success. To Plotius Grypus, whom Vespasian had lately elevated to senatorial rank and put in command of a legion, and to all other officers who were loyal, he wrote admonishing them more frankly; and they all replied, putting the haste of Primus and Varus in an unfavourable light and saying what was likely to please Mucianus. By sending these letters to Vespasian, Mucianus succeeded in preventing the plans and acts of Antonius from being estimated so highly as the latter had hoped.

LIII. Aegre id pati Antonius et culpam in Mucianum conferre, cuius criminationibus eviluissent pericula sua; nec sermonibus temperabat, immodicus lingua et obsequii insolens. Litteras ad Vespasianum composuit iactantius quam ad principem, nec sine occulta in Mucianum insectatione: se Pannonicas legiones in arma egisse; suis stimulis excitos Moesiae duces, sua constantia perruptas Alpis, occupatam Italiam, intersepta Germanorum Raetorumque auxilia. Quod discordis dispersasque Vitellii legiones equestri procella, mox peditum vi per diem noctemque fudisset, id pulcherrimum et sui operis. Casum Cremonae bello imputandum: maiore damno, plurium urbium excidiis veteres civium discordias rei publicae stetisse. Non se nuntiis neque epistulis, sed manu et armis imperatori suo militare; neque officere gloriae eorum qui Daciam[1] interim composuerint: illis Moesiae pacem, sibi salutem securitatemque Italiae cordi fuisse; suis exhortationibus Gallias Hispaniasque, validissimam terrarum partem, ad Vespasianum conversas. Sed cecidisse in inritum labores si praemia periculorum soli adsequantur qui periculis non adfuerint. Nec fefellere ea Mucianum;

[1] Daciam *Sisker*: asiam *M*.

LIII. At this Antonius was indignant, and put the blame on Mucianus, whose base insinuations, as he maintained, had made the dangers that he had run seem trifling; nor did he pick and choose his words, being as he was immoderate in speech and unaccustomed to defer to another. He drew up a letter to Vespasian in a strain too boastful to use to an emperor; and he did not fail to attack Mucianus covertly: "It was I who armed the Pannonian legions. It was I who roused the commanders in Moesia and spurred them on. It was my bold action that broke through the Alps, seized Italy, and blocked the road against any assistance to Vitellius from Germany and Raetia." As for the disaster inflicted on the discordant and scattered legions of Vitellius by a whirlwind of cavalry and the rout of those troops by a great force of infantry which pursued them for a day and a night, Antonius claimed that these were glorious achievements of which he deserved all the credit. The fate of Cremona he charged up to the chances of war; and pointed out that civil discord in earlier days had caused greater loss and had destroyed more cities. He declared that he did not fight for his emperor with despatches and letters, but with deeds and arms; he made no attempt to dim the glory of those who meantime had quieted Dacia; their desire had been to give Moesia peace, his to give Italy safety and security. It was due to his exhortations that the Gauls and Spains, the strongest part of the world, had turned to Vespasian's side. "But," he added, "my efforts will come to nothing if the rewards for dangers run are to be gained only by those who did not face the dangers." Of all this

inde graves simultates, quas Antonius simplicius, Mucianus callide eoque implacabilius nutriebat.

LIV. At Vitellius fractis apud Cremonam rebus nuntios cladis occultans stulta dissimulatione remedia potius malorum quam mala differebat. Quippe confitenti consultantique supererant spes viresque: cum e contrario laeta omnia fingeret, falsis ingravescebat. Mirum apud ipsum de bello silentium; prohibiti per civitatem sermones, eoque plures ac, si liceret, vere narraturi, quia vetabantur, atrociora vulgaverant. Nec duces hostium augendae famae deerant, captos Vitellii exploratores circumductosque, ut robora victoris exercitus noscerent, remittendo; quos omnis Vitellius secreto percontatus interfici iussit. Notabili constantia centurio Iulius Agrestis post multos sermones, quibus Vitellium ad virtutem frustra accendebat, perpulit ut ad viris hostium spectandas quaeque apud Cremonam acta forent ipse mitteretur. Nec exploratione occulta fallere Antonium temptavit, sed mandata imperatoris suumque animum professus, ut cuncta viseret postulat. Missi qui locum proelii, Cremonae vestigia, captas legiones ostenderent. Agrestis[1] ad Vitellium remeavit ab-

[1] adgrestis *M*.

Mucianus was fully aware, and the result was bitter enmity, fostered more openly by Antonius, with cunning and therefore the more implacably by Mucianus.

LIV. Vitellius, however, after the loss of his cause at Cremona, concealed the news of the disaster, and by foolish dissimulation delayed the remedies for his misfortunes rather than the misfortunes themselves. For if he had only acknowledged the truth and sought counsel, he had still some hope and resources left; but when, on the contrary, he pretended that all was well, he made his situation worse by his falsehoods. A strange silence concerning the war was observed in his presence; discussion in the city was forbidden, with the result that more people talked. If they had been allowed to speak, they would have told only the truth; but as they were forbidden, they spread abroad more frightful reports. The generals of the Flavian forces did not fail to increase the rumours by escorting round their camp the Vitellian spies whom they had captured, showing them the strength of the victorious army and then sending them back to Rome. All these Vitellius questioned in secret and promptly had them put to death. Julius Agrestis, a centurion, exhibited notable courage. After many conversations, in which he tried in vain to rouse Vitellius to bold action, he persuaded the emperor to send him to see in person the enemy's forces and to observe what had happened at Cremona. He did not try to deceive Antonius by any secret investigation, but frankly made known his emperor's orders and his own purpose, and demanded to see everything. Men were despatched to show him the battle-ground, the ruins of Cremona, and the captive legions. Agrestis

nuentique vera esse quae adferret, atque ultro corruptum arguenti "quando quidem" inquit "magno documento opus est, nec alius iam tibi aut vitae aut mortis meae usus, dabo cui credas." Atque ita digressus voluntaria morte dicta firmavit. Quidam iussu Vitellii interfectum, de fide constantiaque eadem tradidere.

LV. Vitellius ut e somno excitus Iulium Priscum et Alfenum Varum cum quattuordecim praetoriis cohortibus et omnibus equitum alis obsidere Appenninum iubet; secuta e classicis legio. Tot milia armatorum, lecta equis virisque, si dux alius foret, inferendo quoque bello satis pollebant. Ceterae cohortes ad tuendam urbem L. Vitellio fratri datae: ipse nihil e solito luxu remittens et diffidentia properus festinare comitia, quibus consules in multos annos destinabat; foedera sociis, Latium externis[1] dilargiri; his tributa dimittere, alios immunitatibus iuvare; denique nulla in posterum cura lacerare imperium. Sed vulgus ad magnitudinem beneficiorum aderat,[2] stultissimus quisque pecuniis mercabatur, apud sapientis cassa habebantur quae neque dari neque accipi salva re publica poterant. Tandem

[1] ternis *M*.
[2] haberat *M*.

---

[1] The Latin is obscure, but it apparently means what the English version attempts to say, *i.e.* that the unthinking part of the populace were delighted and dazzled by his apparent liberality. J. F. Gronovius read *hiabat* ("gaped with wonder at") for *aderat*, but with no manuscript warrant.

returned to Vitellius; and when the emperor denied the truth of his report, and even went so far as to charge him with having been bribed, he said, "Since I must give you a convincing proof of my statements, and you can have no other advantage from my life or death, I will give you evidence that will make you believe." With these words he left the emperor's presence, and made good his words by suicide. Some have reported that he was put to death by the orders of Vitellius, but all agree as to his fidelity and courage.

LV. Vitellius was like a man wakened from a deep sleep. He ordered Julius Priscus and Alfenus Varus to block the passes of the Apennines with fourteen praetorian cohorts and all the cavalry. A legion of marines followed them later. These thousands of armed forces, consisting too of picked men and horses, were equal to taking the offensive if they had had another leader. The rest of the cohorts Vitellius gave to his brother Lucius for the defence of Rome, while he, abating in no degree his usual life of pleasure and urged on by his lack of confidence in the future, held the comitia before the usual time, and designated the consuls for many years to come. He granted special treaties to allies and bestowed Latin rights on foreigners with a generous hand; he reduced the tribute for some provincials, he relieved others from all obligations—in short, with no regard for the future he crippled the empire. But the mob attended in delight on the great indulgences that he bestowed[1]; the most foolish citizens bought them, while the wise regarded as worthless privileges which could neither be granted nor accepted if the state was to stand. Finally Vitellius listened to the

flagitante exercitu, qui Mevaniam insederat, magno senatorum agmine, quorum multos ambitione, pluris formidine trahebat, in castra venit, incertus animi et infidis consiliis obnoxius.

LVI. Contionanti—prodigiosum dictu—tantum foedarum volucrum supervolitavit ut nube atra diem obtenderent. Accessit dirum omen, profugus altaribus taurus disiecto sacrificii apparatu, longe, nec ut[1] feriri hostias mos est, confossus. Sed praecipuum ipse Vitellius ostentum erat, ignarus militiae, improvidus consilii,[2] quis ordo agminis, quae cura explorandi, quantus urgendo trahendove bello modus, alios rogitans et ad omnis nuntios vultu quoque et incessu trepidus, dein temulentus. Postremo taedio castrorum et audita defectione Misenensis classis Romam revertit, recentissimum quodque[3] vulnus pavens, summi discriminis incuriosus. Nam cum transgredi Appenninum integro exercitus sui robore et fessos hieme atque inopia hostis adgredi in aperto foret, dum dispergit viris, acerrimum militem et usque in extrema obstinatum trucidandum capiendumque tradidit, peritissimis centurionum dissentientibus et, si consulerentur, vera dicturis. Arcuere[4] eos intimi amicorum Vitellii, ita formatis principis

[1] ut *Schneider*: vi *M.*
[2] consiliis *M.*
[3] quoque *M.*
[4] arcuere *Lipsius*: arguere *M.*

---

[1] Bevagna.

demands of his army which had stopped at Mevania,[1] and left Rome, accompanied by a long line of senators, many of whom were drawn in his train by their desire to secure his favour, most however by fear. So he came to camp with no clear purpose in mind, an easy prey to treacherous advice.

LVI. While Vitellius was addressing the troops an incredible prodigy appeared—such a flock of birds of ill omen flew above him that they obscured the day with a black cloud. Another dire omen was given by a bull which overthrew the preparations for sacrifice, escaped from the altar, and was then despatched some distance away and in an unusual fashion. But the most outstanding portent was Vitellius himself; unskilled in war, without foresight, unacquainted with the proper order of march, the use of scouts, the limits within which a general should hurry on a campaign or delay it, he was constantly questioning others; at the arrival of every messenger his face and gait betrayed his anxiety; and then he would drink heavily. Finally, weary of the camp and hearing of the defection of the fleet at Misenum, he returned to Rome, panic-stricken as ever by the latest blow and with no thought for the supreme issue. For when the way was open to him to cross the Apennines while the strength of his forces was unimpaired, and to attack his foes who were still exhausted by the winter and lack of supplies, by scattering his forces he delivered over to death and captivity his best troops, who were loyal to the last extremity, although his most experienced centurions disapproved, and if consulted, would have told him the truth. But the most intimate friends of Vitellius kept

auribus ut aspera quae utilia, nec quidquam nisi iucundum et laesurum acciperet.

LVII. Sed classem Misenensem (tantum civilibus discordiis etiam singulorum audacia valet) Claudius Faventinus centurio per ignominiam a Galba dimissus ad defectionem traxit, fictis Vespasiani epistulis pretium proditionis ostentans. Praeerat classi Claudius Apollinaris, neque fidei constans neque strenuus in perfidia; et Apinius Tiro praetura functus ac tum forte Minturnis agens ducem se defectoribus obtulit. A quibus municipia coloniaeque impulsae, praecipuo Puteolanorum in Vespasianum studio, contra Capua Vitellio fida, municipalem aemulationem bellis civilibus miscebant. Vitellius Claudium Iulianum (is nuper classem Misenensem molli imperio rexerat) permulcendis militum animis delegit; data in auxilium urbana cohors et gladiatores, quibus Iulianus praeerat. Ut conlata utrimque castra, haud magna cunctatione Iuliano in partis Vespasiani transgresso, Tarracinam occupavere, moenibus situque magis quam ipsorum ingenio tutam.

LVIII. Quae ubi Vitellio cognita, parte copiarum

---

[1] The successor of Bassus. Cf. iii. 12.

[2] At the mouth of the Liris, on the border between Latium and Campania.

[3] Pozzuoli, on the bay of Naples.

[4] Terracina, on the coast south of the Pontine marshes.

them away from him, and so inclined the emperor's ears that useful counsel sounded harsh, and he would hear nothing but what flattered and was to be fatal.

LVII. The action of the fleet at Misenum is an illustration of the weight that a bold stroke on the part of a single individual may have in time of civil strife. It was Claudius Flaventinus, a centurion dishonourably discharged by Galba, who brought the fleet to revolt by forging letters from Vespasian in which he held out to the men a reward for their treason. The fleet was commanded by Claudius Apollinaris,[1] who was neither strong in loyalty nor determined in treachery; and Apinius Tiro, an ex-praetor who at that time happened to be at Minturnae,[2] offered himself to lead the rebels. These moved the municipal towns and colonies to action. The people of Puteoli[3] became ardent supporters of Vespasian; Capua, on the other hand, was faithful to Vitellius; and so rivalry between communities became a part of the civil war. Vitellius selected Claudius Julianus to reconcile the troops, for when Julianus shortly before had commanded the fleet at Misenum, he had exercised his authority in a mild fashion. The emperor gave him to support his efforts one of the city cohorts and the gladiators that Julianus then commanded. When the two forces were encamped over against each other, Julianus did not long hesitate to join Vespasian's party; then the combined forces occupied Tarracina,[4] a town which was better defended by its walls and situation than by any ability on the part of the soldiers.

LVIII. On learning this, Vitellius left part of his

Narniae cum praefectis praetorii relicta L. Vitellium fratrem cum sex cohortibus et quingentis equitibus ingruenti per Campaniam bello opposuit. Ipse aeger animi studiis militum et clamoribus populi arma poscentis refovebatur, dum vulgus ignavum et nihil ultra verba ausurum falsa specie exercitum et legiones appellat. Hortantibus libertis (nam amicorum eius quanto quis clarior, minus fidus) vocari tribus iubet, dantis nomina sacramento adigit. Superfluente multitudine curam dilectus in consules partitur; servorum numerum et pondus argenti senatoribus indicit. Equites Romani obtulere operam pecuniasque, etiam libertinis idem munus ultro flagitantibus. Ea simulatio officii a metu profecta verterat in favorem; ac plerique haud perinde Vitellium quam casum locumque principatus miserabantur. Nec deerat ipse vultu voce lacrimis misericordiam elicere, largus promissis, et quae natura trepidantium est, immodicus. Quin et Caesarem se dici voluit, aspernatus antea, sed tunc superstitione nominis, et quia in metu consilia prudentium et vulgi rumor iuxta audiuntur. Ceterum ut omnia inconsulti impetus coepta initiis valida spatio lan-

---

[1] Terni.

[2] Vitellius had hitherto declined to be called Caesar or Augustus (i. 62; ii. 55–62), possibly prompted by a desire to appear modest; but now the imperial name seemed to him a support in his misfortunes.

troops at Narnia[1] with the prefects of the praetorian guard; his brother Lucius Vitellius he sent with six cohorts and five hundred horse to oppose the threatened outbreak in Campania. He himself was sick at heart, but the enthusiasm of the soldiers and the shouts of the people demanding arms gave him fresh spirit, while he addressed the cowardly rabble, whose courage would not extend beyond words, under the unreal and pretentious names of an army and legions. On the advice of his freedmen (for the more distinguished his friends were, the less he trusted them), he ordered the people to assemble in tribes, and administered the oath to the members as they enrolled. Since the numbers were too great, he divided between the consuls the selection of the recruits. On the senators he imposed a contribution of slaves and cash. The knights offered assistance and money, while even the freedmen demanded to be allowed the same privilege. This pretended devotion, which was in reality prompted by fear, resulted in enthusiasm for the emperor; yet most men felt sorry not so much for Vitellius as for the unfortunate position to which the principate had fallen. Nor did he fail personally to appeal to their pity by look, voice, and tears; he was generous and even prodigal in his promises, after the manner of the timid. Nay, he even went so far as to wish to be called Caesar, a title which he had rejected before, but now accepted from a superstitious feeling with regard to the name,[2] and because in time of fear the counsels of the wise and the words of the crowd obtain a like hearing. However, since all movements that arise from thoughtless impulses are strong at first but

guescunt, dilabi paulatim senatores equitesque, primo cunctanter et ubi ipse non aderat, mox contemptim et sine[1] discrimine donec Vitellius pudore inriti conatus quae non dabantur remisit.

LIX. Ut terrorem Italiae possessa Mevania ac velut renatum ex integro bellum intulerat, ita haud dubium erga Flavianas partis studium tam pavidus Vitellii discessus addidit. Erectus Samnis Paelignusque et Marsi aemulatione quod Campania praevenisset, ut in novo obsequio, ad cuncta belli munia acres erant. Sed foeda hieme per transitum Appennini conflictatus exercitus, et vix quieto agmine nives eluctantibus patuit quantum discriminis adeundum foret, ni Vitellium retro fortuna vertisset, quae Flavianis ducibus non minus saepe quam ratio adfuit. Obvium illic Petilium Cerialem habuere, agresti cultu et notitia locorum custodias Vitellii elapsum. Propinqua adfinitas Ceriali cum Vespasiano, nec ipse inglorius militiae, eoque inter duces adsumptus est. Flavio quoque Sabino ac Domitiano patuisse effugium multi tradidere; et missi ab Antonio nuntii per varias fallendi artis penetrabant, locum ac praesidium monstrantes. Sabinus inhabilem

[1] contemptim et sine *Pichena* : contempti mesti ne *M.*

---

[1] His return to Rome, described in chapter 56.

[2] Later he crushed the uprising led by the Batavian Civilis (books iv. and v.).

[3] Vespasian's brother, who was city-prefect at this time. Cf. below, chapters 64–75.

slacken with time, the senators and knights gradually began to fall away, at first with hesitation and when Vitellius was not present, later in open scorn and indifference, until in shame at the failure of his attempts he excused them from the services which they would not render.

LIX. While the occupation of Mevania had terrified Italy and had seemed to start a new war, it was also true that the timid retreat of Vitellius [1] had increased the favourable feeling toward the Flavian party. The Samnites, Paelignians, and Marsians were jealous because Campania had anticipated them, and eagerly undertook all services required by war with the enthusiasm that attaches to every new devotion. Nevertheless, the army had been greatly exhausted by a severe winter storm while crossing the Apennines, and when the troops, though undisturbed by any enemy, found difficulty in struggling through the snow, the leaders realized what risks they would have run, had not that fortune which often served the Flavian commanders quite as much as wisdom turned Vitellius back. In the mountains they met Petilius Cerialis, who had escaped the pickets of Vitellius by disguising himself as a peasant and using his knowledge of the district. Cerialis was closely connected with Vespasian, and being himself not without reputation in war, was made one of the commanders.[2] Many have reported that Flavius Sabinus [3] also and Domitian had an opportunity to escape opened to them. Emissaries of Antonius by various cunning arts made their way to them and showed them the place to which to flee and the protection that they would have. Sabinus offered the excuse that his health

labori et audaciae valetudinem causabatur: Domitiano aderat animus, sed custodes a Vitellio additi, quamquam se socios fugae promitterent, tamquam insidiantes timebantur. Atque ipse Vitellius respectu suarum[1] necessitudinum nihil in Domitianum atrox parabat.

LX. Duces partium ut Carsulas venere, paucos ad requiem dies sumunt, donec aquilae signaque legionum adsequerentur. Et locus ipse castrorum placebat, late prospectans, tuto copiarum adgestu, florentissimis pone tergam municipiis; simul conloquia cum Vitellianis decem milium spatio distantibus et proditio sperabatur. Aegre id pati miles et victoriam malle quam pacem; ne suas quidem legiones opperiebantur, ut praedae quam periculorum socias. Vocatos ad contionem Antonius docuit esse adhuc Vitellio viris, ambiguas, si deliberarent, acris, si desperassent. Initia bellorum civilium fortunae permittenda: victoriam consiliis et ratione perfici. Iam Misenensem classem et pulcherrimam Campaniae oram descivisse, nec plus e toto terrarum orbe reliquum Vitellio quam quod inter Tarracinam Narniamque iaceat. Satis gloriae proelio Cremonensi partum et exitio Cremonae nimium invidiae: ne

[1] respectus varus *M.*

---

[1] Casigliano, ten Roman miles north of Terni.
[2] From Verona. Cf. chapter 52.
[3] At Narnia (Terni).

was not fitted to stand fatigue or to engage in a bold enterprise; Domitian had the courage, but, in spite of the fact that the guards Vitellius set over him promised to join him in flight, he feared that they were planning treachery. And yet Vitellius himself out of regard for his own relatives, cherished no cruel purpose against Domitian.

LX. On arriving at Carsulae,[1] the leaders of the Flavian party rested a few days and waited for the eagles and standards of the legions to come up.[2] They also regarded with favour the actual situation of their camp, which had a wide outlook, and secured their supply of stores, because of the prosperous towns behind them; and at the same time, as the troops of Vitellius were only ten miles away,[3] they hoped to have conferences with them and to bring them over. The soldiers objected to this policy and preferred a victory to peace; they were opposed to waiting even for their own legions, which would share in the booty as well as the dangers. Antonius assembled his troops and pointed out that Vitellius still had an army whose allegiance to him would be doubtful if the soldiers were given a chance to deliberate, but which would be dangerous if driven to despair. "The beginning of civil war," he said, "is necessarily left to fortune; but victory is always secured by strategy and wise counsel. The fleet at Misenum and the lovely district of Campania have already deserted Vitellius, and he now has nothing left out of the whole world but the land that lies between Tarracina and Narnia. We gained a full measure of glory in the battle of Cremona, but by the destruction of Cremona won greater unpopularity than we could wish. Therefore we should

concupiscerent Romam capere potius quam servare. Maiora[1] illis praemia et multo maximum decus, si incolumitatem senatui populoque Romano sine sanguine quaesissent. His ac talibus mitigati animi.

LXI. Nec multo post legiones venere. Et terrore famaque aucti exercitus Vitellianae cohortes nutabant, nullo in bellum adhortante, multis ad transitionem, qui suas centurias turmasque tradere, donum victori et sibi in posterum gratiam, certabant. Per eos cognitum est Interamnam proximis campis praesidio quadringentorum equitum teneri. Missus extemplo Varus cum expedita manu paucos repugnantium interfecit; plures abiectis armis veniam petivere. Quidam in castra refugi cuncta formidine implebant, augendo rumoribus[2] virtutem copiasque hostium, quo amissi praesidii dedecus lenirent. Nec ulla apud Vitellianos flagitii poena, et praemiis defectorum versa[3] fides ac reliquum perfidiae certamen. Crebra transfugia tribunorum centurionumque; nam gregarius miles induruerat pro Vitellio, donec Priscus et Alfenus desertis castris ad Vitellium regressi pudore proditionis cunctos exsolverent.

LXII. Isdem diebus Fabius Valens Urbini in

[1] maior *M.*
[2] augendorum oribus *M.*
[3] versa *Freinsheim*: verba *M.*

---

[1] The prefects of the praetorian guards. Cf. chap. 58.
[2] Cf. chap. 43. [3] Urbino.

not long to capture Rome so much as to save it. You will have greater rewards and the greatest possible fame if you aim to secure without bloodshed the safety of the senate and the Roman people." These arguments and others to the same effect quieted the soldiers' impatience.

LXI. Not much later the legions arrived at Carsulae. The terrifying report that the Flavian army had been reinforced caused the cohorts of Vitellius to waver: no officer urged them to fight, but many to desert, rivalling one another in handing over their centuries and squadrons as a gift to the victors and a security for their own reward later. From them the Flavians learned that Interamna in the neighbouring plain was defended by four hundred horse. Varus was despatched at once with a force in light marching order. He killed a few of the garrison when they resisted; the majority threw down their arms and begged for pardon. Some, escaping to the main camp, caused utter consternation there by exaggerated accounts of the bravery and the numbers of their enemies, which they gave to mitigate their own disgrace for having failed to hold their post. With the Vitellians there was no punishment for cowardice; those who went over to the Flavians received the rewards of their treachery; the only rivalry left was in perfidy. Among the tribunes and centurions desertions were frequent; for the common soldiers had remained steadfastly loyal to Vitellius until now Priscus and Alfenus[1] by abandoning the camp and returning to Vitellius set them all free from any shame of treachery.

LXII. During these same days Fabius Valens[2] was killed at Urbinum,[3] where he was under guard.

custodia interficitur. Caput eius Vitellianis cohortibus ostentatum ne quam ultra spem foverent; nam pervasisse in Germanias Valentem et veteres illic novosque exercitus ciere credebant: visa caede in desperationem versi. Et Flavianus exercitus immane quantum aucto[1] animo exitium Valentis ut finem belli accepit. Natus erat Valens Anagniae equestri familia. Procax moribus neque absurdus ingenio ni[2] famam urbanitatis per lasciviam peteret. Ludicro Iuvenalium[3] sub Nerone velut ex necessitate, mox sponte mimos actitavit, scite magis quam probe. Legatus legionis et fovit Verginium et infamavit; Fonteium Capitonem corruptum, seu quia corrumpere nequiverat, interfecit: Galbae proditor, Vitellio fidus et aliorum perfidia inlustratus.

LXIII. Abrupta undique spe Vitellianus miles transiturus in partis, id quoque non sine decore, sed sub signis vexillisque in subiectos Narniae campos descendere. Flavianus exercitus, ut ad proelium intentus ornatusque, densis circa viam ordinibus adstiterat.[4] Accepti in medium Vitelliani, et circumdatos Primus Antonius clementer adloquitur: pars Narniae, pars Interamnae subsistere[5] iussi. Relictae

[1] aucto *add. Haase.* [2] ni *add. Halm.*
[3] Iuvenalium *Lipsius*: iuvenum *M.*
[4] adsisterat *M.* [5] substitere *M.*

---

[1] Anagni.
[2] Cf. *Ann.* xiv. 15. A festival established by Nero, in which the youth of the Equestrian order took part.
[3] Cf. i. 7 f. [4] Cf. i. 8.

His head was exhibited to the cohorts of Vitellius to keep them from cherishing any further hope, for hitherto they had believed that Valens had made his way to the German provinces, where he was setting in motion the old forces and enrolling new. The sight of his head turned them to despair; and it was extraordinary with what an enormous increase of courage the execution of Valens inspired the Flavian troops, who regarded it as the end of the war. Valens was born at Anagnia[1] of an equestrian family. He was a man of loose morals but not without natural ability, save that he sought a reputation for wit by buffoonery. At the Festival of Youth[2] under Nero he appeared in mimes, at first apparently under compulsion, but later of his own free will, acting in a manner more clever than decent. As a legate of a legion he courted Verginius and then defamed him.[3] He put Fonteius Capito[4] to death after corrupting him—or it may have been because he could not corrupt him. A traitor to Galba, he was faithful to Vitellius and gained glory from the perfidy of others.

LXIII. Now that every possible hope from any source was destroyed, the troops of Vitellius were ready to come over to Vespasian's side; but they wished to do it with honour, and so came down into the plain below Narnia with their ensigns and standards. The Flavian troops, all equipped and ready for the battle, were drawn up in close order along the sides of the road. The Vitellians were allowed to advance between the Flavian lines; then Antonius drew his forces about them and addressed them in kindly terms. Half of them were ordered to stay at Narnia, the other half at Interamna. At

simul e victricibus legiones, neque quiescentibus graves et adversus contumaciam validae. Non omisere per eos dies Primus ac Varus crebris nuntiis salutem et pecuniam et secreta Campaniae offerre Vitellio, si positis armis seque ac liberos suos Vespasiano permisisset. In eundem modum et Mucianus composuit epistulas; quibus plerumque fidere Vitellius ac de numero servorum, electione litorum loqui. Tanta torpedo invaserat animum ut, si principem eum fuisse ceteri non meminissent, ipse oblivisceretur.

LXIV. At primores civitatis Flavium Sabinum praefectum urbis secretis sermonibus incitabant, victoriae famaeque partem capesseret: esse illi proprium militem cohortium urbanarum, nec defuturas vigilum cohortis, servitia ipsorum, fortunam partium, et omnia prona victoribus: ne Antonio Varoque de gloria concederet. Paucas Vitellio cohortis et maestis undique nuntiis trepidas: populi mobilem animum et, si ducem se praebuisset, easdem illas adulationes pro Vespasiano fore; ipsum Vitellium ne prosperis quidem parem, adeo ruentibus debilitatum. Gratiam patrati belli penes eum qui urbem occupasset: id

[1] The vigiles acted both as city police and as firemen.

the same time some of the victorious legions were left behind, not to oppress the Vitellians if they remained quiet, but in sufficient strength to meet any rebellious movement. During this time Antonius and Varus did not fail to send frequent messages to Vitellius offering him safety, money, and a retreat in Campania, provided he would lay down his arms and give himself and his children up to Vespasian. Mucianus also wrote to him to the same effect; and Vitellius was often inclined to trust these proposals and spoke of the number of slaves he should take with him and the place he should choose for his retreat. Such a lethargy had fallen on his spirit that, but for others remembering that he had been emperor, he would have forgotten it himself.

LXIV. On the other hand, the leading citizens began secretly to urge Flavius Sabinus, the city prefect, to claim his share of victory and glory. "You have," they said, "your own military force in the city cohorts, and the cohorts of the police[1] also will not fail you, nor will our slaves; in your favour are the good fortune of the Flavian party and the readiness with which all things become easy for the winning side. Do not yield in glory to Antonius and Varus. Vitellius has only a few cohorts, and those are in a panic because of the gloomy news from every quarter. The people are fickle, and if you but offer yourself as their leader, they will bestow the same flattery on Vespasian that they have bestowed on Vitellius, while Vitellius himself, unable to bear even success, is still more enfeebled by disaster. Gratitude for ending the war will belong to the man who seizes the city. It is for

Sabino convenire ut imperium fratri reservaret, id Vespasiano ut ceteri post Sabinum haberentur.

LXV. Haudquaquam erecto animo eas voces accipiebat, invalidus senecta[1]; sed[2] erant qui occultis suspicionibus incesserent, tamquam invidia[3] et aemulatione fortunam fratris moraretur. Namque Flavius Sabinus aetate prior privatis utriusque rebus auctoritate pecuniaque Vespasianum anteibat, et credebatur adfectam eius fidem parce iuvisse[4] domo agrisque pignori acceptis; unde, quamquam manente in speciem concordia, offensarum operta metuebantur. Melior interpretatio, mitem virum abhorrere a sanguine et caedibus, eoque crebris cum Vitellio sermonibus de pace ponendisque per condicionem armis agitare. Saepe domi congressi, postremo in aede Apollinis, ut fama fuit, pepigere. Verba vocesque duos testis habebant, Cluvium Rufum et Silium Italicum: vultus procul visentibus notabantur, Vitellii proiectus et degener, Sabinus non insultans et miseranti propior.[5]

LXVI. Quod si tam facile suorum mentis flexisset Vitellius, quam ipse cesserat, incruentam urbem Vespasiani exercitus intrasset. Ceterum ut quisque Vitellio fidus, ita pacem et condiciones abnuebant,

[1] *Sequuntur in Mediceo* seu ferebatur lecticula (*c.* 67) . . . in Capitolium accivit (*c.* 69): *verum ordinem restituit Puteolanus.*

[2] sed *Haase*: seu *M.*

[3] invidiae *M.*

[4] parce iuvisse *Halm*: praeiuvisse *M.*

[5] proprior *M.*

---

[1] Built by Augustus on the Palatine.

[2] Governor of Spain. Cf. i. 8; ii. 58, 65.

[3] The author of the extant epic *Punica.*

you to guard the imperial power for your brother, for Vespasian to put you before all others."

LXV. Sabinus, however, listened to such appeals without enthusiasm, for he was impaired by old age. Indeed there were some who attacked him, covertly insinuating that, prompted by ill-will and envy, he was inclined to delay his brother's success. For Sabinus was the elder, and so long as they were both private citizens, he was superior to Vespasian in influence and fortune; moreover, there was a report that once, when Vespasian's credit had been affected, Sabinus had given him some scanty assistance and taken a mortgage on his city house and farms for security. So then, in spite of the apparent cordial feeling between them, there was a fear of secret misunderstandings. A kinder explanation of his hesitation is that he was a gentle spirit who shrank from blood and slaughter, and for this reason he discussed many times with Vitellius the question of peace and of laying down his arms under terms. They had frequent private interviews; finally, as the story went, they came to an agreement in the temple of Apollo.[1] Only two men, Cluvius Rufus [2] and Silius Italicus,[3] actually witnessed their words and statements; but those who were at a distance marked their faces and noted that Vitellius seemed downcast and humiliated, while Sabinus had a look of pity rather than of triumph.

LXVI. Now if Vitellius could have persuaded his followers to withdraw as easily as he brought himself to do so, Vespasian's army would have entered the city without bloodshed. But as it was, his most faithful adherents rejected peace and terms with their opponents, pointing out that in such a policy

discrimen ac dedecus ostentantes et fidem in libidine victoris. Nec tantam Vespasiano superbiam ut privatum Vitellium pateretur, ne victos quidem laturos: ita[1] periculum ex misericordia. Ipsum sane senem[2] et prosperis adversisque satiatum, sed quod nomen, quem statum filio eius Germanico fore? Nunc pecuniam et familiam et beatos Campaniae sinus promitti: set ubi imperium Vespasianus invaserit, non ipsi, non amicis eius, non denique exercitibus securitatem nisi extincto aemulatore redituram. Fabium illis Valentem, captivum et casibus dubiis[3] reservatum, praegravem fuisse, nedum Primus ac Fuscus et specimen partium Mucianus ullam in Vitellium nisi occidendi licentiam habeant. Non a Caesare Pompeium, non ab Augusto Antonium incolumis relictos, nisi forte Vespasianus altiores spiritus gerat, Vitellii cliens, cum Vitellius collega Claudio foret. Quin, ut censuram patris, ut tres[4] consulatus, ut tot egregiae domus honores deceret,[5] desperatione saltem in audaciam[6] accingeretur. Perstare militem, superesse studia populi; denique nihil atrocius eventurum quam in quod sponte ruant.

[1] laurosita *M*. [2] sanem *M*.
[3] captium et captis diebus *M*. [4] ut res *M*.
[5] degeret *M*. [6] audacia *M*.

---

[1] Neither statement is true.

[2] Possibly Vespasian owed something to the influence of L. Vitellius, the father of Vitellius, who had been a colleague of Claudius in the consulship 43 A.D. and in the censorship 47–51.

lay danger and disgrace, and that they had only the victor's caprice as guarantee. "Vespasian has not self-assurance enough," they said, "to endure Vitellius as a private citizen, and not even the defeated party will allow it: their pity will be a source of danger. It is true that you are an old man yourself, who has had his fill of success and adversity; but what name and position is your son Germanicus to have? At this moment they promise you money, slaves, and delightful retreats in Campania. But when Vespasian has once grasped the imperial power, neither he nor his friends nor even his army will feel that they have any security unless his rival is destroyed. Fabius Valens, though a captive, reserved as a hostage for a possible crisis, has proved too great a burden for his captors. Will Primus and Fuscus or that leading representative of their party, Mucianus, have any liberty in dealing with you except the liberty of killing? Caesar did not leave Pompey unharmed or Augustus Antony.[1] What hope is there now for you, unless perchance Vespasian has a loftier soul—this Vespasian, who once was a client of a Vitellius, when a Vitellius was colleague of Claudius.[2] No. You must prove yourself worthy of your father's censorship, of the three consulships,[3] and all the honours belonging to your famous house. In desperation at least you must gird yourself to bold action. The soldiers are loyal, the people enthusiastic in their support. Finally, nothing worse can happen than that to which we are rushing of our free will.

[3] L. Vitellius was consul in 43 and 47 A.D. according to Suet. *Vitell.* 2; the date of his third consulship is unknown. Cf. i. 52.

Moriendum victis, moriendum deditis: id solum referre, novissimum spiritum per ludibrium et contumelias effundant an per virtutem.

LXVII. Surdae ad fortia consilia Vitellio aures: obruebatur animus miseratione curaque, ne pertinacibus armis minus placabilem victorem relinqueret coniugi ac liberis. Erat illi et fessa aetate parens; quae tamen paucis ante diebus opportuna morte excidium domus praevenit, nihil principatu filii adsecuta nisi luctum et bonam famam. XV kalendas Ianuarias audita defectione legionis cohortiumque,[1] quae se Narniae dediderant, pullo amictu Palatio degreditur, maesta circum familia[2]; ferebatur[3] lecticula parvulus filius velut in funebrem pompam: voces populi blandae et intempestivae, miles minaci silentio.

LXVIII. Nec quisquam adeo rerum humanarum immemor quem non commoveret illa facies, Romanum principem et generis humani paulo ante dominum relicta fortunae suae sede per populum, per urbem exire de imperio. Nihil tale viderant, nihil audierant. Repentina vis dictatorem Caesarem oppresserat, occultae Gaium insidiae, nox et ignotum rus fugam Neronis absconderant, Piso et Galba tamquam in

[1] legiones cohortium quaeque *M.* [2] famia *M.*
[3] seu ferebatur *M*, *vide ad c.* 65.

We must die if conquered; die likewise if we surrender. The only question is whether we shall breathe our last breath amid mockery and insults or in valorous action."

LXVII. Vitellius's ears were deaf to all sterner counsels. His mind was overwhelmed by pity and anxiety for his wife and children, since he feared that if he made an obstinate struggle, he might leave the victor less mercifully disposed toward them. He had also his mother, who was bowed with years; but through an opportune death she anticipated by a few days the destruction of her house, having gained nothing from the elevation of her son to the principate but sorrow and good repute. On December eighteenth, when Vitellius heard of the defection of the legion and cohorts that had given themselves up at Narnia, he put on mourning and came down from his palace, surrounded by his household in tears; his little son was carried in a litter as if in a funeral procession. The voices of the people were flattering and untimely; the soldiers maintained an ominous silence.

LXVIII. There was no one so indifferent to human fortunes as not to be moved by this sight. Here was a Roman emperor who, but yesterday lord of all mankind, now, abandoning the seat of his high fortune, was going through the midst of the people and the heart of the city to give up his imperial power. Men had never seen or heard the like before. A sudden violent act had crushed the dictator Caesar, a secret plot the emperor Gaius; night and the obscurity of the country had concealed the flight of Nero; Piso and Galba had fallen, so

acie cecidere: in sua contione Vitellius, inter suos milites, prospectantibus etiam feminis, pauca et praesenti maestitiae congruentia locutus—cedere se pacis et rei publicae causa, retinerent tantum memoriam sui fratremque et coniugem et innoxiam liberorum aetatem miserarentur—simul filium protendens, modo singulis modo universis commendans, postremo fletu praepediente adsistenti consuli (Caecilius Simplex erat) exsolutum a latere pugionem, velut ius necis vitaeque civium, reddebat. Aspernante consule, reclamantibus qui in contione adstiterant, ut in aede Concordiae positurus insignia imperii domumque fratris petiturus discessit. Maior hic clamor obsistentium penatibus privatis, in Palatium vocantium. Interclusum[1] aliud iter, idque solum quo[2] in sacram viam pergeret patebat: tum consilii inops in Palatium rediit.

LXIX. Praevenerat rumor eiurari[3] ab eo imperium, scripseratque Flavius Sabinus cohortium tribunis ut militem cohiberent. Igitur tamquam omnis res publica in Vespasiani sinum cecidisset, primores senatus et plerique equestris ordinis omnisque miles urbanus et vigiles domum Flavii Sabini complevere. Illuc de studiis vulgi et minis Germanicarum cohortium adfertur. Longius iam progressus erat quam

[1] inter clausum *M.* [2] quod *M.*
[3] iurari *M.*

---

[1] Cf. ii. 60.
[2] That is, three cohorts made up of soldiers from the German army. Cf. ii. 93ff.

to say, on the field of battle. But now Vitellius, in an assembly called by himself, surrounded by his own soldiers, while even women looked on, spoke briefly and in a manner befitting his present sad estate, saying that he withdrew for the sake of peace and his country; he asked the people simply to remember him and to have pity on his brother, his wife, and his innocent young children. As he spoke, he held out his young son in his arms, commending him now to one or another, again to the whole assembly; finally, when tears choked his voice, taking his dagger from his side he offered it to the consul who stood beside him, as if surrendering his power of life and death over the citizens. The consul's name was Caecilius Simplex.[1] When he refused it and the assembled people cried out in protest, Vitellius left them with the intention of depositing the imperial insignia in the Temple of Concord and after that going to his brother's home. Thereupon the people with louder cries opposed his going to a private house, but called him to the palace. Every other path was blocked against him; the only road open was along the Sacred Way. Then in utter perplexity he returned to the palace.

LXIX. The rumour had already spread abroad that he was abdicating, and Flavius Sabinus had written to the tribunes of the cohorts to hold the troops in check. Therefore, as if the entire state had fallen into Vespasian's arms, the leading senators, a majority of the equestrian order, and all the city guards and watchmen crowded the house of Flavius Sabinus. Word was brought there concerning the temper of the people and the threats of the German cohorts;[2] but by this time Sabinus had already gone

ut regredi posset; et suo quisque metu, ne disiectos eoque minus validos Vitelliani consectarentur, cunctantem in arma impellebant: sed quod in eius modi rebus accidit, consilium ab omnibus datum est, periculum pauci sumpsere. Circa lacum Fundani descendentibus qui Sabinum comitabantur armatis occurrunt promptissimi Vitellianorum. Modicum ibi proelium improviso tumultu, sed prosperum Vitellianis fuit. Sabinus re trepida, quod tutissimum e praesentibus, arcem Capitolii insedit mixto milite et quibusdam senatorum equitumque, quorum nomina tradere haud[1] promptum est, quoniam victore Vespasiano multi id meritum erga partis simulavere. Subierunt obsidium etiam feminae, inter quas maxime insignis Verulana Gratilla, neque liberos neque propinquos sed bellum secuta. Vitellianus miles socordi custodia clausos circumdedit; eoque concubia nocte suos liberos Sabinus et Domitianum fratris filium in Capitolium accivit, misso per neglecta ad Flavianos duces nuntio qui circumsideri ipsos et, ni[2] subveniretur, artas res nuntiaret. Noctem adeo quietam egit ut digredi sine noxa potuerit: quippe miles Vitellii adversus pericula ferox, laboribus et vigiliis parum intentus erat, et hibernus imber repente fusus oculos aurisque impediebat.

[1] aut tradere haud *M*.
[2] ipsos et ni *Pichena*: ipsos se Ini *M*.

---

[1] On the Quirinal.
[2] The south-western height on the Capitoline is here meant, on which stood the temple of Jupiter Capitolinus.

too far to retreat; and everyone, fearing for himself lest the Vitellian troops should attack the Flavians when scattered and therefore weak, urged the hesitating prefect to armed action. But, as generally happens in such cases, while all gave advice, few faced danger. As Sabinus and his armed retinue were coming down by the reservoir of Fundanus,[1] they were met by the most eager of the supporters of Vitellius. The conflict was of trifling importance, for the encounter was unforeseen, but it was favourable to the Vitellian forces. In his uncertainty Sabinus chose the easiest course under the circumstances and occupied the citadel on the Capitoline[2] with a miscellaneous body of soldiers, and with some senators and knights, whose names it is not easy to report, since after Vespasian's victory many claimed to have rendered this service to his party. Some women even faced the siege; the most prominent among them was Verulana Gratilla, who was not following children or relatives but was attracted by the fascination of war. While the Vitellians besieged Sabinus and his companions they kept only a careless watch; therefore in the depth of night Sabinus called his own sons and his nephew Domitian into the Capitol. He succeeded also in sending a messenger through his opponents' slack pickets to the Flavian generals to report that they were besieged and in a difficult situation unless help came. In fact the night was so quiet that Sabinus could have escaped himself without danger; for the soldiers of Vitellius, while ready to face dangers, had little regard for hard work and picket duty; besides a sudden downpour of winter rain rendered seeing and hearing difficult.

LXX. Luce prima Sabinus, antequam in vicem hostilia coeptarent, Cornelium Martialem e primipilaribus ad Vitellium misit cum mandatis et questu quod pacta turbarentur: simulationem prorsus et imaginem deponendi imperii fuisse ad decipiendos tot inlustris viros. Cur enim e rostris fratris domum, imminentem foro et inritandis hominum oculis, quam Aventinum et penatis uxoris petisset? Ita privato et omnem principatus speciem vitanti convenisse.[1] Contra Vitellium in Palatium, in ipsam imperii arcem regressum; inde armatum agmen emissum, stratam innocentium caedibus celeberrimam urbis partem, ne Capitolio quidem abstineri. Togatum nempe se et unum e senatoribus: dum inter Vespasianum ac Vitellium proeliis legionum, captivitatibus[2] urbium, deditionibus cohortium iudicatur, iam Hispaniis Germaniisque et Britannia desciscentibus, fratrem Vespasiani mansisse in fide, donec ultro ad condiciones vocaretur. Pacem et concordiam victis utilia, victoribus tantum pulchra esse. Si conventionis paeniteat, non se, quem[3] perfidia deceperit, ferro peteret, non filium Vespasiani vix puberem—quantum occisis uno sene et uno iuvene profici?—: iret obviam legionibus et de summa rerum illic certaret: cetera secundum eventum proelii cessura. Trepidus ad haec Vitellius pauca purgandi sui causa

[1] contemnisse *M.* [2] captivitatus *M.*
[3] seque *M.*

LXX. At daybreak, before hostilities could begin on either side, Sabinus sent Cornelius Martialis, a centurion of the first rank, to Vitellius with orders to complain that he had broken their agreement. This was his message: "You have made simply a pretence and show of abdicating in order to deceive all these eminent men. For why did you go from the rostra to your brother's house which overlooks the Forum and invites men's eyes, rather than to the Aventine and to your wife's home there? That was the action proper to a private citizen who wished to avoid all the show that attaches to the principate. On the contrary, you went back to the palace, to the very citadel of the imperial power. From there an armed band has issued; the most crowded part of the city has been strewn with the bodies of innocent men; even the Capitol is not spared. I, Sabinus, am of course only a civilian and a single senator. So long as the question between Vespasian and Vitellius was being adjudged by battles between the legions, by the capture of cities and the surrender of cohorts, although the Spains, the Germanies, and Britain fell away, I, Vespasian's own brother, still remained faithful to you until I was invited to a conference. Peace and concord are advantageous to the defeated; to the victors they are only glorious. If you regret your agreement, you should not attack me whom your treachery has deceived, or Vespasian's son, who is as yet hardly more than a child. What is the advantage in killing one old man and one youth? You should rather go and face the legions and fight in the field for the supremacy. Everything else will follow the issue of the battle." Vitellius was disturbed by these words and made a brief reply to

respondit, culpam in militem conferens, cuius nimio ardori[1] imparem esse modestiam suam; et monuit Martialem ut per secretam aedium partem occulte abiret, ne a[2] militibus internuntius invisae pacis interficeretur: ipse neque iubendi neque vetandi potens non iam imperator sed tantum belli causa erat.

LXXI. Vixdum regresso in Capitolium Martiale furens miles aderat, nullo duce, sibi quisque auctor. Cito agmine forum et imminentia foro templa praetervecti erigunt aciem per adversum collem usque ad primas Capitolinae arcis fores. Erant antiquitus porticus in latere clivi dextrae subeuntibus, in quarum tectum egressi saxis tegulisque Vitellianos obruebant. Neque illis manus nisi gladiis armatae, et arcessere tormenta aut missilia tela longum videbatur: faces in prominentem porticum iecere et sequebantur ignem ambustasque Capitolii fores penetrassent, ni Sabinus revulsas undique statuas, decora maiorum, in ipso aditu vice muri obiecisset. Tum diversos Capitolii aditus invadunt iuxta lucum asyli et qua Tarpeia rupes centum gradibus aditur. Improvisa utraque vis; propior atque acrior per asylum ingruebat. Nec sisti poterant scandentes per con-

[1] nimio ardori *Puteolanus*: nimius ardor *M*.
[2] a *om*. *M*.

---

[1] In the saddle between the two peaks of the Capitoline hill, where, according to tradition, Romulus had established a refuge. It is to-day the Piazza del Campidoglio.
[2] At the south-western point of the hill.

excuse himself, putting the blame on his soldiers, with whose excessive ardour, he declared, his own moderation could not cope. At the same time he advised Martialis to go away privately through a secret part of the palace, that the soldiers might not kill him as the mediator of a peacc which they detested. As for himself, he was powerless to order or to forbid; he was no longer emperor, but only a cause of war.

LXXI. Martialis had hardly returned to the Capitol when the soldiers arrived in fury. They had no leader; each directed his own movements. Rushing through the Forum and past the temples that rise above it, they advanced in column up the hill, as far as the first gates of the Capitoline citadel. There were then some old colonnades on the right as you go up the slopes; the defenders came out on the roofs of these and showered stones and tiles on their assailants. The latter had no arms except their swords, and they thought that it would cost too much time to send for artillery and missiles; consequently they threw firebrands on a projecting colonnade, and then followed in the path of the flames; they actually burned the gates of the Capitol and would have forced their way through, if Sabinus had not torn down all the statues, memorials to the glory of our ancestors, and piled them up across the entrance as a barricade. Then the assailants tried different approaches to the Capitol, one by the grove of the asylum [1] and another by the hundred steps that lead up to the Tarpeian Rock.[2] Both attacks were unexpected; but the one by the asylum was closer and more threatening. Moreover, the defenders were unable to stop those who climbed through neighbour-

iuncta aedificia, quae ut in multa pace in altum edita solum[1] Capitolii aequabant. Hic ambigitur, ignem tectis obpugnatores iniecerint, an obsessi, quae crebrior fama, dum nitentis ac progressos depellunt.[2] Inde lapsus ignis in porticus adpositas aedibus; mox sustinentes fastigium aquilae vetere[3] ligno traxerunt flammam alueruntque. Sic Capitolium clausis foribus indefensum et indireptum conflagravit.

LXXII. Id facinus post conditam urbem luctuosissimum foedissimumque rei publicae populi Romani accidit, nullo externo hoste, propitiis, si per mores nostros liceret, deis, sedem Iovis Optimi[4] Maximi auspicato a maioribus pignus imperii conditam, quam non Porsenna dedita urbe neque Galli capta temerare potuissent, furore principum excindi. Arserat et ante Capitolium civili bello, sed fraude privata: nunc palam obsessum, palam incensum, quibus armorum causis? Quo tantae cladis pretio? Stetit dum[5] pro patria bellavimus. Voverat Tarquinius Priscus rex bello Sabino, ieceratque fundamenta spe magis futurae magnitudinis quam quo modicae adhuc populi Romani res sufficerent. Mox Servius Tullius socio-

[1] sonum *M.*
[2] fama . . . depellunt *Heraeus*: famam . . . depulerint *M.*
[3] vertere *M.* [4] optimum *M.* [5] dum *add. Haase.*

---

[1] Apparently supports, shaped in the form of eagles.
[2] 507 B.C. [3] 387 B.C.
[4] During the struggle between Marius and Sulla, 83 B.C.

ing houses, which, built high in time of peace, reached the level of the Capitol. It is a question here whether it was the besiegers or the besieged who threw fire on the roofs. The more common tradition says this was done by the latter in their attempts to repel their assailants, who were climbing up or had reached the top. From the houses the fire spread to the colonnades adjoining the temple; then the "eagles" which supported the roof, being of old wood, caught and fed the flames.[1] So the Capitol burned with its doors closed; none defended it, none pillaged it.

LXXII. This was the saddest and most shameful crime that the Roman state had ever suffered since its foundation. Rome had no foreign foe; the gods were ready to be propitious if our characters had allowed; and yet the home of Jupiter Optimus Maximus, founded after due auspices by our ancestors as a pledge of empire, which neither Porsenna, when the city gave itself up to him,[2] nor the Gauls when they captured it,[3] could violate—this was the shrine that the mad fury of emperors destroyed! The Capitol had indeed been burned before in civil war,[4] but the crime was that of private individuals. Now it was openly besieged, openly burned—and what were the causes that led to arms? What was the price paid for this great disaster? This temple stood intact so long as we fought for our country. King Tarquinius Priscus had vowed it in the war with the Sabines and had laid its foundations rather to match his hope of future greatness than in accordance with what the fortunes of the Roman people, still moderate, could supply. Later the building was begun by Servius Tullius with the enthusiastic help

rum studio, dein Tarquinius Superbus capta Suessa Pometia hostium spoliis exstruxere. Sed gloria operis libertati reservata: pulsis regibus Horatius Pulvillus iterum consul dedicavit ea magnificentia quam immensae postea populi Romani opes ornarent potius quam augerent. Isdem rursus vestigiis situm est, postquam interiecto quadringentorum quindecim annorum spatio L. Scipione C. Norbano consulibus[1] flagraverat. Curam victor Sulla suscepit, neque tamen dedicavit: hoc solum felicitati eius negatum. Lutatii Catuli nomen inter tanta[2] Caesarum opera usque ad Vitellium mansit. Ea tunc aedes cremabatur.

LXXIII. Sed plus pavoris obsessis quam obsessoribus intulit. Quippe Vitellianus miles neque astu neque constantia inter dubia indigebat: ex diverso trepidi milites, dux segnis et velut captus animi non lingua, non auribus competere, neque alienis consiliis regi neque sua expedire, huc illuc clamoribus hostium circumagi, quae iusserat vetare, quae vetuerat iubere: mox, quod in perditis rebus accidit, omnes praecipere, nemo exsequi; postremo abiectis armis fugam et fallendi artis circumspectabant. Inrumpunt Vitelliani et cuncta sanguine ferro flammisque miscent. Pauci

[1] norbanacos *M*. [2] ta *M*.

---

[1] On the history of the Capitol, see Livy, Book I. 38. 53. 55.

[2] Actually 425 years.

[3] As Sulla himself said. Pliny, *N. H.* vii. 138.

[4] Who dedicated the new temple in 69 B.C. Although Augustus spent great sums on the decoration of the Capitol, he did not displace the inscription containing the name of Catulus.

of Rome's allies, and afterwards carried on by Tarquinius Superbus with the spoils taken from the enemy at the capture of Suessa Pometia. But the glory of completing the work was reserved for liberty: after the expulsion of the kings, Horatius Pulvillus in his second consulship dedicated it; and its magnificence was such that the enormous wealth of the Roman people acquired thereafter adorned rather than increased its splendour.[1] The temple was built again on the same spot when after an interval of four hundred and fifteen years it had been burned in the consulship of Lucius Scipio and Gaius Norbanus.[2] The victorious Sulla undertook the work, but still he did not dedicate it; that was the only thing that his good fortune was refused.[3] Amid all the great works built by the Caesars the name of Lutatius Catulus[4] kept its place down to Vitellius's day. This was the temple that then was burned.

LXXIII. However, the fire terrified the besieged more than the besiegers, for the Vitellian troops lacked neither skill nor courage in the midst of danger. But on the opposing side, the soldiers were frightened, the commander, as if stricken, could neither speak nor hear; he would not be guided by others' advice or plan for himself; swayed this way and that by the enemies' shouts, he forbade what he had just ordered, ordered what he had just forbidden. Presently, as happens in time of desperation, all gave commands, none obeyed them; finally they threw away their arms and began to look about for an opportunity to flee and a way to hide from their foes. The Vitellians broke in and wrought utter carnage with fire and sword. A few experienced

militarium virorum, inter quos maxime insignes Cornelius Martialis, Aemilius Pacensis, Casperius Niger, Didius Scaeva, pugnam ausi obtruncantur. Flavium Sabinum inermem neque fugam coeptantem circumsistunt, et Quintium Atticum consulem, umbra honoris et suamet vanitate monstratum, quod edicta in populum pro Vespasiano magnifica, probrosa adversus Vitellium iecerat. Ceteri per varios casus elapsi, quidam servili habitu, alii fide clientium protecti[1] et inter sarcinas abditi. Fuere qui excepto Vitellianorum signo, quo inter se noscebantur, ultro rogitantes respondentesve audaciam pro latebra haberent.

LXXIV. Domitianus prima inruptione apud aedituum occultatus, sollertia liberti lineo amictu turbae sacricolarum immixtus ignoratusque, apud Cornelium Primum paternum clientem iuxta Velabrum delituit. Ac potiente rerum patre, disiecto aeditui contubernio, modicum sacellum Iovi Conservatori aramque posuit casus suos in marmore expressam; mox imperium adeptus Iovi Custodi templum ingens seque in sinu dei sacravit. Sabinus et Atticus onerati catenis et ad Vitellium ducti nequaquam infesto sermone

[1] protecti *Nipperdey*: contecti *M*.

---

[1] One of the consuls for November and December.

[2] There was a shrine of the Egyptian goddess Isis on the Capitol.

soldiers, among whom Cornelius Martialis, Aemilius Pacensis, Casperius Niger, and Didius Scaeva were the most distinguished, dared to fight and were killed. Flavius Sabinus, who was unarmed and did not attempt to flee, the Vitellians surrounded; they likewise took Quintus Atticus, the consul.[1] He was marked out by his empty title and his own folly, for he had issued proclamations to the people, in which he had spoken in eulogistic terms of Vespasian, but had insulted Vitellius. The rest of the defenders escaped in a variety of ways, some dressed as slaves, others protected by their faithful clients and hidden among the baggage; there were some who caught the password by which the Vitellians recognised one another, and then, taking the lead in asking it or giving it on demand, found a refuge in audacity.

LXXIV. Domitian was concealed in the lodging of a temple attendant when the assailants broke into the citadel; then through the cleverness of a freedman he was dressed in a linen robe and so was able to join the crowd of devotees[2] without being recognized and to escape to the house of Cornelius Primus, one of his father's clients, near the Velabrum, where he remained in concealment. When his father came to power, Domitian tore down the lodging of the temple attendant and built a small chapel to Jupiter the Preserver with an altar on which his escape was represented in a marble relief. Later, when he had himself gained the imperial throne, he dedicated a great temple to Jupiter the Guardian, with his own effigy in the lap of the god. Sabinus and Atticus were loaded with chains and taken before Vitellius, who received them with no angry word or look, although the crowd cried out

vultuque excipiuntur, frementibus qui ius caedis et praemia navatae[1] operae petebant. Clamore a[2] proximis orto sordida pars plebis supplicium Sabini exposcit, minas adulationesque miscet. Stantem pro gradibus Palatii Vitellium et preces parantem pervicere ut absisteret: tum confossum conlaceratumque et absciso capite truncum corpus Sabini in Gemonias trahunt.

LXXV. Hic exitus viri haud sane spernendi. Quinque et triginta stipendia in re publica fecerat, domi militiaeque clarus. Innocentiam iustitiamque eius non argueres; sermonis nimius erat: id unum septem annis quibus Moesiam, duodecim quibus praefecturam urbis obtinuit, calumniatus est rumor. In fine vitae alii segnem, multi moderatum et civium sanguinis parcum credidere. Quod inter omnis constiterit, ante principatum Vespasiani decus domus penes Sabinum erat. Caedem eius laetam fuisse Muciano accepimus. Ferebant plerique etiam paci consultum dirempta[3] aemulatione inter duos, quorum alter se fratrem imperatoris, alter consortem imperii cogitaret. Sed Vitellius consulis supplicium poscenti populo restitit, placatus ac velut vicem reddens, quod interrogantibus quis Capitolium in-

[1] enovatae *M.* [2] a *om. M.* [3] direpta *M.*

---

[1] A flight of steps leading from the Capitol to the Forum, on which the bodies of executed criminals were exposed.

in rage, asking for the right to kill them and demanding rewards for accomplishing this task. Those who stood nearest were the first to raise these cries, and then the lowest plebeians with mingled flattery and threats began to demand the punishment of Sabinus. Vitellius stood on the steps of the palace and was about to appeal to them, when they forced him to withdraw. Then they ran Sabinus through, mutilated him, and cut off his head, after which they dragged his headless body to the Gemonian stairs.[1]

LXXV. Thus died a man who was far from being despicable. He had served the state for thirty-five years, winning distinction in both civil and military life. His upright character and justice were above criticism; but he talked too easily. This was the only thing that mischievous gossip could say against him in the seven years during which he governed Moesia or in the twelve years while he was prefect of the city. At the end of his life some thought that he lacked energy, many believed him moderate and desirous of sparing the blood of his fellow-citizens. In any case all agree that up to the time that Vespasian became emperor the reputation of the house depended on Sabinus. According to report his death gave Mucianus pleasure. Most men felt that his death was in the interests of peace also, for it disposed of the rivalry between the two men, one of whom thought of himself as the brother of the emperor, the other as a partner in the imperial power. But Vitellius resisted the people when they demanded the punishment of the consul, since he felt kindly toward Atticus, and wished, as it were, to repay him; for when people asked who had set fire

cendisset, se reum Atticus obtulerat eaque confessione, sive aptum tempori[1] mendacium fuit, invidiam crimenque agnovisse et a partibus Vitellii amolitus videbatur.

LXXVI. Isdem diebus L. Vitellius positis apud Feroniam castris excidio Tarracinae imminebat, clausis illic gladiatoribus remigibusque, qui non egredi moenia neque periculum in aperto audebant. Praeerat, ut supra memoravimus, Iulianus gladiatoribus, Apollinaris remigibus, lascivia socordiaque gladiatorum magis quam ducum similes. Non vigilias agere, non intuta moenium firmare: noctu dieque fluxi et amoena litorum personantes, in ministerium luxus dispersis militibus, de bello tantum inter convivia loquebantur. Paucos ante dies discesserat Apinius Tiro donisque ac pecuniis acerbe per municipia conquirendis plus invidiae quam virium partibus addebat.

LXXVII. Interim ad L. Vitellium servus Verginii[2] Capitonis perfugit pollicitusque, si praesidium acciperet, vacuam arcem traditurum, multa nocte cohortis expeditas summis montium iugis super caput hostium sistit: inde miles ad caedem magis quam ad pugnam decurrit. Sternunt inermos aut arma capientis et quosdam somno excitos, cum tenebris,

[1] temporis *M.* [2] Verginii *Puteolanus*: vergilii *M.*

[1] Three miles from Tarracina. [2] Cf. chap. 67.

to the Capitol, Atticus had assumed the guilt, and by this confession—or possibly it was a falsehood to meet the situation—seemed to have accepted the odium of the crime and to have freed the party of Vitellius.

LXXVI. During these same days Lucius Vitellius, who had pitched camp at Feronia,[1] threatened to destroy Tarracina, where he had shut up the gladiators and seamen, who did not dare to leave their walls or to run any risks in open ground. As I have stated above,[2] Julianus commanded the gladiators, Apollinaris the crews, but the profligate habits and lazy characters of both these made them seem more like gladiators than leaders. No watch was kept; no effort made to strengthen the weak parts of the walls. Day and night they wandered about, making the pleasant parts of the shore echo with the noise of their festivals; their soldiers were scattered to seek materials for their pleasures, while the leaders talked of war only at their dinners. A few days earlier Apinius Tiro had left Tarracina, and now was gaining more unpopularity than strength for his cause by the harsh way in which he collected gifts and money in the towns.

LXXVII. In the meantime a slave of Verginius Capito escaped to Lucius Vitellius and promised that if he could have a force, he would hand over the citadel, which was empty. Accordingly, late at night he guided some light cohorts and got them on the heights above their foes; from this position they poured down to massacre rather than to fight. They slew their opponents, some unarmed, others just taking their arms, and some just roused from sleep, while all were confused by the darkness, the

pavore, sonitu tubarum, clamore hostili turbarentur. Pauci gladiatorum resistentes neque inulti cecidere: ceteri ad navis ruebant, ubi cuncta pari formidine implicabantur, permixtis paganis, quos nullo discrimine Vitelliani trucidabant. Sex Liburnicae inter primum tumultum evasere, in quis praefectus classis Apollinaris; reliquae[1] in litore captae, aut[2] nimio ruentium onere pressas mare hausit. Iulianus ad L. Vitellium perductus et verberibus foedatus in ore eius iugulatur. Fuere qui uxorem L. Vitellii Triariam incesserent, tamquam gladio militari cincta[3] inter luctum cladisque expugnatae Tarracinae superbe saeveque egisset. Ipse lauream gestae prospere rei ad fratrem misit, percontatus statim regredi se an perdomandae Campaniae insistere iuberet. Quod salutare non modo partibus Vespasiani, sed rei publicae fuit. Nam si recens victoria miles et super insitam pervicaciam secundis ferox Romam contendisset, haud parva mole certatum nec sine exitio urbis foret. Quippe L. Vitellio quamvis infami inerat industria, nec virtutibus, ut boni, sed quo modo pessimus quisque, vitiis valebat.

LXXVIII. Dum haec in partibus Vitellii geruntur, digressus Narnia Vespasiani exercitus festos[4] Saturni dies Ocriculi per otium agitabat. Causa

[1] reliquas *M.* [2] ut *M.*
[3] cinctam *M.* [4] festo *M.*

---

[1] Cf. chaps. 63 and 64 above.
[2] Tacitus here resumes from chap. 63.
[3] Dec. 17–23. [4] Otricoli.

terror, the sound of the trumpets, and the shouts of their enemies. A few of the gladiators resisted and fell not without vengeance on their foes. The rest rushed to the ships; but there an equal panic caused utter confusion, for the Vitellians slew without distinction the townspeople who joined the soldiers in their flight. Six Liburnian galleys escaped at the first alarm with Apollinaris the prefect of the fleet on board; the rest of the ships were captured at the shore, or else were swamped by the excessive weight of those who rushed on board. Julianus was taken before Lucius Vitellius, flogged, and slain before his eyes. Some accused Triaria,[1] wife of Lucius Vitellius, with girding on a soldier's sword and behaving haughtily and cruelly in the horrible massacre that followed the capture of Tarracina. Vitellius himself sent laurels to his brother to announce his success, and at the same time asked whether he directed him to return or to press on to the conquest of Campania. The consequent delay helped not only Vespasian's party but the state, for if the troops had hurried to Rome while fresh from their victory and with their natural stubbornness confirmed by their pride over their success, the struggle which would have ensued could not have been slight, and indeed would have destroyed the city. For all his infamous nature, Lucius Vitellius possessed industry, and drew strength not like good men from their virtues, but like the basest from his vices.

LXXVIII. While these things were happening on the side of Vitellius,[2] Vespasian's forces left Narnia and quietly celebrated the Saturnalia[3] at Ocriculum.[4] The excuse given for such unseemly delay was that

tam pravae morae ut Mucianum opperirentur. Nec defuere qui Antonium suspicionibus arguerent tamquam dolo cunctantem post secretas Vitellii epistulas, quibus consulatum et nubilem filiam et dotalis opes pretium proditionis offerebat. Alii ficta haec et in gratiam Muciani composita; quidam omnium id ducum consilium fuisse, ostentare potius urbi bellum quam inferre, quando validissimae cohortes a Vitellio descivissent, et abscisis omnibus praesidiis cessurus imperio videbatur: sed cuncta festinatione, deinde ignavia Sabini corrupta, qui sumptis temere armis munitissimam Capitolii arcem et ne magnis quidem exercitibus expugnabilem adversus tris cohortis tueri nequivisset. Haud facile quis uni adsignaverit culpam quae omnium fuit. Nam et Mucianus ambiguis epistulis victores morabatur, et Antonius praepostero obsequio, vel dum regerit[1] invidiam, crimen meruit; ceterique duces dum peractum bellum putant, finem eius insignivere. Ne Petilius quidem Cerialis, cum mille equitibus praemissus, ut transversis itineribus per agrum Sabinum Salaria via urbem introiret, satis maturaverat, donec obsessi Capitolii fama cunctos simul exciret.

LXXIX. Antonius per Flaminiam ad saxa rubra

[1] regerit *Pichena*: regeret *M.*

---

[1] Apparently Tacitus here refers to the sad results of the inaction on the part of the Flavian leaders—the burning of the Capitol, the murder of Sabinus, etc.

[2] About six miles north of Rome.

they were waiting for Mucianus. There were also some who suspected Antonius, alleging that a treasonable purpose made him delay, after he had secretly received letters from Vitellius offering him a consulship, the hand of his daughter, and a great dowry as rewards for treachery on his part. Others, however, regarded these tales as sheer inventions devised for the advantage of Mucianus; some held that all the leaders proposed to threaten Rome with war rather than make war on her, since the strongest cohorts had already abandoned Vitellius, and it seemed probable that if all his resources were cut off, he would give up the imperial power. "But all plans," they said, "had been spoiled first by the haste of Sabinus and then by his weakness; for he had rashly taken up arms, and later had been unable to defend against even three cohorts the citadel of the Capitoline, which, with its strong fortifications, could have resisted the attacks of even great armies." But it would not be easy to fix on any individual the fault that was common to all. Mucianus held back the victors by ambiguous letters, while Antonius, by his untimely compliance or in his efforts to shift the blame to him, rendered himself culpable, and the rest of the commanders, by assuming that the war was over, made its close notorious.[1] Not even Petilius Cerialis, who had been sent on in advance with a thousand horse under orders to proceed by the roads across the Sabine country and to enter Rome by the Salarian Way, advanced with proper speed until the report that the Capitol was besieged spurred all to action at the same time.

LXXIX. Antonius, advancing along the Flaminian Road, reached Rubra Saxa[2] late at night; but the

multo iam noctis serum auxilium venit. Illic interfectum Sabinum, conflagrasse Capitolium, tremere urbem, maesta omnia accepit; plebem quoque et servitia pro Vitellio armari nuntiabatur. Et Petilio Ceriali equestre proelium adversum fuerat; namque incautum et tamquam ad victos ruentem Vitelliani, interiectus equiti pedes, excepere. Pugnatum haud procul urbe inter aedificia hortosque et anfractus viarum, quae gnara Vitellianis, incomperta hostibus metum fecerant. Neque omnis eques concors, adiunctis quibusdam, qui nuper apud Narniam dediti fortunam partium speculabantur. Capitur praefectus alae Iulius[1] Flavianus; ceteri foeda fuga consternantur, non ultra Fidenas secutis victoribus.

LXXX. Eo successu studia populi aucta; vulgus urbanum arma cepit. Paucis scuta militaria, plures raptis[2] quod cuique obvium telis signum pugnae exposcunt. Agit grates Vitellius et ad tuendam urbem prorumpere iubet. Mox vocato senatu deliguntur legati ad exercitus ut praetexto rei publicae concordiam pacemque suaderent. Varia legatorum sors fuit. Qui Petilio Ceriali occurrerant extremum discrimen adiere, aspernante milite condiciones pacis.

[1] Iulius *Agricola*: tulius *M.* [2] rapti *M.*

assistance he brought was not in time. At Rubra Saxa he heard only the sad news that Sabinus had been killed, the Capitol burned, that the city was in a panic; it was further reported that the common people even and the slaves were arming to support Vitellius. Moreover, the horsemen of Petilius Cerialis had been worsted in an engagement, for when he advanced carelessly and in haste, as if he were proceeding against a defeated foe, the Vitellians met him with a force in which foot and horse were ranged together. The battle took place not far from the city among buildings and gardens and winding streets, which were familiar to the Vitellians but strange to their opponents, who were consequently frightened. Moreover, not all of Cerialis's horsemen had the same sentiments, for some had been assigned to his troop who had lately surrendered at Narnia and who consequently were watching the fortunes of the two parties. Julius Flavianus, prefect of a squadron, was captured; all the rest fled in shameful flight, but the victors did not pursue them beyond Fidenae.

LXXX. This success increased the enthusiasm of the people. The populace at Rome took up arms. A few had shields; the majority hastily seized whatever weapons came to hand and demanded the signal for battle. Vitellius thanked them and ordered them to sally forth to defend the city. Later the senate was convened and selected representatives to go to the armies and to persuade them in the interests of the state to agree on peace. The fortunes of these envoys varied. Those who met Petilius Cerialis ran the greatest dangers, for his soldiers scorned all terms of peace. They

Vulneratur praetor Arulenus Rusticus: auxit invidiam super violatum legati praetorisque nomen propria dignatio viri. Pulsantur[1] comites, occiditur proximus lictor, dimovere turbam ausus: et ni dato a duce praesidio defensi forent, sacrum etiam inter[2] exteras gentis legatorum ius ante ipsa patriae moenia civilis rabies usque in exitium temerasset. Aequioribus animis accepti sunt qui ad Antonium venerant, non quia modestior miles, sed duci plus auctoritatis.

LXXXI. Miscuerat se legatis Musonius Rufus equestris ordinis, studium philosophiae et placita Stoicorum aemulatus; coeptabatque permixtus manipulis, bona pacis ac belli discrimina disserens, armatos monere. Id plerisque ludibrio, pluribus taedio: nec deerant qui propellerent proculcarentque, ni admonitu modestissimi cuiusque et aliis minitantibus omisisset intempestivam sapientiam. Obviae fuere et virgines Vestales cum epistulis Vitellii ad Antonium scriptis: eximi supremo certamini[3] unum diem postulabat: si moram interiecissent, facilius omnia conventura. Virgines cum honore dimissae; Vitellio rescriptum

[1] pulsantur *Kiessling*: palantur *M*.
[2] in *M*. [3] certamine *M*.

---

[1] A prominent Stoic who was put to death by Domitian in 94 A.D.

[2] The teacher of Epictetus. His complete works have been lost, but large parts exist in quotations by other writers.

actually wounded the praetor Arulenus Rusticus.[1] His high personal character increased the indignation naturally felt at this violence done an envoy and this insult inflicted on a praetor. His attendants were driven off; the lictor nearest him was killed when he dared to try to make a way through the crowd; and in fact if Cerialis had not given the envoys a guard to protect them, the persons of ambassadors, whose sanctity is respected even among foreign nations, would have been violated in the madness of civil strife, and the envoys killed before the very walls of their native city. A fairer hearing was given the delegates who went to Antonius, not because his soldiers were less violent, but because the general had more authority.

LXXXI. Musonius Rufus[2] had joined these delegates. He was a member of the equestrian order, a man devoted to the study of philosophy and in particular to the Stoic doctrine. Making his way among the companies, he began to warn those in arms, discoursing on the blessings of peace and the dangers of war. Many were moved to ridicule by his words, more were bored; and there were some ready to jostle him about and to trample on him, if he had not listened to the warnings of the quieter soldiers and the threats of others and given up his untimely moralizing. The troops were also met by Vestals who brought letters from Vitellius to Antonius. Vitellius asked that the decisive conflict be put off for one day only, and urged that if they only delayed, they could come more easily to a complete agreement. The Vestals were sent back with honour; the reply to Vitellius was that by killing Sabinus and burning the Capitol he had

Sabini caede et incendio Capitolii dirempta[1] belli commercia.

LXXXII. Temptavit tamen Antonius vocatas ad contionem legiones mitigare, ut castris iuxta pontem Mulvium positis postera die urbem ingrederentur. Ratio cunctandi, ne asperatus proelio miles non populo, non senatui, ne templis quidem ac delubris deorum consuleret. Sed omnem prolationem ut inimicam victoriae suspectabant; simul fulgentia per collis vexilla, quamquam imbellis populus sequeretur, speciem hostilis exercitus fecerant. Tripertito agmine pars, ut adstiterat,[2] Flaminia via, pars iuxta ripam Tiberis incessit; tertium agmen per Salariam Collinae portae propinquabat. Plebs invectis equitibus fusa; miles Vitellianus trinis et ipse praesidiis occurrit. Proelia ante urbem multa et varia, sed Flavianis consilio ducum praestantibus saepius prospera. Ii tantum conflictati sunt qui in partem sinistram urbis ad Sallustianos hortos per angusta et lubrica viarum flexerant. Superstantes maceriis hortorum Vitelliani ad serum usque diem saxis pilisque subeuntis arcebant, donec ab equitibus, qui porta Collina inruperant, circumvenirentur. Concurrere et in campo Martio infestae acies. Pro Flavianis[3] fortuna et parta totiens victoria: Vitelliani

[1] direpta *M*. [2] adsisterat *M*. [3] prosluvianus *M*.

---

[1] The Ludovisi quarter, in the north part of the city.
[2] Over the Salarian Way.

made all communication between the two sides impossible.

LXXXII. None the less, Antonius assembled his legions and tried to calm and persuade them to camp by the Mulvian bridge and enter the city the next day. He desired this delay, for he feared that his troops, exasperated by battle, might have no regard for the people, the senate, or even for the temples and shrines of the gods. But his men suspected every delay as inimical to their victory; at the same time the standards which gleamed among the hills, although followed by an unarmed crowd, had presented the appearance of a hostile army. The Flavian forces advanced in three columns: part continued in their course along the Flaminian Way, part along the bank of the Tiber; the third column approached the Colline gate by the Salarian Way. The mass of civilians was dispersed by a cavalry charge; but the troops of Vitellius also advanced in three columns to defend the city. There were many engagements before the walls with varied results, yet the Flavian forces, being more ably led, were more often successful. The only troops that met with serious trouble were those who had moved through narrow and slippery streets toward the left quarter of the city and the gardens of Sallust.[1] The Vitellian forces, climbing on top of the walls that surrounded the gardens, blocked their opponents' approach with a shower of stones and javelins until late in the day, when they were finally surrounded by the cavalry that had broken in through the Colline gate.[2] The hostile forces met also in the Campus Martius. The Flavians had good fortune and many victories on their side; the

desperatione sola ruebant, et quamquam pulsi, rursus in urbe congregabantur.

LXXXIII. Aderat pugnantibus spectator populus, utque in ludicro certamine, hos, rursus illos clamore et plausu fovebat. Quotiens pars altera inclinasset, abditos in tabernis aut si quam in domum perfugerant, erui iugularique expostulantes parte maiore praedae potiebantur: nam milite ad sanguinem et caedis obverso spolia in vulgus cedebant. Saeva ac deformis urbe tota facies: alibi[1] proelia et vulnera, alibi balineae popinaeque; simul cruor et strues corporum, iuxta scorta et scortis similes; quantum in luxurioso otio libidinum, quidquid in acerbissima captivitate scelerum, prorsus ut eandem civitatem et furere crederes et lascivire. Conflixerant et[2] ante armati exercitus in urbe, bis Lucio Sulla, semel Cinna victoribus, nec tunc minus crudelitatis: nunc inhumana securitas et ne minimo quidem temporis voluptates intermissae: velut festis diebus id quoque gaudium accederet, exultabant, fruebantur, nulla partium cura, malis publicis laeti.

LXXXIV. Plurimum molis in obpugnatione castrorum fuit, quae acerrimus quisque ut novissimam spem retinebant. Eo intentius victores, praecipuo

[1] alii *M.* [2] et *add. Ritter.*

---

[1] In 88, 87, and 82 B.C.

Vitellians rushed forward, prompted only by despair, and even though beaten, they kept forming again within the city.

LXXXIII. The populace stood by watching the combatants, as if they were at games in the circus; by their shouts and applause they encouraged first one party and then the other. If one side gave way and the soldiers hid in shops or sought refuge in some private house, the onlookers demanded that they be dragged out and killed; for so they gained a larger share of booty, since the troops were wholly absorbed in their bloody work of slaughter, while the spoils fell to the rabble. Horrible and hideous sights were to be seen everywhere in the city: here battles and wounds, there open baths and drinking shops; blood and piles of corpses, side by side with harlots and the compeers of harlots. There were all the debauchery and passion that obtain in a dissolute peace, every crime that can be committed in the most savage conquest, so that men might well have believed that the city was at once mad with rage and drunk with pleasure. It is true that armed forces had fought before this in the city, twice when Lucius Sulla gained his victories and once when Cinna won.[1] There was no less cruelty then than now; but now men showed inhuman indifference and never relaxed their pleasures for a single moment. As if this were a new delight added to their holidays, they gave way to exultation and joy, wholly indifferent to either side, finding pleasure in public misfortune.

LXXXIV. The greatest difficulty was met in taking the Praetorian Camp, which the bravest soldiers defended as their last hope. The resistance

veterum cohortium studio, cuncta validissimarum urbium excidiis reperta simul admovent, testudinem tormenta aggeres facesque, quidquid tot proeliis laboris ac periculi hausissent, opere illo consummari clamitantes. Urbem senatui ac populo Romano, templa dis reddita: proprium esse militis decus in castris[1]: illam patriam, illos penatis. Ni statim recipiantur, noctem in armis agendam. Contra Vitelliani, quamquam numero fatoque dispares, inquietare victoriam, morari pacem, domos arasque cruore foedare suprema victis solacia amplectebantur. Multi semianimes super turris et propugnacula moenium expiravere: convulsis portis reliquus globus obtulit se victoribus, et cecidere omnes contrariis vulneribus, versi in hostem: ea cura etiam morientibus decori exitus fuit.

Vitellius capta urbe per aversam Palatii partem Aventinum in domum uxoris sellula defertur, ut si diem latebra vitavisset, Tarracinam ad cohortis fratremque perfugeret. Dein mobilitate ingenii et, quae natura pavoris est, cum omnia metuenti praesentia maxime displicerent, in Palatium regreditur

---

[1] Cf. the note on chap. 27 above.

made the victors only the more eager, the old praetorian cohorts being especially determined. They employed at the same time every device that had ever been invented for the destruction of the strongest cities—the "tortoise,"[1] artillery, earthworks, and firebrands—shouting that all the labour and danger that they had suffered in all their battles would be crowned by this achievement. "We have given back the city to the senate and the Roman people," they cried; "we have restored the temples to the gods. The soldier's glory is in his camp: that is his native city, that his penates. If the camp is not at once recovered, we must spend the night under arms." On their side the Vitellians, unequal though they were in numbers and in fortune, by striving to spoil the victory, to delay peace, and to defile the houses and altars of the city with blood, embraced the last solace left to the conquered. Many, mortally wounded, breathed their last on the towers and battlements; when the gates were broken down, the survivors in a solid mass opposed the victors and to a man fell giving blow for blow, dying with faces to the foe; so anxious were they, even at the moment of death, to secure a glorious end.

On the capture of the city Vitellius was carried on a chair through the rear of the palace to his wife's house on the Aventine, so that, in case he succeeded in remaining undiscovered during the day, he might escape to his brother and the cohorts at Tarracina. But his fickle mind and the very nature of terror, which makes the present situation always seem the worst to one who is fearful of everything, drew him back to the palace. This he

vastum desertumque, dilapsis etiam infimis servitiorum aut occursum eius declinantibus. Terret solitudo et tacentes loci; temptat clausa, inhorrescit vacuis; fessusque misero errore et pudenda latebra semet occultans ab Iulio Placido tribuno cohortis protrahitur. Vinctae pone tergum manus; laniata veste, foedum spectaculum, ducebatur, multis increpantibus, nullo inlacrimante: deformitas exitus misericordiam abstulerat. Obvius e Germanicis militibus Vitellium infesto ictu per iram, vel quo maturius ludibrio eximeret, an tribunum adpetierit, in incerto fuit: aurem tribuni amputavit ac statim confossus est.

LXXXV. Vitellium infestis mucronibus coactum modo erigere os et offerre contumeliis, nunc cadentis statuas suas, plerumque rostra aut Galbae occisi locum contueri, postremo ad Gemonias, ubi corpus Flavii Sabini iacuerat, propulere. Una vox non degeneris animi excepta, cum tribuno insultanti se tamen imperatorem eius fuisse respondit; ac deinde ingestis vulneribus concidit. Et vulgus eadem pravitate insectabatur interfectum qua foverat viventem.

LXXXVI. Patria illi Luceria[1]: septimum et quinquagensimum aetatis annum explebat, consulatum, sacerdotia, nomen locumque inter primores nulla sua

[1] Patria illi Luceria *Oberlin*: patrem illi luceriā *M.*

---

[1] The date was either Dec. 20 or 21, 69 A.D.

found empty and deserted, for even the meanest of his slaves had slipped away or else avoided meeting him. The solitude and the silent spaces filled him with fright: he tried the rooms that were closed and shuddered to find them empty. Exhausted by wandering forlornly about, he concealed himself in an unseemly hiding-place; but Julius Placidus, tribune of a cohort, dragged him to the light. With his arms bound behind his back, his garments torn, he presented a grievous sight as he was led away. Many cried out against him, not one shed a tear; the ugliness of the last scene had banished pity. One of the soldiers from Germany met him and struck at him in rage, or else his purpose was to remove him the quicker from insult, or he may have been aiming at the tribune—no one could tell. He cut off the tribune's ear and was at once run through.

LXXXV. Vitellius was forced at the point of the sword now to lift his face and offer it to his captors' insults, now to see his own statues falling, and to look again and again on the rostra or the place where Galba had been killed. Finally, the soldiers drove him to the Gemonian stairs where the body of Flavius Sabinus had recently been lying. His only utterance marked his spirit as not ignoble, for when the tribune insulted him, he replied, "Yet I was your Emperor." Then he fell under a shower of blows; and the people attacked his body after he was dead with the same base spirit with which they had fawned on him while he lived.[1]

LXXXVI. His native city was Luceria. He had nearly completed the fifty-seventh year of his age. The consulate, priesthoods, a name and place

industria, sed cuncta patris claritudine adeptus. Principatum ei detulere[1] qui ipsum non noverant: studia exercitus raro cuiquam bonis artibus quaesita perinde adfuere quam huic per ignaviam. Inerat tamen simplicitas ac liberalitas, quae, ni adsit modus, in exitium vertuntur. Amicitias dum magnitudine munerum, non constantia morum contineri[2] putat, meruit magis quam habuit. Rei publicae haud dubie intereat Vitellium vinci,[3] sed imputare perfidiam non possunt qui Vitellium Vespasiano prodidere, cum a Galba descivissent.

Praecipiti[4] in occasum die ob pavorem magistratuum senatorumque, qui dilapsi ex urbe aut per domos clientium semet occultabant, vocari senatus non potuit. Domitianum, postquam nihil hostile metuebatur, ad duces partium progressum et Caesarem consalutatum miles frequens utque erat in armis in paternos penatis deduxit.

[1] ei detulere *Rhenanus*: eidem tulere *M*.
[2] contineri *Acidalius*: continere *M*.
[3] vicinis *M*.
[4] precipit *M*.

among the first men of his day, he acquired by no merit of his own but wholly through his father's eminence. The men who gave him the principate did not know him. Seldom has the support of the army been gained by any man through honourable means to the degree that he won it through his worthlessness. Yet his nature was marked by simplicity and liberality—qualities which, if unchecked, prove the ruin of their possessor. Thinking, as he did, that friendships are cemented by great gifts rather than by high character, he bought more friends than he kept. Undoubtedly it was to the advantage of the state that Vitellius should fall, but those who betrayed him to Vespasian cannot make a virtue of their own treachery, for they had already deserted Galba.

The day hurried to its close. It was impossible to summon the senate because the senators had stolen away from the city or were hiding in their clients' houses. Now that he had no enemies to fear, Domitian presented himself to the leaders of his father's party, and was greeted by them as Caesar; then crowds of soldiers, still in arms, escorted him to his ancestral hearth.

MAPS

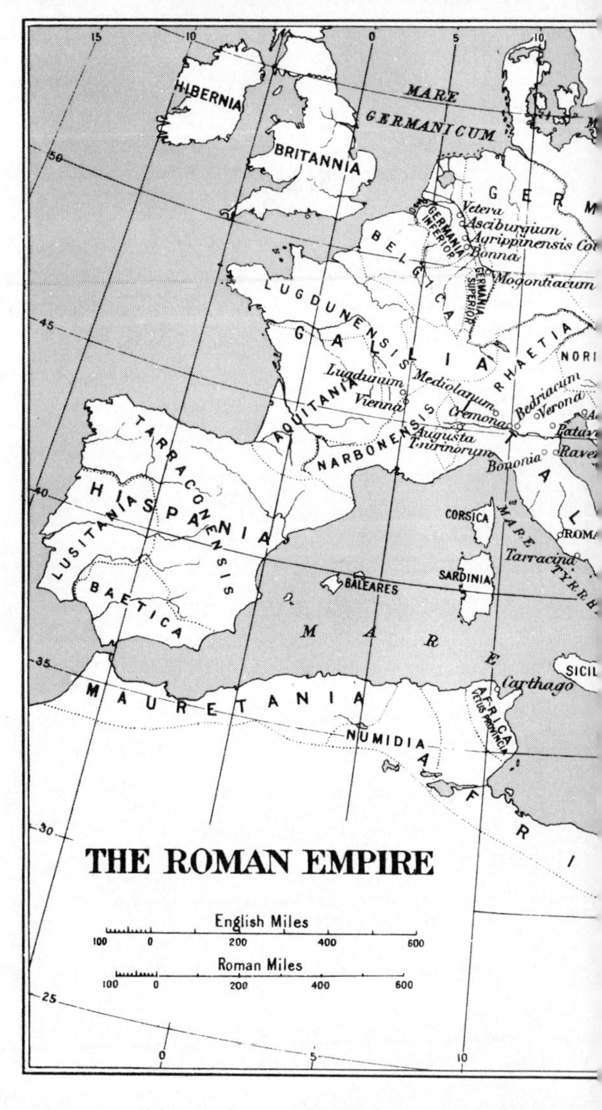

THE ROMAN EMPIRE
English Miles
100 0 200 400 600
Roman Miles
100 0 200 400 600
HIBERNIA
BRITANNIA
MARE
GERMANICUM
GERMANIA INFERIOR
GERMANIA SUPERIOR
Vetera
Asciburgium
Agrippinensis Col
Bonna
Mogontiacum
BELGICA
LUGDUNENSIS
GALLIA
AQUITANIA
NARBONENSIS
RHAETIA
NORI
Lugdunum
Vienna
Mediolanum
Cremona
Bedriacum
Verona
Augusta Taurinorum
Bononia
Ravei
ROMA
Tarracina
CORSICA
SARDINIA
BALEARES
TARRACONENSIS
HISPANIA
LUSITANIA
BAETICA
MARE
SICIL
Carthago
AFRICA VETUS PROVINCIA
MAURETANIA
NUMIDIA

Edward Stanford Ltd., London

NORTHERN ITALY
English Miles
0 10 20 30 40 50 60 70 80
Rhodanus F.
Alpes Poeninae
Alpes Rhae
Addua F.
Alpes Poeninae (Great St Bernard)
Alpes Graiae (Little St Bernard)
Duria maior
Comum
Eporedia
Novaria
Mediolanum
GALLIA TRANSPADA
Vercellae
Ticinum
Cremona
Duria minor
Augusta Taurinorum
Placentia
Alpes Cottiae
Padus F.
Parma
GALLI
LIGURIA
Alpes Maritimae
Albintimilium
Monoecus
SINUS LIGUSTICUS
Pisae
Forum Iulii
MAR
TYRR
7
8
9
10
45
44
43